The New History

The New History
The 1980s and Beyond

Studies in
Interdisciplinary
History

Edited by
Theodore K. Rabb and Robert I. Rotberg

Contributors
Peter H. Smith
Jacques Julliard
Peter Clarke
Jacques Revel
Lawrence Stone
Miles F. Shore
David Herlihy
Allan G. Bogue
Peter Temin
Barry Supple
E. A. Wrigley
Bernard S. Cohn
John W. Adams
Natalie Z. Davis
Carlo Ginzburg
William J. Bouwsma
Joel Colton
Arnold Thackray
Theodore K. Rabb

Princeton University Press
Princeton, New Jersey

Published by
Princeton University Press,
41 William Street,
Princeton, New Jersey
08540
In the United Kingdom:
Princeton University Press,
Guildford, Surrey
Introduction copyright ©
1982 by
Princeton University Press
LCC 82-47634
ISBN 0-691-05370-7
ISBN 0-691-00794-2 pbk.
Printed in the
United States of America by
Princeton University Press,
Princeton, New Jersey

FIRST PRINCETON PAPERBACK, 1982

Contents

The New History
The 1980s and Beyond (I)

Introduction

As a rule, historians concern themselves with the affairs of man's past. They are often uncomfortable with the present, and little exercised about the future. It is almost a contradiction in terms to ask historians to analyze the future needs of their craft, speculating knowledgeably and from an informed base about the ways in which historians of the later 1980s and 1990s will decipher the codes of earlier years. However, at the beginning of the present decade, the editors of this volume and of the *Journal of Interdisciplinary History*, the better to serve their readers and the historical profession as a whole, sought to understand how and in what ways the writing of history had progressed since the late 1960s, when the *Journal* was founded, and where it will and should be going.

We asked a diverse collection of leading scholars to gather at the Villa Serbelloni in Bellagio, Italy, in early 1980. There we posed a series of questions: Is political history still a relevant sub-discipline? Is the practice of intellectual history passé? Have we gone as far as possible with quantification in history? Are formal proofs central to the newest history? Can more be done with family history? Is biography still a worthwhile genre? Can past personality be understood best only by practicing retrospective psychoanalysis? In what direction should historians of science head? What contribution can anthropology and folklore make to the understanding of history? Is economic history beyond history and should it continue to be?

We asked each contributor to discuss the current practices and trends in his sub-discipline. We then urged each—and for some the task was uncongenial—to be prescriptive. Upon what topics should historians focus? What avenues of research should prove most attractive? What methods will historians need to pursue their research options in the coming decades? And how, we asked, should new generations of historians be trained? Should graduate schools emphasize numeracy at the expense of traditional skills? Should all new historians be equipped to use a computer intelligently, to understand and employ in their writing a choice of psychoanalytical approaches, and to be sophisticated in economics? How, in sum, should Clio's muse be acculturated and directed?

The discourse at Bellagio was spirited, international, and frequently inventive. The papers originally discussed have been revised and originally appeared in two issues of Volume XII of the *Journal of Interdisciplinary History*. So did several, but not all, of the oral comments and short essays that arose from the ensuing dialogue among the collectivity of historians, anthropologists, political scientists, and psychoanalysts that was brought together thanks to the support of the Rockefeller Foundation.

We believe that these essays raise questions which are central to the study and teaching of history in at least this decade. We anticipate that the book will provoke fierce debate. We are prepared for them to be as controversial as we know them to be seminal. When the *Journal* enters its third decade, we expect still to be benefiting from the research, revision, and criticism which they will have initiated.

—R.I.R., T.K.R.

Political History in the 1980s

Peter H. Smith

A View from Latin America   One might expect this
essay to be very brief. Political history, as everyone knows, has
come to be old-fashioned and outmoded. Especially in the United
States, and to a substantial extent in Europe as well, attention has
turned from authority figures and policy-makers to common people and popular masses. Explorations in economic history have
continued to shed light on the origins and transformations of
feudalism, capitalism, and socialism. Investigations of social history have opened up entirely new vistas of awareness and inquiry—with conspicuous emphasis on sex differences, sexuality,
the family, and other areas of intimate, day-to-day existence.
Interest in the mighty and powerful appears to be declining fast.
The new concern is with the daily lives of ordinary people, a
trend that offers a clear prognostication for political history in the
1980s: there will not be much of it.

This tendency comes from diverse origins. One is the identification of new issues and problem-areas, as in the case of
women's history. Another is the discovery of hitherto unused
records and sources. Still another factor is technology: computerization has made it possible to handle masses of data—and hence
to ask questions—that seemed unthinkable only two decades ago.
The development of econometrics has produced powerful tools
for analyzing crucial aspects of economic change, and the application of demographic techniques to historical materials has offered novel insights into the dynamics of social transition. For all
of these reasons, substantive and methodological, historians in
Europe and America are concentrating energies on social and
economic (rather than political) dimensions of the past.

But the turn away from politics is more than a sign of
disinterest. It is also an act of rejection—a stance that derives from

Peter Smith is Head of the Department of Humanities and Professor of History and
Political Science at M.I.T. His most recent book is *Labyrinths of Power: Political Recruitment
in Twentieth-Century Mexico* (Princeton, 1979).

0022-1953/81/0103-25 $02.50/0

two distinct lines of argumentation. One stresses the ineffective-
ness and (excuse the term) the irrelevance of politics. Today's
leaders have shown their utter inability to deal with crucial contemporary issues, such as unemployment and stagflation, while
social inequities persist. Whatever the statesmen do or say, they
do not (and perhaps cannot) alleviate patterns of oppression and
deprivation. Republicans look just like Democrats, and turbulent
upheavals, even revolutions, lead to false illusions: they, too, end
up perpetuating continuities. Socioeconomic structures endure, in
this view, and common people fashion strategies for survival and
self-protection in recognition of this simple principle. It is on this
humble level that one can glimpse the dignity of struggle, and it
is here, in daily tests of endurance, that we can best observe the
drama of humanity's predicament.

The second source of disenchantment arises from the premise
that, although politics is both effective and relevant, political
power has tended to serve the forces of regression, benightedness,
and evil. Vietnam and Watergate have so tinged our vision of the
past that it is difficult to reconcile denunciation of present-day
politics with appreciation of creative governance in history. Indeed, the manipulations and deceptions of the Johnson-Nixon era
have instilled an entire generation of U.S. historians with skepticism and disdain, while the implantation of repressive regimes
in Argentina, Brazil, Chile, and other Latin countries provoked
both horror and distaste throughout the hemisphere. Politics is
seen as the art of the immoral, and therefore as a subject not
worth inquiry.

So who wants to study politics? Historical research involves
long-term commitments of energy and time, and psychologically
it is desirable, and probably even necessary, for historians to take
a favorable view of the value of their topic—if not of the actors
themselves. The disenchantment with politics is pervasive and
widespread, and, especially in the United States, it has played a
significant part in the historiographical shift toward socioeconomic concerns.

The prospects for third-world history present a sharply contrasting picture. In Latin America, at least, politics continues to
represent power, and the immense variation in popular ideologies
means that political authority can serve widely differing ends. In
a society where Roman Catholic corporatism coexists and com-

petes with liberal pluralism and radical Marxism, where neofas-
cists fight with socialists, one can hardly afford to dismiss politics
as irrelevant or politicians as self-serving. The stakes are too high
and the conflicts too real. In these parts of the world politics
constitutes a vital force, and this perception will almost certainly
lead scholars to sustain their interest in and commitment to the
writing of political history.

What constitutes political history is, partly, a matter of definition. It can be defined as the study of government: as the
narration of laws and regulations passed by those in power. It can
be construed as the study of institutions invested with authority.
It can unravel ideas and conceptions about justice, order, and the
role of the state. It can focus on the ways in which people choose
their leaders, especially through elections and other analogous
mechanisms. And it can deal with broad patterns of change, as in
longstanding (but fast-fading) efforts to detect origins and levels
of democratization or modernization.

For the purposes of this article I define politics as behavior
that affects both the bases of authority and the authoritative allocation of public goods. At the heart of politics lies power, and
the distinguishing feature of political power is that it ultimately
rests on the more or less legitimate control of violence (whether
or not it is employed). Political action entails not only the quest
for power, but also the exercise of authority through the allocation
of goods—goods in multiple forms, ranging from national defense
to patronage to economic benefits to symbolic gratification. It can
take place on local as well as national levels, and it can revolve
around informal arrangements as well as formal institutions.

Political history is, self-evidently enough, the study of past
politics. But it is at this point that historians' categories of their
trade—e.g., political history, economic history, social history—
begin to sow confusion. An economic historian might analyze the
effect of tariff regulations on a country's balance of payments or
rate of inflation but, despite the preoccupation with an overtly
political act (the imposition of tariffs), the inquiry would be neatly
categorized as *economic* history. A social historian could examine
the effect of military mobilization on female labor-force participation and family structures, and, despite the concern with politics
and economics, the result would still be put into the *social* history
compartment. In terms of causal modeling, it is as though his-

torians were to identify their fields of interest by the nature of the dependent variable. The independent variables, no matter how great their importance, do not play any such role in the process of self-identification. It is a curious state of affairs.

What it means is that almost all historians, whatever their field or persuasion, will probably have to pay some attention to politics, at least as I have defined it. The acquisition and use of political power, as cause or effect, have simply been too crucial to ignore, and colleagues who describe themselves as social and economic historians will acknowledge this fact with increasing explicitness in the course of the decade ahead. This quest for integrated explanation should prove to be a most welcome development, and one that will enrich our understanding of political behavior as well as of economic patterns and social processes.

Having expressed all of these caveats, I focus on likely trends in the historical study of politics under four general headings: (1) inputs, (2) structures and processes, (3) outputs, and (4) ideas and attitudes. I limit my citations to Latin America, although my tacit frame of reference is the third world as a whole. I anticipate probable trends, and also offer suggestions and hopes about directions that they might take.

Narration has a time-honored place in political history, especially in areas such as Latin America, where so much spadework is still to be done. (Biography and other forms of narrative history within Latin America often have a partisan ring, which diminishes their reliability, but they nevertheless help clear away the forests.) My concern focuses on approaches that seek to identify specific connections between two or more variables and, eventually, to construct workable models of causal processes. Oddly, or mistakenly, this kind of work has often been labelled as behavioral, empirical, or quantitative—that is, according to its secondary characteristics—although its primary distinction entails the systematic quest for correlations, associations, and causal connections. My focus deals with conceptualization, not technique, an emphasis which will itself become a major feature of political history within the next decade or so.

INPUTS   The analysis of inputs into a political system—the articulation, aggregation, and promotion of citizen interests—has established a distinguished tradition in the discipline of political science. Within the United States, especially, attention has focused on that most conspicuous of democratic institutions: the political election. Countless articles and monographs have delved into patterns of voting behavior, party allegiance, ticket-splitting, and other electoral phenomena. Behind the sophisticated statistical manipulation of voting returns there appears to lurk a basic, sometimes ethnocentric judgment: the conscientious casting of a ballot is the highest form of political participation.

One of the most instructive examples of this genre is Burnham's classic article, "The Changing Shape of the American Political Universe." Through a longitudinal study of election returns from 1848 to 1964, Burnham demonstrates that voter participation has undergone marked patterns of "surge and decline," that the proportion of partisan-minded "core voters" has dropped far below its nineteenth-century level, and that the share of "peripheral" voters has correspondingly increased. Burnham's apprehensive warnings about the consequent potential for mass mobilization may indeed reflect an ideological preference, but his empirical approach provides an outstanding model for long-run analyses of at least one form of political participation.[1]

Methodological as well as substantive concerns have given further impetus to the study of electoral performance. Efforts to deduce individual behavior from aggregate data prompted an arcane series of argumentative articles in the *Journal of Interdisciplinary History,* and it appears that the ecological regression technique, pioneered by Kousser, has become an accepted tool of the trade. Other U.S. historians have conducted relentless searches for individual voting returns or party preferences, and Hammarberg's study of the mid-nineteenth-century Indiana electorate aptly illustrates the richness of these possibilities.[2]

1   Walter Dean Burnham, "The Changing Shape of the American Political Universe," *American Political Science Review,* LIX (1967), 7–28.
2   E. Terrence Jones, "Ecological Inference and Electoral Analysis," *Journal of Interdisciplinary History,* II (1971), 249–262; J. Morgan Kousser, "Ecological Regression and the Analysis of Past Politics," *ibid.,* IV (1973), 237–262; Allan J. Lichtman, "Correlation, Regression, and the Ecological Fallacy: A Critique," *ibid.,* IV (1974), 417–434; Jones, "Using Ecological Regression," *ibid.,* IV (1974), 593–596; John L. Hammond, "New Approaches to Aggregate Electoral Data," *ibid.,* IX (1979), 473–492. Kousser, *The Shaping of Southern Politics: Suffrage Restriction and the Establishment of the One-Party South, 1880–1910* (New Haven, 1974). Melvyn Hammarberg, *The Indiana Voter: The Historical Dynamics of Party Allegiance during the 1870s* (Chicago, 1977).

The North American fascination with voter performance seems faintly quixotic to Latin Americans, who tend to assume that elections are rigged (if they take place at all) and that voters cast ballots more under coercion than out of conviction. But the whole question of political participation, broadly construed, represents a major line of inquiry that will unquestionably be pursued in the decade ahead. The salience of the topic no one doubts: in societies with large-scale peripheral or marginal populations the possibilities for widespread mobilization are immense, and yet, paradoxically enough, the effects of mass action have rarely been observed. Appreciation of these complexities requires historical investigation of the multiple modes, levels, and forms of political participation in Latin American society.

Recent research on contemporary Latin America has yielded a number of suggestive findings. When elections occur, for example, voter participation is higher than in the United States (over 90 percent of eligible Venezuelans took part in the presidential election of 1973, compared to average rates of 55–60 percent in the United States). Groups and collectivities adopt deliberate strategies in accordance with structural contexts—such as the presence or absence of mass-based parties, or the nature of struggle among the elites—and they mold their behavior on rational lines. Middle- and upper-class strata dominate the national arena, whereas the poor and dispossessed concentrate upon local, communal domains. The lower classes may refrain from national-level participation, not because of cultural bias, but because of realistic calculations of the possibilities for benefits. As Booth has observed, "modernization may not mean acquiring a new predisposition to participate, but simply perceiving that the national arena has potential utility. . . . Parochial nonparticipation in national politics is probably a consequence of position in the social system, not a psychocultural attribute of certain individuals." Exit the notion of the civic culture![3]

Serious assessment of the historical dimensions of political

3 John A. Booth, "Political Participation in Latin America: Levels, Structure, Context, Concentration, and Rationality," *Latin American Research Review*, XIV (1979), 48. See also Mitchell A. Seligson and Booth, "Political Participation in Latin America: An Agenda for Research," *ibid.*, XI (1976), 95–119; Booth and Seligson (eds.), *Political Participation in Latin America*, I: *Citizen and State*; II: *Politics and the Poor* (New York, 1978 and 1979). The civic culture concept was made famous by Gabriel A. Almond and Sidney Verba, *The Civic Culture: Political Attitudes and Democracy in Five Nations* (Princeton, 1963).

participation in Latin America could very well begin with a Burn-ham-like treatment of voting patterns over time. It would be necessary to focus on countries with established traditions of recurrent if not always regular elections (Argentina, Brazil, Chile, Colombia, and Costa Rica) and to foreshorten time perspectives in some instances (Peru and Venezuela). Results would require cautious and careful interpretation, but they would nonetheless produce extremely useful information about one central type of citizen action.

We need, in addition, considerable research into the varieties of participatory modes. We must go beyond elections and governmental processes to investigate kinds and types of community action, popular movements, and authority relationships. Political currency takes many forms in Latin America, and in order to appreciate its acquisition we will have to broaden the range of our analyses.

One topic that cries for research is violence. Almost everyone agrees that Latin America has a long history of violence, especially political violence, but we do not yet have a longitudinal study of its changing levels, shapes, and functions. Under certain circumstances particular types of violence do not represent challenges to the established order. They constitute, instead, workable and widely acknowledged instruments for promoting group interests within the order itself, and one of the analytical challenges is to detect and define the thresholds of acceptability. In Argentina, for example, the assassination of targeted individuals, as horrendous as it was, appeared to be a recognized aspect of political conflict in the late 1960s and early 1970s. Activists understood and accepted the risk. From the mid-1970s onward, however, the character of violence changed, as the circle of victims spread far beyond the core of activists. The pattern of killing nearly approached the random murders of, say, Northern Ireland, and this violation of the accepted rules of political contention has inflicted one of the greatest traumas—and obstacles to reconciliation—that the Argentines have yet had to endure.[4]

The detection and interpretation of violent behavior, from

4 For one study of violence in Latin America based on contemporary data see Ernest A. Duff and John E. McCamant, *Violence and Repression in Latin America: A Quantitative and Historical Analysis* (New York, 1976). See also James E. Payne, *Labor and Politics in Peru: The System of Political Bargaining* (New Haven, 1965).

crimes to strikes to riots to rebellions, demand painstaking research and exquisite sensibilities. Fortunately there is a model for such undertakings in the Tillys' pathbreaking study, *The Rebellious Century*. Focusing on France, Italy, and Germany, the Tillys blend quantitative and qualitative modes of analysis to expose the underpinnings of collective violence during extended periods of industrialization and urbanization. It is a provocative, original, and imaginative work, and one that provides a comparative frame of reference—as well as a research design—for similar studies on Latin America.[5]

Another fruitful line of investigation might concern the differentiation of domains for authority, and, by extension, political participation. Chaney has recently demonstrated that the political participation of women in Latin America is usually confined to extensions of their roles as mothers—health, education, and welfare, for example—and then mainly on the lower levels of policy-making. Attributing this self-limitation to Latin women's voluntary acceptance of the *supermadre* self-image, Chaney invokes a variant of false-consciousness argumentation. But if one were to think of alternative power domains, one might come to quite a different conclusion. The "supermother" myth might not fit too well in the national political arena, but it might operate with considerable efficacy on the local level, and, more important, it would grant women the right to claim exclusive authority within the household. The family can be construed as a power arena and within this domain the female figure reigns supreme. A historical understanding of the dynamic interrelations between polity and family offers a major challenge for research in the 1980s.[6]

STRUCTURES AND PROCESSES   Throughout its recent history Latin America has displayed extraordinary variation in its assemblage of political regimes, from competitive multiparty systems (as in pre-coup Chile) to single-party structures (postrevolutionary Mexico) to anti-party military monoliths (present-day Argentina). Corporatist alliances coexist and compete with class-based movements; conservative forces struggle openly with revolutionary

5 Charles Tilly, Louise Tilly, and Richard Tilly, *The Rebellious Century, 1830–1930* (Cambridge, Mass., 1975).
6 Elsa M. Chaney, *Supermadre: Women in Politics in Latin America* (Austin, 1979). On the role of "centralizing women" see Larissa Adler Lomnitz and Marisol Pérez Lisaur, "The History of a Mexican Urban Family," *Journal of Family History*, III (1978), 392–409.

tendencies. Individual countries, such as Argentina and Brazil, have undergone fundamental transitions from aristocratic governance to limited democracy to populist experimentation to military rule. One of the most intimidating and irresistible tasks for political historians has been to impose intellectual order on this bewildering array of data. What are the regularities underlying this variety? What are the determinants of political structure? What factors shape the processes of change?

In the optimistic hubris of the 1960s students of Latin American political history, especially those from the United States, found ready and congenial answers in what had come to be known as modernization theory. As applied to Latin America by Johnson and others, the argument posited simple causal connections. Economic development creates middle-class sectors which in turn espouse political democracy, either as a tactical means of gaining power or as an expression of enlightened values (the difference did not seem to matter at the time). The greater the level of economic development, the greater the likelihood of democratic practice. The paradigm possessed internal coherence and logical structure, it linked political processes to social and economic forces, it appeared to find empirical support in the cross-national analyses of Lipset and Cutright, and it offered bright hopes for the future. It seemed to be too good to be true—and so, alas, it was.[7]

Reality proved to be harsh. Instead of dispensing prosperity, economic development (such as it was) accentuated the concentration of wealth and exacerbated existing inequalities. The middle strata, relatively privileged, forged little if any sense of class consciousness and, in critical moments of decision, joined with the ruling classes in opposition to the popular masses. Political outcomes took a decidedly authoritarian turn, as shown by the lamentable experiences of Brazil (1964), Argentina (1966), and Chile (1973). And in stark contradiction of modernization theory, these patterns emerged in the most developed—and most rapidly developing—countries of the continent. What could have gone wrong?

Two sets of answers came forth. One focused on the cultural

7 John J. Johnson, *Political Change in Latin America: The Emergence of the Middle Sectors* (Stanford, 1958). Seymour Martin Lipset, *Political Man: The Social Bases of Politics* (Garden City, 1963), 27–63; Phillips Cutright, "National Political Development: Measurement and Analysis," *American Sociological Review*, XXVIII (1963), 253–264.

traditions of Latin America and argued, in effect, that anti-democratic politics was (and remains) entirely consistent with a Catholic and Mediterranean worldview that stressed the need for harmony, order, and the elimination of conflict. By failing to grasp these continuities, scholars had confused form with substance and rhetoric with reality. Latin America's constitutions were never as democratic as they appeared; party politics were not as representative as they might have looked. There had been no downfall of democracy because there had not been much upsurge in the first place. The academic community, afflicted by its own myopia and biases, had simply misread the social facts.[8]

A second approach accepted modernization theory's linkage of socioeconomic causes with political outcomes but turned the answer upside down: since Latin America's economic development was qualitatively different from that of North America and Western Europe, it produced different political results. Specifically, this argument maintained, Latin America's experience was determined by the pervasive fact of its dependency. "By dependency," as Theotonio dos Santos has explained,

> we mean a situation in which the economy of certain countries is conditioned by the development and expansion of another economy to which the former is subjected. The relation of inter-dependence between two or more economies, and between these and world trade, assumes the form of dependence when some countries (the dominant ones) can expand and be self-sustaining, while other countries (the dependent ones) can do this only as a reflection of that expansion, which can have either a positive or a negative effect on their immediate development.[9]

Because of its intrinsic character, dependent development intensifies inequities, allocating benefits to sectors involved in the world market and denying them to marginal groups.

The proponents of *dependencia* theory, as it quickly came to be known, insisted from the start that economic dependency led to political authoritarianism, but the precise form of this relationship remained unclear. It was not until the early 1970s that

8 For one influential example of this argument, see Howard J. Wiarda, "Toward a Framework for the Study of Political Change in the Iberic-Latin Tradition: The Corporative Model," *World Politics,* XXV (1973), 206–235.
9 As quoted in Ronald H. Chilcote, "A Critical Synthesis of the Dependency Literature," *Latin American Perspectives,* I (1974), 4.

O'Donnell, an Argentine political scientist, presented a coherent rationale for this position. According to O'Donnell's analysis the dependent location of Latin America's economies has placed inherent limitations on the region's capacity for industrial growth. As expansion declines conflict ensues, and ruling elites confront a clear-cut choice: they can sacrifice growth or they can pursue it by repressing the working classes. The preference, almost invariably, is for the latter course, even if it means violent assaults upon already-organized working-class groups. Thus occurred the vicious coups and repressive regimes in Brazil, Argentina, and Chile. They did not emerge in spite of Latin America's economic development; they emerged because of it.[10]

The *dependencia* approach has great potential as an explanatory tool, but it has weaknesses, at least in current form, and stands in need of refinement. Ironically enough the principal obstacles have come from *dependentistas* themselves who have seized upon the concept as a kind of political creed, as a badge of radical honor. This is particularly true in the United States, where dependency thinkers (and their opponents) argue endlessly about the ideological content of obscure conceptual positions that, as often as not, are mere exercises in semantics. The curious result is that there has been much discussion of dependency ideas, but there has been relatively little effort to provide empirical tests for their validity. Almost everyone talks about it but, as in so many other areas of human endeavor, hardly anyone does it.[11]

What we need are serious historical studies of the precise

---

10 Guillermo A. O'Donnell, *Modernization and Bureaucratic-Authoritarianism: Studies in South American Politics* (Berkeley, 1973). For further discussion of such relationships see the various essays in David Collier (ed.), *The New Authoritarianism in Latin America* (Princeton, 1979).

11 See, for example, C. Richard Bath and Dilmus D. James, "Dependency Analysis of Latin America," *Latin American Research Review*, XI (1976), 3–54; Richard R. Fagen, "Studying Latin American Politics: Some Implications of a *Dependencia* Approach," *ibid.*, XII (1977), 3–26; Fernando Henrique Cardoso, "The Consumption of Dependency Theory in the United States," *ibid.*, XII (1977), 7–24; Chilcote, "A Question of Dependency," *ibid.*, XIII (1978), 55–68; Steven Jackson, Bruce Russett, Duncan Snidal, and David Sylvan, "An Assessment of Empirical Research on *Dependencia*," *ibid.*, XIV (1979), 7–28; D.C.M. Platt, "Dependency in Nineteenth-Century Latin America: An Historian Objects," and ensuing exchange with Stanley J. Stein and Barbara H. Stein, *ibid.*, XV (1980), 113–149; Robert A. Packenham, "The New Utopianism: Political Development Ideas in the Dependency Literature," *Working Papers* of the Latin American Program, Woodrow Wilson International Center for Scholars, 19 (1978); articles by James Caporaso, Raymond Duvall, Albert O. Hirschman, and Theodore H. Moran in *International Organization*, XXXII (1978), 13–100; various issues of *Latin American Perspectives*.

relationships in dependent societies between economic development and social classes and political regimes. For the elaboration of a usable dependency approach we need to reach a clear understanding of these interconnections during the phases of accelerated export-driven growth, roughly from 1880 to 1930, through the processes that defined and consolidated Latin America's subordinate and dependent position in the modern world economy. There have been a few efforts of this kind, most notably in the works of Bergquist, Halperín Donghi, and the Steins. But a great deal remains to be done, and this should constitute a high priority on the historiographical agenda for the years ahead.[12]

One ultimate goal of such inquiries would be to establish a solid foundation for rigorous and systematic comparative historical analysis. The dependency approach conveys an implicit argument for cross-national comparison, since it argues that national experiences must necessarily be understood within their international context, and it purports to identify crucial variables and causal processes. Within this framework it should become feasible to isolate and comprehend variations in political structure that can be explained by variations in the intensity and forms of dependency relations.

Take, for example, the question of revolution. Why have some Latin American countries had successful socialist revolutions whereas others have not? To illustrate one means of attacking this problem, Figure 1 identifies key "social actors" in a broad conceptual scheme. In addition to specifying urban and rural social-class groups, the model identifies two other crucial agents: the state, which may or may not be the property of one or more social strata; and the foreign sector, public and private. (Solid arrows represent relatively firm alliances; broken arrows represent fragile or partial coalitions.) It is my contention that relationships among these social actors can be understood largely as a result of their functional location within the world economy, and these

12 Charles W. Bergquist, *Coffee and Conflict in Colombia, 1886–1910* (Durham, 1978); Tulio Halperín Donghi, *Historia contemporánea de América Latina* (Madrid, 1969); S.J. and B.H. Stein, *The Colonial Heritage of Latin America: Essays on Economic Dependence in Perspective* (New York, 1970). Although cast in a modernization framework, my own early work on *Politics and Beef in Argentina: Patterns of Conflict and Change* (New York, 1969) attempts to assess the political implications of export-import economics, as does Michael Monteón, *Chile in the Nitrate Era, 1880–1930: The Evolution of Dependence* (forthcoming).

Fig. 1 Social Configurations in Contemporary Latin America

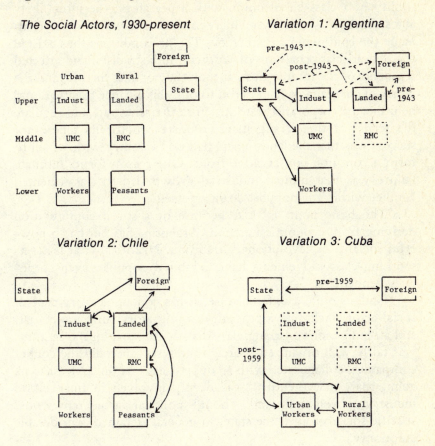

relationships in turn condition (but do not determine) political arrangements and regimes.[13]

In demonstration of one variation on this theme, Argentina's beef-and-wheat economy produced two critical social results: the absence of a peasantry, especially in the pampa region, and the importation of working-class labor from Europe. Both the state and the foreign sector, in the early part of this century, were mostly in league with landed interests. For economic and demographic reasons the working class suddenly began exerting pres-

13 On the role of the state see Alfred Stepan, *The State and Society: Peru in Comparative Perspective* (Princeton, 1978), 3–113.

sure on the political system in the 1930s, but there was no possibility of a class-based union with a peasantry; the most likely allies, instead, were newly emergent industrialists ready to challenge the landowning aristocracy. The preconditions thus existed for a multi-class coalition of workers, industrialists, and affected segments of the middle class. It took the populist rhetoric and the personal charisma of Juan Perón to pull this alliance together, and he utilized a corporatist state structure to orchestrate and regulate the terms of this arrangement. One reason for its temporary success was that the landowners had no peasantry with which to form a common conservative front. One reason for its ultimate failure was that limited industrial growth led to class-oriented conflict within the populist coalition itself.

The basic point is that, because of a social configuration deriving from economic function, Argentina has not had a powerful socialist or revolutionary tradition. Historically, at least, its working-class movements have exhibited populist, even corporatist tendencies.

Chile is quite a different case. It has contained every type of social actor, including a peasantry, a migratory rural proletariat, and an indigenous working class that, by the turn of the century, was fairly well organized. Foreign interest, especially the copper companies, collaborated with an upper class that (in contrast to its counterpart in Argentina) was deeply involved in finance and industry as well as in land. Though political parties represented specific social groups, the state, in general, retained considerable autonomy.

There existed elements of a powerful socialist movement. Party politics could (and did) lead to ideological polarization. The visible presence of the foreign sector, and its alliance with the upper class, added nationalistic tinges to anti-aristocratic resentments. There was hope for a broad-based coalition of workers and peasants: thus the triumph and euphoria of the Salvador Allende government. In the long run, however, Chile's socialist movement failed because its fundamental social basis was restricted mainly to the industrial working class. Urban and rural components of the upper class maintained their solidarity, partly through close kinship ties, and landowners managed to resuscitate some measure of support from one of the most traditionally conservative elements in Latin American society: the peasantry. To the everlasting discredit of the United States, external intervention strengthened the opposition and hastened the downfall of Allende's regime. Chilean socialism was bound to succeed, but it was also doomed to fail.

Cuba's monocultural society displays yet another combination. Foreign (that is, United States) domination of the sugar industry meant that, for all practical purposes, there was no local upper class. Workers in the mills and on plantations comprised an active proletariat, and labor migration enhanced the opportunities for lower-class cohesion and self-consciousness. Unions were weak, the army was corrupt, and the state, under Fulgencio Batista, was a pitiful plaything of United States interests.

Cuba therefore possessed elements of a socialist movement, one that could capitalize on anti-imperialist sentiments and one that would meet with relatively little resistance—except from the foreign sector, which did not mobilize all the resources at its disposal. To this extent the Cuban experience may well have been unique. It bears some resemblance to Nicaragua, and possibly to other Central American countries, but it differs sharply from Argentina, Chile, and many other nations of the hemisphere. For it is not only the common fact of *dependencia* that makes a difference. It is also the type, the level, and the form.

A schematic outline of my basic line of argument appears in Figure 2. The arrows represent causal relationships that occur both within and between distinct time periods (t_0 and t_1). In contrast to most other dependency models, this one seeks to integrate political decision-making with economic determinants. Elites (or others) can select among various responses to economic opportunities; the social structure lays down conditions for plausible (but not necessary) social coalitions; and political strategies and leadership can make or unmake effective alliances. As in Figure 1, I construe the state as a separate social entity with substantial degrees of potential autonomy. Economic dependency, in short, can delimit the context of decisions and the range of workable options. The choice among alternatives lies at the core of politics.[14]

It is my hope that political history in the 1980s will pursue

14 Compare this scheme to the heuristic representations depicted in Jackson et al., "An Assessment." Among the standard models, my approach comes closest to the analytical mode of Cardoso and Enzo Faletto (trans. Marjory Mattingly Urquidi), *Dependency and Development in Latin America* (Berkeley, 1979). This book first appeared in Spanish in 1969 and has remained ever since the classic exposition of the dependency approach.

Fig. 2 Schematic Outline of a Modified Dependency Approach

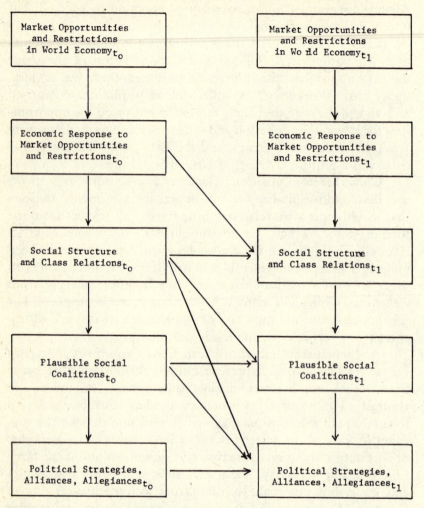

the potentials of dependency analysis, more or less in the fashion
that I have sketched out. It is time for historians of Latin America
and other third-world areas to explore dependency hypotheses in
empirical contexts, to strive for generalizations at the middle
range, and to consider economic dependency as one variable
among many—not as the sole explanation of reality. Within such
conceptual perspective comparative dependency analysis can
greatly enrich our comprehension of structures, processes, and
the dynamics of political change.

OUTPUTS   State policy offers yet another promising avenue for Latin American and third-world history. Indeed a trend toward public policy analysis has recently become something of a social-science fad, and I hesitate to advocate pursuit of passing fashion or an empty slogan: what passes for much-touted policy analysis is, in many cases, what students of politics have been doing for some time. But there is much to be said for deliberate and self-conscious concentration on the *content* of policy decisions, as distinguished from the processes by which they are reached. The focus here would be not so much on the properties of the system itself—its representativeness, authoritarianism, centralization, or whatever—as on the policies or outputs that the system produces. Instead of asking who governs or how, the policy analyst would ask: What is the substance of decisions that emerge? What determines that substance? And what is its effect?

United States scholars have formulated numerous hypotheses about the determinants of public policy. One, predictably enough, has to do with the popular will: as the electorate chooses, so goes public policy. Voters select leaders to represent their views, and politicians survive by keeping in close touch with their constituencies. It would be easy to parody this position, which seems so thoroughly inapplicable to the political realities of Latin America, but it may well find empirical support in specified moments or contexts.[15]

A second approach to public policy stresses socioeconomic determinants. In this perspective, social and economic conditions shape (or at least circumscribe) policy content in three basic ways: by articulating the locus of economic power and *class relations,* which, according to orthodox Marxism, would necessarily find reflection in the substance of governmental decisions; by presenting available *resources,* such as the amount of income or goods that could be taxed by the authorities; and by defining *needs* or social problems that attract official concern. Thus Sharkansky some time ago found that, for states within the United States, the

15   See J. Rogers Hollingsworth and Ellen Jane Hollingsworth, *Dimensions in Urban History: Historical and Social Science Perspectives on Middle-Size American Cities* (Madison, 1976), esp. ch. 3, "The Impact of Voting on Public Policy," which shows that electoral variables "have virtually no influence on any of the major kinds of municipal spending" (141). See also Brian R. Fry and Richard F. Winters, "The Politics of Redistribution," *American Political Science Review,* LXIV (1970), 508–522; Bernard H. Booms and James R. Halldorsen, "The Politics of Redistribution: A Reformulation," *ibid.,* LXVII (1973), 924–933.

relationship between indicators of economic development and state government expenditures per capita actually came out to be negative (the higher the development, the lower the expenditure). To resolve this apparent paradox, Sharkansky argued that the greater needs of less industrialized areas would more than compensate for the relative scarcity of resources.[16]

A third general model assumes that political elites are relatively immune to popular pressure, that they possess broad ranges of discretion, and that they formulate policy according to ideological predisposition, group solidarity, or desire for personal (usually economic) gain. Such premises have furnished a starting point for a mounting tide of research on the social composition and career patterns of ruling elites in Latin America, but the specific linkages to policy outputs have yet to be explored.[17]

Students of Latin America have just begun to enter the field of public policy. And Malloy, in his recent study of social security systems in Brazil, has cautioned against a headlong rush toward premature theorizing. As Malloy maintains,

> the "state of the art" of public policy analysis is so underdeveloped that the construction and application of elaborate models or frames of analysis rarely clarifies matters and often creates little more than an intellectual artifact which actually distorts perceptions and hinders effective analysis. Since most models and frameworks were created from analysis of public policies in the United States and Western Europe, the potential problems are compounded when these models are uncritically exported to other geographical and cultural settings.[18]

Malloy proceeds to relate the development of social security in twentieth-century Brazil to the reassertion of executive power and the dominance of a bureaucratized patrimonial state. In this view the state does not merely process electoral results, reflect class interests, or respond to societal needs: it constitutes a relatively independent entity that can shape policy of its own accord.

16 Ira Sharkansky, *Spending in the American States* (Chicago, 1968), 60–63. On this general question see also Thomas R. Dye, *Politics, Economics, and the Public: Public Outcomes in the American States* (Chicago, 1966); Harold L. Wilensky, *The Welfare State and Equality: Structural and Ideological Roots of Public Expenditures* (Berkeley, 1975).

17 Such as my own *Labyrinths of Power: Political Recruitment in Twentieth-Century Mexico* (Princeton, 1979).

18 James M. Malloy, *The Politics of Social Security in Brazil* (Pittsburgh, 1979), 8.

Whatever their conceptual persuasion, political historians of Latin America have much to learn from the analysis of public policy. We lack sufficient serious, careful research on the formation and evolution of policies on such critical issues as education, health, welfare, taxes, lands, labor, crime, and housing. The points of origin of these policies might prove to correspond with moments of popular agitation, economic crisis, or political transition, in which case they could yield considerable insight on the dynamics of governmental process and elite response. Occurrences of natural catastrophe—volcanic eruptions, hurricanes, or epidemics—frequently reveal the mechanics of policy-making at uniquely transparent moments, since a response to an emergency displays clear-cut priorities and, in some instances, a governmental intent to rebuild or transform entire portions of the social order. Eventually it might be possible to correlate policy content to variations in the structures of regimes, either across countries or over time, but at this point the need is for primary investigation.[19]

What are the effects of social policy? What difference does it make? It is essential to make a clear distinction between the substance of public policy and its results—or, in other words, between policy *output* and *outcome*. This path of inquiry leads to tangled conceptual thickets, especially in connection with the question of causality (not to mention ulterior motivation and the possibility of intentional failure).

Studies on the degrees and determinants of inequality, for example, have led to debate and disputation on the causal properties of economic conditions, political structures, and party movements. In the mid-1960s Cutright employed cross-national comparisons to argue that political democracy, as well as economic development, had a strong and positive impact on equality,

---

19 See the forthcoming dissertations by John I. Laun, "The Politics of Housing in Colombia, 1940–1970" (University of Wisconsin, Madison); for comparative purposes, Frances Gouda, "Poverty and Poor Relief in the Netherlands and France, 1815–1855" (University of Washington, Seattle). An illustration of the attempt to identify social pressures on policy formation appears in Thomas E. Skidmore, "Workers and Soldiers: Urban Labor Movements and Elite Responses in Twentieth-Century Latin America," in Virginia Bernhard (ed.), *Elites, Masses, and Modernization in Latin America, 1850–1930* (Austin, 1979), 79–126, 141–156. Donald B. Cooper dealt with moments of natural catastrophe in his fascinating monograph, *Epidemic Disease in Mexico City, 1761–1813: An Administrative, Social, and Medical Study* (Austin, 1965), but few have picked up his lead.

but reanalysis of the same data has challenged this view. Still another study dismisses a simple relationship between democratic structure and economic equality, but purports to offer empirical confirmation for a social-democratic view: "Strong socialist parties acting within a democratic framework appear to have reduced inequality in industrial societies," as Hewitt concludes, and this observation "encourages optimism about the possibilities of political action to reduce inequality." Social outcome, according to this interpretation, is not merely a function of economics. It is also a matter of politics and public policy.[20]

Historians of Latin America and third-world areas will, in all likelihood, pursue the study of policy causes and effects. It remains to be seen whether recent cross-sectional findings, debatable as they are, have any application to longitudinal patterns of change over time. (Indeed, much of the sociological literature appears to accept or expound the fallacious assumption that static, synchronic associations reflect and reveal dynamic, diachronic processes: *caveat historicus*). Over a decade ago Wilkie published a pathbreaking study on the social consequences of federal expenditure in Mexico, and, although his analysis was flawed, it offered an admirable model for this general type of inquiry. The territory is uncharted, and the prospects for discovery are genuine.[21]

IDEAS AND ATTITUDES   Political processes bear a close and reciprocal connection to the ideas and attitudes of political actors. As cause, ideology or worldview can shape and sometimes determine individual and collective responses to stimuli; as effect, political outlooks and ideology ultimately adjust to long-run changes in power relationships and systemic environments. The study of *mentalité* has become a major preoccupation in European

20 Cutright, "Inequality: A Cross-National Analysis," *American Sociological Review*, XXXII (1967), 562–578; Robert W. Jackman, "Political Democracy and Social Equality: A Comparative Analysis," *American Sociological Review*, XXXIX (1974), 29–45; Richard Rubinson and Dan Quinlan, "Democracy and Social Inequality: A Reanalysis," *ibid.*, XLII (1977), 611–623; Christopher Hewitt, "The Effect of Political Democracy and Social Democracy on Equality in Industrial Societies: A Cross-National Comparison," *ibid.*, XLII (1977), 450–464.
21 James W. Wilkie, *The Mexican Revolution: Federal Expenditure and Social Change since 1910* (Berkeley, 1967); for a methodological critique see Skidmore and Smith, "Notes on Quantitative History: Federal Expenditure and Social Change in Mexico since 1910," *Latin American Research Review*, V (1970), 71–85.

historiography, and it offers substantial contributions to our understanding of Latin American politics. Yet it has not, in my view, received the attention that it deserves.

Which is not to ignore the widespread recognition of cultural factors. Recent literature on corporatism and authoritarianism assigns a prominent role to the legacy of Catholic social doctrine and the Iberian (or Mediterranean) ethos, to the point, indeed, where the explanations often seem deterministic. This search for elementary patterns has consistently stressed the commonalities of the Iberian cultural heritage, articulating and defining the widely shared assumptions that would help account for similar patterns of political behavior. Such codification has produced considerable insight, but it has not prompted serious research into the history of political ideas in Latin America. In point of fact, the apparent clarity (and occasional simplicity) of the culture-as-cause line of argumentation may well have discouraged the systematic and critical study of intellectual currents.

There are other obstacles too. As Hale pointed out some time ago, the history of ideas in Latin America lacks a strong historiographical tradition. Most work on prominent thinkers has been partisan, slipshod, or patently hagiographical. As a result, Hale observed, "the study, or better the exploitation, of nineteenth-century ideas has long been central to the traditional partisan interpretations of the national experience . . . any focus on ideas becomes associated with historiography that serves political and not professional ends."[22]

The problem and the need both remain. Indeed, the scarcity of intensive work on ideas is made all the more conspicuous by the exceptional breadth and variety of political strains in the Latin American heritage: corporatism, liberalism, socialism, and anarchism have all had articulate and powerful exponents. We can learn from the examination of popular views and refined *belles lettres,* of attitudes or outlooks and beliefs and ideologies. At present Hale is himself a lonesome leader in this field, and he has precious few followers.

Two trends offer hope of improvement. One is the recent renaissance in political philosophy, especially in the United States.

22   Charles A. Hale, "The Reconstruction of Nineteenth-Century Politics in Latin America: A Case for the History of Ideas," *Latin American Research Review,* VIII (1973), 66.

Rawls, Nozick, and others have opened up fundamental and far-reaching inquiries into the ethical relationships between individuals, collectivities, and the state. It is a vibrant and immensely significant discourse, and one that should capture the attention of historians before too long.[23]

I am not suggesting that the Rawls–Nozick exchange has any direct applicability to the appreciation of moral philosophy in Latin America. The implications are important but indirect. In the brilliantly constructed bargaining game that underlies his theory of "justice as fairness," for example, Rawls postulates parity among the actors: that is, "their capacities are comparable in that no one among them can dominate the rest." A hypothetical "veil of ignorance" would prevent the actors from knowing their own (and each other's) relative positions of advantage. And they would function, moreover, within autonomous and "well-ordered" societies. Such conditions are so far removed from the self-consciously hierarchical, asymmetrical, and occasionally turbulent realities of Latin America that it becomes difficult to imagine empirical connections for an argument that is in the first instance highly abstract. Nozick, too, pitches his theory of the "minimal state" on a lofty plane. "Individuals have rights," he declares at the outset," and there are things no person or group may do to them." It is a ringing affirmation, but it does not have much resonance in Latin America.[24]

Nonetheless this recent surge of philosophical inquiry fastens upon a crucial theme, the state and the individual, which occupies the center of political discourse throughout Latin American history. And it is the style, if not always the substance, of this exploration that can offer guides for the study of ideas. The emphasis on logical precision, the pursuit of corollaries, and the insistence on analytical rigor furnish admirable examples for the kind of work that we need. We should search not only for the widespread common themes. We must also examine variations

23 John Rawls, *A Theory of Justice* (Cambridge, 1971); Robert Nozick, *Anarchy, State, and Utopia* (New York, 1974).
24 Rawls, *Theory of Justice*, 4–5, 127, 136–142, 453–462. On abstractness, see Robert Paul Wolff, *Understanding Rawls: A Reconstruction and Critique of A Theory of Justice* (Princeton, 1977). Other critiques of Rawls include Brian Barry, *The Liberal Theory of Justice: A Critical Examination of the Principal Doctrines in* A Theory of Justice *by John Rawls* (Oxford, 1973); Norman Daniels (ed.), *Reading Rawls: Critical Studies on Rawls'* A Theory of Justice (New York, 1974). Nozick, *Anarchy,* ix; Nozick's analysis of Rawls appears on 183–231.

upon those central themes, and, in so doing, accord them serious treatment.

The second positive trend comes from the fact that students of Latin American literature, if not historians, are making substantial advances in the critical analysis of political and social thought. Garrels provides a persuasive and revisionist interpretation of José Carlos Mariátegui, for example, and such journals as *Hispamérica* have encouraged and promoted the social analysis of Latin American literature. After all, many of the region's most prominent thinkers expressed themselves through novels or other fictional forms, instead of polemical tracts, partly in order to evade censorship and partly to minimize political and personal risk. (One might even posit a causal connection: the greater the level of authoritarianism, the more indirect the artistic modes.) It thus seems wholly logical for literary scholars to enter the domain of political history.[25]

Mass culture offers further opportunities for imaginative historical inquiry, and here there is much to be done. Most of Latin America's masses have been illiterate throughout most of history, but this does not mean that they have been inarticulate. On the contrary, it means that historians must search for attitudinal traces in nonliterate forms of expression: oral tradition, political slogans, popular music, paintings, cartoons, comic strips, and even televised soap operas. Enormous possibilities exist.[26]

Eventually it should become possible to make empirically grounded and suggestive (if imprecise) statements about the determinants and roles of attitudes in politics. If we suspect that schooling subjected students to indoctrination and thus helped shape their outlooks, we must turn to the study of civics texts and teaching materials. If we hypothesize that ideology affects decision-making, as it almost certainly does, then we need to grasp the variety of alternative explanations and solutions available to decision-making groups. We can reach analytical judgments only after we have examined the range and difference in political ideas, within the corporate tradition as well as outside it, and I think that the time has arrived.

25   Elizabeth Garrels, "Mariátegui y la Argentina," forthcoming.
26   As further demonstrated by the essays in John Higham and Paul K. Conkin (eds.), *New Directions in American Intellectual History* (Baltimore, 1979).

Political history may be an endangered species in Europe and the United States, but it is hardly so near to the verge of extinction in Latin America and other third-world areas. There is too much that we do not know. As one colleague quipped, only half in jest: On Latin America, we haven't done enough traditional-style research in order to reject it yet. More important, the contemporary concerns of Latin American societies continually point to politics and political action as crucial determinants of societal well-being and everyday existence. Extremes compete with each other, the stakes remain inordinately high, and politics offers more than emphasis or nuance. It can be, quite literally, a matter of life and death.

As political history continues its development throughout the 1980s, practitioners may change their working habits. First, we may witness the formation of collaborative research teams. The various themes that I have touched on in this essay—inputs, structures and processes, outputs, ideas, and attitudes—are eminently interdisciplinary in nature, and they might be most efficiently confronted through collective effort. This mode of operation is standard practice in the basic sciences, fairly common in the social sciences—and anathema to most historians. Transition, if it comes, will probably be slow.

Second, I hope we will see an increasing trend toward comparative historical analysis. The dependency approach, as I have tried to indicate, contains ingredients of systematic and fruitful comparisons of Latin American societies, but there is no overwhelming reason to restrict the approach to single geographical or cultural areas. A comparison to Turkey, let us say, might reveal more about revolutionary and postrevolutionary processes in Mexico than a comparison to Cuba or Bolivia. The Chilean labor movement might be more similar to those in Italy or France than to those in Peru or Brazil. The political economy of Argentina might be more like that of Australia or Canada than that of Venezuela or Colombia. And so on. The point is to select cases according to clearly identified criteria. As this takes place, we may observe a movement away from the confines of area studies toward broad-based, multi-regional comparisons.[27]

27 See John Fogarty, Ezequiel Gallo, and Hector Diéguez, *Argentina y Australia* (Buenos Aires, 1979).

Third, I suspect that we will see a continuing decline in professional infatuation with quantification per se and an emphasis, instead, on conceptualization and theory. Statistical technique is merely one tool among many: it can be useful, but its application does not constitute an intellectual revolution. Political historians of the 1980s will employ a wide range of sources and approaches, and they will probably be inclined to define their work according to its subject-matter rather than its methodology. This strikes me as a thoroughly wholesome development.

Finally, and most generally, I believe that political history will continue to develop new forms, and, more specifically, that historiographical trends in Latin America and other third-world areas will have a decided impact on scholarly work in (and on) Europe and the United States. Nothwithstanding the recent disaffection with politics in the North Atlantic community, historians will find it difficult to ignore the intellectual and social importance of power. Sympathy with the oppressed and dispossessed does not provide an escape from the study of authority, control, and domination; on the contrary, it makes all the more necessary a clear understanding of the power relationships that give rise to deprivation in the first place. Those who have endured or witnessed suffering do not forget this point. As we enter the decade of the 1980s, it may be especially fitting for Latin America to become a central source for the revitalization of political history around the globe.

Political History in the 1980s

Jacques Julliard

Reflections on its Present and Future   Political history measures the contribution of voluntary actions in the unfolding of history. Of course, not every voluntary act is political, but once a collective action takes on a concerted form, the political aspect is there. We have acquired the habit, since Sigmund Freud, of considering psychic activities as an enormous iceberg, of which the visible, or conscious part, is only a superficial layer of the whole. In the same way, we normally regard history as a formidable monolithic block—a mountain subject to slow and powerful subterranean movements. At its peak, tiny characters dance and writhe in a shadow show, imagining themselves to be the source of the profound movements at their feet.

As long as decision making appears as an integrated social function, alongside such other spheres as production or contemplation, then it is no longer self-evident that all history is political. On the contrary, political history is no more than one sphere among many, which should be studied for itself. History itself becomes more specialized and begins, under cover of an avalanche of facts, to dodge the question of the relative weight of each of these spheres in the making of history. As historians we are generally accustomed to an infrastructuralist view of history which sees in politics a simple epiphenomenon, largely determined by a collection of economic and social conditions that cannot be modified by human will. Yet at the same time, as actors and as citizens, we act as if our intervention had a certain effect.

A school of history that claims allegiance to Marxism has given us many examples of these inconsistencies. Furet, in his recent work, has convincingly shown how an overemphasis on the economic aspect of the causes of the French Revolution leads eventually, at the outbreak of revolution in 1789, to a naively

Jacques Julliard is Director of Studies at l'Ecole des Hautes Etudes en Sciences Sociales in Paris. He is author of, among other books, *Contre la politique professionnelle* (Paris, 1978). This article has been translated from French by Rebecca A. McCormick.

0022-1953/81/01029-16 $02.50/0

évènementiel political and ideological narrative, where the method of the historian limits itself to the consciousness of the actors: a paltry end for those inspired by Karl Marx's *The German Ideology* (London, 1938). The conspiratorial view of revolutionary history is not the sole domain of such reactionary historians as Augustin de Barruel. It can also be the view of social historians who see in conservative governments the simple executive committee of the grande bourgeoisie, or even of economic historians who see in the arrangement of economic facts a plot to create a particular situation.[1]

We find the same difficulty in the position of a Marxist theoretician like Althusser, who, after advancing the view of the fundamental contradiction as that between productive forces and relations of production, still maintains that this contradiction can hold in reserve a revolutionary structure or an actual revolution. I do not reject the idea that so complex an event as a revolution is the result of an exceptional accumulation of diverse factors, all contributing to the same end. The point is rather than it is an admission of defeat for a basically infrastructuralist theory to take refuge in "overdetermination": in this way there would be one historical causality for everyday, and another for special occasions.[2]

The greatest difficulty in a Marxist or more generally causalist conception of the making of history, which keeps the political dimension in reserve as long as possible, is to go *from cause to effect*. By denying a specifically *political* explanation, the infrastructuralist historians condemn themselves to impotence when faced with new, decisive moments when the slow fermentations of the long term suddenly appear to burst, according to this scheme, like bubbles on the surface of history. To say that the revolutionary outbreak, for example, was precipitated by gradual movements in demography or the economy, does not explain either how or why the passage from the "lower" to the "higher" sphere was effected. These historians then resort to tautologies or trivialities: "unique situations," or "the convergence of circumstances," or even the actions of great men.[3]

1   François Furet, *Penser la révolution française* (Paris, 1978), 26–27, 124–125.
2   Louis Althusser (trans. B. Brewster), *For Marx* (New York, 1968), 99–100.
3   On the causalist conception of history see the suggestive analyses of Cornelius Castoriadis, *L'Institution imaginaire de la société* (Paris, 1975), 233–302.

This interpretation of history is constantly torn between the most rigorous mechanistic and the most bewildered psychological explanations. We leap from the profit curve without transition to the exploits of heroes. Thrown out the door, politics sneaks back in by the window. And this is still politics in the most traditional sense, the politics that has been identified, not without reason, with narrative *évènementiel* history. This schizophrenia bases itself, one cannot help but wonder how, on "historical materialism."

From this perspective we can perceive how the pioneers of the *Annales* school were able, without too much injustice, to condemn in one fell swoop those associated with positivist narrative history as it was practiced in France in the late nineteenth and early twentieth centuries, and those representative of a Marxist history, who floundered in the meandering revolutionary recounting of events or in militant apologetics.[4]

In whatever way it is presented, the argument is essentially the same: political history is psychological, biographical, qualitative, ideological, *évènementiel,* in a word, *narrative.*It is the expression of a naive consciousness, which regards painting as an effort to reproduce its model and which, in the same way, is persuaded that the past exists, buried somewhere underneath the dust or archives or the layers of experience; that it is only a question of rediscovering it, of resuscitating it as a whole. It would not occur to this naive consciousness *that its historical object must be constructed* and that, if this is not done, the historian condemns himself to share all the errors of perspective and all the deforming passions of the original actors. If it is not to build something entirely new, then the famous "historical distance" is nothing other than the gradual impoverishment of information along the course of time.[5]

It is no longer possible to condemn in the same breath or regard with the same disdain types of history that are really different, under the pretext that it is customary to label them with the same term. This would not only be unjust, but also would leave in place an inhibition that too often relegates historical renovation to remain in the cellar. In truth, this movement has

4 I have summarized this argument in a contribution to Jacques Le Goff and Pierre Nora (eds.), *Faire de l'histoire* (Paris, 1974), II, 228–250.
5 Lawrence Stone, "The Revival of Narrative: Reflections on a New Old History," *Past & Present,* 85 (1979), 3–24.

reversed itself somewhat in recent years, but the renewal of political and ideological history carries its own risk, that of taking
the form of a backlash against infrastructuralist history, a dis-
guised return to the most conventional types of history.

For these reasons I make a distinction between the different types
of political history. Within this category, one can distinguish four
different areas: first, traditional narrative history, in which politics
is dominant in the chronology of events; second, history where
politics constitutes the principal explicative hypothesis; third, political history as the sociology of power; and finally, political
history over the long term, which emphasizes not events and
mutations, but cultural characteristics and enduring traits.

POLITICAL HISTORY AS NARRATIVE HISTORY   can take two forms:
either the narrow recounting of political events; or a broader
narrative in which political history provides the connecting link.

We have as an example l'Histoire du Parti Communiste Français
by Fauvet, currently editor-in-chief of Le Monde, as well as a
political scientist and one of the most respected exponents of
contemporary French politics. The PCF is a political party, and it
is not surprising that political questions are at the heart of this
book. But these questions are the object of a narration in which
events follow one another in rapid succession. The chapter headings are in themselves significant: "A Slow Gestation," "A Difficult Birth," "A Troubled Childhood," and "Maturity," the
third part of Volume I. This political monograph is presented,
even in its vocabulary, as a biography.[6]

Behind every narrative history it is not difficult to discern,
with more or less ease, the biographical model, which, along with
its other advantages, has a well-defined homogeneous subject and
a construction like those in fiction: a beginning, the development
of the plot, and an end, or at least an epilogue. When we compare
this work to Les Communistes Français by Kriegel, a historian and
political scientist, we find no chronological narrative, but rather
an analysis across time of the different "circles" that make up the
French Communist Party. It is not that chronology is absent: it

6 Jacques Fauvet, with Alain Duhamel, l'Histoire du Parti Communiste Français (Paris,
1965), 2v.

is what makes sense of her arguments concerning party membership and the succeeding generations of party militants. Party politics is not absent either, but it is integrated into the organic
growth of an institution, the PCF, that the author analyzes as a
counter society. From the perspective of political narration, the
history of the PCF becomes that of its élite and, first of all, of its
first leader, Maurice Thorez.[7]

The biography of Thorez by Robrieux can, as much as Fauvet's work, be considered a history of the PCF: the approach is the
same, even if the value judgments are different. The rhythm is
the same, not only because Thorez became so identified with the
PCF that their stories overlap, but also because the narrative history
of an institution like the PCF has been conceived as a biography.[8]

POLITICAL HISTORY AS A SYSTEM OF EXPLANATION   can best be
demonstrated in the case we have just evoked: Is it not appropriate
to the fundamental nature of the object of inquiry to give pride
of place to political narrative when examining a party? Further,
when studying a centralized party run from the top down, is it
not appropriate to emphasize the top group, and in so doing
implicitly criticize its pretence that the party is really run by its
base? The problem is how to express this "preference for the
political" when, instead of an individual or a party, the object of
study is a historic period in its entirety. Fauvet has written, under
the title of *La Quatrième République* (Paris, 1959), an almost entirely partliamentary history of the years 1944–1958. This parliamentary recitation is considered the very stuff of the collective
fate of France during this period simply on the basis of the central
role that Parliament took at that time in the process of decision—
or of indecision. This approach equates the history of a collectivity
with the deliberate expressions of will of its élites. The presence
of a representative régime with universal suffrage does permit one
to conceive of the political history of the masses as the narration
of the words and deeds of their elected representatives.

Traditional ideological history is but a variant of this political
history founded at the same time on psychology and will. It can

7 Annie Kriegel (trans. by E. P. Halperin), *The French Communists: Profile of a People*
(Chicago, 1972; orig. pub. 1968).
8 Philippe Robrieux, *Maurice Thorez, vie secrète et publique* (Paris, 1975). See also the
work of Harvey Goldberg, *The Life of Jean Jaurès* (Madison, 1962).

confer on the 'movements of ideas' a direct historical effect, as others would to the movement of capital, or it can see in the actions of political leaders the application of a previously set program. And yet, the Reformation quickly escaped the original intentions of Martin Luther; the USSR of Vladimir Ilich Lenin bore little resemblance to the ideas expressed shortly before the October Revolution in *The State and Revolution* (New York, 1919). This linear system of causality, which goes from first intentions to the act or which seeks to determine the intellectual responsibility of an act (Who wanted it?), sends us back to the biographical and anthropomorphic model described above. It pictures society as an organic whole endowed with a certain number of characteristics, among them will. Intellectual history can no more be reduced to this naive model than can political history.[9]

THE HISTORICAL SOCIOLOGY OF POWER   In this approach, the historian owes much to neighboring disciplines, most notably to sociology. Veyne has seen in the writings of Weber "the most exemplary historical work of our century." I would add: the most exemplary work in political history. In Weber's work, which embraces the economic, religious, and social aspects with so much power, the political is not erased or reduced to a pale reflection of other forces, and the autonomy of the political is affirmed with particular vigor by the author of *Politik als Beruf.* The celebrated distinctions in *Wirtschaft und Gesellschaft* between the different forms of legitimate domination (traditional, charismatic, and rational) are not merely "ideal types" which would derive from one another, but are also historic figures with all that that implies of risks, ambiguities, and defeats. One could imagine no more radical a break with unbroken linear history. The political history of Weber, like all conceptual efforts, introduces three essential and related elements: discontinuity, typology, and comparison.[10]

One should not minimize the considerable contributions of the founders of the sociology of political organization such as

9   See on this point the reflections of Roger Chartier in "Histoire intellectuelle ou histoire socio-culturelle: les trajectoires françaises," unpub. ms. (Ecole des Hautes Etudes en Sciences Sociales, Paris); William J. Bouwsma, "Intellectual History in the 1980s," in the second of these two special issues of the *Journal of Interdisciplinary History,* XII (1981), forthcoming.
10   Paul Veyne, *Comment on écrit l'histoire, essai d'épistémologie* (Paris, 1971); Max Weber, *Politik als Beruf* (Munich, 1919); *idem, Wirtschaft und Gesellschaft* (Tübingen, 1922).

Roberto Michels and Moisei Iakolevich Ostrogorski. With them, suspicion entered the study of democracy and political history was enriched by a new dimension: one could now measure the distance between words and deeds, latent and surface functions, and finally, sociology and ideology.

Under the influence of sociology and political science, history has turned more and more to the underlying meaning of politics at the occasional expense of politics itself; the analysis of the structure of power, of its language, overshadows the study of its effects. In this sense, the way to study the politics of a government is not only to study its method of conducting public business and making decisions in matters of defense, economy, internal order, and culture, but also to study the strategies of ruling groups to win or conserve power. In a democratic country, the art of governing can be summarized as a permanent arbitration between the desire to make the best—if not always the most popular—decision in terms of the interests of the country and the temptation to make the decision which will most favor the re-election of the leaders.

POLITICAL HISTORY OVER THE LONG TERM   No matter how strong the link between politics and events—to the point that, although not all events are political, one can hardly conceive of events with no political implications—it is still true that political beliefs take deeper root in the individual and collective consciousness, where they become connected to the religious, or at least to the general system of beliefs. The question of politics is part of the problem of the "third floor" of Agulhon. Indeed, should one speak at all of the third floor if one agrees with Ernest Labrousse, the great structural historian, who considers that the social lags behind the economic and the intellectual behind the social, or would it be more appropriate to speak of the first floor, or even the cellar? In reality, now that the infrastructuralist system has shown its impotence, or at least its inadequacy, the idea of a linear causality where the economic, social, and intellectual aspects of history succeed one another in the manner of biblical geneaology has become less and less acceptable. For proof, we can look at politics as it is manifest not only in the very short term, but also over time.[11]

11 Maurice Agulhon, *La République au village* (Paris, 1970; 2nd. ed. 1979).

Using voting behavior as an example of the ambivalence of politics, we find, at first glance, that there is nothing more conjunctural, more prey to economic and other fluctuations of the moment, or to the caprice of public opinion, than voting. Further, it is in principle an example of "weak political behavior," to use the expression of Bertrand de Jouvenel, as opposed to "strong political behavior" such as popular movements or revolutions. But unlike popular movements and revolutions, voting still has the methodological advantage of being by nature quantifiable, with a long, continuous and relatively homogeneous source of data. Yet electoral behavior, where so many accidents and idiosyncrasies intervene, cannot be explained without recourse to the long term, combining the effects of public opinion and mental structures.[12]

At the end of *Tableau politique de la France sous la Troisième République* (Paris, 1913), a pioneering work of electoral geography and sociology, André Siegfried, noting the relative weakness of the geo-social explanations advanced to account for the political behavior of voters, spoke of the "mystery of ethnic temperaments." This is, to be sure, a confession of failure and an open if not proud recourse to tautology. But beyond that, it is the admission by a rigorous, even positivist mind, that politics, in whatever way one approaches it, always escapes the limitations of a simple system of causality, and thus touches on the psychology of the unconscious and the geological strata, as it were, of individuals and social groups. In this sense, politics escapes the unsettled froth of the history of events and finds itself, paradoxically, in the realm of the history of the immovable. It is remarkable that this political map of France is nearly unchanged since the beginning of universal suffrage.

Many others have noted, since Goguel, the striking similarity between the distribution of votes obtained by the Democratic-Socialists in the legislative elections of 13 May, 1849 and that of votes in the referendum of 5 May, 1946 in favor of the new constitution. The similarity has endured to this day, if one com-

12 I say in principle, since elections can at times be the site of major political confrontations. It has been said that the Czech Communists in February 1948 unleashed the series of events now called the coup of Prague in order to avoid a defeat in the forthcoming elections predicted by the polls. Cf. François Fejtö, *Le coup de Prague, 1948* (Paris, 1976). We should therefore join François Goguel in distinguishing between "elections of appeasement" and "elections of combat."

pares the maps of these two elections to that of the votes obtained by François Mitterrand in the second round of the presidential election of 19 May, 1974. But we should not press this comparison too far. Besides, since these maps are drawn up at the level of departments, they may lead to error by concealing many local disputes. Nevertheless, the general outline of the Left-Right cleavage remains; it appears to have resisted any change.[13]

In many respects these maps, which are those of the French Left for the past 130 years, constitute the inverse of the well known map of religious observance in rural France drawn up by Boulard, suggesting a strong correlation between religiosity and votes for the Right. This has been confirmed by the results of opinion surveys. In spite of the decline in church attendance over the past quarter century, religious observance has remained the strongest indicator of voting behavior, stronger in any case than any socio-professional indices one could construct.[14]

The temptation is great to see in politics a crystallization and in some sense a secularization of religion. But it is a temptation one must resist, if only because, in the urban environment, the usefulness of the religious variable has diminished along with religious observance itself. Furthermore, this variable is hardly everywhere what Labrousse has called "the least substitutable antecedent." In the end, its singular effectiveness in France is because, in the society of the nineteenth century, of which traces remain most visible in the countryside, the religious question was the primary conflict. Elections expressed and even reinforced it.

Electoral competition, as its name implies, is a *confrontation* which derives strength from whatever it finds in society: profound trends, opinions, and aspirations which are in some way arranged and organized. The vote is a simple form of expression, reducing the multiplicity of conflicts to a single choice—the reds against the whites, Left against Right. One might ask whether, locally at

13 There are many works referring to this similarity: Goguel, *Géographie des élections françaises de 1870 à 1951* (Paris, 1951); *idem, La politique des partis sous la IVème République* (Paris, 1970; 4th ed.); René Rémond, *La vie politique en France depuis 1789* (Paris, 1965–1969), 2 v.; Goguel and Alfred Grosser, *La Politique en France,* (Paris, 1970; 4th ed.); Frédéric Bon, *Les élections en France,* (Paris, 1978).

14 Fernand Boulard, *An Introduction to Religious Sociology* (London, 1960), 36. The same conclusions were reached by Guy Michelat and Michel Simon in *Classe, religion et comportement politique* (Paris, 1977), a dual investigation by non-directive interviews and opinion surveys.

least, particular electoral behavior in a particular place, which often outlives modifications in the religious or social context, does not depend also on other factors leading to oppositions or even conflicts. For example, there are geographical factors: opposition between town and country, mountain and plain or valley, bocage and open field, areas where circulation is easy and those where it is difficult, the coast and the inland; or administrative factors: the frontier effect created over time by more or less artificial divisions leading to different political consequences (a problem well known in post-colonial Africa), or the rivalry of two cities for regional hegemony. In the same manner, one could raise the question of the role of notables in elections, not as a specific factor so much as a more or less contingent support of particular positions the implications of which can be much more profound.[15]

The intention is not to exhaust the list of theoretically possible determinants of electoral behavior, but rather to indicate those which may have at some moment given support to political bipolarity. It may even be that the confrontation itself creates this effect and not, as is generally believed, the reverse. The idea is to view suffrage as a universal symbolic language, a reduction of the conflicts across society. Thus the link established by historians between this political behavior and that problem, conflict, or mentality, may indeed be spurious, as is clearly shown by Agulhon in his inquiry into the establishment of the republic in the countryside of the Var. His problem was to explain how a people, in less than half a century, could have gone from one end of the political spectrum to the other. The role of contingency in the choice of a political system is clearly described. In the space of half a century, peasant discontent is expressed now on the Right, now on the Left. A few hundred kilometers away, the contrast is still more striking, as has been brilliantly demonstrated by Bois in the case of the Sarthe.[16]

15 Cf. the study, still in progress, initiated by François Furet and Jacques Ozouf, in which I took part, at the Ecole des Hautes Etudes en Sciences Sociales, Paris, on the historical origins of the distribution of voting behavior in contemporary France. Alain Corbin, *Archaisme et modernité en Limousin au XIXeme siecle, 1845–1880* (Paris, 1975), is not "far from thinking" that the town-country opposition "was the most important factor conditioning the political behavior of the Limousin population from 1845 to 1880." One could draw similar conclusions from the study of Paul Bois on the Sarthe (see below, note 16).

16 Agulhon, *La République au village*; Bois, *Paysans de l'ouest. Des structures économiques et sociales aux options politiques depuis l'époque révolutionnaire* (Paris, 1960; abridged ed., Paris, 1971).

Compared with many of his predecessors, who on the whole limited themselves to describing the economic and social conditioning of political behavior, Agulhon, while taking this conditioning into account, has tried to establish the specifically political factors in political behavior: in the case of Var, the role of intellectual and bourgeois activists in inciting the popular classes on behalf of democracy. "The influence of the 'political' is then, in other terms, the influence of classes bearing the very features of national history." As Agulhon takes pains to point out, this approach is not necessarily generalizable. But to our mind it has the great merit of tackling politics head on—for itself—and showing that with comparable social and economic structures, it is culture that makes the difference.[17]

But what is political culture? This question is of some moment in France, where it has led to new historical projects and essays, and has even entered into political debate.[18] The work of Bois, cited above, tries to show how a political tradition strongly identified with the Right, that of the west of France and in particular the department of the Sarthe, goes back to an original event, the French Revolution. To the peasants hungry for land, the sale of the nationalized lands was a great disappointment, because for the most part it was the urban bourgeoisie that was able to purchase them. This basic frustration made the peasantry susceptible to the appeals of the counter-revolution and was the starting point for an uninterrupted chain of political attitudes and voting behavior from the nineteenth century to our time. Of course, the revolutionary trauma took place in a particular socio-economic context. In emphasizing a formative event, as Le Roy Ladurie put it: "the narrative-structural historian that is Paul Bois" has not overlooked traditional factors of conditioning. But he has shown how inside these "the fleeting event secreted a lasting mentality: the short term secreted the long term."[19]

17 Among Agulhon's predecessors are A. Armengaud, *Les populations de l'Est acquitain au début de l'époque contemporaine* (Paris, 1961); Georges Dupeux, *Aspects de l'histoire sociale et politique du Loir et Cher, 1848–1914* (Paris, 1962); Philippe Vigier, *la seconde République dans la région alpine, étude politique et sociale* (Paris, 1963); to which one must add the studies of Corbin and Bois, already cited. Agulhon, *La Republique au village,* 473.

18 Pierre Rosanvallon and Patrick Viveret, *Pour une nouvelle culture politique* (Paris, 1977). Most notably in the remarks of Michel Rocard to the Socialist Congress in Nantes (1977) stating, within the Socialist Party, the existence of "two cultures," the one centralist and Jacobin, the other decentralist and *autogestionnaire*.

19 Emmanuel Le Roy Ladurie, "Evènement et longue durée dans l'histoire sociale: l'exemple chouan," in *Communications,* 18 (1972), 72–84.

The connection between structures and events does not go only in one direction. Normally, one considers the first as having ignited the second; the example of the Sarthe shows also that, on the contrary, a passing sociopolitical circumstance can give way to a durable and even fossilized political culture, to the extent that it has nothing more to do with the event that served as its inspiration.

This formal causality does not always work in the same sense. In the neighboring Limousin studied by Corbin, the resentment of the town by the countryside, comparable in nature to that in the Sarthe but making its appearance during the Revolution of 1848, gave birth to a political culture of the extreme Left, not of the extreme Right.

Another example of the formative role of an event and its later consequences leading to the foundation of a genuine political tradition, this time not only regional, but also national in scope, is the commentary of Furet on the theory of Jacobinism elaborated by Auguste Cochin, a forgotten and then rediscovered theoretician of the French Revolution. In the end, even bearing in mind the advances in historical work on the French Revolution—and one thinks immediately of the work of Labrousse—what remains most mysterious in this great affair is not the short or long term conditions that set the Revolution in motion; is it the motion itself—its "torrent" as Furet puts it. The example of so many other Western nations suggests to us that the "profound causes" could have led to a roughly identical modern France without having taken the revolutionary path. But, where the French Revolution can be said to be irreplaceable is at the level of *politics*: here its work is indelible; French political society is steeped in it. One is almost tempted to say that political culture is what is left when all else has been tried.[20]

As Tocqueville said over and over again, there existed in France a "pre-Jacobinism" before the Revolution. In this sense, the Revolution was a continuation of the Ancien Régime by other means. That the tradition of the Ancien Régime was completely absorbed by the new political culture established after 1789, and that this monarchical conduct became an essential component of the new democratic ideal, justifies the prominence of the Revolution in French history. Of this analysis, I retain three elements which we have already encountered: first, the frequent occurrence

20 Furet, *Penser la révolution française* (Paris, 1978).

of a formative event at the origin of a political tradition; second, the role of "circles of thought" in the elaboration of Jacobinism; last, and most important, the express wish not to reduce the political dimension to a crystallization, more or less superficial, and more or less parasitic, of the economic or the social dimension. On the contrary we make the political dimension the very object of analysis: "In the end," writes Furet, "the Marxist Vulgate of the history of the French Revolution turns the world upside down: It situates the revolutionary break at the level of the economic and social, when nothing resembles the society of Louis XVI so much as the society of Louis Philippe."[21]

In an attempt to define the possible meanings of political history and to describe its recent expressions, I have admittedly taken the easiest course. But the very object of this effort impels me to go beyond this exposition and to imagine, not what will be—prediction has never been a strong point of historians—but what could be political history in the years to come.

To put the question differently, what is the relationship between political and contemporary history and do they have something particular in common? The re-examination of the issues and methods of history that took place in France under the aegis of Marc Bloch and Lucien Febvre of the *Annales* appears to have bypassed both political and contemporary history. At its inception, however, *Annales* attached particular importance to the study of the contemporary world; Febvre even wished for a reverse history that would begin with the present day and go back in time. At the same time, the journal manifested a certain mistrust of political history.[22] But contemporary history soon lost ground as well, falling into the same disregard as political history, and the new history skirted them both. This dismissal was hardly accidental since it is genuinely difficult, when studying the present day, to set aside the intentions and wills of actors. Is this because, without the distance of time, these intentions and wills are the only explanations at our disposal? Or is it, in a more serious vein, because they have acquired in the world of today an importance that they lacked in former times?

21 Alexis de Tocqueville, *L'ancien régime et la révolution* (Paris, 1856); Furet, *Penser la révolution*, 41.
22 Cf. André Burguière, "Histoire d'une histoire: la naissance des *Annales*," *Annales*, XXXIV (1979), 1347–1359.

Two hypotheses can now be presented: the first is the continued increase of the number of actors implicated in political decision making; the second is the continued extension of the sphere of application of these decisions.

The first hypothesis challenges historians to reflect on what they think about the democratic credo, which over the past thirty years has come to hold the allegiance of the majority of people: it is the masses, whether by regular and peaceable means, through the exercise of universal suffrage, or by sudden and violent means, who make history—and make it with greater and greater consciousness. "The history of a revolution," wrote Trotsky, "is for us first of all a history of the forcible entrance of the masses into the realm of rulership over their own destiny." The claim of universal suffrage is that it establishes the rule of popular sovereignty. No one has ever claimed, not even Jean Jacques Rousseau, that popular sovereignty can rule over the physical world as it can over society; that it can eliminate the realm of necessity. But if the dogma of popular sovereignty is valid, then with the coming of universal suffrage the true social history has become political history.[23]

As proof *a contrario,* one need only remark that the destruction of liberal and democratic society by totalitarianism, far from liquidating the dogma of the power of the masses, has on the contrary based itself on it. Most assuredly, the parody of democracy acted out by nearly all the tyrants on the surface of the earth is like the compliment that vice pays to virtue.[24]

But must historians become systematically neo-Machiavellian along the lines of Vilfredo Pareto, and see everywhere in the forms of democratic participation a mere camouflage of the power of élites? It is true that the first, the most illustrious, and the most influential of the neo-Machiavellians was Marx himself, in his denunciation of the illusions of political democracy. And yet, in Marxism, politics got its revenge in the end; the democratic skepticism changed in a flash into socialist idealism. What then is socialism if not the moment when the political is placed, to join Mao Tse Tung, at "the command post" of society, where the people's will becomes the true infrastructure of society? The essential point is that contemporary historians are obliged to give

23 Leon Trotsky, *The Russian Revolution* (New York, 1959), ix-x.
24 See the work of Hannah Arendt, *The Origins of Totalitarianism* (New York, 1951), Pt. 3.

pride of place, if only to unmask its illusions, to democratic decision making.

The second hypothesis is closely linked to the first. Does not the increasing weight of science and technology in the modern world tend to increase, if only modestly, the role of the conscious and the voluntary in social life? Alongside the economy as something endured by men, should not the student of contemporary history give greater weight to the attempts of governments and social institutions to master the economy—in other words, give due credit to strategies, in effect to policies? In the same way, we attempt today to master demographic change, to regulate it by influencing fertility and sterility, instead of leaving this regulation to the "natural" forces of famine, war, and epidemic. This action extends even into the realm of culture, which is now, alas, the object of a strategy—that is, a policy.

For the moment, the results are still meager. In spite of the means of analysis, prediction, and intervention at our disposal, modern economies have been unable either to predict or to vanquish the crises that beseige them. The scales still tilt in the direction of necessity, not of will. In the demographic realm, not only do the great catastrophes of the past remain historical agents of the first order, but the demographers confess their inability to explain satisfactorily the changes in the attitudes and behavior of populations in life questions.

However, we are now entering an era of "programmed societies" in which collective political decisions weigh ever more heavily in the life of the individual. And should it not be considered a turning point in the history of mankind and the coming of age of politics, itself the child of science and technology, that for the first time the greatest cataclysm threatening humanity is no longer natural, but the product of human will: the nuclear holocaust?

For the contemporary historian, above and beyond the traditional approaches to politics (such as narrative accounts and critical sociologies of power), which there is no question of eliminating, there are two particularly effective ways to make use of political studies to understand societies under scrutiny: to measure the weight of the past through the political cultures that issue from it; and to evaluate the weight of the future through the different implications of social programming.

What is the relation of political history to change? Change

can hardly be said to be popular today among historians; most prefer the study of continuities and structures, glancing only briefly at the conditions of passage from one state to another, from one system to another. For the man of action, however, the factors of change are the essential question. The detachment of today's historians from anything that could be a guide for action was perhaps the condition for the attainment by the discipline of scientific status, or was perhaps simply an escape from the problems of today; but in any case this detachment is already well established. In closing the renowned, perhaps too well renowned book by Febvre on the religion of François Rabelais, one cannot help but wonder when and how atheism could have ever arisen in contemporary France, so much did the old mentalities keep everything under lock and key. And yet, mentalities change.[25]

The search for causality in history, or even more modestly, the revelation of structures and persistences, leads one to forget that there is always more to an event than its causes; that in history there is permanent innovation. At the risk of imagining the historical unfolding of events as the unending and inexorable development from an initial "big bang," one must admit that social history is in part a continuous creation. To say this is in no way to imply the negation of determinism, but only to reject the linear conception, in imitation of Newtonian physics, of historical evolution, in favor of a more analytical, or rather, cybernetic view of this evolution.

The analysis of a maze of independent yet converging sequences in an original fused whole, not reducible to the sum of its parts, is in modern society the task of political history, precisely because political history takes into account the strategies of actors in the face of historical necessity. In modern societies, the inter-relations are sufficiently numerous to give birth to events, institutions, and even structures that are sufficiently complex for the word *political* to remain the only one capable of describing them.

25 Jacques Revel, "Histoire et science sociale: les paradigmes des *Annales*," *Annales*, XXXIV (1979), 1371: "The history dominant in the *Annales* is divorced from any analysis of social change." Lucien Febvre, *Le problème de l'incroyance au XVIe siècle: la religion de Rabelais* (Paris, 1947).

Political History in the 1980s

Peter Clarke

Ideas and Interests   The contribution of political science to the study of political history has been in introducing a beneficial rigor to the definition of concepts and the specification of problems. It is also, and not coincidentally, associated with the application of quantitative methods and schematic models. But the social sciences as such deal in abstractions and regularities, especially those which can be approached within a quantitative and comparative perspective. The use of the particular here may legitimately be through case studies in order to enlarge and enhance the body of theory. This procedure, however, imports an illegitimate objective for historians. They can certainly learn from comparative studies and from theory, but as historians they are actually and ultimately concerned with what happened once. They draw upon theory in order to enlarge and enhance their understanding of the particular, in all its historical richness.[1] And if historians are concerned with "what happened once" there is an inescapable role for contingency in their causal explanations, especially in political history. They may be forced to discover causes of particular developments, not in deep structural regularities, but in what is trivial.[2]

Politics, seen as part of real history, is inevitably intertwined with social and economic conditions. Powicke, in the preface of a book which dealt at length with such subjects as war, diplomacy, and public finance, wrote: "This book is a study in social history, not in the sense in which the term is generally used, but in the sense of social life, relations, and forces in political action.

Peter Clarke is a Fellow of St. John's College, Cambridge. His most recent book is *Liberals and Social Democrats* (Cambridge, 1978).

0022-1953/81/01045-3 $02.50/0

1   It goes without saying that if the subject of investigation falls below a certain threshold of significance it will hardly repay historical study in itself.

2   I am happy to find much the same point argued in the text of the valedictory lecture by Hugh Trevor-Roper, "History and Imagination," *Times Literary Supplement* (July 25, 1980), 833–835.

Political history and social history are, in my view, two aspects of one process. Social life loses half its interest and political movements lose most of their meaning if they are considered apart."[3]

It is helpful to speak of social and economic conditions, not as determinants, but as constraints which limit the available political strategies. But if we are to understand this process we must also allow for the influence of political ideas. One of the problems central to politics is that of adjusting conflicting interests and conflicting ideas. It is not just that both have a sociological dimension; they share a sociological interface. Interests may be an expression of the social structure, but this should not be taken as given in static, concrete, material terms. We need to be concerned also with social consciousness as the perceptions of that structure, for they determine the agenda of politics.

The role of ideas is not so much as doctrine but as ideology. By doctrine I mean a formally articulated, and probably sophisticated, system of political thought. By ideology I mean the social purchase of political ideas, in relating to different social groups and in making sense of their social position and interests in a convincing way. And the "fit" here constitutes the verisimilitude of an ideology, as a vision of the world and its possibilities, speaking to certain economic and social needs but also possessing an internal coherence.

There are three accounts of the political process with immediate claims on our attention. First, there is the view of politics as realized intentions. This is part of what has been referred to as the linear system of causality. The interpretation of public policy as the people's voice is another variant. This is a teleological populism in which cause and effect operate in a simple chain—too simple by half, as the obvious retort would have it.

Second is the view of politics as economically determined. This is the classical Marxist position, pointing to the relations of production as an all-embracing explanation of all political structures and all political actions. In this form it ought to be clear that the sort of explanation which is offered is a functional one. Relationships, developments, and events are to be explained by their effects, especially in permitting or encouraging capitalism to continue. It is useful to have attention directed to the outcome of politics in this way. But what is missing, as in all functionalist

3 F. Maurice Powicke, *King Henry III and the Lord Edward* (Oxford, 1947), I, v.

interpretations, is an explanation of *how* the functional outcome was reached. Cohen, as a philosopher, is content to defend functional explanation by establishing the claim: "It is possible to know *that* x explains *y*, and yet find it very puzzling that *x should* explain *y*, through failure to see *how* *x* explains *y*." Yet the historian's curiosity over how things happened cannot so easily be appeased.[4]

Third is the view of politics as manipulation by elites. This focuses attention on the strategies adopted for getting and keeping power, a problem largely evaded by "teleological populism." It points to the role of insiders (and challengers) who seek to manipulate the system in order to advance their own interests, as a class, or as competitive individuals. The salience of ambition and maneuver has recently received attention in several notable studies of "high politics." This is salutary so far as it goes, and only unsatisfying when "high politics" is presented as the whole of politics. It is little gain to replace an account that is politically naive with one that is psychologically and sociologically naive in its analysis of the role of political leaders and the forces which they seek to mobilize.[5]

Although each of these approaches in itself may be flawed, each offers important insights. It would be a curious history which did not discuss people's own understanding of what they were doing, and therefore dismissed intentions. But the recognition that these intentions might well not be realized in ways that had been foreseen also points to the importance of outcomes and the general constraints of the social structure. In explaining how the outcomes were decided, the role of political maneuver also demands attention. My suggestion is that a full rendering of political history will pay more attention to the problem of ideology, which is relevant in all three respects. The conditions making for the verisimilitude of an ideology are at once those of social structure and social consciousness and also of political mobilization and leadership. All of these aspects therefore merit consideration in the sort of political history capable of exploring the tension between ideas and the interests that they serve.

4 I am much indebted to the lucid study by G. A. Cohen, *Karl Marx's Theory of History: A Defence* (Oxford, 1978), esp. 249–296.
5 The outstanding contributions from this school are: Maurice Cowling, *1867: Disraeli, Gladstone and Revolution* (Cambridge, 1967); idem, *The Impact of Labour, 1920–1924* (Cambridge, 1971); idem, *The Impact of Hitler* (Cambridge, 1975); Alistair B. Cooke and John Vincent, *The Governing Passion* (Brighton, 1974).

Political History in the 1980s

Jacques Revel

A Comment Does an examination of the status of political history have a place in a collection of essays devoted to "History in the 1980s"? I would not have raised the question had not Jacques Julliard and Peter Smith done so themselves in their contributions to this volume. Smith suggests that political history has been declared old-fashioned and outmoded, and Julliard says that it is reputed to be superficial and largely irrelevant.

This unfortunate reputation that the field seems to have acquired does not, in my opinion, correspond to the actual situation. Even in France where the *Annales* tradition and its sphere of influence could be thought to have dominated the directions of history, political history remains a vital field both in terms of the output of articles and the faculty positions held by political historians within academic institutions. Why then the bad reputation?

It is true that political history has not featured in the general revival of historical scholarship that has marked the past thirty to fifty years and that the revival has actually taken a sharply critical stance towards political history. The criticisms leveled against political history have focused on three points. First was the reappraisal of historical fact. Those historians who sought scientific status for their discipline or some integration of history within the social sciences claimed that only repetitive facts constituted in a series could provide a rigorous basis for scientific observation. The unique event—a political occurrence for example—was irrelevant.

Second, the critics claimed that politics remained only at the surface of the social reality which historians were purporting to comprehend as a whole. As such political history was asserted, without justification, to be mainly contemporary history—and, in particular, an analysis of short-term phenomena.

Jacques Revel is co-editor of *Annales*. He has co-authored *La nouvelle histoire* (Paris, 1978).

0022-1953/81/01049-2 $02.50/0

The third aspect of this critical appraisal identified political history with a literary genre, the so-called chronicle, in which narrative rhetorical devices replaced an articulated analysis of rigorous sets of questions.

These criticisms leveled at the field in the early twentieth century did not succeed in eradicating the study of political history. The reasons for this failure were many: historiographical changes (or fashions) proceed slowly; politics are so obviously present in our daily lives that it would be impossible to remove them from historical experience; the leading challenges in the field of socioeconomic history were not able to reduce politics to the mere output of basic determination, nor to equate political analysis with social, economic, or cultural analysis. Remarkable monographic studies (for example, the work of Agulhon on southern France) have proceeded not by building a general formal system of relations between politics and socioeconomic conditions, but by making those relations more complex to the point that those abstractions—politics, society, and the economy—need to be redefined and comprehended through real social forms. The articles of Smith and Julliard lead us to the same conclusions, with the example of *dependancia* in Latin America and the case of the Revolution in French historiography.[1]

Political history is alive and, what is more, it seems to be changing. What is striking is that both Smith and Julliard are advocating a larger and more complex definition of politics. This means that whereas historians were accustomed to view politics as a mere superficial level of the social reality, they now recognize a most (and perhaps the most) complex arrangement of social forms, which may explain the most recent attempts to incorporate sociological and anthropological concepts or patterns into the study of political history.

This expansion of the field does not mean that sociology or anthropology will provide political historians with ready-made solutions; but it does demonstrate that the definition of politics and of political analysis is no longer straightforward—not for historians, not for political historians, and not for their critics. It may be rather that it is political history that is again a central value in historical analysis.

1 Maurice Agulhon, *La République au village* (Paris, 1970).

Family History in the 1980s

Lawrence Stone

Past Achievements and Future Trends

GROWTH, SOURCES, AND TYPOLOGY   Within the field of history, social history has been the greatest growth industry since World War II, with its sub-field family history having undergone an even more spectacular expansion. Although this growth has taken place all over the world, it has been most heavily concentrated in America, France, and England, which together account for nearly 40 percent of the total world output. The books and articles produced in these three countries, which are almost equal in the total volume of their respective output, have been outstanding in quality as well as quantity, for this is where most of the important and innovatory work has been done.[1]

The output for these three countries is an indicator of how the field has grown. The number of significant books and articles published about family history rose in England and France from under ten every five years in the 1920s, 1930s, and early 1940s to between 200 and 240 from 1972 to 1976—a twentyfold increase in thirty years (Table 1). What is so remarkable is the dizzy acceleration of growth in the 1970s, at a time when the total output of scholarly publications was leveling off as the economic crisis of academia began to affect both authors and publishers.

In America the growth curve is basically similar, although it differs in some significant respects. The pre-war output, mostly devoted either to sociological theory or to the history of the post-1890 period, was already higher than that of England or France,

Lawrence Stone is the Dodge Professor of History and the Director of the Shelby Cullom Davis Center for Historical Studies, Princeton University. Among his books is *The Family, Sex and Marriage in England, 1500–1800* (London, 1977).

0022-1953/81/01051-37 $02.50/0

1   These observations are derived from the comprehensive study of Gerald L. Soliday (ed.), *History of Family and Kinship: A Select International Bibliography* (New York, 1980). I am deeply indebted to Soliday for his kindness in providing me with an advance copy of this magnificent bibliographical tool while it was still in proof.

Table 1 Books and Articles on the History of the Family Published Between 1922 and 1976[a]

PERIOD	ENGLAND	FRANCE	U.S.A.	TOTAL
1922–26	8	6	6	20
1927–31	10	8	13	31
1932–36	8	9	22	39
1937–41	7	10	23	40
1942–46	5	11	20	36
1947–51	22	22	16	60
1952–56	47	61	44	152
1957–61	65	72	40	177
1962–66	104	107	76	287
1967–71	145	147	144	436
1972–76	212	252	338	802

[a] Extracted from an analysis of *History of the Family and Kinship: a Select International Bibliography* (ed.) Gerald L. Soliday (New York, 1980). Note that this bibliography is "select," not complete.

but the take-off only began in earnest after 1961, almost a decade later than in the other two countries. Since then, however, growth has occurred at an even faster pace, reaching a peak of 340 publications during the period 1972 to 1976. In all three countries over 800 books and articles on family history appeared in those five years.

In the last 100 years many outside influences have stimulated this rapid growth of interest in family history. The first was sociology, as Engels in England tried to link the family to industrialization, and as Le Play in France established a typology of family structures, from the extended to the stem to the nuclear. These scholars set the historians on the track of what have been two central areas of inquiry ever since.[2]

A second early influence, which has strongly affected family history in France, but is hardly visible elsewhere, has come from legal history. French law schools have long been turning out doctoral dissertations on local marriage customs and laws of inheritance. They have been based on legal documents and on folklore, which has been highly developed in that country. As a result, it is only in France that it has so far been possible to

2 Friedrich Engels, *The Origins of the Family, Private Property and the State* (New York, 1972); Pierre G. F. Le Play, *L'Organisation de la Famille* (Paris, 1871).

produce a national survey of local variations in inheritance customs.[3]

In America, and to a lesser degree in England, anthropology has had a considerable impact on the historical profession. Anthropologists have always been intensely concerned with such matters as kinship structures, incest taboos, and endogamy and exogamy in marriage, and it is from them that the historians developed their interest in such matters as marriage customs and the roles of the patriarch, lineage, and kin.

In the late 1940s, as social history got under way, it became clear that a key methodology was going to be local community studies, since only by strict geographical limitation could these attempts at "total history" become manageable. As soon as these studies became limited to a single village community, as happened in America where the time available for the completion of dissertations is much shorter than in Europe, attention was almost automatically directed at the family, since it was almost the only institution still visible in this narrow microscopic focus.[4]

In the 1950s and 1960s the most important influence in shaping the field was historical demography, one major consequence of which has been, until very recently, the strongly quantitative character of much of family history. Studies based on literary or qualitative evidence have been, and still are, regarded in many quarters with considerable suspicion, as being both unscientific in methodology and elitist in content. They violate the norms of the two fashionable current ideals: scientific history and history from below.

In the 1970s other, more topical concerns came into play. It was evident by then that the Western family was undergoing rapid change. Sexual mores were being transformed by penicillin and the pill, which removed the two main hazards of extra-marital sex; divorce rates were soaring to 50 percent as feminist demands for equality increased the strains of cohabitation, and as the ro-

---

3 Jean Yver, *Egalité entre héritiers et exclusion des enfants dotés: essai de géographie coutumière* (Paris, 1966); Emmanuel Le Roy Ladurie, "Family Structures and Inheritance Customs in Sixteenth Century France," in Jack Goody, Joan Thirsk, and Edward P. Thompson (eds.), *Family and Inheritance* (Cambridge, 1976).

4 John Demos, *A Little Commonwealth: Family Life in Plymouth Colony* (New York, 1970); Philip J. Greven, Jr., *Four Generations: Population, Land, and Family in Colonial Andover, Massachusetts* (Ithaca, 1970); Kenneth Lockridge, "The Population of Dedham, Mass., 1636–1736," *Economic History Review*, XIX (1966), 318–344.

mantic expectations of couples about marriage proved unrealistic. The desired number of children shrank dramatically, as prospective parents reckoned up their cost, in money, time, energy, and affection. Married women abandoned the nursery and the kitchen and poured into the work force. Some saw these massive changes as a threat to the social fabric, others as a welcome adjustment to the new conditions of modern life. In order to put these urgent contemporary problems into perspective, everyone wanted to know what family life was really like in the past. Was there a golden age of the family somewhere out there, or merely a dismal record of male chauvinist tyranny, child abuse, cruelty, economic exploitation, emotional coldness, and sexual frustration? It seemed—and still seems—important to find out.

In America, but hardly at all elsewhere as yet, the Women's Liberation Movement generated a flurry of historical interest in women in the past. It was pointed out—rightly—that standard history books had largely ignored one half of the human race, unless its members happened to be queens or the wives or mistresses of prominent men. The history of gender, sex-roles, and feminist ideas and movements has become the subject of American university courses, books, articles, and collections of historical pamphlet literature. Defeated feminists from the past, like Mary Wollstonecraft, have suddenly emerged from the obscurity in which they had long languished.

The sexual liberation of the 1970s has meant that a subject which had hitherto been on everyone's minds but was never publicly spoken about, least of all in history books, suddenly became very fashionable. Not only were the major pornographic classics of the eighteenth or nineteenth century, like James Cleland's *Fanny Hill* (London, 1749) or the anonymous *My Secret Life* (Amsterdam, c. 1882–94), suddenly reproduced in their hundreds of thousands; almost for the first time historians began investigating changes in sexual behavior in the past, both inside and outside marriage. They have studied changes in the principle and practice of the double sexual standard, the frequency of bastardy and prenuptial conceptions, the treatment of sexual deviants like homosexuals, the scale of prostitution, and the history of menarche, menopause, masturbation, female orgasm, and so on.

Finally, partly under the stimulus of psychology and cultural anthropology, there has occurred first in France and then in England and America, a new interest in the history of *mentalité*—in the values, beliefs, emotions, and passions of individuals and groups. This interest has stimulated a new kind of family history, concerned as much with emotional as with economic or social relationships. New questions have been asked about the nature and quality of personal bonds among the members of the nuclear family and the kin, and within the family between husband and wife, and parents and children.

Since these influences have been the main inspirations behind the astonishing growth of family history, it is easy to understand why the historiography can be classified into five broad types, characterized by different data, different methodologies, and different questions. The first is demographic, establishing the parameters of birth, marriage, and death, with all that these entail. The second type is legal, setting out the laws and customs which have governed marriage arrangements, the influence of the lineage and the kin, the power of the patriarch, the rules governing payment for marriage (whether bride price was paid by the groom or dowry paid by the bride), and the transmission of property by inheritance (whether partible or impartible or somewhere in between). The third type is economic, treating the family either as it was in the past as a unit of production, and studying the effect upon it of female and child labor inside or outside the home, working together in a joint family enterprise or separately as wage laborers; or treating it as it is today as a unit of consumption of the cornucopia of goods poured out by modern Western capitalist economies. The fourth type is social; this may look at the evolving structure of various groupings—lineage, kin, household, and family, whether extended or nuclear; or it may concern itself with specific age groups, such as children, adolescents, or the elderly. The fifth and last type is psychological and behavioral, concerned with how people have treated one another, parents and children, husbands and wives, the nuclear family and the kin, the old and the young; how they have behaved sexually before and after marriage, and how they have thought they *ought* to behave; and finally their values, states of mind and emotions, and their degree of responsiveness to marital affection, love, lust, respect for the aged, or devotion to little children.

These five types are themselves subdivided into two broad, and unfortunately largely water-tight, categories: history from above and history from below. Until the nineteenth century we know little about 90 percent of all who have lived in the past except the bare facts of their births, their deaths, and perhaps their marriages. Family history of the bottom 90 percent of the population has consequently been largely quantitative and statistical in nature. If not, it has been drawn from the possibly biased reports of middle-class observers, from testimony in law-suits, or has been dubiously extrapolated from the attitudes and behavior of the literate elite.

These latter, the top 5 or 10 percent, have left behind them a vast mass of documentation—laws, lawsuits, wills, marriage settlements, didactic literature, newspapers, novels, poems, love letters, family correspondence, autobiographies, and diaries. In this discrepancy between the overwhelming evidence for a small minority, and the wholly inadequate evidence for the vast majority lies one of the major unsolved weaknesses of family history.

HISTORIOGRAPHY

Demography   In reviewing the development of family history, it is wise to start with historical demography, since it provides the basic factual infrastructure, and comprises a high proportion of the total output. There have been three main sources for work on historical demography: parish registers of baptisms, marriages, and burials; pre-nineteenth century censuses of villages and a few towns, listing the inhabitants house by house; and nineteenth-century official nation-wide censuses. None are without their problems; the first are particularly unreliable, especially in England and America, and record linkage presents intractable problems. In 1967 Flynn concluded gloomily that "in view of all the difficulties of aggregation, one is left wondering whether it will ever be possible to derive conclusions of any real value from the employment of this technique." [5]

5 Major general works include: Louis Henry, "Historical Demography," *Daedalus,* XCVII (1968), 385–396; Thomas H. Hollingsworth, *Historical Demography* (Ithaca, 1969); Peter Laslett and Richard Wall (eds.), *Household and Family in Past Time* (Cambridge, 1972). See also, Lutz K. Berkner, "The Use and Misuse of Census Data for the Historical Analysis of Family Structure," *Journal of Interdisciplinary History,* V (1975), 721–738; David V. Glass and D. E. C. Eversley (eds.), *Population in History: Essays in Historical Demography* (London, 1965); Richard T. Vann, "History and Demography," *History and Theory,* IX (1969), 64–78; E. Anthony Wrigley, *Population and History* (New York, 1959); Jean-Louis

More promising than aggregation of recorded baptisms, marriages, and burials for family history is the laborious and time-consuming technique of family reconstitution, which consists in taking a parish register and using it to reconstruct the vital genealogical facts of individual families over several generations. The results are difficult to interpret, but if only we can rely on it, this technique allows us to obtain precise information about the crucial demographic indicators which form the basic parameters of family life. We can establish age-specific fertility and nuptiality rates, the median age of marriage of men and women; the frequency of remarriage; age-specific infant, child, and adult mortality rates; prenuptial conception rates; indications of the use or non-use of contraceptive measures; and so on.[6]

Investigations using these methods have been in progress in France for many years now, under the leadership of Henry and Goubert. Many of the results have been published, and the findings of a comprehensive, collective nation-wide sampling will soon appear. For England, nothing has yet been published except the puzzling data for the single, possibly atypical, village of Colyton in Devon, although work on some other villages and one or two small towns is in progress. For colonial America, the procedure is limited by the inadequacy of the records, especially of burials, but some useful conclusions have been drawn from a number of studies of New England villages and towns.[7]

Flandrin, *Familles: parenté, maison, sexualité dans l'ancienne société* (Paris, 1976); Wrigley (ed.), *Identifying People in the Past* (London, 1973); *idem*, "Clandestine Marriage in Tetbury in the Late Seventeenth Century," *Local Population Studies*, X (1973), 15–21; Michael W. Flynn, "Population in History," *Economic History Review*, XX (1967), 141. For a more optimistic view, see Eversley, "Exploitation of Anglican Parish Registers by Aggregative Analysis," in Laslett et al. (eds.), *An Introduction to English Historical Demography* (London, 1966); David Levine, "The Reliability of Parochial Registration and the Representativeness of Family Reconstitution," *Population Studies*, XXX (1976), 107–122.

6   Henry, *Manuel de démographie historique* (Geneva, 1970); Roger S. Schofield, "La reconstitution de la famille par ordinateur," *Annales*, XXVII (1972), 1071–1082; *idem*, "The Representativeness of Family Reconstitution," *Local Population Studies*, VIII (1972), 13–17; Wrigley, "Family Reconstitution," in Laslett et al., *Introduction to English Historical Demography*, 96–159; Antoinette Chamoux, "La reconstitution des familles: espoirs et réalités," *Annales*, XXVII (1972), 1083–1090.

7   Henry, "Ducs et pairs sous l'Ancien Régime: charactéristiques démographiques d'une caste," *Population*, XV (1960), 807–830; *idem*, "The Population of France in the Eighteenth Century," in Glass and Eversley (eds.), *Population in History*, 434–456; Pierre Goubert, *Beauvais et le Beauvaisis de 1600 à 1730* (Paris, 1960). Wrigley, "Family Limitation in Pre-Industrial England," *Economic History Review*, XIX (1966), 82–109; *idem* "Mortality in

Certain facts are now clear. Everywhere among the bottom 95 percent of the population, marriage for both sexes came late, grew later still in England and France in the seventeenth and early eighteenth centuries, and then became a little earlier again. Men in their late twenties married women in their mid-twenties. The same situation has been found in New England in the seventeenth century. This late marriage pattern, which is unique to the West, coupled with a relatively low and declining level of nuptiality, is the most startling and significant finding of the past two decades of demographic history as it affects the family.

That families were only formed very late seems beyond dispute, but what still remains uncertain is when the pattern established itself, and why. What induced men and women in northwest Europe and America to delay marriage some ten years or more after puberty, a decision involving heroic self-control in the sphere of sexual gratification? We do not know, but it obviously must have had an immediate economic cause. And, indeed, we find that everywhere in these areas young couples set up house by themselves, instead of moving in with the parents of one or other spouse as was normal elsewhere. To marry they therefore needed to save up capital to buy furniture and tools, and to acquire the necessary skills to pay the rent or to buy a house. This could only be done by a long period of hard work and abstemious living to accumulate the necessary capital and qualifications.

The next question, however, is why and when this pattern of neo-local residence, as it is called, established itself in the first place. About this we are almost wholly ignorant although there are indications that it was established by the fifteenth or even fourteenth century. Associated with this custom is that of the female dowry. Instead of a bride-price, whereby the groom paid money to the parents of the bride, the Western custom was for the bride and/or her parents to pay money to the groom or his parents, to give the new couple a start in life. Once again we are not sure when or why the dowry rather than the bride-price became the norm, although we know that it was prescribed under

Pre-Industrial England: The Example of Colyton, Devon over Three Centuries," *Daedalus*, XCVII (1968), 546–580. Demos, *A Little Commonwealth*; Greven, *Four Generations*; Robert V. Wells, "Household Size and Composition in the British Colonies in America, 1675–1775," *Journal of Interdisciplinary History*, IV (1973–74), 543–570; idem, "Quaker Marriage Patterns in a Colonial Perspective," *William and Mary Quarterly*, XXIX (1972), 415–442.

classical Roman law, and was standard in eleventh-century Italy. The facts are clear, but the reasons for them remain obscure.

Family reconstitution has enabled scholars to prove convincingly that infant and child mortality were in general very high, and also that they declined in the sixteenth century, rose in the late seventeenth and early eighteenth centuries, and then declined again after about 1750. The reasons for these cyclical swings, however, remain obscure. Whatever may have been the causes of early death, some—including myself—have argued that there were significant limiting psychological results. A fully child-oriented society, we say, is not likely to develop in a situation in which one third of all children are dead by the age of one, and one half do not survive into adulthood, although no one claims a direct and crude inverse correlation between infant mortality and maternal love. The anthropological evidence is clearly opposed to any such view. But if there were a link of some sort, which way did it go? Did greater parental care reduce infant mortality in the mid-eighteenth century, or vice-versa?

Whatever the answer, evidence is mounting that infanticide, by deliberate or semi-deliberate neglect or direct abandonment to almost certain death in foundling hospitals, was perhaps the most important element in family limitation by the poor in early modern Europe, if only because the main alternatives, contraception and abortion, were unavailable. This general prevalence of infant neglect and abandonment, and the extraordinary expansion of the use of wet-nursing by both of upper and lower urban groups in eighteenth- and early nineteenth-century France, despite its known lethal consequences, undermine the argument of those who believe that maternal love is a historical constant in all cultures, as well as a biological given.[8]

The other important finding about mortality as it affected family history is that it was high among young adults, especially women exposed to the perils of childbirth. As a result, the ex-

8 On infanticide: William L. Langer, "Infanticide: A Historical Survey," *History of Childhood Quarterly*, I (1974), 353–365; Barbara A. Kellum, "Infanticide in England in the Later Middle Ages," *History of Childhood Quarterly*, I (1974), 367–388; K. Wrightson, "Infanticide in Earlier Seventeenth-Century England," *Local Population Studies*, XV (1975), 10–22; Emily R. Coleman, "L'infanticide dans le haut Moyen Age," *Annales*, XXIX (1974), 315–335. On abandonment: Claude Delasselle, "Les enfants abandonnés à Paris au XVIIIe siècle," *Annales*, XXX (1975), 187–218; François Lebrun, "Naissances illégitimes et abandons d'enfants en Anjou au XVIIIe siècle," *Annales*, XXVII (1972), 1183–1189.

pectation of a durable marriage in the past was even lower than today, despite our high divorce rate. Divorce, in fact, serves as a modern functional substitute for death. On the average, a seventeenth-century peasant marriage in France could be expected to last only about twelve to seventeen years. This meant that less than half of all fathers were still alive at the marriage of their eldest son, and that it was a society with very many orphans who, dependent on circumstances, were taken in by their nearest relatives, paid for by the parish, or else abandoned to starve in the gutter.

Family reconstitution can both tell us about the average family size and also throw some flickering light on the vexed problem of the timing, social specificity, causes, and scale of the practice of family limitation. Statistics about mean fertility of completed families, that is of couples who remained alive and together until the wife's menopause, prove that the notion of the average house swarming with children and a new baby being born every year are without foundation in fact. Because of lactation, which provides some protection, births were in most societies naturally spaced at about two-year intervals, and many infants soon died.[9]

An early age of the mother at the conception of her last child, and longer and longer intervals between conceptions after the birth of the first two or three children, regardless of the mother's age, are both plausible indications of contraceptive practices. At the higher levels of society, among the Genevan or Lyons bourgeoisie or the European aristocracy, aggregate evidence of a

9 Norman Himes, *Medical History of Contraception* (Baltimore, 1936); James T. Noonan, *Contraception: A History of its Treatment by the Catholic Theologians and Canonists* (Cambridge, Mass., 1966); Hélène Bergues (ed.), *La prévention des naissances dans la famille: ses origines dans les temps modernes* (Paris, 1960); Flandrin, "Contraception, mariage et relations amoureuses dans l'Occident chrétien," *Annales,* XXIV (1969), 1370–1390; *idem, L'église et le contrôle des naissances* (Paris, 1970); Orest and Patricia Ranum (eds.), *Popular Attitudes toward Birth Control in Pre-Industrial France and England* (New York, 1972); Edward Shorter, "Female Emancipation, Birth Control, and Fertility in European History," *American Historical Review,* LXXVIII (1973), 605–640; J. A. Banks, *Prosperity and Parenthood: A Study of Family Planning among the Victorian Middle Classes* (London, 1954); Alain Croix and C. Dauphin, "La contraception avant la révolution," *Annales,* XXIV (1969), 662–684; Jacques Dupâquier and M. Lachiver, "Sur les débuts de la contraception en France, ou les deux malthusianismes," in *ibid.,* 1391–1406; Wells, "Family Size and Fertility Control in Eighteenth-Century America: A Study of Quaker Families," *Population Studies,* XXV (1971), 73–82; Linda Gordon, *Woman's Body, Woman's Right: A Social History of Birth Control in America* (New York, 1976); Daniel Scott Smith, "Family Limitation, Sexual Control, and Domestic Feminism in Victorian America," in Mary Hartman and Lois Banner (eds.) *Clio's Consciousness Raised* (New York, 1974), 119–136.

decline in marital fertility after the late seventeenth century indicates a growing practice in these circles of family limitation.[10]

The evidence for birth control among the poor is much weaker and is riddled with problems. One difficulty about drawing firm conclusions from aggregate data about completed fertility is that evidence is growing to show that the necessity for both wives and husbands of the poor to go out to work, often to live in the houses of their employers, meant that very many marriages of the poor were constantly being interrupted by long separations. Any growth of this practice, for example any expansion of live-in domestic service by married women at the expense of needle-work or clothing manufacture in the home, would produce the same aggregate result of declining fertility as the practice of contraception. Others argue, on the basis of virtually no evidence, that libido was low and sexual abstinence common among married couples. The inherently implausible theory that contraception began among the peasantry in England in about 1650, and was abandoned again by them in about 1740, is based on suspect data from the single village of Colyton. There are now those who believe that there was no contraception at all in England before the nineteenth century.[11]

In France, however, contraception seems to have been widely practiced first in Paris and the southwest in the early eighteenth century, and to have become general after 1790. Indeed, another of the remarkable discoveries of historical demography is that the French poor were unique among industrializing societies in practicing birth control both in rural and urban areas at a very early stage, at least half a century before England. The reasons for this extraordinary fact are still obscure, but the social and demographic results were profound. In the late seventeenth century France had four times the population of England and Wales; by the late nineteenth it had the same.

Household Structure   The second problem in family history, which has been vigorously pursued, especially in England, has been that of the size and composition of the household and its

---

10 Sigismund Peller, "Births and Deaths among Europe's Ruling Families Since 1500," in Glass and Eversley (eds.), *Population in History,* 87–100; M. Garden, *Lyons et les lyonnais au XVIIIe siècle* (Paris, 1975).
11 Wrigley, "Family Limitation." Vann, for one, is now very sceptical about the use of birth control in any class in England before the nineteenth century.

relation to the life cycle. The stimulus to such studies came from sociology and the data are drawn from household censuses. Since these are most common in English records, it is not surprising that it has been Laslett of the Cambridge Group for the Study of Population and Society who has been the leading entrepreneur in these studies since 1964.[12]

What this work has shown without possibility of doubt is that the standard household to be found in northwest Europe and New England was not an extended family of kin, relatives, or several married generations, as hypothesized by Le Play, but the familiar isolated nuclear family of parents and children. This model, suitably modified, can survive the discovery that it does not fit anywhere around the Mediterranean basin, or indeed anywhere south of the river Loire (where much larger and more complex households existed in considerable number, assembled in huge farmhouses which could accommodate several nuclear families at a time). Its significance, however, has been undermined by the demonstration that a high adult mortality rate is alone sufficient to explain the absence of elderly parents, and has been virtually destroyed by the realization that the fact that few households contained grandparents does not mean that few grandparents lived with their children. Thus, in nineteenth-century Preston, only 9 percent of households contained grandparents, but 80 percent of persons over sixty-five who had living children were residing with them.[13]

The second finding claimed to have emerged from a study of household censuses is that in seventeenth- and eighteenth-century England, but not in New England, the population was extraordinarily mobile, village populations changing in composition

12 Goody (ed.), *The Developmental Cycle in Domestic Groups* (Cambridge, 1971); Eugene A. Hammel and Laslett, "Comparing Household Structure over Time and between Cultures," *Comparative Studies in Society and History*, XVI (1974), 73–109; Laslett and Wall, *Household and Family*; Tamara Hareven (ed.), *Transitions: The Family and the Life Course in Historical Perspective* (New York, 1978); Jean Cuisenier and Martine Segalen (eds.), *The Family Life Cycle in European Societies* (The Hague, 1977); Wells, "Demographic Change and the Life Cycle of American Families," *Journal of Interdisciplinary History*, II (1971), 273–282; *idem*, "Household Size and Composition."

13 Michael Anderson, *Family Structure in Nineteenth-Century Lancashire* (Cambridge, 1971); *idem*, "Household Structure and the Industrial Revolution: Preston in Comparative Perspective," in Laslett and Wall, *Household and Family*, 215–235. See also Valerie Smith, "The Analysis of Census-Type Documents," *Local Population Studies*, II (1969), 12–24.

by 50 percent or more in a period of ten years. But the data themselves were first shown to be riddled with ambiguities because of problems of record linkage from one census to another. Utterly devastating to the conclusion was the demonstration by Prest that the extraordinary mobility among the population at large was caused not only by the natural processes of birth and death, but also by very rapid mobility among one small sector of the population—adolescents sent out to work in other peoples' homes as domestic servants, farm laborers, or apprentices. The turn-over among heads of households was not particularly striking and scarcely any greater than that in New England.[14]

The major and insuperable objection to most aspects of this work on households derives from a realization that family size and composition are not fixed over time, but oscillate throughout the family life cycle. A new nuclear family is formed by a marriage and neo-local residence; children are born; the children either die or grow up and leave home; the parents grow old and retire; one of them dies and the widow takes up residence with a married child. And so the cycle revolves, the family contracting and expanding like a concertina to absorb these constant changes. A census provides little more than a snapshot taken at a single moment in time, which completely misses this ever-changing rhythm in family life and thus in household size. A diachronic picture of change over time is not easily derived from a single census.

Another criticism of these studies concerns household composition. The data rarely enable one to distinguish lodgers from servants from stray kin such as spinster aunts, widowed mothers, or young nieces, nephews, or cousins. Economic necessity forced parents to hire live-in workers to take the place of children as a field labor force when the latter left home. It also forced urban and even rural dwellers to fill the empty nest with lodgers, the importance of whom has only recently been established. Under these circumstances, elaborate calculations of household size lose all meaning. The answer, whatever it may be, is true but trivial. What is important is that it is only in the twentieth century that

---

14 Laslett, *Family Life and Illicit Love in Earlier Generations* (Cambridge, 1977), 50–101; Wilfred R. Prest, "Stability and Change in Old and New England: Clayworth and Dedham," *Journal of Interdisciplinary History*, VI (1976), 359–374.

the isolated nuclear family has truly emerged, free from servants, workers, and lodgers.[15]

Moreover a moment's thought makes it obvious that average household size and composition varied with the economic resources of the family. The seat of a nobleman was spacious and full of children, stray kin, and a plethora of servants. At the other end of the scale, the one or two room hovel of the poor cottager was necessarily confined to himself, his wife, and his young children. In between the rich and the poor, key economic variables determining household size were the size of the farm and whether it was pasture or arable, both of which directly affected the size of the labor force required to work it.

The final blow to the whole household size and composition enterprise has been the realization that residence under one roof is not very meaningful. We do not know whether or not these household members cooked or ate together, whether or not they worked in the same field or enterprise, or whether their loyalties and affections were directed to those inside the house or outside to kin or friends living down the road or in the next village.[16]

Economics   The economic function of the poor family has changed radically over time. Up to as late as the seventeenth century it was a unit of production, its members working mostly in or around the home, or in nearby fields. Today, it is a unit of consumption, productive labor being carried on individually for a wage and outside the home. Despite intensive work, the stages of this major transformation of the family economy are still obscure.[17]

15 David J. Rothman, "A Note on the Study of the Colonial Family," *William and Mary Quarterly*, XXIII (1966), 627–634.
16 The major critic of household size and composition studies based on census data is Berkner, "Use and Misuse of Census Data."
17 Theodore W. Schultz (ed.), *Economics of the Family: Marriage, Children, and Human Capital* (Chicago, 1974); Engels, *Origins of the Family*; William J. Goode, *World Revolution and Family Patterns* (New York, 1963); Hareven, "Modernization and Family History: Reflections on Social Change," *Signs*, II (1976), 190–206; H. John Habakkuk, "Family Structure and Economic Change in Nineteenth Century Europe," *Journal of Economic History*, XV (1955), 1–2; Hans Medick, "The Proto-Industrial Family Economy: The Structural Function of Household and Family during the Transition from Peasant Society to Industrial Capitalism," *Social History*, III (1976), 291–316; Louise A. Tilly and Joan W. Scott, *Women, Work, and Family* (New York, 1978); E. Richards, "Women in the British Economy Since about 1700: An Interpretation," *History*, LIX (1974), 337–357; Anderson,

The characteristics of the pre-industrial peasant family are clear enough from the massive local studies of the sixteenth and seventeenth centuries carried out in France and elsewhere. The second and subsequent stages are less clear. A central puzzle is the significance of proto-industrialization, the provision of ample and sufficient work for young women and children in cottage textile industries. What effect did this or later changes in economic opportunities have upon family structure and domestic behavior? Braun has argued from a Swiss example that it was proto-industrialization which first freed young people from parental and kin control, since it permitted early marriage without the need to wait for a plot of land. It also turned children into a positive economic asset as early contributors to the family wage-packet.[18]

Other scholars working on the urbanizing and industrializing societies of the nineteenth century have revealed a far more complex development, and the discovery of a fully developed, large-scale factory flourishing in late nineteenth-century New England in close harmony with the most traditional of patriarchal and lineage family systems casts some doubt on the causal model which posits economic development as the key variable in family change. Even today the modern factory and office seem to be less disruptive of traditional family life than they were once believed to be. All agree, however, that once child labor laws were introduced, and children once again became an economic burden instead of an asset, there was a clear and strong incentive to birth control.[19]

Recent studies of women in history have either traced the history of feminist movements in the past, or have been devoted to this question of changes in female involvement in the labor force, and the effect of these changes on the position of wives in the family. The generally accepted theory is that married women were withdrawn from productive labor by the bourgeoisie and even lower bourgeoisie for status reasons in the eighteenth and

"Household Structure and the Industrial Revoltuion"; Hareven (ed.), *Family Kin in Urban Communities: 1700–1930* (New York, 1977); Frank F. Furstenberg, Jr., "Industrialization and the American Family: A Look Backward," *American Sociological Review,* XXXI (1966), 326–337.

18 Rudolf Braun, "The Impact of Cottage Industry on an Agricultural Population," in David Landes (ed.), *The Rise of Capitalism* (New York, 1966), 53–64.

19 Hareven, *Family and Kin.*

early nineteenth centuries, and have only returned in force in the twentieth century. It is also argued that this withdrawal was very damaging to the status of women, since their psychological independence, their self-esteem, and their power within the family was directly related to their economic participation in production.[20]

As for the poor, it is difficult to demonstrate that twelve to fourteen hours of backbreaking labor in the field or in domestic industry improved a women's respect or power in the home. Many societies have used women as economic (and sexual) slaves, and treated them accordingly. It may be that the rise or fall of patriarchy as a cultural norm has been as important as female labor participation in determing the position of women at all levels of society.

Lineage, Kin, and Family   One of the central questions asked by anthropologists has always concerned the relation of lineage and kin to the nuclear family. They have stressed the importance for social structure of determining whether or not the family of orientation, that is the one in which one is raised, continues to be more important than the family of procreation, the family which one forms by marriage. They patiently investigate marriage taboos, exchange systems, and the degrees to which the patriarch and the clan continue to guide the affairs of each nuclear household. They also study the degree of patriarchy within each nuclear household—the extent to which, in theory and in practice, the wife and children are subordinate to the male head.

These are questions which historians have addressed, espe-

20   David Herlihy, "Land, Family and Women in Continental Europe, 701–1200," in Susan Mosher Stuard (ed.), *Women in Medieval Society* (Philadelphia, 1976), 13–45; Jean E. Gagen, *The New Woman: Her Emergence in the English Drama, 1600–1730* (New York, 1954); Patricia Branca, *Silent Sisterhood. Middle-Class Women in the Victorian Home* (Pittsburg, 1975); Lenore Davidoff, *The Best Circles: Women and Society in Victorian England* (London, 1973); Oliver Hufton, "Women and the Family Economy in Eighteenth-Century France," *French Historical Studies,* IX (1975), 1–23; Hartman and Banner (eds.), *Clio's Consciousness Raised*; Nancy F. Cott, "Divorce and the Changing Status of Women in Eighteenth-Century Massachusetts," *William and Mary Quarterly,* XXX (1976), 586–614; Carol Smith-Rosenberg and Charles Rosenberg, "The Female Animal: Medical and Biological Views of Woman and Her Role in Nineteenth-Century America," *Journal of American History,* LX (1973), 332–356. For a challenge of the accepted view, see Mary Beth Norton, *Liberty's Daughters: the Revolutionary Experience of American Women, 1750–1800* (Boston, 1980).

cially with respect to the landed aristocracy, where clan alliances, nepotism, and patriarchy have been most powerfully developed. The investigations of Duby in France have shown the centrality of such issues for the French nobility of the early Middle Ages. McFarlane explored these matters for the late medieval English nobility, and Habakkuk, James, Slater, Trumbach, and Stone for the sixteenth to eighteenth century greater English landowners. So far, however, relatively little has been done to explore such problems at a lower social level, although in England a beginning has been made for the seventeenth century clergy by Macfarlane in his study of the Josselin family, and by Spufford and others for the peasantry. The strongly legalistic bias of much French scholarship on family history has also done a good deal to illuminate these questions, although few of these publications have probed very deeply beneath the surface of the law. The most valuable information on French peasant lineage, kin, and family relations has come from the great local histories, such as those of Goubert and Le Roy Ladurie, and from recent research by Flandrin.[21]

In America the most important study of these matters was by Greven on Andover in the seventeenth and eighteenth centuries, tracing the evolution of patriarchy as it responded to a situation of first limitless and then limited land resources. In more recent times, Anderson has offered the intriguing speculation that the importance of kin actually increased, as an aid to mobility, in the early stages of urbanization and industrialization.[22]

21 For e.g., Georges Duby, *Hommes et structures au Moyen Age* (Paris, 1973). K. Bruce McFarlane, *The Nobility of Later Medieval England* (Oxford, 1973); Goode, "Marriage among the English Nobility in the Sixteenth and Seventeenth Centuries: A Comment," *Comparative Studies in Society and History*, III (1960–61), 207–214; Habakkuk, "Marriage Settlements in the Eighteenth Century," *Transactions of the Royal Historical Society*, XXXII (1950), 15–30; Mervyn James, *Family, Lineage, and Civil Society: A Study of Society, Politics, and Mentality in the Durham Region, 1500–1640* (New York, 1974); Miriam Slater, "The Weightiest Business: Marriage in an Upper-Gentry Family in Seventeenth-Century England," *Past & Present*, 72 (1976), 25–54; Stone, *The Family, Sex and Marriage in England 1500–1800* (London, 1977); Randolph Trumbach, *The Rise of the Egalitarian Family: Aristocratic Kinship and Domestic Relations in Eighteenth-Century England* (New York, 1978). Alan Macfarlane, *The Family Life of Ralph Josselin: An Essay in Historical Anthropology* (Cambridge, 1970); Margaret Spufford, *Contrasting Communities: English Villagers in the Sixteenth and Seventeenth Centuries* (Cambridge, 1974); Goody et al. (eds.), *Family and Inheritance*; Goubert, *Beauvais*; Le Roy Ladurie, *Les paysannes de Languedoc* (Paris, 1966), 2 v.; Flandrin, *Les amours paysannes: amour et sexualité dans les campagnes de l'ancienne France, XVIᵉ–XIXᵉ siècle* (Paris, 1975); idem, *Familles*.
22 Greven, *Four Gnerations*; Anderson, *Family Structure*; idem, "Household Structure."

Stages of Life   Of the three stages of life which have come under close examination, none is free from dispute. Recent work is beginning to question whether or not Ariès was right to argue that the concept of children as clearly distinguished from adults only evolved in the seventeenth century. Few can see any validity in deMause's mono-causal psychological hypothesis that there has been a steady linear increase through the ages in the quality of child care, as each generation treats its children a little better and therefore produces more loving parents in the future.[23]

On the contrary, it is difficult to deny that the first result of greater concern about the upbringing of children was to treat them more harshly in order to break their stubborn wills, since it was then generally believed that the child was born with Original Sin. It was the substitution of the Lockean *tabula rasa* for Calvinist Original Sin which transformed the greater interest in the child into greater affection and permissiveness. The revival of the doctrine of Original Sin in about 1800 caused a swing back to harsher treatment of children in the nineteenth century, before the unprecedented age of permissiveness of the twentieth century. Even if the Ariès concept remains valid, its practical effect in child-treatment has varied over time. Another unsolved problem with the Ariès model concerns the simultaneous development of the school, which removed from the family much of the responsibility for socialization, and even the physical presence of the child. Ariès sees no contradiction in these two trends toward the recognition of the child and the delegation of the child's education to an external institution. Others find the two trends contradictory and puzzling. Maybe the two were merely coincidental in time, the demand for literacy and classical learning making the school

23 Philippe Ariès, *Centuries of Childhood* (London, 1962); Lloyd deMause, "The Evolution of Childhood," in *idem* (ed.), *History of Childhood* (New York, 1974), 1–74. Other works on childhood and child rearing include Demos, "Developmental Perspectives on the History of Childhood," *Journal of Interdisciplinary History,* II (1972), 315–327. Robert Forster and O. Ranum (eds.), *Family and Society: Selections from the Annales* (Baltimore, 1976); C. John Sommerville, "Towards a History of Childhood and Youth," *Journal of Interdisciplinary History,* III (1973), 438–447; David Hunt, *Parents and Children in History: The Psychology of Family Life in Early Modern France* (New York, 1970); Ross W. Beales, Jr., "In Search of the Historical Child: Miniature Adulthood and Youth in Colonial New England," *American Quarterly,* XXVII (1975), 379–398; Greven (ed.), *Child-Rearing Concepts, 1628–1861: Historical Sources* (Ithasca, Ill., 1973); *idem, The Protestant Temperament: Patterns of Child-Rearing, Religious Experience, and the Self in Early America* (New York, 1977); Michael Gordon (ed.), *The American Family in Social-Historical Perspective* (New York, 1973).

inevitable, just at the time when other cultural forces were causing increased concern for the welfare and moral upbringing of the child.

Far more controversial is the dating of the emergence of the concept of adolescence as a clearly defined period of life after puberty during which a young person remains in a position of dependence. Hall saw it emerge only in the late nineteenth century. Demos and Gillis place it in the early nineteenth century, Kett puts it later, and others—including myself—much earlier. Duby and others point to the medieval concept of "youth" and to its strong peer group organizations. They argue that apprentices formed a large, dependent, often riotous sub-culture which was well recognized at least as early as the sixteenth century. The dispute seems to be more about boundaries and definitions than about concrete social realities, and the difference between "youth" and "adolescence" to be mainly one of terminology.[24]

Similar uncertainty exists about old age. Fischer holds that the role of and respect for the old has steadily decreased in the last two centuries. He argues that we now unceremoniously relegate our aged relatives to nursing homes and forget about them, instead of taking them into our homes and looking after them ourselves, as we used to do. He points to the current cult of youth and the denigration of the old as out-dated and useless, as opposed to an earlier period when merely being old was thought to confer wisdom and respect.

I have denied the reality of this golden age for the old, arguing that attitudes were always ambiguous, a combination of respect for endurance and power over economic resources, and a contempt for physical weakness and disagreeable psychological traits such as avarice. The incredibly minute directions left in the past by dying men in their wills to protect the rights of their

---

24 Duby, "In Northwestern France: The 'Youth' in Twelfth-Century Aristocratic Society," in F. L. Cheyette (ed.), *Lordship and Community in Medieval Europe* (New York, 1968), 198–209; Natalie Z. Davis, "The Reasons of Misrule: Youth Groups and Charivaris in Sixteenth-Century France," *Past & Present*, 50 (1971), 41–75; G. Stanley Hall, *Adolescence: Its Psychology and its Relations to Physiology, Anthropology, Sociology, Sex, Crime, Religion, and Education* (New York, 1904), 2 v.; J. Demos and Virginia Demos, "Adolescence in Historical Perspective," in Gordon (ed.), *American Family*, 209–221; John R. Gillis, *Youth and History: Tradition and Change in European Age Relations, 1770 to Present* (New York, 1974); Joseph Kett, *Rites of Passage: Adolescence in America, 1790 to the Present* (New York, 1977).

widows in their sons' houses after their deaths suggest that they had little or no confidence in a child's sense of filial obligation. Moreover, whatever our motives, the fact remains that we are today paying unprecedented sums in taxes to prolong the life of the aged through free medical care, and to provide them with adequate inflation-proof pensions to live on, as a result of which the vast majority live fairly comfortably in their own homes. This indicates to me that we do still accept our social responsibilities for the old, although now through more institutional and less familial arrangements. The debate remains unresolved.[25]

Religion So far, the problems and variables which have been discussed have been primarily materialistic in character, and statistical in methodology. A great deal of work had been done, however, on the effects of less concrete matters on family life. In particular, ever since Weber much effort has been directed to studying the effects of Protestantism, and especially Calvinism, on the family. The literature has centered upon four problems. The first has been the effect of the substitution of "holy matrimony" for virginity as the ideal, the argument being that this was an important factor in stimulating a demand for marital affection and in sanctifying the home. I have also argued that, by substituting the head of the household for the priest, and by domesticating religion through family prayers led by the head, it stimulated the revival of patriarchy and the decline of the position of women. The second has been the effect of Puritanism on the treatment of children. On the one hand Puritans cared about children, since upon them was based their hopes of creating a City upon a Hill; and on the other hand they feared them as imbued with Original Sin. The third question has concerned the attitude taken by Puritans to sexuality in general, and deviant sexuality in particular. The fourth and final issue is the Weberian problem of the effects of Protestantism, and the "Puritan ethic" of thrift and diligence in the calling, in stimulating the growth of capitalism. Here too the work has been intense and of high quality, but no consensus is yet in sight.[26]

25 David H. Fischer, *Growing Old in America* (New York, 1977); Stone "Walking over Grandma," *New York Review of Books* (12 May, 1977), 36–38; J. Demos, "Old Age in Early New England," in Gordon (ed.), *American Family*, 209–221.
26 Christopher Hill, "The Spiritualization of the Household," in his *Society and Puritanism in Pre-Revolutionary England* (London, 1964), 443–481; James T. Johnson, *A Society Ordained*

Greven has recently erected a complete framework of family emotional life, based on the single variable of the "Protestant temperament." He identifies three distinct religious types—evangelical, moderate, and genteel—attaches them to different social classes, and uses them to explain the development of widely different types of family life style. His model is thus based on the concept of a fixed class matrix and a variable religious imprint. The validity and utility of this model is discussed below.[27]

Values and Emotions   As has already been pointed out, the family history of the bottom 90 percent of the population, because of the nature of the records, has to be largely statistical in methodology and, consequently, very materialistic in the questions that can be asked. The values and beliefs of this segment of the population have largely to be deduced from statistical data about age of marriage, frequency of marriage with older women, retention or abandonment of children, care of widows, prenuptial pregnancy, bastardy, and so on. Based essentially on the two sources of parish registers and censuses, these studies offer a thin and watery gruel to those who wish to penetrate deeper into the rich psychological content of family life. For the poor, the only direct evidence about such matters comes from reports by middle-class doctors, clergymen, or charitable workers, and their testimony is immediately suspect as being as much a product of class prejudice as objective observation.

Some scholars, like Shorter, have used this evidence extensively, whereas others angrily deny its utility. The truth probably lies somewhere in between. As Le Roy Ladurie's *Montaillou* has proved, ecclesiastical court records, which contain written interrogations of witnesses, can throw a flood of light on lineage ties, household loyalties, family relations, and sexual behavior, even at a very remote period in time. In England, wills are of limited value, since only a minority of the population drew them up, but the proportion was much higher in France and America. The

---

by God: *English Puritan Marriage Doctrine in the First Half of the Seventeenth Century* (Nashville, 1970); Levin L. Schücking, *The Puritan Family: A Social Study from the Literary Sources* (London, 1969); André Burgière, "De Malthus à Max Weber: le mariage tardiff et l'esprit d'enterprise," *Annales,* XXVII (1972), 1128–1138; Edmund S. Morgan, *The Puritan Family: Religion and Domestic Relations in Seventeenth-Century New England* (New York, 1966; rev. ed.).

27 Greven, *Protestant Temperament.*

problem of assessing the quality of family life among the poor in the past, of penetrating their bedrooms, hearing them talk, and understanding how they felt about their wives, their children, their relatives, and their mothers-in-law, thus presents methodological difficulties that have not yet been satisfactorily overcome.[28]

With the literate elite and middle class, the problem is infinitely easier. Here there are available huge quantities of family correspondence, often of a most intimate nature, as well as diaries, autobiographies, and love-letters. Wills and marriage settlements survive in great numbers and hundreds of law suits for separation in the ecclesiastical and secular courts throw a searchlight upon the web of relationships that bonded families together and the tensions which ripped them apart. Finally, there is a wealth of didactic literature, written first by clergymen, then by philosophers, and finally by doctors, about such matters as household management, the choice of a wife, the relations between spouses, appropriate sexual behavior, and how to bring up children. This advice literature may or may not approximate actual behavior, but at least some of it was widely read and thus seems to have struck a sympathetic chord in its readers.

From all of this material a very different kind of family history has begun to emerge from that of the historical demographers and students of household structure. The first to open up this new territory was Ariès. His *Centuries of Childhood* has probably done more to stimulate interest in family history in the last twenty-five years than any other single book. Despite its loose use of evidence, especially iconographic, its maddening lack of specificity about time, place, and class when it made a point or offered an example, it nevertheless presented a wholly new vista on the nature of human experience in the past; it led directly into the great issue of the timing and nature of family change from the traditional to the modern. Where, and when, did the modern bourgeois family emerge and what are its defining characteristics? No amount of counting by the historical demographers or household sociologists is going to reach into the heart of the matter. It is now widely agreed that psychological attitudes, just as much

28 Shorter, *The Making of the Modern Family* (New York, 1975); Le Roy Ladurie, *Montaillou, village occitan de 1294 à 1324* (Paris, 1975).

as economic functions, social structures, or demographic changes, characterize the change in family type to the one we know today. On both sides of the Atlantic these attitudinal changes can be proved to have occurred before the economic changes, and in classes unaffected by those changes, and they therefore must to some extent have enjoyed an independent history. Reductionist attempts to attribute them all to economic causes do not fit the historical facts.

There is general agreement about the nature of these changes. First was the decline of the external influence from kin, parents, friends, and neighbors on the nuclear family, a change of the latter from a porous and outward-looking institution to a closed and inward-turned one. The critical change was a weakening of the bonds of kinship. Second, there developed greater emotional bonding between spouses, as marriage became a matter of free choice based on personal affection and sexual attraction rather than the result of a mercenary arrangement made between the parents. This in turn, together with the increased expectation of life of young adults, generated a demand for divorce. If these new expectations for married love were not fulfilled, now that the prospects of life together for thirty years or more had become the statistical norm, the demand for a right to legal separation became overwhelming, despite much moral and religious opposition.[29]

Attitudes toward children also changed, although when and in what classes remains uncertain. There was an abandonment of the concept of the child as an immature adult, and his emergence as a creature recognized as having special needs and aptitudes; the shift was from an exploitative to a nurturant attitude toward the child, so that the balance of economic transfer changed from an upward flow from the children to the parents to a downward flow from the parents to the children. The result was the emer-

29   Goody (ed.), *The Character of Kinship* (London, 1973); Edward E. Evans-Pritchard, "The Study of Kinship in Primitive Societies," *Man*, XXIX (1969), 190–193; James, *Family, Lineage, and Civil Society*; Duby, "Lignage, noblesse et chevalerie au XIIᵉ siècle dans la région mâconnaise: une révision," *Annales*, XXVII (1972), 803–823; Hareven, *Family amd Kin*; C. Kenny, "Wife-Selling in England," *Law Quarterly Review*, XLV (1929), 494–497; Oliver R. McGregor, *Divorce in England* (London, 1957); Griselda Rowntree and Norman H. Carrier, "The Resort to Divorce in England and Wales, 1858–1957," *Population Studies*, XI (1958), 188–232; Alain Lottin, *La désunion du couple sous l'ancien régime: l'exemple du Nord, Lille* (Paris, 1975); Herman R. Lantz, *Marital Incompatibility and Social Change in Early America* (Beverly Hills, 1976).

gence of the child-oriented society of today, in which parents cheerfully make a heavy economic and emotional investment in their children in order to launch them successfully into the world, with little or no expectation of return in their old age, except in terms of psychic satisfaction. Not surprisingly, it was among the bourgeoisie and landed elite, where economic transfers between parents and children had always been downward, that this great emotional shift was first experienced.

This child-orientation inevitably led to a growing specialization of the woman's activities in child care and education within the home, leaving economic production more to the men. The sexes divided into two spheres, both spatially and functionally. In the end, another by-product of child-orientation was contraception, since the quality of the children produced became more highly prized than the quantity, and only a limitation in numbers would enable the mother to devote her full energies to child-rearing.

Another aspect of the growth of the bourgeois family type was the slow evolution of the concept of privacy, the withdrawal from public rooms and promiscuous bedrooms. Sex, excretion, and conversation all for the first time gradually became more private in the eighteenth and nineteenth centuries. People withdrew to private bedrooms behind locked doors, water closets were installed to replace the ubiquitous close stool and chamber pot, and small dining rooms supplied with dumb-waiters replaced the great hall where one feasted in public, attended by servants who could hear every word that was said. Individualism—affective individualism—became the prized ideal of both husband and wife, and parent and children, once the sixteenth-century phase of reinforced patriarchy, supported by both church and state, began to fade away in the late seventeenth century. This ideal of affective individualism slowly induced parents to relinquish, more or less voluntarily, their age-old veto over the spouse choice of their children, and the children to make their free choice on the basis of affection rather than economic calculation. The normal practice of social endogamy, and a common-sense recognition that love on a crust of bread in a garret is not a satisfying way of life, prevented gross disparities in social and economic backgrounds of marriage partners, just as it had always done, and just as it still does today.

If one examines the theories of all those who have attempted a general overview of this question of the evolution of the modern family—Engels, Ariès, Flandrin, deMause, myself, Shorter, Greven, and now Degler and Norton—it seems clear that there is fairly general agreement that the changes described took place sometime between 1680 and 1850. It is also agreed that they were highly class specific in origin. But there is no agreement in sight about which were the leading sectors in the change, nor when or why the changes occurred. As leading sectors, Ariès, myself, and Greven favor the gentry and the bourgeoisie, Trumbach the aristocracy, and Degler and Norton the middle class; we are therefore in rough agreement. DeMause ignores class altogether; and Engels and Shorter focus on the industrial proletariat. This is a question of fact which further research should be able to settle once and for all, although the considerable evidence already available strongly indicates the bourgeoisie, the gentry, and soon after the nobility as the foremost sectors.

The second issue is that of timing, for if the new family type can be shown to have existed before industrialization and urbanization, as well as among classes unaffected by these movements, then the economic modernization argument fails. It has been suggested that the new family type first emerged with the Florentine bourgeoisie in the fifteenth century, the Amsterdam bourgeoisie of the early seventeenth century, and then the London bourgeoisie of the late seventeenth century. Trumbach and Stone have demonstrated that the changes occurred among the bourgeoisie, upper squirearchy, and aristocracy in England between 1680 and 1780; in America Smith and Greven identify them among the gentry in the eighteenth century; and Smith, Degler, and Norton among the middle classes between 1760 and 1820.[30]

Some of the explanations offered for these extraordinary shifts in attitudes and behavior within the family are strictly monocausal. DeMause bases everything on a Freudian psychological hypothesis about a weakening of the traumatic effects of early child-rearing from generation to generation. Macfarlane attributes everything to a particular form of economic individualism, the will and capacity to buy and sell property, which he identifies as

30 Daniel Blake Smith, *Inside the Great House* (Ithaca, 1981); Carl N. Degler, *At Odds: Women and the Family in America, 1776 to the Present* (New York, 1980); Norton, *Liberty's Daughters*.

peculiar to England and which he traces, with some difficulty, back to the early Middle Ages. Both of these hypotheses have met with little approval. In America Norton and, apparently, Degler attribute the change to the experience of the Revolution and the impact of egalitarian and republican ideology. Greven offers a purely religious explanation. It is almost lacking a sense of change over time, since each of his three religious modes seems to attach itself to a different social class. His theory is interesting but is of strictly limited utility, since it stops well before the age of industrialization, is applicable by definition solely to the Protestant parts of Europe, and in practice is applied exclusively to America.[31]

My own model is multicausal, involving the rise and fall of religious piety; changes in concepts of the nature of the state and society; economic change, with the development of a money economy and possessive individualism; social change with the rise of a wealthy middle class of bourgeois, professionals, and squires; cultural evolution; and the influence of key thinkers such as John Locke. It is dependent upon the principle of cultural diffusion, starting from near the top and drifting first upward to the aristocracy and much later downward into lower social strata. It envisions, as does Greven's model, a multiplicity of family types extant at any one time and prevalent in different layers of the society. Change is seen as both slow and erratic. The main difference between this model, which in this respect is very similar to that of Degler and Norton, and that of scholars such as Shorter, is that it sees the change operating from the top down rather than from the bottom up, and that it identifies the prime influences as religious, political, and cultural as well as social and economic. Its weakness is its heavy dependence on the hoary method of argument by example, and elite example at that.[32]

Those who place the main stress on economic modernization stress different aspects of that process. Habakkuk, Easterlin, and Berkner have emphasized different land use and inheritance patterns. Braun believes that the new family type was a product of

31 L. deMause, "The Evolution of Childhood"; Macfarlane, *The Origins of English Individualism: The Family, Property and Social Transition* (Cambridge, 1979). Herlihy has rightly described the latter as "a silly book founded on faulty method and propounding a preposterous thesis," *Journal of Family History,* V (1980), 236.
32 Stone, *Family, Sex and Marriage*; Shorter, *Modern Family.*

proto-industrialization. The spread of cottage industry allowed the young to abandon social and sexual restraints and, since work was now plentiful, and fear of unemployment and starvation minimal, to marry when and whom they pleased. Cottage industry thus liberated the poor from parental control, marriage ages went down, and prenuptial conception (and bastardy) went up. Scott and Tilly have focused on the possibilities of employment for women and children in the urban industries of the late eighteenth and early nineteenth centuries as the critical factor in liberating children from their parents, allowing free and early mate choice, and stimulating family planning. Shorter has introduced a key intervening variable, sexual liberation, caused, according to him, by this new economic freedom, but he has not managed to persuade many scholars to accept it. Degler ties his story to a slow but relentless drive by American women since 1790 to secure autonomy, first over marriage, then the home, child-rearing, birth-control, sexuality, and finally equality of opportunity in the workplace. The stages of the drive are well defined but the causes are left obscure.[33]

Nor is there consensus about the effect of the whole complex of Enlightenment thought on family life. A traditional view is that it has been a progressively liberating influence, with an enormously beneficial effect in promoting the greatest happiness of the greatest number. But liberalism soon ran into head-on conflict with the destructive effects upon the disoriented urban proletariat of laissez-faire capitalism. As a result it was forced to turn to state intervention to alleviate the misery and degradation of the poor, creating a top-heavy bureaucracy to administer the paternalistic legislation of the welfare state. The result has been to elevate the family into the idealized sanctuary of personal happiness in a cut-throat world. But when it failed to live up to expectations, the state relieved the family of many of its functions and regulated abuses within it with laws and agencies for the protection of

33 Habakkuk, "Family Structure and Economic Change"; Richard Easterlin, "Factors in the Decline of Farm Family Fertility in the United States: Some Preliminary Research Results," *Journal of American History*, LXIII (1976), 600–614; *idem*, "Does Human Fertility Adjust to the Environment?" *American Economic Review*, LXI (1971), 399–407; Berkner, "Inheritance, Land Tenure, and Peasant Family Structure: A German Regional Comparison," in Goody et al. (eds.), *Family and Inheritance*, 71–95. Braun, "The Impact of Cottage Industry." Tilly and Scott, *Women, Work and Family*. Degler, *Women and the Family in America*.

children and women. The result has freed the family to concentrate on child-rearing and emotional satisfaction, and done much to alleviate cruelty and misery.

The alternative view, which is now the fashionable one, is that the whole welfare enterprise, from compulsory schooling to juvenile courts, is an aspect of bourgeois ideological hegemony, molding the poor in the ideal image of the dominant class of capitalists; that the institutions set up to deal with deviants, such as lunatic asylums and prisons—and for many even grade schools—are deliberately depersonalizing and oppressive; that the only real beneficiaries are the new "helping professions"—doctors, psychoanalysts, social workers, teachers, prison guards, juvenile court judges, and the rest; and that the family has become helpless in their hands, and has lost almost all its older functions to these new oppressors. This view, advocated by Donzelot in France and Lasch in America, has turned upside-down conventional notions about the relationship of the family to the modern state apparatus. There does, however, seem to be space for a middle ground, a view that post-Enlightenment intervention has indeed improved the quality of the family and reduced the sum of human misery and ignorance. One can also readily admit that state interference in all aspects of domestic life in the last century has also produced a vast impersonal bureaucracy, that the helping professions have gained great power, and that the social functions of the family have been greatly restricted.[34]

Sexuality   The final area of research and contention in family history concerns the history of sexuality. Here it is not only the causes but also the facts which are in dispute. There are those who argue, from statistics about bastardy and pre-nuptial conception, and from the shame punishments ruthlessly meted out to fornicators and adulterers, that the Puritan ideology of the late sixteenth and early seventeenth centuries had a considerable effect in repressing the libido, partly by terror, and partly by ideological indoctrination. Even within marriage, Puritan preachers thundered about the evils of "matrimonial whoredom," meaning excessive sexual enthusiasm for a spouse, and any of the

34 Jacques Donzelot, *The Policing of Families* (New York, 1979); Christopher Lasch, *Haven in a Heartless World* (New York, 1977).

practices of polymorphous perversity which are recommended in marriage manuals available today in every bookstore.[35]

Others, like Hill and Morgan, deny that the Puritans were particularly hostile to sexuality. Quaife has argued that prosecutions for sexual delinquency in seventeenth-century ecclesiastical courts in one English county indicate a very tolerant attitude toward such matters by the public at large, and even the judges themselves. All have correctly pointed out that the Puritans stressed "holy matrimony" and recognized that one purpose of marital sexual intercourse was for mutual comfort, as well as for the avoidance of fornication and for the procreation of children.[36]

The same debate rages over the Victorian period, when the middle classes in England, Europe, and America took an even more repressive view of sexuality. Some point to the weight of medical and religious texts attacking masturbation and sexual excess, and alleging that normal women either did not experience sexual desire, or at any rate less so than men—a dramatic reversal of previous theory. Others stress the huge expansion of prostitution, the rising bastardy rate, and the production of the most erudite and obscene pornography the world has ever seen as evidence that the anti-sexual drive of the Victorian middle class was in practice a failure.

Those who accept that there was a real and marked relaxation

35 The literature on this subject is already huge. General works are Shorter, *Modern Family* ; Gordon Rattray Taylor, *Sex in History* (New York, 1954; rev. ed., 1959); Flandrin, "L'attitude à l'égard du petit enfant et les conduites sexuelles dans la civilisation occidentale: structures anciennes et évolution," *Annales de démographie historique* (1973), 143–210; *idem,* "Contraception, mariage et relations amoureuses; *idem, Familles*; Michel Foucault, *Histoire de la sexualité* (Paris, 1976), I; Shorter, "Illegitimacy, Sexual Revolution, and Social Change in Modern Europe," *Journal of Interdisciplinary History,* II (1971), 237–272; Stone, *The Family, Sex and Marriage*; Peter T. Cominos, "Late-Victorian Sexual Respectability and the Social System," *International Review of Social History,* VIII (1963), 18–48, 216–250; Ronald Pearsall, *The Worm in the Bud: The World of Victorian Sexuality* (New York, 1969); E. Trudgill, "Prostitution and Paterfamilias," in Harold J. Dyos and Michael Wolff (eds.), *The Victorian City* (London, 1973), 693–705; Martha Vicinus, *Suffer and Be Still: Women in the Victorian Age* (Bloomington, 1972); Ben Barker-Benfield, *The Horrors of the Half-known Life: Male Attitudes toward Women and Sexuality in Nineteenth-Century America* (New York, 1976); *idem,* "The Spermatic Economy; A Nineteenth-Century View of Sexuality," *Feminist Studies,* I (1972), 45–74; Degler, "What Ought to Be and What Was: Women's Sexuality in the Nineteenth Century," *American Historical Review,* LXXIX (1974), 1468–1490.

36 Hill, "Sex, Marriage and the Family in England," *Economic History Review,* XXXI (1978), 453–455; Morgan, *Puritan Family*; G. R. Quaife, *Wanton Wenches and Wayward Wives* (London, 1979).

in sexual behavior in eighteenth-century England and New England, shown by the abrupt rise in pre-nuptial conceptions, and probably also in bastardy, are sharply divided about the causes. Some point to the rise of religious indifference in late seventeenth-century England and perhaps New England and in late eighteenth-century France. They ascribe the rise in pre-nuptial conceptions to an increased willingness of young girls to allow themselves to be seduced by their suitors. They explain this by a decline of moral inhibitions against pre-marital sexual intercourse, at the same time that traditional social constraints were maintained which obliged most couples who had conceived a child to get married before the child was born. The moderate increase in the eighteenth century both of serving maids and of unmarried women living away from their families and working in factories probably raised the number of lonely girls exposed to male seduction, and thus may have helped somewhat to increase the amount of pre-nutpial pregnancy and bastardy.[37]

The alternative explanation, put forward by Shorter, is that there was a great unleashing of the libido. The poor, psychologically freed in some rather mysterious way by "laissez-faire industrial organization, capitalist production and the beginnings of proletarianization, threw themselves into each others arms in an urgent quest for sexual gratification. The libido unfroze in the blast of the wish to be free." This is a bold but wholly unproven thesis which has not yet succeeded in attracting many converts.[38]

The two main conclusions of this debate are, first, that there must have been some relaxation of moral controls on pre-marital sex for pre-nuptial conception to have risen so dramatically in the eighteenth century. And, second, that the increased willingness

37 Shorter, "Illegitimacy, Sexual Revolution"; *idem,* "Sexual Change and Illegitimacy: The European Experience," in Robert Bezucha (ed.), *Modern European Social History* (Lexington, Mass., 1972), 231–269; Laslett, *Family Life*; P. E. H. Hair, "Bridal Pregnancy in Earlier Rural England, Further Examined," *Population Studies,* XXIV (1970), 59–70; Pierre Caspard, "Conceptions prénuptiales et développement du capitalisme dans la Principauté de Neuchâtel (1678–1820)," *Annales,* XXIX (1974), 989–1008; Jacques Depauw, "Amour illégitime et société à Nantes au XVIIIe siècle," *Annales,* XXVII (1972), 1155–1182; Lottin, "Naissances illégitimes et filles-mères à Lille au XVIIIe siècle," *Revue d'histoire moderne et contemporaine,* XVII (1970), 278–322; D. S. Smith and Michael S. Hindus, "Premarital Pregnancy in America 1640–1971: An Overview and Interpretation," *Journal of Interdisciplinary History,* V (1975), 537–570; Laslett, Karla Oosterveen, and Richard M. Smith (eds.), *Bastardy and its Comparative History* (London, 1980).
38 Shorter, *Modern Family,* chs. 3, 7.

of young girls to allow full intercourse before marriage was probably not due to any release of the libido, but to the traditional desire, now operating under new rules, to catch a husband—a desire which in most cases was in fact fulfilled.

Other aspects of sexuality have so far been barely touched upon. Our knowledge of attitudes toward infantile sexuality is still largely confined to one unique document about a very untypical child, a doctor's diary about the education of the young King Louis XIII of France.

There is still no serious history of either lesbianism or homosexuality in the modern West, although a pioneer study has appeared on homosexuality in the Middle Ages. We can now recognize the rise and the decline in nineteenth-century America of "sorority"—passionate but usually non-physical relationships between women, characteristically one married and one spinster. We also have the extraordinary new book about homosexuality as a dominant culture in fifth-century B.C. Greece. It shows what can be done by the application of imagination and patience in extracting information from every possible type of evidence— from plays, philosophy, and legal texts to painting and sculpture.[39]

From this torrential outpouring of historical investigation on a wide range of issues, four things have emerged very clearly. First, there is no such thing as a single national family type at any given period. There never has been a French family or an English family or an American family, but rather a plurality of families. In the past there were enormous regional differences which have only recently been diminished.

Second, there is not even such a thing as a New England family or a Languedoc family, or whatever, since there were at any given time a series of very different family types specific to different social strata and to different religious persuasions. There has nearly always been an aristocratic type, an urban upper bourgeois type, a lower middle class type, a respectable laboring class type, and a non-respectable laboring class type, each of which may differ radically from all of the others. There is seepage of

39 John Boswell, *Christianity, Social Tolerance and Homosexuality: Gay People in Western Europe from the Beginning of the Christian Era to the Fourteenth Century* (Chicago, 1980); Kenneth J. Dover, *Greek Homosexuality* (Cambridge, Mass., 1978).

cultural modes from group to group, but the trend to uniformity may be spread over many hundreds of years, and is never fully complete, not even today. Moreover, a major change in family practice can drift geographically from region to region, taking centuries to cross the expanse of Western Europe: the abandonment of swaddling, for example, took place in England by the end of the eighteenth century, but only reached Russia in the early twentieth.

Third, changing religious views on family ethics, which are also very specific to class and region, have evidently had an enormous influence on family life at different periods. All future research is going to have to be much more sensitive to these problems of class, regional, and religious diversity than has previously been the case. Future studies will have to recognize and identify a plurality of competing family options extant within any single society and region.

The last thing which has become clear is that family history is inextricably involved in the great issue of the change from traditional to modern society. No other question is more important to historians of the West than the causes, nature, timing, and consequences of this transition. Early sixteenth-century society was sparse, with high birth and high mortality rates, and was poor, rural, agrarian, illiterate, small-scale, communitarian, hierarchical, authoritarian, pious, weakly governed, and amateurish. Late twentieth-century society is dense, with low birth and death rates, and is rich, urban, industrial, literate, large-scale, individualistic, depersonalized, egalitarian, democratic, agnostic, bureaucratized, and professional. There is hardly a single one of these transformations in which the family has not played a key role as an agent, subject, catalyst, or transmitter of changing values and experience.

THE FUTURE

New Methods and Sources   Finley has observed that "all the possible statistics about age of marriage, size of family, rate of illegitimacy will not add up to a history of the family." It seems likely that the contribution of historical demography to family history will be much less in the 1980s than it has been in the 1960s and 1970s, if only because the main outlines of the demographic story as it affects family life are now fairly clear. It is safe to say that studies of household size and composition based on censuses have an even less promising future. They have now reached an intellectual and conceptual dead end, unless radically new ways of using them can be devised. The most hopeful new approach is a highly ingenious use of statistics to indicate changes of values, as developed by Smith.[40]

A fruitful source for future research about intimate details of family life lies in the vast body of data in the records of ecclesiastical or other courts dealing with litigation over breach of contract, separation, or divorce. It may be that this will turn out to be the single most important untapped body of qualitative information about family life in the past. The documents provide precisely the kind of information that historians of *mentalité* are looking for, and work upon them is likely to bring rich rewards in the 1980s.

Unsolved Problems   The central, unresolved questions—the core program for the 1980s—are first, where, when, and in what classes did the new 'bourgeois' family type first emerge; and second, were the key independent variables attitudinal or economic, or both. What effect, in short, did modernization in the broadest sense of the word have upon family life or family life upon modernization? Many more detailed studies of working-class families undergoing the industrializing and urbanizing process, using mainly statistical but also literary evidence, are needed to solve this complicated and difficult question.

But other social groups must not be neglected. So far, almost nothing is known about bourgeois families in the pre-modern period. The two books on Florentine patriciate families, by Goldwaite and Kent, come to radically different conclusions. Virtually nothing is known about the family structure and values of the Amsterdam or London bourgeoisie of the seventeenth century, and this is a lacuna that urgently needs filling. Two books about the English landed elite in the eighteenth century have come to much the same conclusion about the facts of change, even if the models of explanation differ. But nothing comparable exists so

40   Moses Finley, "Progress in Historiography," *Daedalus,* CVI (1977), 139; Wells, "Family History and Demographic Transition," *Journal of Social History,* IX (1975), 1–19; D. S. Smith, "Parental Power and Marriage Patterns," *Journal of Marriage and the Family,* XXXV (1973), 419–428.

far for the landed elite of France or any other European country. This too is a gap that must be filled as soon as possible.[41]

Everyone recognizes the enormous importance of inheritance customs in determing the character of family life among the propertied classes, but only in France has the pattern been fully elucidated. In England little is known for certain about regional inheritance customs among the yeomanry and smallholders. As for the greater English landowners, the significance of the late seventeenth-century strict settlement, which for twenty-five years has been regarded as the key legal innovation governing inheritance among the elite, has recently been brought into question. Only a series of intensive studies of local elites will clear up this problem. In America we know a good deal about New England inheritance customs, but much less about the middle colonies or the Chesapeake Bay area. This discrepancy is already being narrowed, and a flood of monographs in the 1980s can be expected to narrow the gap still further.[42]

Other problems in every time and every place are still awaiting solutions. For the medieval period, much more work needs to be done to elucidate the significance of lineage in the early stages of feudalism, a field pioneered by Duby in France. The timing of the emergence of both childhood and adolescence as distinctive periods of life needs much more investigation, as do attitudes toward the aged. The influence of the state on the family needs more study on a comparative transnational basis, in order to test the validity of the association of patriarchy with authoritarian kingship, and of limited familial equality with limited political participation. A great deal of work has already been done on the relationship of Protestantism, and especially Puritanism, to the family, but we still know very little about the effects of post-Tridentine Catholicism.

41 Richard A. Goldthwaite, *Private Wealth in Renaissance Florence* (Princeton, 1968); Francis W. Kent, *Household and Lineage in Renaissance Florence* (Princeton, 1977); Stone, *Family, Sex and Marriage*; Trumbach, *Rise of the Egalitarian Family*.
42 Habakkuk, "Marriage Settlements"; *idem*, "The Rise and Fall of English Landed Families," *Transactions of the Royal Historical Society*, XXIX (1979), 187–207; C. Clay, "Marriage, Inheritance and the Rise of Large Estates in England, 1660–1815," *Economic History Review*, XXI (1968), 503–518; John V. Beckett, "English Landownership in the Later Seventeenth and Eighteenth Centuries," *Economic History Review*, XXX (1977), 566–581; Lloyd Bonfield, "Marriage Settlements and the 'Rise of Great Estates'; The Demographic Aspect," *Economic History Review*, XXXII (1979), 483–493.

The changing position of women in the family has been intensely studied in recent years in America, and to a lesser extent in England, but is still very undeveloped in France. The central issues are the facts, the causes, and the consequences of change: change in women's power over general family decision-making, over property, and over birth control and child-rearing; and change in women's participation in productive economic activity inside or outside the home, involving change in the concept of the double sphere, the male as the bread-winner and the female as the homemaker. None of these issues has been definitively resolved. For example, the eternal conflict between women's responsibilities in the home and in the work-force needs re-evaluation in the light of more intensive historical research. The creation of the "cult of true womanhood" in the early nineteenth century may turn out to have been as liberating in its time as has been its overthrow under the changed conditions of the late twentieth century.[43]

America has a special problem, that of the black family before and after slavery, on which an enormous amount of work has been done in recent years. So far, however, there are few signs of an emerging consensus, and yet it seems inherently implausible that a problem in so recent a period of history should not be soluble by a well-planned strategy of research using all available documents.[44]

Now that the Pandora's Box of the history of sexuality has been opened, it must be vigorously rummaged until the major problems are resolved. We still know far too little about class-specific sexual attitudes, and even less about class-specific extra-marital or marital sexual behavior. Serious histories of homosexuality or lesbianism in the medieval, early modern, and modern periods are only just beginning to be written, and the controversies about the allegedly sexually repressive nature of Puritanism

43   Degler, *Women and the Family in America.*
44   Herbert G. Gutman, *The Black Family in Slavery and Freedom, 1750–1925* (New York, 1976); *idem,* "Persistent Myths about the Afro-American Family," *Journal of Interdisciplinary History,* VI (1975), 181–210; John W. Blassingame, *The Slave Community: Plantation Life in the Antebellum South* (New York, 1972); Robert W. Fogel and Stanley Engerman, *Time on the Cross: The Economics of American Negro Slavery* (Boston, 1974), 2v.; Furstenberg et al., "The Origins of the Female-Headed Black Family: The Impact of the Urban Experience," *Journal of Interdisciplinary History,* VI (1975), 211–233; Eugene D. Genovese, *Roll, Jordan, Roll: The World the Slaves Made* (New York, 1974).

and Victorianism have yet to be settled. About the realities of sexual practice, we have a good many theories but little more than a handful of detailed case studies of sexual behavior among the elite, some controversial and dubious statistics about bastardy, and some firm data about prenuptial conception among the masses. And that is all. We do not even have a serious and well-documented book about the history of venereal disease and its treatment, or the use of mechanical or chemical contraceptives.

This survey suggests that, one way or another, family history is now inextricably bound up with virtually all of the major debates over historical sources, methods, problems, and interpretations. It is a cockpit for the battle between the quantifiers and the qualifiers—the cliometricians and those who prefer to rely upon personal and literary documents. In fact this is an absurd quarrel, since no serious history is possible without a combination of both. Family history could not begin until the demographic ground-work had been laid by the quantifiers. Once that had been accomplished, and family structure elucidated, questions of changes in attitudes and affections rose to the surface, answers to which are going to require the use of quite different sources and techniques. Even here, however, quantification can be used to suggest trends, besides being necessary in order to sort out the typical from the eccentric. As for literary sources, there is the serious problem of whether changes in the amount and character of the documenta-tion may not lead to false conclusions about changes in attitudes.

Family history also raises questions of interpretation; are monocausal explanations satisfying in themselves, or is history such a complicated and messy business that only multicausal ex-planations have much hope of proving to be even moderately convincing? Any historian of the family is confronted with the decision whether or not to accept a functionalist view of society as a linked set of organic subsystems, the family being primarily an agency for socialization and biological reproduction. But in family history, as elsewhere, similar structures may conceal dif-ferent functions: for example, the nuclear family as an economic unit of production clearly preceded the nuclear family as a unit of affective relations.

Family historians also have to make a series of critical choices: whether to accept Freudian, Eriksonian, or some other model of psychological development; whether to accept or reject the theory of a simple demographic transition from high birth rate/high death rate to low birth rate/low death rate; to decide whether the family of today is falling apart, or whether it has never been stronger; whether it serves as a "haven in a heartless world," or as a unit for profligate consumerism, or as a demoralized and devitalized institution almost all functions of which have been taken over by the ever-increasing numbers in the medical and counseling professions. Family historians are also forced to take some position on the uniqueness or otherwise of Western culture and society; on the historical effects upon domestic affairs of Protestantism, Puritanism, the Enlightenment, industrialization, technology, and the modern state; on the role and significance of women in history; on theories about the nature of the new-born child; on sexual behavior and its relation to sociobiology, ethics, religion, and technology. There is thus scarcely any major problem in our lives, or any major dispute about the nature of change in the past, upon which family history does not somehow impinge.

In view of this, and of the exponential growth of the literature in recent years, two things are fairly certain; first, the current astonishing rate of growth cannot continue indefinitely, and is certain to slow down before very long; second, for the foreseeable future the volume of activity is unlikely to decline, if only because the number of important unsolved problems still far exceed those which have now been more or less satisfactorily accounted for. Thanks to the intensive work on family history over the past quarter of a century, we now know the questions we ought to be asking. But we do not yet have many indisputable answers.

Biography in the 1980s

Miles F. Shore

A Psychoanalytic Perspective   Biography as a Western literary form began with fragments of lives in early Greek literature, but was launched as a professional endeavor by Plutarch, Suetonius, and Tacitus in the first century, A.D. Since then, the significance of biography as a literary genre has waxed and waned. Bent to the purpose of ecclesiastical exhortation in its medieval incarnation, the lives of saints, biography was revived in the Renaissance by Sir Thomas More, William Roper, and George Cavendish, and assumed a variety of forms, both distinguished and scurrilous, in the seventeenth and eighteenth centuries. Its Victorian version, the official tome of deadly propriety was replaced by the irreverent "new biography" which, by the late 1920s and early 1930s, made biography a major literary form, at least in terms of sales. Since then it has continued steadily to interest both popular and scholarly readers.

Located somewhere between literature and history, biography has always been regarded with misgivings by its artistic and historical neighbors. Frequently the work of gifted amateurs, it has been viewed as simply an assemblage of facts requiring little in the way of literary art. Its potential subjects have regarded it apprehensively; not a few have taken pains to cover their tracks by destroying letters, diaries, and other shards of their existence. Historians have viewed it with even more concern, for some biographers, motivated to capture and recreate a life, have fashioned literary triumphs which are historical humbug. Further, there is considerable difference of opinion about the role of the individual person in determining the course of events. For Ralph Waldo Emerson "there is properly no history: only biography,"

Miles F. Shore is Bullard Professor of Psychiatry and Head of the Department of Psychiatry, Massachusetts Mental Health Center, Harvard Medical School. He is the author of "Cecil Rhodes and the Ego Ideal," *Journal of Interdisciplinary History,* X (1979), 249–265.

0022-1953/81/01089-25 $02.50/0

whereas Tolstoy argued that history could not be explained by a simple transfer of collective power to the great individual.[1]

Well before Langer officially placed mastery of the theories and tools of psychoanalysis on the docket as the next agenda for historians, biography had been stirred by controversy over the use of psychoanalytic ideas in the writing of lives. Beginning with Freud's "Leonardo da Vinci" in 1910, the first formal psychoanalytic life study, psychobiography has been subject to the same mix of credulity and rejection as has psychoanalysis; like psychoanalysis, it has suffered at least as much from its aficionados as its opponents.[2]

The simplest definition of "psychology" is "the mental, attitudinal, motivational, or behavioral characteristics of an individual or a type, class, or group of individuals." By that definition it is difficult to imagine a non-psychobiographical biography. The narrower definition of psychology is "the science of mind or of mental phenomena and activities: systematic knowledge about mental processes." It is the application of this definition which has led to the idea that psychobiography can exist as a separate genre which explicitly uses scientifically derived concepts and data to understand the subject. This development is a result of the evolution of biography and certain special characteristics of psychoanalytic psychology.

Since the earliest biographies there has been a continuum of approach ranging from idealizing or heroic works at one end of the spectrum, through those which strove for realism, to the reductionist, debunking type at the other. Plutarch's aim was to provide for his readers instruction and enlightenment about moral virtue. Suetonius, by contrast, focused on the intimate details of the lives of the Caesars, the courtesans, and the others of whom he wrote, to capture the total reality of his subjects' lives. He was less interested in enhancing the moral capacities of his readers

1 Leon Edel, "The Cult of Biography: The Figure Under the Carpet," *New Republic* (Feb. 10, 1979), 25–29. Emerson is quoted in Marc Pachter, "The Biographer Himself: An Introduction," in Pachter (ed.), *Telling Lives, The Biographer's Art* (Washington, D.C., 1979). Leo Tolstoy, *War and Peace* (New York, 1938; orig. pub. 1868), 809.
2 William Langer, "The Next Assignment," *American Historical Review*, LXIII (1958), 283–304; Sigmund Freud, "Leonardo Da Vinci and a Memory of His Childhood," in James Strachey (ed.), *The Standard Edition of the Complete Psychological Works of Sigmund Freud* (London, 1955).

than in cataloging, like an assiduous naturalist, every trait, habit, or idiosyncrasy of the person being studied through the microscope of his curiosity.[3]

Both themes, idealization and realism, can be traced in the works which followed these two biographical progenitors. James Boswell, when chided for his realistic portrayal of Samuel Johnson, advised his critics that he would not "cut off his claws, nor make a tiger a cat to please anybody."[4] Even so, his primary aim was to celebrate a colorful and distinguished character and his work is thus an amalgam of the two approaches. It was classic Victorian biography which developed the idealizing theme to an extreme which ultimately proved too much for critics and for an increasingly sophisticated public. Strachey, with characteristic pungency, epitomized the genre as "those two fat volumes with which it is our custom to commemorate the dead—who does not know them, with their ill-digested masses of material, their slipshod style, their tone of tedious panegyric, their lamentable lack of selection, of detachment, of design? They are as familiar as the cortege of the undertaker, and wear the same air of slow, funeral barbarism."[5]

Victorian idealizing biography was replaced by the "new biography" heralded by Froude's four-volume epic on Carlyle, which presented a candid account of Carlyle's fierce personality and his stormy marriage. But it is Strachey who is generally regarded as the founder and uniquely skilled practitioner of the new realism which captured biography at the time of World War I. His goal was to achieve "a becoming brevity—a brevity which excludes everything that is redundant and nothing that is significant." Strachey was criticized for deliberately eroding the image of public persons by exposing their nether aspects, and it is true that he was acerbic and enjoyed puncturing the pompous. He was saved from dismissal as a sensationalist crank by his literary gifts and the novelty of his approach. In view of his association with the Bloomsbury group, Strachey should have reflected Freudian ideas in his work. Actually, although he was interested in human relationships and the nuances of character, his goal was the literary

3 Arthur Hugh Clough, *Plutarch's Lives* (New York, 1909), 37–38. Joseph Gavorse (ed.), *The Lives of the Twelve Caesars by Suetonius* (London, 1931), x.
4 Quoted in Pachter, *Telling Lives*, 5.
5 Lytton Strachey, *Eminent Victorians* (London, 1918), vi–vii.

resuscitation of biography, not the transplantation of psycho-analysis.[6]

That other new biographers would use psychoanalytic ideas was inevitable because of the unique suitability of psychoanalytic psychology for life studies. Psychiatry before Freud was concerned with illnesses which happened to people; that is illnesses which were extraneous to the person in the same way as gout, tuberculosis, or appendicitis. That psychoanalysis gave conceptual form to the continuum between normal and abnormal psychology and that it offered a developmental theory made it possible to construct a framework upon which a personal psychological narrative could be hung. The framework related intrapsychic events to the external manifestations of attitudes and behavior. The psychological narrative paralleled life events from cradle to grave and thus had the potential to be a subtle and enriching accompaniment to the life story.

Both brief sketches and full-fledged biographical studies were done by psychoanalysts in the first three decades of this century. Flugel, Hitschman, Clark, and others contributed to this literature. Since psychoanalysis at the time was primarily concerned with the id, instinctual drives, primitive mental mechanisms, and the intricacies of unconscious conflict, early psychoanalysis fitted easily into the reductionist school of biography. Despite Freud's warnings in his "Leonardo," and some notable exceptions such as Clark's sensitive biography of Abraham Lincoln, most of these works focused on the id and drives, featured primitive sexual content and conflicts, and became part of the contentious battle for acceptance which was the major theme in the history of psychoanalysis as a discipline.[7]

There was substantial spillover of a psychological approach into professional biography during this period: Krutch on Poe, Anthony on Alcott, Ludwig on Goethe and Napoleon, and Zweig on Marie Antoinette. Although only Krutch was openly psychoanalytical, all of them were interested in psychological development and conflicts and the influence of personality on events.[8]

6 James Anthony Froude, *Thomas Carlyle* (London, 1882–1884), 4v; L. Strachey, *Victorians*, vii.

7 J. C. Flugel, "On the Character and Married Life of Henry VIII, *International Journal of Psychoanalysis*, I (1920), 24–55; Edward Hitschman, *Great Men: Psychoanalytic Studies* (New York), 1955; L. Pierce Clark, *Lincoln: A Psychobiography* (New York, 1933).

8 Joseph Wood Krutch, *Edgar Allan Poe: A Study in Genius* (New York, 1926); Katherine Anthony, *Louisa May Alcott* (New York, 1938); Emil Ludwig, *Goethe: The History of a*

In the meantime, psychoanalytic theory was evolving beyond its early interest in the id to focus on ego psychology, the study of those psychological functions which channel mental activity into meaningful and comfortable patterns of experience and which make possible the development of character traits and patterns. The earlier psychoanalytic emphasis on instinctual drives and psychological conflict was particularly useful to unravel symptomatology and the pathological sequelae of poorly resolved conflict; ego psychology expanded the capacity to study normal development and behavior including productive functioning and outstanding achievement. It set the stage for the extraordinary work of Erikson in his schematization of psychological development which integrated the "timetable of the organism with the structure of social institutions." Among other things, Erikson's schema postulated continued psychological development of significant dimensions beyond childhood and adolescence through the entire life cycle. Thus the conceptual tools available to the investigator of lives and the biographer were vastly expanded and it became possible to understand human behavior without resorting to a pathological model. This line of research was extended into studies of adult development by Levinson and his collaborators, and the sophisticated longitudinal studies of Vaillant.[9]

The result has been a spate of biographical works which make explicit use of psychoanalytic concepts, led by Erikson's own studies of Martin Luther and Mohandas Gandhi. Many, such as the Sterbas on Ludwig von Beethoven, Greenacre on Lewis Carroll and Jonathan Swift, Cody on Emily Dickinson and Mack on T. E. Lawrence have been written by psychiatrists or psychoanalysts. Historians and professional biographers have contributed their share; notably Edel with his five-volume life of Henry James, Kearns on Lyndon Johnson, Mazlish on the Mills, and Rogow on James Forrestal.[10]

Man (New York, 1928); Stefan Zweig, *Marie Antoinette: The Portrait of an Average Woman* (New York, 1933).

9 Erik Erikson, *Childhood and Society* (New York, 1963; 2nd ed.), 246. Daniel J. Levinson, Charlotte N. Darrow, Edward B. Klein, Maria H. Levinson, and Braxton McKee, *The Seasons of a Man's Life* (New York, 1978); George E. Vaillant, *Adaptation to Life* (Boston, 1977).

10 Erikson, *Young Man Luther* (New York, 1958); *idem, Gandhi's Truth* (New York, 1969); Edith Sterba and Richard Sterba, *Beethoven and His Nephew* (New York, 1954); Phyllis Greenacre, *Swift and Carroll: A Psychoanalytic Study of Two Lives* (New York, 1963); John Cody, *After Great Pain: The Inner Life of Emily Dickinson* (Cambridge, Mass.,

As the use of psychoanalytic concepts in biography has spread, opposition has, predictably, been vigorous and distinguished. The opposition has not come only from opponents of psychoanalysis; deep concern has been expressed within the psychoanalytic community about the validity and appropriateness of applied psychoanalysis, i.e., the transplantation of psychoanalytic formulations and concepts to any settings outside the consulting room, and, more narrowly, to relationships other than the transference neurosis.

The specific concerns have been several, and substantive; their dissemination has helped considerably to raise standards in psychobiography. The first has to do with the rules of evidence and clinical methodology. In work with live patients, it is the interaction between patient and therapist which is the unit of study. The transference neurosis and its congeners serve as a model of the patient's psychopathology as well as the fulcrum of change. And the opportunity to gauge the reaction of the patient—his or her associations and emotional response—is the touchstone of validity. Nonverbal data—tone of voice, body movements, and facial expression—are important clues to meaning. The relationship is sheltered in confidentiality and the patient is motivated, at least consciously, to divulge what the therapist indicates will be most helpful. In contrast, the biographer's data are usually written material, produced by the subject for some purpose other than the elucidation of psychological reality, as well as accounts of behavior and relationships by persons other than the subject, with their own biases and special relationship to the subject. There may also be such archival materials as wills, accounts, memoranda, and travel itineraries. Major objections have been raised because the use of this material does not allow for the interaction between therapist and patient which is the domain within which psychoanalytic data customarily have their existence and meaning. Even in those cases where the biographer interviews the subject or knows the subject personally, the relationship and

1971); John E. Mack, *A Prince of Our Disorder: The Life of T. E. Lawrence* (Boston, 1976); Edel, *The Life of Henry James* (New York, 1953–1972), 5v.; Doris Kearns, *Lyndon Johnson and The American Dream* (New York, 1977); Bruce Mazlish, *James and John Stuart Mill: Father and Son in the Nineteenth Century* (New York, 1975); Arnold Rogow, *James Forrestal* (New York, 1963).

setting can never reproduce the special characteristics of the analytic hour.

A second objection has to do with the relationship of the
biographer to his subject, a relationship which is the biographical
analogue of countertransference. Bowen has stated that she can
only write about a person she can love, by which she clearly
means something quite different from the idealization characteristic of Victorian biographies. By contrast, examples abound of
works which are seriously flawed by the author's animus, Bullitt
and Freud's book on Wilson being the prime case. This issue has
been thoroughly discussed and understood and there is now substantially greater sophistication about an author's unwitting bias
toward a subject.[11]

A third problem is what Donald has called "imperfect articulation"—the inability to relate psychological data to historical
events based on inadequate mastery of both disciplines by the
biographer. A well-known example is Freud's gaffe in his study
of Leonardo, in which he based a good deal of his formulation on
a mistranslation of the Italian word for "kite" which rendered it
"vulture." For biographers without psychoanalytic training, the
analogous mistake is an over-literal application of psychoanalytic
concepts to explain isolated behavioral incidents rather than an
attempt to understand broad behavioral themes supported by the
kind of data compiled by the clinician working with a patient. A
subset of this problem is the attempt to explain creative works or
historical achievement as the direct and simply-linked result of
early childhood traumata. Great achievement may be shaped by
early trauma or even psychopathology, but it is rarely its result.[12]

These criticisms have had some effect in refining the use of
psychological data in biography and there are now much more
sophisticated works, such as Mack's biography of Lawrence,
which bring together careful historical scholarship and keen clinical acumen in a mutually enriching and convincing blend. It is
also true, despite the controversy, that a completely event-cen-
tered biography such as Morris' Roosevelt is vaguely unsatisfac-

11 Catherine Drinker Bowen, *Biography: The Craft and the Calling* (Boston, 1968). C. D.
Bullitt and Sigmund Freud, *Thomas Woodrow Wilson: A Psychological Study* (Boston, 1966).
12 David H. Donald, "Between History and Psychology: Reflections on Psychobiography," lecture at the American Psychiatric Association Meeting, 1972. Lionel Trilling,
"Art and Neurosis," in his *The Liberal Imagination* (New York, 1953), 159–183.

tory because we fail to find in it the modern equivalent of Plutarch's "particular attention to the marks and indications of the souls of men" which we have come to expect.[13]

Although psychobiography continues to generate controversy, the contribution of psychological understanding to the study of lives is sufficiently well accepted that one may anticipate the eventual disappearance of psychobiography as a separate genre. Instead, all biographies will be expected to include a consideration of personality factors as they affect the subject's life and contribution. The extent to which psychological matters are presented will depend upon: (1) the degree to which otherwise inexplicable events can be elucidated by considering psychological data, i.e., the true importance of psychological factors in the life story; (2) the extent to which data are available in the record of the subject upon which valid inferences about psychological matters can be based; (3) the degree of mastery of psychological concepts achieved by the author; and (4) the state of development of psychoanalytic and other explanatory concepts which can be fruitfully applied to the particular life under consideration.

It is possible even at this point to set out a number of criteria to measure the success of a biography which uses modern psychological knowledge to portray a life: a biography which recognizes that every human being, however ordinary or extraordinary, has certain basic needs for love and self-esteem from others, must struggle with hatred and self-centeredness which interfere with essential relationships, has had parents of a certain type and a life story marked by good and bad luck, by painful and rewarding experiences, and has unconscious residues from psychological development which influence behavior. The criteria which can be used to assess such a modern biography thus reflect both developments in psychodynamic theory and derivatives of clinical work appropriately adapted to biographical literature.

First, the basis of any endeavor, biographical or clinical, which aims to portray psychological reality must be an empathic approach which seeks an appreciation of the inner experience of the other person. Empathy is "the capacity for participating in or

13 Edmund Morris, *The Rise of Theodore Roosevelt* (New York, 1979); Plutarch, "Life of Alexander," in *The Lives of Nobel Grecians and Romans* (Chicago, 1952), 541.

a vicarious experiencing of another's feelings, volitions, or ideas and sometimes another's movements to the point of executing bodily movements resembling his." In this definition, some permeability of the boundary between self and object is implied in the vicarious experiencing of the other's feelings and the imitation of bodily movements. But the main emphasis is upon the appreciation of the psychological experience of the other person: the subject's state of mind is deliberately tuned out or set aside. This self-effacing empathy is the major clinical tool for gathering data about complex psychological configurations.[14]

Its effectiveness is enhanced by knowledge of the subject's past history, present mood, and current concerns. It seeks to answer the question, "if I were this other person with a certain background of life experience, desires, vulnerabilities, and a certain way of looking at things, how might I feel under these circumstances, at *this* moment?" Thus an immersion both in the subject's life and in the moment is central.

Clinicians are trained in empathic immersion by a complex process of experiential and theoretical education. Some pre-existing capacity to empathize helps—usually developed out of painful interpersonal experience in which gauging the psychological state of some significant other person was of importance. Experience with a wide variety of patients is the major route to the development of empathic skills, but close supervision by a more experienced clinician is a necessary additional ingredient. Overlapping, but distinctly secondary is acquaintance with the clinical and theoretical literature to provide a conceptual framework into which data can be fitted. Awareness that the data include observations about oneself as well as the patient develops *en passant*. That aspect can be enhanced by personal therapy, a frequent accompaniment to training.

A second definition of empathy is "the imaginative projection of a subjective state whether affective, conative, or cognitive into an object so that the object appears to be infused with it: the reading of one's own state of mind or conation into an object (as an artistic object)." That definition, which implies a loss of the boundary between self and object, describes "self-involved" empathy which poses a serious danger for the collection of data

14   Heinz Kohut, *The Analysis of the Self* (New York, 1971), 300.

about complex psychological processes. A major pitfall for the investigator of inner experience is the confusion of his or her own state with that of the subject; a goal of training in empathy is to avoid that mistake.

Second, there should be conveyed a sense of the development of the person through the life cycle. The work of Erikson, Levinson, Jaques, and Vaillant makes it clear that psychological development proceeds throughout life. Although there are characteristic features which persist from stage to stage, the person may be very different in attitudes, interests, and reactions to events in adolescence, middle, and old age. Too many biographies make no differentiation of character as it evolves; they fail to paint in the lines and wrinkles of life experience; they frequently confuse reactions to the life-long process of aging with psychopathology. The result is a distortion of the trajectory of normal psychological development.

As a corollary, the modern biographer should be aware of the importance of developmental crises, those naturally-occurring periods of emotional upheaval and instability which may be manifested in varying degree in different persons. In some cases there is relatively little overt disturbance of the pattern of life and relationships in response to such crises as demonstrated in Offer and Offer's studies of male adolescence. In other cases there is little in the way of symptomatology but substantial effects on work and marital relationships of the kind revealed in Jacques' work on the profound changes in the pattern of creativity in artists and composers in their mid-thirties. However, developmental crises may precipitate serious symptoms of pathology in vulnerable individuals. Thus the "identity diffusion" described by Erikson occurs in adolescents whose identity crises supervene on a base of inadequate resolution of earlier developmental issues.[15]

Gross symptomatology is difficult for biographers to overlook; the manifestations of developmental crises in the form of pathological or destructive behavior are much less likely to be recognized and understood by the biographer. For instance, Henry VIII's romance with Anne Boleyn, who had been at court and potentially available for more than three years, only began

15   Daniel Offer and Judith Barkin Offer, *From Teenage to Young Manhood* (New York, 1975); Elliott Jaques, "Death and the Mid-Life Crisis," *International Journal of Psychoanalysis,* XLVI (1965), 502–513; Erikson, *Childhood and Society,* 247–274.

after a series of major military and political disappointments and after the frustration of his wish to have a son by Catherine of Aragon. The relationship of his infatuation to issues in his psychological development was overlooked until an understanding of the phenomena associated with mid-life crises became available.

Erikson alluded to the mid-thirties stage of generativity as the need to be needed which results in "Care . . . the widening concern for what has been generated by love, necessity or accident." According to Erikson the crisis associated with that period results from an imbalance between self-interest and interest in others. Similarly, but separately, Jaques concluded that the mid-life period consisted of a working-through of depression set off by the failure of defensive idealization, activity, and denial to ward off the realization of aging and eventual death signalling the ultimate defeat for even healthy self love.[16]

One cannot expect every biographer to be a developmental psychologist. But one can hope that any biographer who aspires to excellence and contemporary relevance will have in mind the basic principles of developmental crises, an awareness of their possible manifestations, and a rough schematization of crisis periods—early and late adolescence, generativity, later middle age, and old age at a minimum. Acquaintance with the work of Erikson, Vaillant, Levinson, Gould, and Neugarten is essential.[17]

Third, the modern biography should reflect an understanding of the central role of object loss, disappointment, and life change in precipitating emotional distress, significant changes in behavior, and clinical symptoms. The critical importance of object loss in hastening disturbances in psychological equilibrium is poorly conveyed in the psychoanalytic and psychiatric literature, although it is the key to clinical assessment and diagnosis and is a major issue in the conduct of treatment. In establishing the precipitating causes of emotional illness, one always explores important emotional relationships and their reflections in self-esteem to establish the shifts which have led to symptoms or to major changes in

16   Shore, "Henry VIII and the Crisis of Generativity," *Journal of Interdisciplinary History*, II (1972), 359–390; Erikson, *Insight and Responsibility* (New York, 1964), 130–132, Jaques, "Death and the Mid Life Crisis."

17   Levinson et al, *The Seasons of a Man's Life*; Vaillant, *Adaptation to Life*; Erikson, *Childhood and Society*; Roger Gould, "The Phases of Adult Life: A Study in Developmental Psychology," *American Journal of Psychiatry*, CXXIX (1972), 521–531; B. L. Neugarten, *Personality in Middle and Late Life* (New York, 1964).

behavior. In work with patients these are validated by sensitive clinical investigation which can trace back and establish emotional connections.

Although the biographer may be limited to presumptive evidence based on the chronological sequence of events, there is such a volume of clinical experience and research data on the effects of life change that connections are justified if stated with appropriate qualifications. For example, Theodore Roosevelt remained depressed for approximately seven months—a normal period of time—after his father's death, when he was a sophomore at Harvard. His father had played a large part in his care from early infancy because of Roosevelt's childhood asthma, and he continued to be admired and relied upon by the young Roosevelt. Roosevelt's recovery from his grief was closely related in time to his falling in love with Alice Lee, who became his first wife. With the intensity which characterized everything he did, he set out to win her despite, or perhaps because of, a significant coolness on her part. His own account of his feelings for her conveys an overestimation of her and a fantasy of perfect happiness which to some extent reflected Victorian hyperbole and his own exuberance, but are also very likely related to her serving as a replacement for his dead father. His frequent separations from her, particularly when she was pregnant, and other shreds of evidence are consistent with a relationship which did not live up to this exaggerated beginning.[18]

One may appropriately ask if establishing such a connection makes any different. In this case, Roosevelt's later behavior toward his first wife is clearer if one includes the possibility that his original estimation of her was exaggerated by grief and a wish to replace his father at whatever cost. For instance, he was away from her a great deal during the nine months of her first pregnancy—absences which seem odd for a devoted young husband. His last trip, a jaunt to Albany during the week she was scheduled to deliver, was climaxed by his hasty recall to find her dying of kidney disease.

Consistent with the requirement of sensitivity to object loss is the need for a biographer to understand the normal grief reaction, its stages, duration, and possible outcomes. Morris, for

18 Morris, *Theodore Roosevelt*, 104–133.

instance, expresses surprise at the depth of Roosevelt's grief for his father, describing it as a "sensitivity so extreme it verges on mental imbalance." Yet its duration was within what we know clinically to be normal limits, and Roosevelt felt all of the pain of the loss in resolving his grief. Thus he recalled vividly his father's holding him in his arms as a child "for hours together, night after night." And he managed out of that successful grief work to construct a helpful internal object. "Years afterward," Corinne, his sister, wrote: "When the college boy of 1878 was entering upon his duties as President of the United States, he told me frequently that he never took any serious steps or made any vital decision for his country without thinking first what position his father would have taken on the questions." [19]

It is also important to understand in a general way the outcomes of grief. In addition to behavior change and symptoms, loss of important persons may lay down a precipitate of character traits. This is particularly true in children where the death of a parent or of siblings may be "metabolized" by character formation in the shape of the lost object. Children rarely show the adult pattern of grieving with its distinguishable stages which were described by Lindemann. Instead their reactions are more often a denial of feelings of grief, or of rapid recovery from acute tearfulness and depression, followed by activity and the development of attitudes and behavior which reflect the loss. [20]

A forty-nine-year-old man sought psychoanalysis because of his inability to settle down to marriage or to a long term job although he had excellent professional training. Despite high paying jobs in his field, he rented apartments, drove a battered car, and had few clothes or other personal possessions. His father had died when he was four, his mother when he was eight. An aunt, with whom he then lived, died when he was ten and, because his remaining uncle was alcoholic, he was placed in foster homes until he went to college.

In analysis his inability to make commitments was traced to memories of his feelings when, instead of crying at his parents' funerals, he was a "brave little man" and resolved never to get trapped in caring for someone again. Thus his character style

19 Ibid., 95–96.
20 See Eric Lindemann's classic article, "Symptomatology and Management of Acute Grief," American Journal of Psychiatry, CI (1944), 141.

reflected an alternative to conscious awareness of losses which are overwhelming.

The fourth desideratum for a modern biographer is the search for what Edel has called the "personal myth," the set of less-than-conscious motivations which lie behind manifest attitudes and behavior, and which are organized into a decipherable pattern based on crucial developmental experiences. Edel cites the example of Ernest Hemingway, who challenged Max Eastman to a fist fight because Eastman asked in print why Hemingway made such a fuss about the hair on his chest. Edel's view, consistent with both psychodynamic and common sense, is that Hemingway's bellicose reaction confirmed the implication of Eastman's question: that deep male insecurity underlay the outer machismo which characterized Hemingway's art and life.[21]

Similarly, Rhodes' life was dominated by a personal myth; it was the idea, expressed in his late adolescent "Confession of Faith," that the evils of the world would be corrected by the formation of a secret society modelled on the Jesuits and the Masons, "with but one object, the furtherance of the British Empire and the bringing of the whole uncivilized world under British rule for the recovery of the United States for the making the Anglo-Saxon race but one empire." The society was to be formed of Englishmen scattered all over the world who would work within their respective countries to spread British control since "more territory simply means more of the Anglo-Saxon race more of the best the most human, most honorable race the world posseses." It was this idea which motivated his territorial ambitions north of the Transvaal, and which, embodied in his will, became the Rhodes scholarships. That myth, with its fraternal aspects, reflected Rhodes' early experience of roaming free as a boy with his brothers in a close-knit band, an experience which had been terminated by the dispersal of Rhodes and his brothers across the British empire.[22]

The highest expression of the biographer's art lies in the elucidation of the nuances of motivation and relationship which form the personal myth and make it possible to see the psychological unity within which action takes on meaning. Central to

21 Edel, "The Figure Under the Carpet," 17.
22 Cecil J. Rhodes, "Confession of Faith," reproduced in John Flint, *Cecil Rhodes* (Boston, 1974), 249–250.

that personal myth, especially in those who lead others, is the role played by guiding ideals. Such ideals are an amalgam of the grandiosity and omnipotent fantasies characteristic of the earliest, primitive precursors of self-awareness and self-esteem. Their modification by experience with others—both gratifying and frustrating—is a crucial determinant of later stages of functioning, for the ideals organize both interpersonal relationships and instrumental behavior. It is here that the demands of art and psychological science coincide to define succinctly the biographer's task.[23]

Fifth, a contemporary biography should have an awareness of the manifestations of psychological and physical illness. Cody in his biography of Dickinson takes pains to establish that her progressive withdrawal from human contact was an evolving psychosis rather than simply the result of an extreme sensitivity to ordinary events characteristic of genius. It is remarkable that Cody is forced to argue the case against what he calls "the tacit 'conspiracy' of present-day authors to fix Emily Dickinson within the sphere of normality." He quotes MacLeish, "most of us are half in love with his dead girl," as a basis for understanding this denial of her pathology.[24]

Without discounting that motivation, one must also acknowledge that without some awareness of the signs and symptoms of mental illness, the biographer is at a disadvantage in portraying and understanding many of the subjects of biography. Psychodynamic formulation has not completely superseded descriptive psychiatry; in fact psychiatric diagnosis of affective disorders, schizophrenia and its variants, borderline personalities, the neuroses and character disorder is increasingly precise and usefully supplements a psychodynamic approach. An awareness of the general features of major syndromes and the habit of using consultants to gain precision in this area should be the goal of every serious biographer.

Similarly, attention to the influence of physical illness on the life story is important. The effects of syphilis on behavior are well

23 Kohut, "Forms and Transformations of Narcissism," *Journal of the American Psychoanalytic Association,* XIV (1966), 243–272.
24 Cody, *After Great Pain,* 36; Archibald MacLeish, "The Private World: Poems of Emily Dickinson," in Richard B. Sewall (ed.), *Emily Dickinson: A Collection of Critical Essays* (Englewood Cliffs, 1963), 40.

known and perhaps even exaggerated by prurience. Hypertension, nephritis, rheumatic heart disease, and endocrine abnormalities all interfere with normal functioning in both general and specific ways. How many ciphers and maps were misread, battles lost, and rendezvous missed because of severe myopia before glasses were available? The delayed effects of subdural hematoma—a clot on the brain—following even mild head injury can be profoundly significant but difficult to diagnose. Ergotism and other natural and intentional intoxications can be exceedingly important. It is essential for the biographer to bear in mind that physical illnesses have always affected human beings, eminent as well as ordinary. To seek consultation is of critical importance: what is required of the consultant is both great clinical experience with the illness (and related illnesses) under consideration, and familiarity with current developments in research on that group of illnesses. Neither clinical nor research expertise alone is sufficient. Consulting more than one expert may be useful in complicated and important cases. Certainly consulting only one's local internist or surgeon is not adequate.

Sixth, some acknowledgement that the unconscious exists and that its subtle influence can change the course of history is also a basic requirement for modern biography. Having passed through the early id period of psychoanalysis with its ingenuous rejoicing that eminent persons could be the pawns of unconscious strivings, it should now be possible to include the signs of unconscious processes in an understanding of biographical subjects without violating the rules of evidence or resorting to jargon. Doing so requires the clinician's careful attention to slips of the tongue, mistakes, and behavior which is inexplicable in ordinary terms. The pursuit of psychodynamic understanding begins where commonsense explanations fail; the manifest myth covers a secret myth which is revealed to those who are alert to the possibilities and relentless in compiling and cross-checking the data. As Edel has put it "there are so many new ways, then, for drawing larger conclusions about an inner life, of which the outer life is a constant expression." [25]

Hand in hand with receptivity to the unconscious, there must be an awareness of the limitations of interpretations which rely exclusively on unconscious processes and infantile strivings. To

[25] Edel, "Figure Under the Carpet," 32–33.

acknowledge the limitations of one's art by giving appropriate weight to reality, to the pressures of public life, and even to coincidence and bad luck is the mark of maturity in the biographer as in the therapist. It is extremely important to recognize that most significant behavior is over-determined; that is, it serves a variety of intrapsychic functions at various levels of the personality and also furthers adaptation to the real world.

How can the biographer prepare for the task of sophisticated manipulation of psychological concepts and data? To what extent will formal training in psychodynamic psychology be necessary? How important is personal psychoanalysis? A variety of models exist: there are historians who have finished special training programs in psychoanalytic institutes; a few psychiatrists have formal graduate training in history; far more common are historians, political scientists, and scholars in the arts who have attended workshops or courses in departments of psychiatry and in psychoanalytic institutes. The natural bent of scholars is theoretical; they have usually read the psychoanalytic literature and are expert in the manipulation of its concepts. What is missing in the psychoanalytic and psychiatric literature is an account of the application of theory to clinical situations; the gathering and validation of data, and the gradual accumulation of material to develop an empathic sense of the inner reality of the patient.

Clinical skill is transmitted by an apprenticeship in which a student/trainee meets with a more experienced supervisor, one hour for every one or two hours with a patient. "Process" notes, a close-to-verbatim account of interactions between patient and therapist, are studied by the supervisor-therapist duo to tease out the latent content of the interaction. This process is rarely described in the literature; the actual learning which evolves from the process is almost impossible to capture and transmit except by participating in it. As a result, clinical methods generally remain inaccessible to scholars. The writing of psychologically sophisticated biography is closely related to clinical work; its major failures reflect a lack of clinical "feel" on the part of its practitioners who clumsily transpose complex theoretical concepts to "explain" behavior or relationships rather than build up a chain of events and behavior which conveys to the empathically-tuned observer a construct which can make sense out of the sequence.

Theodore Roosevelt's romantic pursuit of Alice Lee so soon

after his father's death is susceptible to a mechanically oedipal interpretation; that freed by his father's death from the second adolescent oedipal situation, Roosevelt was able to realize his heterosexual strivings and win the hand of Alice Lee. That interpretation would ignore a more empathic reading of what it felt like to be Roosevelt reacting to the death of his father, with whom he had had a relationship marked predominantly by admiration, respect, closeness, and a need to be reassured that his father approved of him. Thus "I felt as if I had been stunned, or as if a part of my life had been taken away, and the two moments of sharp, bitter agony, when I kissed the dear dead face and realized that he would never again on this earth speak to me or greet me with his loving smile," and, later, "all through the sermon, I was thinking of Father. I could see him sitting in the corner of the pew as distinctly as if he were alive, in the same dear old attitude, with his funny little 'warlike curl'! and his beloved face. Oh, I feel so sad when I think of the word never." [26]

Rather than oedipal competition, it was support, encouragement, and approval which he sought from his father. A rote oedipal interpretation would miss the special quality of the relationship which is revealed by empathic awareness to have many persisting pre-oedipal features which were transformed into a positive and sustaining aspect of Roosevelt's adult character. For the clinician, theory serves the ordering of the data, not the other way around.

Thus, some actual experience with real patients is extremely important for the contemporary biographer. This experience might be simply observing skilled clinicians interviewing patients for diagnostic purposes. The observation of group psychotherapy, a commonly available didactic experience, would make it possible to observe the behavioral manifestations of unconscious processes and the unfolding of free associations. Close supervision of these experiences would supply the final step: ordering the data using theoretical constructs. One is reminded of Renault's self-imposed training as a novelist which included becoming a nurse to expose herself to a wide range of human experience. Similiarly the biographer's training should consist not only of wide real experience with human life, and the information about human psychology

---

26 Morris, *Theodore Roosevelt*, 95.

and its development from the literature. It should also include a familiarity with clinical situations in which it is uniquely possible to develop an empathic awareness of the inner experience of another human being. One's own therapy or psychoanalysis can provide some of this empathic exposure and is useful. But therapy is not a substitute for clinical experience in understanding someone else, for it is that experience which is the closest real-life counterpart of biographical work.[27]

What theoretical system should the biographer adopt—Freudian, Jungian, Gestalt, behaviorist, or some other? Although theoretical orientation clearly affects clinical work by influencing methods of observation and what is observed, clinicians in actual practice are not theoretically pristine. The major part of the process of diagnosis and of therapy consists of relating isolated observations to a larger conceptual scheme which makes sense for that patient and which can serve to guide intervention. The choice is determined by the nature of the patient's problems and character, the schemata with which the therapist is familiar and the exigencies of the patient's reality. For example, classical oedipal dynamics are less relevant to the treatment of a borderline character problem than is the work of Kernberg which stresses an understanding of early object relationships—not that oedipal dynamics are refuted by the case: they are simply less relevant at crucial phases of the treatment. The modern biographer should have a general acquaintance with various theoretical approaches, and work back from the particular subject to the most useful schema with a great deal of help from consultants.[28]

However, the subjects of biography, those "individuals who have aroused in the world a particular curiosity," are not a representative sample of personality types. Although outstanding persons vary in many psychological characteristics, they tend to be persons in whom narcissism is an important feature. Thus the recent developments in psychoanalytic theory relating to narcissism, its normal development and manifestations as well as its pathological variants, are extremely important for the biographer.

27 Mary Renault, *Persian Boy* (New York, 1972).
28 Leston Havens, *Approaches to the Mind: Movement of the Psychiatric Schools from Sects Toward Science* (Boston, 1973); Otto Kernberg, *Object Relations Theory and Clinical Psychoanalysis* (New York, 1976); *idem, Borderline Conditions and Pathological Narcissism* (New York, 1975).

In addition to the work of Kernberg previously mentioned, that of Kohut should be familiar to the scholarly biographer. Kohut postulates that narcissism undergoes a separate development, parallel to the developments of love for others. The nature and extent of their eventual fusion determines the guiding ideals, and the degree of grandiosity, or vulnerability to shame and humiliation, characteristic of the adult. For individuals of outstanding achievement these are crucial matters; a sensitive and informed awareness of their dynamics is essential for most writing of lives.[29]

We tend to think of biography like most creativity, as the enterprise of a creative individual working alone. In fact, as Meyer has pointed out, collaboration in the creative process is common if not invariable, even in cases where there is little differentiation of function or expertise between the collaborators. Biography which includes psychological data is a natural endeavor for collaboration between the historian or literary biographer and a psychodynamically oriented clinician. And it is equally clear that consultation by a host of experts in history, medicine, psychiatry, and other special fields is a necessary prerequisite to the presentation of any life story if it is to achieve the verisimilitude in multiple-dimensions which modern scholarship demands. Other than the ill-fated Freud-Bullitt work on Wilson, there are few examples of this kind of collaboration—a surprising matter in view of the obvious indications for such joint efforts.[30]

To project the absorption of psychobiography into biographical literature is a simple extrapolation of trends which are already well developed. It is in a sense to predict what has already occurred. What about the farther reaches of developments in biography—biography beyond the 1980s?

The development of psychobiography was the result of advances in the understanding of human life and behavior and is simply the latest version of what has always been the case, that the writing of lives reflects the state of knowledge about the conception of man characteristic of an age. It would not have

---

29 Kohut, "Forms and Transformations"; *idem, The Restoration of the Self* (New York, 1977); *idem, Analysis of the Self.*
30 Bernard C. Meyer, "Some Reflections on the Contribution of Psychoanalysis to Biography," in Robert R. Holt and Emmanuel Peterfreund (eds.), *Psychoanalysis and Contemporary Science* (New York, 1972), 373–391.

been possible to hypothesize that George III was a victim of porphyria until that metabolic disorder was described as an entity. As knowledge of human behavior and development grows, data and new conceptions will be available to enrich the biographical literature.[31]

Chief among these new sources will be contributions from neurobiology. It is already clear that depression has a biological base in the physiological life cycle/metabolism of monoamine neurotransmitters, the substances which are involved in the transmission of the nerve impulse from one nerve to the next in the central nervous system. The concentration of these substances at different locations in the central nervous system, which seems to influence the presence or absence of depression, is in turn dependent upon a sequence of chemical reactions which govern the production, distribution, and destruction of the neurotransmitters. These chains of crucial chemical reactions can be influenced at various points in the sequence by changes in the chemical environment which can have a number of causes. This provides a theoretical basis for the intriguing observation that clinically similar states of depression can be brought about by psychological events such as disappointment, physical illnesses such as hepatitis, or from physiological states such as sleep deprivation. The depression which results from these causes is usually reversible. In some cases, for reasons that are not yet clear, but which probably involve a genetically transmitted predisposition, a less easily reversible process results: so-called endogenous depression. Antidepressant drugs alter the activity of these monoamines by interfering at different points along the chain of physiological reactions. Thus amphetamines counteract depression and stimulate euphoria by releasing monoamines in the brain. Other antidepressants inhibit the processes for inactivating the monoamines, thus increasing brain levels to reduce depression and produce euphoria.[32]

Neurotransmitters have also been studied in relationship to schizophrenia. The capacity of certain drugs to produce schizophrenia-like symptoms has led to intensive study of their properties. Some are chemically related to monoamine neurotrans-

31 Richard Hunter and Ida McAlpine, *George III and the Mad Business* (New York, 1969).
32 Joseph J. Schildkraut and Seymour S. Kety, "Biogenic Amines and Emotion," *Science,* CLVI (1967), 21–30.

mitters. Thus mescaline is a slightly changed version of dopamine, a neurotransmitter. Monoamine oxidase, an enzyme which breaks down neurotransmitters, is decreased in the blood cells (platelets) of certain schizophrenic patients who hallucinate. The idea is that in these schizophrenics, monoamines which are produced under normal circumstances by the body are not broken down because of the decreased enzyme in the body and are thus free to circulate and cause the hallucinations. Obviously this finding is only a fragment of a much more complicated story spelling out the biological basis of schizophrenia, which has not yet been discovered. A fascinating sidelight is a study of the platelet monoamine oxidase enzyme levels of a group of male college students who were unselected as regards psychopathology. Those with low monoamine oxidase levels, compared to the rest of the group, saw psychiatrists more often, had an increased amount of trouble with the law, and increased histories of suicide and suicide attempts among their relatives. Thus biochemical markers may be associated with patterns of behavior outside the range of overt symptoms of schizophrenia.[33]

What relevance does all this have for the biography of the future? First, it will not replace the psychodynamic, empathic, developmental view of human character and behavior which is now dominant. All of the biological theories leave ample room for the influence of life experience on biological mechanisms. In fact, the influence of biological factors so far elucidated by the most sophisticated epidemiological and genetic studies is characteristically very small, accounting for only 15–20 percent of the variance in the phenomena being studied. Rather than replacing psychosocial determinants, the clear implication of this work is a much more subtle and sophisticated blending of nature and nurture than has ever been possible before.

Second, it does mean that it may be possible to understand in greater depth the susceptibility and resilience to life experience which has always been such a puzzle. Why did Abraham Lincoln respond to his early losses by becoming a chronically depressed man with recurrent bouts of deep melancholy, whereas Theodore Roosevelt's reaction to his somewhat later losses was denial, hy-

33 M. S. Buchsbaum, R. D. Coursey and D. L. Murphy, "The Biochemical High Risk Paradigm: Behavioral and Family Correlates of Low Platelet Monoamine Oxidase Activity," *Science*, CXCIV (1976), 339–341.

peractivity, and belligerant exuberance? And how did it come about that neither was incapacitated by either the losses or their reactions, but, using different styles, pressed on to great achievement? Those are matters which cannot be fully explained on the basis of psychological development.

Third, it indicates a greater role for a new kind of archival material in the study of the lives of the eminent. To the subject matter of archive-based quantitative history will be added the biological remnants of existence. The study of court records, wills, account books, and letters will be supplemented by the scrutiny and in some cases the biochemical analysis of tissues and secretions. A prototype of such investigation is the chemical analysis of Napoleon's hair which purported to demonstrate on the basis of arsenic levels that he was systematically poisoned by his British jailers on the island of St. Helena. However questionable the result, the aim is clearly identical with what will increasingly be a new direction for historians and archivists.[34]

All of the genetic information from which it may someday be possible to unravel the complexities of neurobiology is contained in cells of the body. Fibroblasts, the basic cells of connective tissue, can be frozen and preserved for long periods of time. When thawed, they can be cultured to grow and multiply to produce identical replicas which can be studied while the originals can be frozen. Thus an immortal biological archive can be created, available for study by new techniques as they arise. In addition, banks of preserved human brains have already been set up to provide material for anatomical, biochemical, and radiographical studies in the future. There is some evidence of correlations between personality factors and blood types. Long-term preservation of blood fractions is currently a reality and will doubtless be refined in the future. All of these developments presage increasingly detailed studies in entirely new dimensions of neurobiology and neurochemistry.[35]

Fourth, it is very likely that included in these biological and genetic aspects of biography will be increased sophistication about the role of physical illness in the life story. For just as knowledge

34 Sten Forshufvud, Hamilton Smith, and Anders Wassen, "The Arsenic Content of Napoleon's Hair," *Nature,* CXCII (1961), 103–105.
35 Steven W. Matthyse, personal communication; Robert W. Shapiro, personal communication.

explodes about neurobiology so does knowledge about other aspects of human biology and pathophysiology, including unanticipated links to character and behavior.

A major area in which it is possible to foresee new developments is that of collective biography. From the earliest days of psychoanalysis there has been interest in understanding group behavior in psychoanalytic terms. Freud's seminal paper, "Group Psychology and the Analysis of the Ego," was the first attempt. It was followed by a host of works related to anthropology, sociology, group psychology, and organizational behavior which have attempted systematic explanations of collective behavior. Most convincing have been those which attempted to articulate the relationship between individual and group motivations, the leader and the led.[36]

Less persuasive have been attempts to explain collective behavior as if the group, especially large groups, were an individual with a common set of child-rearing experiences leading to a collective outcome. Thus Kardiner and the culture and personality school of anthropology sought to locate the roots of national character in basic personality structure which was influenced by institutionalized and related child-rearing practices. deMause has put forward the "Psychogenic Theory of History" which asserts that history since antiquity can be divided into six periods according to the predominance of certain child-rearing modes.[37]

The problem with these approaches is methodological. Inferences about collective attitudes, motivation, and life experience drawn from works of art, individual diaries, letters, and memoirs, are not valid since these traces of the recent or distant past are rarely generated by a representative sample of the population. Instead, they overwhelmingly reflect the lives of individuals who are exceptional in one way or another.

The technical basis for true collective biography has only been available for the past forty years in the form of public

36 Freud, "Group Psychology and the Analysis of the Ego" (1912), in James Strachey (ed.), The Standard Edition of the Complete Psychological Works of Sigmund Freud (London, 1955), 67. Fred Weinstein and Gerald Platt, The Wish to Be Free (Berkeley, 1969); Harry Levinson, Organizational Diagnosis (Cambridge, 1972); Jaques, "Social Systems as a Defense Against Persecutory and Depressive Anxiety," in Melanie Klein (ed.), New Directions in Psychoanalysis (New York, 1955).

37 Abram Kardiner, The Psychological Frontiers of Society (New York, 1945); Lloyd deMause, "Historical Group Phantasies," Journal of Psychohistory, VII (1979), 1–70.

opinion research. Developments in sampling methodology, statistical techniques, and conceptualizing questions has made it possible for the first time to acquire data about attitudes, motivation, and even fantasy which represent large groups of people. The base of data accumulated from this source can serve as the foundation of the collective biography and collective psychohistory of the future. It is not too soon for historians and the more sophisticated practitioners of public attitude surveys to cooperate in this endeavor by relating the public attitude data which already exist in archives to other social and economic data and, more important, to frame questions of psychohistorical and prosopographical interest so that public attitude data can be gathered now which will be of interest to historians in the future.

Biography as a literary form related to history has, since its inception, been a major source of understanding about the forces which move the affairs of human beings. Its appeal, although based in part on this academic purpose, has also rested upon our steady fascination with the lives of other people in which we can find reflections of ourselves, warnings about the pitfalls of existence, and simple satisfaction of our curiosity about the experiences of other humans in exotic times and places.

As in the rest of history, the growth of new knowledge will continue to enrich and complicate the biographer's narrative. It will be the task of the biographer of the future to integrate these data into a narrative which persuasively captures and transmits the experience of persons whose lives are of historical interest and significance.

Quantification in the 1980s

David Herlihy

Numerical and Formal Analysis in European History
"La connaissance des faits n'est jamais complète sans leur analyse numérique."[1]

What contributions for the premodern periods of European history will the computer and computational methods make to historical research in the 1980s? To answer such a question even partially requires a quick review of computer applications in all fields of history over the past two and more decades.

Already in the late 1950s, in the view of many historians, the computer seemed destined to work a revolution in their venerable discipline. In now famous words, Le Roy Ladurie, the distinguished French historian, predicted: "The historian of tomorrow will be a programmer, or he will not be a historian." "In the last analysis . . .," he further affirmed, "only the quantifiable admits of a scientific history." Today in contrast, many scholars, including some enthusiasts of yesteryear, look upon computation as a fashion that has faded. Even Le Roy Ladurie now expresses concern about an "excess of mathematical rigor" and cautions that "the job of the historian, even when equipped with computers, remains a craftsmanship of art." Stone, another distinguished scholar, has recently recommended that in historical work "the computer . . . should only be employed as the choice of last resort."[2]

What then is the future of computation in historical studies? The thesis that I advocate here is that both the enthusiasm which

David Herlihy is the Henry Charles Lee Professor of History at Harvard University. Among other books he is the co-author of *Les Toscans et leur familles. Une étude du Catasto florentin de 1427* (Paris, 1978).

0022-1953/81/010115-21 $02.50/0

1 Ferdinand Lot, "Conjectures démographique sur la France au IXe siècle," *Le Moyen Age*, XXXII (1921), 1.
2 Emmanuel Le Roy Ladurie, *Le territoire de l'historien* (Paris, 1973), 19, 22. My translations. *Idem*, "Recent Historical 'Discoveries'," *Daedalus*, XVI (1977), 141–155. Lawrence Stone, "History and the Social Sciences in the Twentieth Century," in Charles Delzell (ed.), *The Future of History* (Nashville, 1977), 27.

greeted computational methods in the late 1950s and 1960s, and the present skepticism concerning their use, were and are exaggerated. Some styles of "quantitative history" were by the 1960s already old and widely applied in the discipline. I further argue that a faulty notion of what computers really do now often mars the discussion of their role in historical studies, and that the critics of computation in history often fail to make certain crucial distinctions among the various types and levels of historical work which computational methods can serve.

Computers are now widely used, indeed indispensable, in many disciplines ancillary to history—in bibliography and lexicography, for example. Then too, since the foundations of their discipline, historians have gathered, interpreted, and argued from the documents of the past in order to say something about the past. Computational methods now assist on all three levels— collection of data, interpretation, and arguing. Clearly, however, the methods applied will differ substantially according to the purposes that they are serving. This conflation of the varied uses of the computer obscures what computation can do for historical science now and in the decade of the 1980s.

FORMAL ANALYSIS   The now vast literature on the use of computers in historical research overflows with references to quantification. The term is conventional and convenient. But it is also inaccurate. The computer is basically a manipulator of symbols. Word processing, for example, is today a major branch of computer sciences, but it does not necessarily or even usually involve counting. That computers work with a larger set of symbols than numbers alone is obvious. But historians—particularly the critics of computer applications in their discipline—sometimes fail to see all of the implications which flow from this fundamental principle of computation.[3]

The term quantification also misleads for two reasons. It assumes that the only raw data that computers accept are figures, and that the only output comes in numbers. Moreover, quanti-

---

3 These remarks draw much inspiration from Walter A. Sedelow Jr. and Sally Yeates Sedelow, "Formalized Historiography: The Structure of Scientific and Literary Texts, Part I: Some Issues Posed by Computational Methodology," *Journal of the History of the Behavioral Sciences,* XIV (1978), 247–263. See also my own previous remarks, "Computation in History: Styles and Methods," *Computer,* XI (1978), 8–18; *idem,* "The Computer-Assisted Analysis of the Statistical Documents of Medieval Society," in James M. Powell (ed.), *Medieval Studies: An Introduction* (Syracuse, 1976), 185–211.

fication inevitably implies aggregation. It suggests that historians who utilize computers are interested only in group behavior, and that only statistical descriptions of aggregates will emerge from the analysis. Some cliometricians readily embrace this notion, and argue that the exclusive concern with collective behavior lends their work the luster of science. They agree, perhaps without knowing it, with Aristotle, who affirmed that there could be no science of the particular, and hence no scientific history. But *pace* Aristotle, *pace* the cliometricians, the assumption is wrong: the productive use of the computer need not be limited to the study of aggregates, as I hope to illustrate.[4]

The computer's services for history's ancillary disciplines offer ample illustration of its power as a manipulator of symbols. Indeed, most historical projects which today enlist computers are designed to generate "research tools," in the terminology of the American National Endowment for the Humanities. Computers now assist in the preparation of bibliographies, inventories, catalogues, archival guides, indices, glossaries, concordances, thesauruses, and so forth. They are commonly used in the edition of records and the preparation of the critical apparatus. There is no space here to list these contributions, and no need here to praise them. Whatever scholars may conclude about the worth of quantitative history, this work in the ancillary disciplines will go forward without faltering, into the 1980s. And this work alone gives to computers an assured place in historical research.[5]

The better term to describe the fundamental processes of

4 Robert W. Fogel, one of the most prominent of the cliometricians, distinguishes between what he calls "traditional" and "scientific" history, and argues that traditional historians are concerned primarily with individuals, and their scientific colleagues with groups. Of his many writings on this topic, see "The Limits of Quantitative Methods in History," *American Historical Review*, LXXX (1975), 329–350. The relations between so-called "nomothetic" and "ideographic" disciplines constitute a classical issue in philosophy. Most recent writers seem agreed that, from the point of view of practical research, the dichotomy is artificial. See the wise remarks, first expressed in 1957, of a medieval scholar, Sylvia L. Thrupp, "History and Sociology: New Opportunities for Cooperation," in Raymond Grew and Nicholas H. Steneck (eds.), *Society and History* (Ann Arbor, 1977), 293–302.

5 For medieval studies, see the special issue, Anne Gilmour Bryson (ed.), "Medieval Studies and the Computer, *Computers and the Humanities*, XII (1978), 1–225. Most of the projects described in the issue involve the development of research aids. The same journal provides with each issue a bibliography of computer-assisted research in all the humanities, including history. For medieval work in particular, see the project descriptions regularly published in *Computers and Medieval Data Processing* published at the Institut d'études médiévales, University of Montréal, Quebec.

computation is formal analysis. Formal analysis may or may not involve numbers, and may or may not lead to aggregation. One example of formal analysis long used in history is genealogical research. (A recent version of the same interest, but with its own particular goals, is family reconstitution.) In linking sons to fathers and parents to children, the genealogist is constructing a formal pattern, in which the set of relationships binding the people that he is studying will be displayed. This is also the kind of work that computers can do with dazzling efficiency. On the assumption that the records utilized are both suitable and suitably edited for machine-processing, the computer can quickly recognize names, establish linkages, and determine lines of descent. The formal pattern which emerges from this work is not primarily based on numbers.

A second example of non-numerical formal analysis in historical research is prosopography, or collective biography. This ancillary discipline is usually concerned with elites of various sorts, political or social. Its basic method is tracking: the researcher collects all references to a particular individual and, on the basis of these observations, he reconstructs his life cycle or career course. Again on the assumption that the records containing the observations are suitable and suitably prepared, the computer can track the same person across them with marvelous speed and efficiency. In collecting and linking observations, the computer enhances and does not obliterate the particular features of the separate careers. Computation does not necessarily mean aggregation. The curious researcher is likely to proceed to the study of the collective behavior of the entire elite, but even this process can enhance individuality, as it allows a comparison between the behavior of individuals and the standards for the entire group. There are, after all, no truly isolated, truly singular actors in history.[6]

Still another example of non-numerical formal analysis would be historical geography and cartography, now also a field in which the computer can make significant contributions. Just as genealogists locate individuals within a descent network stretching over time, so the cartographers reconstruct the spatial distri-

6 For a brief description of the method, see Stone, "Prosopography," in Felix Gilbert and Stephen R. Graubard (eds.), *Historical Studies Today* (New York, 1972), 107–140.

bution of properties, populations, or the qualities associated with them both. Through references to owners and boundaries, the computer can reconstruct past patterns of land distribution. Here again, the computer enhances the distinctive qualities of past landscapes. On a higher level, Russell has studied the distribution of medieval cities within their regions—an analysis partially numeric, but obviously spatial too.[7]

Limited space, and the author's limited competence, does not allow comment on still other uses of the computer in the formal analysis of historical documents, data, and phenomena. Content analysis and the stylistic analysis of literary texts will certainly be widely applied in the 1980s. The computer simulation of social processes, such as the development cycle of households, has obvious relevance for the study of historic communities. And there may be uses for artificial intelligence, a major branch of computational science, in historical reasoning.[8]

I stress the following: historians must rid themselves of the prejudice that computers work only with aggregates and speak only in numbers. If most quantitative historians have analyzed aggregates, that is a choice they have freely made, not one which the machine imposes.

Moreover, if we are to clarify the present status of computational methods in historical research, and also peer into the future, we must distinguish the use of formal analysis at three levels of historical method: formal argument, or the development through explicit reasoning of large statements concerning the past; formal interpretation, or the determination of what particular

---

7 See, for example, Le Roy Ladurie, "Quantitative and Cartographical Exploitation of French Military Archives," *Historical Studies Today,* 62–106; the maps contained in Herlihy and Christiane Klapisch-Zuber, *Les Toscans et leurs familles. Une étude du Catasto florentin de 1427* (Paris, 1978). Josiah Cox Russell, *Medieval Regions and Their Cities* (Bloomington, 1972).

8 For an introduction to stylistic analysis, see the studies contained in Alan Jones and R. F. Churchhouse (eds.), *The Computer in Literary and Linguistic Studies* (Cardiff, 1977); Donald Ross, Jr., "Computer Aided Study of Literary Language," *Computer,* XI (1978), 32–39. Hammel and Wachter, of the University of California, Berkeley, have undertaken a study of the household development cycle through computer simulation. For a partial report on this continuing research, see Kenneth W. Wachter with Eugene A. Hammel and Peter Laslett, *Statistical Studies of Historical Social Structure* (New York, 1978). The possible uses of artificial intelligence in historical reasoning were recently examined at a conference. See the report of Mario Borello, "Knowledge Representation and Reasoning in the Humanities: A Conference Report," *Computers and the Humanities,* XIV (1980), 115–116.

records are saying; and formal editing, or the preparation for further processing of records which already possess a set structure. The distinction is essential, as most present criticisms of quantitative history apply to only one of these three levels—the level of argument.

FORMAL ARGUMENT   Formal analysis on the level of argument is the favored although not the exclusive terrain of the "new economic historians," or cliometricians, as they are now inelegantly called. The principles and pretenses of cliometrics have often been stated and require here only a short summary. The claim of the cliometricians to originality is their explicit use of theory—of mathematical or of logico-mathematical models in explaining what happened in history. These theories are proposed, developed, and tested through the use of historical data. The principal criticism which they mount against the "old" economic history, and now against traditional historiography as a whole, is that historians have usually worked with implied theoretical assumptions and loose quantitative estimates. The new economic historians maintain that all theories should be explicitly presented, all terms in the argument specified, and all quantities defined. They contend that in place of vague verbal statements, historians should define relationships in terms of explicit functional equations. The equations also should identify all of the terms operative in the analysis, with their respective weights. These equations or formulas in turn allow the researcher to explore all of the implications of his theory or hypothesis. Through sensitivity analysis it should be possible to measure the contribution which various factors make to the conclusion, and to exclude those of little significance. The field of historical scrutiny can thus be freed of clutter. Through the use of equations, it is also possible to judge whether surviving sets of historical data are consistent with the analysis, or whether the analysis itself requires further refinement.[9]

9   For a recent, favorable review from a French perspective, see Jean Heffer, "Une histoire scientifique: la nouvelle histoire économique," *Annales*, XXXII (1977), 824–841. See, among many discussions of the method, Charlotte Erikson, "Quantitative History," *American Historical Review*, LXXX (1975), 351–364: Robert P. Swieringa, "Computers and Comparative History," *Journal of Interdisciplinary History*, V (1974), 265–276; Charles Tilly, "Computers in Historical Analysis," *Computers and the Humanities*, VII (1973), 323–335.

Through exact formulations, historical argumentation can be rendered fully explicit and thoroughly rigorous and precise. But the computation required in developing and testing these equations is often formidable, and here the computer renders invaluable services. It is used, however, not primarily to link observations across long runs of documents but to execute formal calculations, estimate values, test results, and the like. The researcher here exploits not so much the computer's capability of reading and recognizing, as its powers of mathematical computation. The art can well claim the name of quantitative history, but it does not exhaust the computer's potential. The grace of Clio lies surely in her form, not in her measurements.

American scholars have been at the forefront in applying formal reasoning to historical issues, and the most sensational products of their work have been in American history—particularly economic history of the nineteenth century. We need hardly allude here to Fogel's and Engerman's famous reassessment of American slavery, *Time on the Cross,* and to the torrents of criticism which have swirled around it. And what about our own principal interest, the history of traditional Europe—of Europe before the great revolutions of the eighteenth century? Works utilizing formal arguments are rare, but not altogether lacking. Kula, a Polish economist, has, for example, presented an economic model of the feudal system based on formal reasoning and substantial imputs of historical data. His nomenclature may be misleading. He examines only the agrarian economy of Poland in the early modern period; makes no effort to apply the model to other, past "feudal" regimes; and does not identify what general characteristics define feudal economies. Still, his astute combination of economic reasoning and historical data make his book deserving of more than casual attention.[10]

Other economists—Americans chiefly—have applied formal reasoning or analysis to the agrarian systems of Western Europe in the Middle Ages and early modern periods. McCloskey has

10 Fogel and Stanley L. Engerman, *Time on the Cross. The Economics of American Negro Slavery* (Boston, 1974), 2v. Among many critical attacks upon it, see Herbert G. Gutman, *Slavery and the Numbers Game: A Critique of* Time on the Cross (Urbana, 1975). Witold Kula, *Théorie économique du système féodale* (Paris, 1970)—(trans. Lawrence Garner), *An Economic Theory of the Feudal System. Toward a Model of the Polish Economy, 1500–1800* (London, 1976).

investigated the logic of open-field agriculture in England before the enclosure movement; he concludes that the scattering of plots over many fields was a means of minimizing the risks of a failed harvest. Fenoaltea disagrees, and has himself sought to elucidate through formal arguments such features of the medieval manorial system as demesne farming and the labor obligation imposed on the dependent cultivators. North and Thomas have similarly examined the economic logic which they believe presided over the rise and fall of the manorial system. Even more ambitiously, the same two authors have attempted to explain the rise of the Western world through the use of formal (though not mathematical) arguments. Gunderson, another economist, has examined historical problems of nearly comparable dimensions: the decline of the Roman empire, and the crisis of Western Europe in the late Middle Ages. His formal reasoning leads him to challenge the conventional view that the late-classical economy was in a state of crisis. The breakup of the empire in the West rather reflected a process of "voluntary decentralization" of the Roman state. His reasoning also instructs him that the crisis of late-medieval Europe—the "economic depression of the Renaissance"—was not rooted in a Malthusian situation of over-population and diminishing real income. That seemingly troubled age appears to him not troubled at all.[11]

Formal reasoning also dominates the special field of historical demography, even for the remote periods of European history. Family reconstitution studies, which now abound, inevitably invite the construction of theoretical models, designed to approximate the behavior of the examined community. Lee has produced several highly sophisticated mathematical models of demographic behavior in traditional European populations, but Lee himself

11 Donald N. McCloskey, "The Enclosure of Open Fields. Preface to a Study of Its Impact on the Efficiency of English Agriculture in the Eighteenth Century," *Journal of Economic History*, XXXII (1972), 15–35; Stefano Fenoaltea, "Risk, Transaction Costs and the Organization of Medieval Agriculture," *Explorations in Economic History*, XIII (1976), 129–151; idem, "Authority, Efficiency and Agricultural Output in Medieval England and Beyond," *Explorations in Economic History*, XXXV (1976), 693–718; Douglass C. North and Robert Paul Thomas, "The Rise and Fall of the Manorial System: A Theoretical Model," *Journal of Economic History*, XXXI (1971), 777–803; idem, *The Rise of the Western World. A New Economic History* (Cambridge, 1973); Gerald Gunderson, "Economic Change and the Demise of the Roman Empire," *Explorations in Economic History*, XIII (1976), 43–68; idem, "Real Incomes in the Late Middle Ages: A Test of the Common Case for Diminishing Returns," *Social Science History*, II (1977), 90–118.

complains of "the tentative or negative nature of many of the empirical results." The theory is vigorous, but the data flabby.[12]

Criticisms of cliometric studies in history are now nearly as extensive as the studies themselves, and require here only a brief review. The cliometricians, say the critics, show scant respect for the sovereignty of the historical record and faulty knowledge of its character. They dare to contrive "counterfactual hypotheses," to pretend that something happened in the past that really did not. Counterfactual history is fictional or "figmented" history, a new form of mythologizing, and the new myth makers are now no more worthy of attention than the old. Classical historical criticism developed largely as an effort to rid history of counterfactual assumptions, of fictions and myths in sum. There may be some broadly human insights to be gained in pretending that the story of Romulus and Remus is true, but the pretense does not advance historical truth.[13]

So too, the functional formulas of the cliometricians, if they are to be tested, often require precise information, which the defective sources of the past cannot supply. Like schoolmen in decadence, they argue over fine points in their doctrine which can never be resolved. Indeed, the most telling deflation of the new economic history has been the frequent failure of its practioners to achieve replicable results, or in other words, to convince substantial numbers of historians, mathematically oriented or not, of the veracity of their conclusions. Cliometric studies often offer marvelous exercises in abstract reasoning, against which colleagues and novices in the trade can tilt their critical lances and sharpen their analytical skills. But how many conclusions of the cliometricians could today be called scientifically compelling? The promise that explicit reasoning would lead to new levels of certainty has not yet been realized.

There is an irony here. Among the cliometricians, refinement on the level of argument is often insufficiently combined with

---

12 Daniel Scott Smith, "A Homeostatic Demographic Regime: Patterns in West European Family Reconstitution Studies," in Ronald Demos Lee (ed.), *Population Patterns in the Past* (New York, 1977), 19–52; Lee, "Methods and Models for Analyzing Historical Series of Births, Deaths, and Marriages," *ibid.*, 337–370, esp. 366.

13 For a more sympathetic view of the use of "counterfactuals" in historical argument, see Lance E. Davis, "'And It Will Never Be Literature'—The New Economic History: A Critique," in Robert P. Swierenga (ed.), *Quantification in American History* (New York, 1970), 274–287.

refinement on the level of collecting and interpreting data—partially through faults in the records themselves, but importantly through the inexperience of the researchers in criticizing historical evidence. In his extended review of *Time on the Cross,* Handlin repeatedly and emphatically posed the question: what is being measured? He alleged that Fogel and Engerman were conflating data from different sources, different regions, and different times. If this be true, then the fault of the two authors was not too much rigor in their methods, but too little. Ingeniously utilizing formal analysis at the level of argument, they failed to apply comparable method in collecting and interpreting their information. And no amount of sophisticated formal argument can correct for fuzzy data.[14]

There is a lesson here too. The new economic historians have clearly been too enamoured by the elegances of abstract reasoning to recognize the special character and the limits of historical data. And historians have been too jubilant in pouncing upon and gloating over this particular error. They have not carried the day; they have not refuted the basic contention of the cliometricians. In any scientific endeavor, formal reasoning—full and explicit statement of the argument—is better than allusive and elusive rhetoric, than efforts to buttress weak cases with strong language.

Ground must be given on both sides. Formal argument need not be mathematical argument, and cliometricians have damaged their own cause by concocting fake figures from the past, because their elegant formulas require them. They have criticized "old" historians for utilizing implied comparisons such as "greater than" or "less than" without specifying values; at the same time, they have conveniently ignored the fact that such terms are appropriate descriptors of relationships in formal analysis. Even computers have no objection to their use. Cliometrics could be considerably softened, with no damage to its essential character. By the same token, traditional historical argument could be rendered considerably more explicit and rigorous, without betraying its traditional form.

Is then a marriage possible between social theorists and historians? Marriages have been attempted. In England, the Cambridge Group for the History of Population and Social Structure

14 Oscar Handlin, *Truth in History* (Cambridge, Mass., 1979), 206–226.

has done exactly this, with notable results. In America, the much larger Social Science History Association, founded in 1975, aims at achieving similar purposes. There are grounds for optimism. Today, both social theorists and traditional historians have frequent recourse to computers, albeit for different purposes. Still, the computer has married them, for better or for worse, for richer or for poorer. In this as in most marriages, some differences between the partners, some tensions even, are to be expected. They may perhaps assure that the union will be long, stable, and fruitful.

FORMAL INTERPRETATION   The formal interpretation of historical data consists in classifying and usually counting distinct but related observations in historical records, in order to describe their collective character and to display trends or patterns running through them—within their "universe," in the language of statistics. Most tables and graphs, which today proliferate in many kinds of history books, are examples of the formal interpretation of data. This is conventional quantitative history, as it has been practiced well beyond the ranks of the cliometricians, and well before their appearance.

In applying this method of interpretation to historical data, the researcher must first define a set of categories into which the observations are to be aggregated. (It should again be noted that the selection of the categories is an exercise in formal, but not necessarily quantitative reasoning.) If the researcher is using a computer, then he or she must devise a code, or collection of appropriate symbols which will identify each set of observations, and each observation within it. Today historians adopt two large strategies in giving the observations a suitably formal identity. These strategies are conventionally called analytical and empirical classifying.

In utilizing analytical categories, historians ask the questions which immediately and directly interest them. Each composes, so to speak, his own questionnaire, and engages in a kind of survey research, an interview with the documents from the past. For example, in studying the concept of community in the writings of St. Augustine and St. Jerome, Adams distinguished five different shades of meaning in the Latin word *populus,* and then determined how often his authors had recourse to each of them.

The current popularity of formal interpretation is reflected in a recent, important book on medieval intellectual history. In his *Reason and Society in the Middle Ages,* Murray classified seventy-one medieval saints by five social categories, ranging from undistinguished to reigning monarch. No computer was needed, but the appreciation of formal analysis is evident, even in the service of medieval cultural history.[15]

By far the most ambitious recent effort to interview the past may be found in the work of the Tillys on riots and social disturbances in France, Italy, and Germany, primarily in the nineteenth century. The flesh of their studies is history, but the spirit sociology. Utilizing newspapers, police reports, and other descriptive accounts, they posed questions: when and where did the riots occur, how many persons participated, what were their social backgrounds, what were the provocations, what kinds and degrees of violence were perpetrated, what damage caused, and so forth. The computer was then enlisted to search for common patterns and correlations in the observed events. How, for example, did the season of the year, wage levels, price of grain, or the extent of unemployment affect the frequency and severity of, or the participation in riots? The conclusions have evident interest, in that they are based upon a systematic survey of a large body of contemporary reports, and not on the arbitrary selection and examination of particular cases of collective violence.[16]

Still, this style of formal interpretation also elicits criticisms.[17] First, the questionnaire necessarily reflects the immediate research purposes of the principal investigators, and so also will the finished, structured, machine-readable file. Although the broad community of historians will presumably be interested in the results of the analysis, probably few will care to reexamine or

---

15 Jeremy Adams, *The Populus of Augustine and Jerome. A Study in the Patristic Sense of Community* (New Haven, 1971); Alexander Murray, *Reason and Society in the Middle Ages* (New York, 1978).

16 Charles Tilly, Louise Tilly, and Richard Tilly, *The Rebellious Century, 1830–1930* (Cambridge, Mass., 1975). A detailed description of the method, omitted in the cited work, appears in Richard Tilly and Gerd Hohorst, "Soziales Protest in Deutschland im 19. Jahrhundert. Skizze eines Forschungsansatzes," in Konrad H. Jarausch (ed.), *Quantifizierung in der Geschichtswissenschaft. Probleme und Möglichkeit* (Dusseldorf, 1976), 232–278. See also Charles Tilly, "How Protest Modernized in France," in William Aydelotte, Allan Bogue, and Fogel (eds.), *The Dimensions of Quantitative Research in History* (Princeton, 1972), 192–255.

17 See the remarks by Stone, "History and Social Sciences," 31.

reuse the supporting documentation. The costs, in other words, of preparing the machine-readable file yield only restricted benefits. Second, in designing the questionnaire, the researcher is often prone to include questions which, albeit of great interest, yet require a judgment on the part of the persons conducting the inquiry. What does *populus* really signify in this passage? Were the saint's parents of undistinguished origins? Who comprised the crowd in a social disturbance, and how many were injured? In these instances, the researcher is not truly collecting the objective data of history, but his own interpretations of the historical accounts. He is conducting a survey of the opinions of present-day observers: what do I, or my assistants, think a passage means? In selecting some accounts over others, and in interpreting their meanings, he runs the risk of introducing biases into the machine-readable file, which will be beyond the powers of men or machines subsequently to rectify. He may strive to be scrupulously objective, but the need to select and to interpret at this early stage in the processing of his records will inevitably weaken the precision of the analysis and lower the credibility of the conclusions. The conclusions are not likely to be replicable by other historians working in the same materials, and thus are likely to fail the prime test of "public science" or scientific history. Historians are thus well advised to use formal interpretation through analytical categories with appropriate caution. The seeming exactitude of the results is in considerable measure specious.

This is not, however, the only or even the better method of formal interpretation of historical data. The historian may choose the categories already present in the records that he is using, and the measurements as well. Thus, historians of population count the numbers of persons found at particular times in particular jurisdictions. Historians of prices record the values of specified commodities, in contemporary measures and moneys. Shifts in boundaries, in measurements, or in the value of money, often complicate their labors, but usually too, through the standard methods of historical criticism, they are able to translate their observations into formal, that is, comparable units.

Scholars, it should be emphasized, have been engaged in this sort of quantitative history for a very long time. The origins of the interest apparently go back to the English and continental Enlightenment of the eighteenth century, which inspired a lively curiosity in social statistics and in "political arithmetic," past and present. In famous words uttered in 1790, Burke already complained: "But the age of chivalry is gone. That of sophisters, economists and calculators, has succeeded, and the glory of Europe is extinguished forever." The earliest compilation and study of the baptismal records of the city of Florence, which begin in 1451, was published in 1775. A great monument in the statistical interpretation of medieval data was Guérard's edition and study, published in 1844, of the *polyptych* of the abbot Irminon, surveying the estates of the monastery of Saint-Germain-des-Prés near Paris, from the first quarter of the ninth century. This magnificent document lists more than 2,700 servile families settled on more than 1,600 tenures, and minutely describes their obligations and possessions. Irminon's *polyptych* has proved to be an inexhaustible mine of information on the early medieval household and manor.[18]

The emergence of a "historical school" of economics, which gained particular prominence in Germany from the middle decades of the nineteenth century, inspired a whole range of statistical studies devoted to the institutions of the past, including the Middle Ages. Historians such as von Inama-Sternegg, Lamprecht, Caro, and others, filled their usually massive tomes with tables and statistical appendices. Through the careful if not always convincing analysis of surveys and charters, they sought to determine the distribution of landownership in medieval Europe, the extent of great and small properties, the density of settlement, size of families, population movements, and so forth. In Russia too, historical economics commanded a large following before World War I, and Russian scholars developed a particular expertise in the history of the medieval English manor. This work continued under Marxist auspices in the Soviet period. The quantitative analysis even of medieval documentation is neither new nor narrow.[19]

18 Edmund Burke, *Reflections on the Revolution in France* (London, 1910), 94; Marco Lastri, *Richerche dell'antica e moderna popolazione della città di Firenze per mezzo dei registri dei battesimi del Battistero di San Giovanni dal 1451 al 1774* (Florence, 1775); B. Guérard (ed.), *Polyptyque de l'abbé Irminon* (Paris, 1844). The edition was reissued with an enlarged introduction in A. Longnon (ed.), *Polyptyque de l'Abbaye de Saint-Germain des Prés* (Paris, 1886–95), 2v.

19 Karl Theodor von Inama-Sternegg, *Deutsche Wirtschaftsgeschichte* (Leipzig, 1879–1891), 2v.; Karl Lamprecht, *Deutsches Wirtschaftsleben im Mittelalter. Untersuchungen über die Entwicklung der materiellen Kultur des Platten Landes auf Grund der Quellen zunächst des Mosel-*

Between the two world wars, historians acquired particular prominence in the quantitative interpretation of historical data. Lot, the great medievalist, whom we cite in the heading to this article, was one of its dedicated advocates. In a medieval context, among the young classics of quantitative history is Déléage's study of rural life in Burgundy, published in 1941 and based principally upon charter evidence, statistically examined. The later, well-known works by Duby on the Mâconnaise, Fossier on Picardy, Bois on eastern Normandy, and others—all of them bristling with tables—stand well within this tradition of French historiography.[20]

Since World War II, French historians associated with the Centre de Recherches Historiques, Ecole des Hautes Etudes, Paris, have made quantitative analysis an integral part of their methods. Chaunu has been eloquent in advocating what he calls, after Fernand Braudel, "serial history." Serial history is the study of movements, usually of population or of prices, over time—time series analysis, in the more familiar English phrase. (Inexplicably, Chaunu does not seem to regard cross-sectional analysis, or the study of large numbers of simultaneous or contemporary observations, as part of quantitative history.) With admirable energy, French scholars have reconstructed movements over time not only of prices and of aggregate populations, but also of tithes, rents, demographic events, and of many other phenomena capable of being counted.[21]

---

landes (Leipzig, 1885–86), 4v.; Georg Caro, *Beiträge zur älteren deutschen Wirtschafts- und Verfassungsgeschichte* (Leipzig, 1905). See, for example, the still useful work by J. M. Kulischer, *Allgemeine Wirtschaftsgeschichte des Mittelalters und Neuzeit* (Munich, 1928), based on lectures given at St. Petersburg before World War I. On the work on the English manor done by P. G. Vinogradoff, A. Savine, D. M. Petrushevsky, E. A. Kosminsky, and other Russian and Soviet scholars, see the bibliographical review in M. A. Barg, *Issledovaniia po istorii angliiskovo feodalizma v XI–XIII vv.* (Moscow, 1962), 5–37. See also E. A. Kosminsky (ed. R. H. Hilton, trans. Ruth Kisch), *Studies in the Agrarian History of England in the Thirteenth Century* (Oxford, 1956).

20 Lot, "Conjectures démographique, 1. Lot is in fact cited with approval in a statement made by another medievalist, Joseph Cuvelier, in 1912. André Déléage, *La vie économique et sociale de la Bourgogne dans le haut Moyen Age* (Mâcon, 1941), 2v.; Georges Duby, *La société aux XI. et XII. siècles dans la région mâconnaise* (Paris, 1953); Robert Fossier, *La terre et les hommes en Picardie* (Paris, 1968), 2 v.; Guy Bois, *Crise du féodalisme. Economie rurale et démographie en Normandie orientale du début du XIVe siècle au milieu du XVIe siècle* (Paris, 1976).

21 Pierre Chaunu, *Histoire quantitative. Histoire sérielle* (Paris, 1978). For bibliography, see Comité français des sciences historiques, *La recherche historique en France de 1940 à 1965* (Paris, 1965).

The arrival of the computer in the 1960s did not create, but it has greatly facilitated, this kind of formal interpretation of historical data. In this as in many areas, the computer has aided historians to do what they long have done—only more quickly and more accurately. Whatever the outcome of the current debate over the new economic history—over formal argument—the formal interpretation of historical data will go forward undisturbed and unimpeded, in the future as in the past. How else can historians objectively find meaning within myriad observations? Then too, the works of Lot and Fogel do not share a common method. Must we predict for them a common fate?

In its memory, and in its supporting libraries, the computer can replicate the logical categories and measurements of the past; it can also preserve an exact record of each observation. We repeat the now familiar point: the computer can as easily preserve individuality as obliterate it. Working with his pencil and contemplating runs of observations, the historian must aggregate. Working with the same series, the computer need not. It can preserve in its memory and in supporting libraries individual observations and runs of observations, available for quick, cheap, and flexible consultation.

To preserve both the original categories and measurements, and the observations too, is in fact to edit, in part or in whole, runs of historical documents. The concept of machine-readable editions of past documentation has particular interest for medievalists. In the nineteenth century, medievalists, together with ancient historians, developed the standards for preparing critical editions of their relatively few documents. These critical editions were also formal editions, in the sense that they all provided essentially the same information: the manuscript tradition, the variant readings, the use of prior sources, the meanings of unusual words, indices and glossaries, and the like. Ancient and medieval historians have a special concern to render their slim documentation accessible and usable. They thus possess an engrossing interest in the computer as editor, librarian, and tireless assistant.

FORMAL EDITING   The kinds of records which are most suitable for computer-editing already possess a set structure because the computer requires of the information presented to it a repetitive, formally structured character. Documents of this sort we shall refer to as serial records.

In our use of the term, a serial record is a logical unit of documentation, forming part of a series, set, or array of comparable logical units. The array is often defined temporally, as in a time series, or spatially, as in a territorial survey; but it can as easily be based on any principle of organization. The records are comparable in the sense that they all respond, as it were, to the same list of questions. They specify or assign values to a common set of variables. Examples of serial records would be entries in baptismal, marriage, or death registers; matriculation lists; household registrations in a census; charters in a medieval chartulary; manorial court rolls; voting returns by ward, county, or state; roll calls in a legislative assembly; and so on endlessly. The raw data at this level of so-called quantitative history is not, it should again be noted, exclusively or even primarily quantities. But the data, even if nominal in character, must be logically related, and must fall within a limited number of discrete categories.

More often than not, serial records resist efficient processing by hand and eye. Many sets of records are so large, so detailed, and so boring, as to tax the energy, time, and patience of the most dedicated researcher. Even the medieval world, usually viewed as a documentary desert, generated many such formidable series. For example, the charters—chiefly donations, exchanges, sales, leases, and other conveyances of land—preserved in separate parchments or in chartularies, antedating the year 1200, surely surpass 100,000.[22]

How can historians master documentary bounties of such magnitude? They may select from out of these large sets those few records which they consider typical of the whole and comment upon them. But this strategy gives great scope to personal impressions and hunches, and more often than not fails to pass the crucial test of scientific inquiry: that the results of one scholar be replicable by others. Or they can attempt to aggregate the observations through manual methods. The latter approach is certainly preferable, as it gives a view of the entire set of surviving documents. In regard to serial records, the whole is almost always larger than the sum of its parts. But aggregation by hand is notoriously slow and tedious, and tedium multiplies error. Here, clearly, is work that the computer can do well, if the documents

22 For bibliography, see Herlihy, "Quantification and the Middle Ages," in Val R. Lorwin and Jacob M. Price (eds.), *The Dimensions of the Past. Materials, Problems, and Opportunities for Quantitative Work in History* (New Haven, 1972), 13–52.

are suitably prepared. Formal editing offers the historian the means of surveying and manipulating lengthy documentary runs, with unprecedented speed and flexibility.

Lured by the promise of rich rewards, medievalists have in recent years energetically sought efficient methods for the conversion of serial documentation into machine-readable form. The strategies that they have elaborated may be identified as three: the integral edition of the complete documentary set; the integral edition of a sampling from the set; and what we shall call, for want of a better name, "track editing."

Formal editing is most easily accomplished when the records are short, carry a fixed and small number of variables, and are very many. The simple structure facilitates coding, and the large numbers of records tips the ratio of benefits to cost in the processing very much in favor of benefits.

Certain serial records readily fulfill these requirements. A team of scholars in Mainz, Germany, working under the direction of Schmid, have edited membership lists, necrologies, and other documents of the medieval monastery of Fulda into parallel registers, containing 38,871 names. Through the computer they can further establish linkages and study the social background of the community which formed within and around this great religious house from the early Middle Ages. Anthony Molho of Brown University and Julius Kirshner of the University of Chicago are currently engaged in preparing a nearly integral, machine-readable edition of the records in the Florentine dowry fund, the *Monte delle doti,* which begins in the early fifteenth century. I am myself preparing integral editions of registers from the *Tratte* deposit of the Florentine state archives, from 1380 to 1530. The registers record the results of the drawings by which the principal offices of the Florentine commune were filled. The typical entry carries a date, the name of the office to be filled, the name of the citizen drawn from the electoral purses, the ward where the candidate resides, and the result of the drawing—either election to office or disqualification for any one of several specified reasons.[23]

Medievalists have also been attempting to edit for machine processing charters, notarial acts, and letters, which have survived

---

23 Karl Schmid (ed.), *Die Klostergemeinschaft von Fulda im früheren Mittelalter* (Munich, 1978), 3v. My project is being supported by a grant from the National Endowment for the Humanities.

in great numbers but which carry complex and shifting information. In Italy, Cinzio Violante and his collaborators have been working for years on editing for the computer the charters of Pisa for the period before 1200. The Ecole Française of Rome has similarly been investigating the feasibility of machine-readable editions of papal letters and responses to petitions (*suppliche*) from the late Middle Ages. Egmont Lee of Calgary University has organized a team of scholars, who will prepare both standard and machine-readable editions of the notarial chartularies of Rome in the fifteenth century. Gervers, of Scarborough College, the University of Toronto, has designed and is now implementing what he calls the DEEDS Project (for "Documents of Essex England Data Set"). The project aims at editing in machine-readable form all the extant charters of Essex County antedating 1400; they are estimated to number between 10,000 and 20,000 acts. The project, when complete, will provide for the first time full control over all of the surviving charters for a significant area of Europe over several centuries.[24]

Still, these efforts to prepare integral editions of entire runs of charters and other complex records have encountered formidable difficulties. The DEEDS project, for example, if I understand the code design correctly, has to create no fewer than eighty-five variables to carry the anticipated information. It must also display the interrelationships of the recorded data. The design of the machine-readable record must perforce be highly elaborate, and the work needed to translate the original act into machine-readable form slow and demanding. To say slow in computational work is also to say expensive. It is unlikely that medievalists will ever command the resources needed to prepare complete editions of even a small part of the extant charters.

One solution would be to omit part of the data, as my co-author and I did in preparing our edition of the Florentine tax survey, the *Catasto* of 1427. But even the systematic omission of data requires that the records possess rigorous consistency from beginning to end. Another response would be to sample the series and edit a certain subset of the total number. Sampling would

24 See the informative collection of studies in Lucie Fossier, André Vauchez, and Cinzio Violante (eds.), *Informatique et histoire médiévale* (Rome, 1977). Michael Gervers, "Medieval Charters and the Computer: An Analysis Using Mark IV," *Computers and the Humanities,* XII (1978), 127–136.

permit acceptable estimates of aggregate values, but precludes the tracking of individuals across the documentary run. The nominal data carried are thus rendered valueless. Sampling, in sum, radically impoverishes the machine-readable edition and its uses.[25]

Intuitively, scholars in several parts of the world have been moving toward a different editorial strategy—"track editing." In track editing, the researcher treats the documentary run as an aggregate of observations. He selects particular targets—persons or objects— and collects and records the observations made upon them. He then proceeds to sort and link the observations, producing strings of data illuminating the history of the selected targets. Track editing is comprehensive, in the sense that all observations on the chosen targets are collected. But it sacrifices the "environment" in which the observations are preserved—the detailed diplomatic information on the documents, and the relationship of the relevant information with the many other bits of data contained in most serial records. The method greatly simplifies the coding of the data and consequently reduces cost. The machine-readable record is short and rigorously formal, and it is possible to process large documentary runs quickly and cheaply.

Utilizing analogous strategy, Higounet-Nadal collected some 80,000 observations on the families of Périgueux in southwest France from about 1300 to 1500, although she seems not to have used the computer to aid her in this labor. Raftis, of the Pontifical Institute of Medieval Studies, the University of Toronto, is preparing a "Regional Data Bank," based largely on court rolls and is tracking the careers of English midland peasants from the late thirteenth century. Zarri is preparing a "collective biography of medieval France," which seems to follow similar principles. All of the above projects choose persons as their targets, but clearly the same method could be used in the tracking of named properties, moneys, villages, geographic references, and the like. By measure of costs and benefits, track editing holds out the best possibilities of bringing the power of the computer to bear on the analysis of long documentary series.[26]

---

25 The *Catasto* project and edition are described in Herlihy and Klapisch-Zuber, *Toscans.*
26 Arlette Higounet-Nadal, *Périgueux aux XIVe et XVe siècles. Etude de démographie historique* (Bordeaux, 1978). Initiating her prodigious labors in the early 1950s, Higounet-Nadal had not then the advantage of advanced computational technology. J. Ambrose

Since the foundations of their discipline, historians have collected, interpreted, and argued from the documents of the past in order to say something about that past. Historians have in consequence urged and applauded the development of technical aids in their work: critical editions of important texts; registers or calendars of records too many to be published *in extenso*; archival inventories; reproductions of documents through microfilm or microfiche; handbooks of diplomatic and paleographical conventions; dictionaries and encyclopedias; and so forth. Today, the computer offers historians flexible and powerful assistance. Much of the skepticism concerning its future focuses upon only one of its several applications in historical research, its use in so-called cliometrics, in the development of formal arguments. But even the defeats of the cliometricians are far from final. Their failure has been, ironically, not too wide but too limited a use of formal analysis. They have subjected their data to rigorous interpretation, but have not applied comparable rigor in collecting and criticizing their information. The historian of the 1980s may not have to be a programmer, but he will have to know how the computer can assist in all phases of his work. Otherwise, he would be derelict in his duties as a scientist and as a historian.

Raftis' Data Bank contains all of the extant information on over a dozen Huntingdonshire communities between 1274 and 1450. See the use made of the data in Edward Britton, *The Community of the Vill. A Study in the History of the Family and Village Life in Fourteenth-Century England* (Toronto, 1977). See the brief announcement of the project by Gian Piero Zarri in *Historical Methods*, 12 (1979), 177. Zarri is associated with the Laboratoire d'Informatique pour les Sciences de l'Homme.

Quantification in the 1980s

Allan G. Bogue

Numerical and Formal Analysis in United States History

"The method of the statistician as well as that of the critic of evidence is absolutely essential." Turner wrote these words in 1904, expressing convictions which this distinguished historian retained throughout his life, as did many of his students and professional colleagues throughout their careers. But, despite the commitment of some American historians to quantitative analysis from the 1890s to the 1930s, their techniques were relatively crude; interest in quantitative evidence was low by the 1940s except among economic historians. Turnerian quantifiers seem not to have used, nor at least emphasized, the word "quantification." It slipped unobtrusively into the working vocabulary of historians in the United States during the late 1950s and early 1960s. In 1959 the Social Science Research Council sponsored a Conference on the History of Quantification in the Social Sciences. The papers presented there were published in a volume entitled *Quantification: A History of the Meaning of Measurement in the Natural and Social Sciences*. In the editor's eyes, "measurement" was a satisfactory synonym for quantification.[1]

To American historians today, quantification still suggests measurement, but it is also a code word that brings related issues to mind involving the identification, processing, and administrative control of quantitative historical evidence in the form of machine-readable data, as well as the conceptual framework and

Allan G. Bogue is the Frederick Jackson Turner Professor of History at the University of Wisconsin, Madison. He is the co-editor of *The History of American Electoral Behavior* (Princeton, 1978).

0022-1953/81/010137-39 $02.50/0

1 Frederick Jackson Turner, "Problems in American History," reprinted in his collected essays, *The Significance of Sections in American History* (New York, 1932), 20. The first wave of quantification is discussed by Richard J. Jensen in "American Election Analysis: A Case Study of Methodological Innovation and Diffusion," in Seymour M. Lipset (ed.), *Politics and the Social Sciences* (New York, 1969), 226–243; Charles M. Dollar and Jensen, *Historian's Guide to Statistics: Quantitative Analysis and Historical Research* (New York, 1971),

research designs in which quantitative research is developed and presented. These matters relate, on the one hand, to the development and availability of quantitative data and to problems of research strategy, theory, and "models" on the other. The development of thinking on these subjects in the United States must be viewed within the context of the behavioral transformation, apparent in the social sciences by the 1950s. Changes in those disciplines helped to stimulate what Aydelotte described as "a sedate, hesitant, circumspect, little behavioral revolution" in the historical profession. In its early stages this reorientation was little influenced by developments in historical studies abroad, although the influence of emigré social scientists was clearly apparent, most notably that of Paul F. Lazarsfeld.[2]

Aydelotte has stated the formal rationale for using quantification in historical analysis with considerable restraint. Although admitting that researchers have abused quantification on occasion, he argued that quantification specifically facilitated the description and management of evidence, contributed to greater accuracy, allowed the testing of hypotheses, and enhanced the perspective of researchers, as well as their ability to reformulate ideas. Since Aydelotte published his collection of essays in 1971, the great number of quantitative contributions in history, and the amount of historical revision and pathbreaking that they represent, suggest that justifications based on logical, methodological, or theoretical grounds need no longer be emphasized. But controversy concerning quantification has not subsided. The work of "quantifiers" has inspired polemical denunciation of those who would subject Clio to artificial insemination or "worship . . . that Bitchgoddess, Quantification" and there has been much sullen disap-

1–26. Harry Woolf (ed.), *Quantification: A History of the Meaning of Measurement in the Natural and Social Sciences* (Indianapolis, 1961), 3. In 1957 the Council sponsored a "Conference on Early American Political Behavior," at Rutgers University under the chairmanship of Richard P. McCormick. Although Lee Benson reported on the use of "detailed election statistics," and other aspects of the new political history are foreshadowed in his report of the proceedings, McCormick does not remember the use of the word quantification at this meeting. By the summer of 1960, however, the Madison conference had occurred and Rowland L. Mitchell, Jr. recalls that "quantification was already the current word" at the Council offices. Social Science Research Council, *Items,* 1 (1957), 49–50; personal communication, McCormick, to author, Feb. 12, 1980; Mitchell, to author, Feb. 25, 1980.

2 William O. Aydelotte, *Quantification in History* (Reading, Mass., 1971), 18.

proval of "that quantification nonsense" in the history profession generally. On occasion, even sometime advocates of quantification have suggested that quantification has been overemphasized.[3]

Fogel has recently distinguished between traditional historians and cliometric practitioners. He has described two ideal types of historians who differ widely in their choice of subject matter, their preferred evidence, their standards of proof, and their attitudes and practices concerning controversy, scholarly collaboration, and "communication with the history-reading public." Such disagreements have been sufficiently deep and acrimonious as to suggest the descriptive phrase "cultural war" to Fogel.[4]

It is curious that "cultural war" should be waged over the efforts of some scholars to introduce a greater degree of quantitative evidence and analysis in history during the last twenty five years. Surely it is a cardinal rule of historical research that historians will—indeed must—use all evidence available and relevant to a full understanding of the historical phenomena under study. But the controversy is even more remarkable because historical evidence of literary or word-form type has much in common with numerical historical evidence. Even setting aside literary evidence that can be easily translated into numbers, both types are almost invariably only parts of the evidence that once existed concerning the past human activity under study. And any given subtype of numerical or word-form evidence has often been incompletely preserved. Both literal and numerical evidence usually contain errors of fact or bias, reflecting the human frailties of those who originally assembled them. In each case also the historian may need special knowledge to exploit the evidence ade-

3 Aydelotte, *Quantification*, 40–42. For an example of root and branch denunciation see Jacques Barzun, *Clio and the Doctors; Psycho-History, Quanto-History, and History* (Chicago, 1974), 14; Carl Bridenbaugh, "The Great Mutation," *American Historical Review*, LXVIII (1963), 315–331. The epithet appears on 326. Note the exchange of correspondence between Jack H. Hexter and Aydelotte in the latter's *Quantification*, 155–179. For second thoughts on such matters see, Samuel P. Hays, "Historical Social Research: Concept, Method, and Technique," *Journal of Interdisciplinary History*, IV (1974), 475–482; Stephen J. Hansen, "The Illusion of Objectivism: A Review of Recent Trends in the New Political History," *Historical Methods*, XII (1979), 105–110. The latter seeks to define the boundaries of quantitative orthodoxy, an all too common exercise in areas of innovative research and one that is all too frequently unproductive.

4 Robert W. Fogel, "'Scientific' History and Traditional History," in L. J. Cohen, J. Łos, H. Pfieffer and K.-P. Podewski (eds.), *Logic, Methodology and Philosophy of Science*, VI (forthcoming).

quately; on occasion, word-form evidence can only be used if the historian possesses appropriate language skills, or a knowledge of specialties like paleography, numismatics, or climatology, and similarly, numerical evidence in many instances is most valuable when subjected to arithmetical or statistical manipulation. Both types of evidence are typically subjected to various forms of winnowing and generalization procedures before the final narrative emerges. In both cases, the scholar's obligation to explain these intermediate stages of research may be the subject of argument. And both literary and quantitative evidence acquire meaning in direct proportion to the perspective of the researchers and their skill in fitting them into a larger context of generalization.

Although observers often dichotomize historians into quantifiers and nonquantifiers, the distinction is misleading. When the literary historian notes that his poet subject lived in the country during most of his lifetime, he has resorted to quantification and a considerable variety of literary adjectives and adverbs testify to the implicit processes of quantification that underlie much conventional history. And those who use quantitative data and analysis explicitly differ among themeselves in great degree. They can for example be scaled in at least two ways: (1) quantifiers—literary, elementary, and advanced; (2) theory users—implicit, in *post hoc* explanation, and in developing or expanding theory.

The boundaries between the scale types in both series are of necessity vague and impressionistic but the elementary quantifier analyzes and presents quantitative data in much the same form that they are found in the sources. Illustrative quantities or amounts, time series of production outputs or current prices, or perhaps data converted to percentages, medians or means, appear in their work. The advanced practitioner, however, displays knowledge of a considerable range of more sophisticated quantitative techniques and measures. The traditional or literary historians use "implicit" or "folk" models to order their evidence. *Post hoc* theorists try to explain historical events by referring to a body of social science theory (laws of human behavior and derivative propositions) but are primarily interested in explaining a particular event or combination of events in past time. The theory builders view historical problems as opportunities to expand the range of cases which they can use in testing and enlarging the body of social science theory. Both of the latter types may consider themselves to be "social scientific historians."

The types in our two scales correlate to some degree but by no means completely. Nor can we assume that any given historian can be pigeon-holed in one and only one position in these scales or in a nine cell table combining them. Scholars may use different strategies in their research at different times. They find relatively simple quantitative methods appropriate in one instance and more elaborate analysis in order in others. It is true also that the number of historians whose work consistently falls in the last category of the second scale is very small. Noting that large numbers of historians simply use quantification to answer long-standing historical questions and fail to posit hypotheses for testing, some have concluded that the revolutionary impact of quantification has been greatly exaggerated. Perhaps so, but this observation ignores the fact that even quantitative historians who fail to develop research designs in which hypotheses are normally tested frequently use statistical techniques that rest upon behavioral or mathematical models of considerable sophistication.[5]

With these definitions and qualifications in mind, what have been the accomplishments of quantification in the United States during the last twenty-five years?

During the last generation quantitative historians—both in history and social science departments—have substantially modified our understanding of the history of the United States. The transformation is more apparent in some areas than others. Diplomatic history, intellectual history, and legal-constitutional history still provide few illustrations of explicit quantitative analysis, despite the activity of the occasional quantifier in these provinces of the discipline. Economic history, political history, and various areas of social history, however, markedly reflect the impact of the quantifier. But even those most deeply involved in these historical provinces disagree about the importance of the transformation. The sophistication of some of the techniques involved, and the definitive nature of some of the answers to perennial questions

5 Douglas N. Sprague, "A Quantitative Assessment of the Quantification Revolution," *Canadian Journal of History*, XIII (1978), 177–192.

provided by new economic historians suggest to outsiders that they have effected a veritable revolution in American economic history. But Fogel, one of the leaders in popularizing econometric history, has recently emphasized the continuities that link traditional economic history and econometric history.[6]

Years ago, Taylor maintained that the changes in transportation technology in the United States during the first seventy years of the nineteenth century constituted a "transportation revolution." That contention still rings true. "The contribution of the new work," writes Fogel, "has been to provide a more detailed and somewhat more precise analysis of the nature of that revolution." This evaluation is overly modest; our understanding of the causal relationships, the systemic functioning, and the equity considerations involved in the transformation of American transportation are greatly different now than was the case during the 1940s and 1950s. Our knowledge of slavery, the development of the economy, the iron and steel industry, public land policy, the growth of cities, and other subjects in economic history in the United States have all been significantly changed by the work of econometric historians.[7]

Quantitative analysts have not been alone in proposing different emphases in political history; the influence of intellectual-cultural historians has been important as well. And to some degree there has been interaction between the two. Some quantifiers have sought to accommodate ideological factors in their work; Kelley's recent writings in cultural history obviously reflect the emphasis of quantitative historians upon ethnocultural factors in explaining

6 In legal-constitutional history for example note, Michael Les Benedict, *A Compromise of Principle: Congressional Republicans and Reconstruction, 1863–1869* (New York, 1974); Gordon M. Bakken, "The Arizona Constitutional Convention of 1910," *Arizona State Law Journal*, I (1978), 1–30, an article illustrative of a number published by this author.

7 George R. Taylor, *The Transportation Revolution, 1815–1860* (New York, 1951). Fogel, "'Scientific' History and Traditional History." Limitations of space prevent a listing of individual monographs and articles in the new economic history. See, rather: Lance E. Davis, "'And It Will Never Be Literature'—The New Economic History: A Critique," *Explorations in Economic History*, VI (1968), 75–92; Peter D. McClelland, "Model-Building in the New Economic History," in Bogue (ed.), *Emerging Theoretical Models in Social and Political History* (Beverly Hills, 1973), 13–33; Donald N. McCloskey, "Does the Past Have Useful Economics?" *Journal of Economic Literature*, XIV (1976), 434–461; Douglass C. North, "The New Economic History After Twenty Years," *American Behavioral Scientist*, XXI (1977), 187–200.

political behavior. But, interaction aside, a generation of political historians has developed which has been strongly influenced by the theoretical and substantive contributions of social scientists interested in political processes as well as by their methods. Most influential of such historians in the early years was Benson, although Aydelotte, a specialist in British history, also made an exceptional early contribution.[8]

Such political historians replaced the seriatim description of presidential elections—the presidential synthesis—with a conception of alternating eras of political stability, separated by periods of systemic realignment, involving one or more elections. Instead of seeking explanations of individual voting behavior, party allegiance, party agendas, and policy outputs primarily in class structure or economic interest groupings, they have tried to measure the importance of a broader range of socioeconomic and ethnocultural variables (including religious-group affiliation and doctrine). The most striking conclusion of these political historians has been that ethnocultural religious variables were generally most important, although the more cautious have emphasized that these were not always salient and that considerable variations in behavior may well have existed at different levels of government and from region to region through time. Some of the

8 Richard Hofstadter, *The Age of Reform: From Bryan to F.D.R.* (New York, 1955) and Bernard Bailyn, *The Ideological Origins of the American Revolution* (Cambridge, Mass., 1967) have been particularly influential. Robert L. Kelley, *The Cultural Pattern in American Politics: The First Century* (New York, 1979). Seminal works by social scientists included Paul F. Lazarsfeld, Bernard Berelson, and Hazel Gaudet, *The People's Choice: How the Voter Makes Up His Mind in a Presidential Campaign* (New York, 1944); V. O. Key, Jr., *Southern Politics in State and Nation* (New York, 1949); *idem,* "A Theory of Critical Elections," *Journal of Politics,* XVII (1955), 3–18; Angus Campbell, Philip E. Converse, Warren E. Miller, and Donald E. Stokes, *The American Voter* (New York, 1960); Robert K. Merton, *Social Theory and Social Structure* (Glencoe, Ill.; rev. ed. 1957). Some of Benson's early ideas appeared in "Research Problems in American Political Historiography," in Mirra Komarovsky (ed.), *Common Frontiers of the Social Sciences* (Glencoe, Ill., 1957), 113–183, and two widely-circulated papers: "An Operational Approach to Historiography," delivered at the American Historical Association meeting (1954), and a preliminary version of the book of 1961, "Public Opinion and the American Civil War: An Essay in the Logic and Practice of Historical Inquiry" (Stanford, 1958). Hays played an important role in the dissemination of the ideas of social science history. See particularly: Hays, "New Possibilities for American Political History: The Social Analysis of Political Life," paper delivered at the Annual Meeting of the American Historical Association (1964).

relations between doctrine and political behavior that have been suggested have become subjects of intense controversy.[9]

Political historians have also devoted much attention to legislative behavior and the characteristics of the political elites on the local, state, and national levels, and have shown some interest in institutionalization and developmental processes. Although much of the new political history cannot be regarded as definitive and many important aspects of past politics demand the attention of the quantifiers, they have greatly altered our understanding of the political history of the United States.[10]

The new social history appeared in the United States somewhat later than its economic and political counterparts. In some respects its antecedents are to be found in the contributions of American scholars, both historians and social scientists, but the influence of European historians, notably those of the *Annales* persuasion and British students of historical demography, has been more directly apparent in some of the constituencies of this

9 See James L. Sundquist, *Dynamics of the Party System: Alignment and Realignment of Political Parties in the United States* (Washington, 1973); Walter Dean Burnham, Jerome M. Clubb, and William H. Flanigan, "Partisan Realignment: A Systemic Perspective," and Benson, Joel H. Silbey, and Phyllis F. Field, "Toward a Theory of Stability and Change in American Voting Patterns: New York State, 1792–1970," in Silbey, Bogue, and Flanigan (eds.), *The History of American Electoral Behavior* (Princeton, 1978), 45–77, 78–105. The early quantitative reorientation in political history is discernible most perceptibly in McCormick, "Suffrage Classes and Party Alignments: A Study in Voter Behavior," *Mississippi Valley Historical Review*, XLVI (1959), 397–410; *idem*, "New Perspectives on Jacksonian Politics," *American Historical Review*, LXV (1960), 288–301; Benson, *The Concept of Jacksonian Democracy: New York as a Test Case* (Princeton, 1961). The latter is essential to an understanding of the later development of the ethnocultural theme. A summary of subsequent developments and listing of key works is to be found in: Bogue, "Recent Developments in Political History: The Case of the United States," in Torgny T. Segerstedt (ed.), *The Frontiers of Human Knowledge* (Uppsala, 1978), 79–110; Bogue, "The New Political History in the 1970's," in Michael Kammen (ed.), *The Past Before Us: Contemporary Historical Writing in the United States* (Ithaca, 1980), 231–251; Philip R. Vandermeer, "The New Political History: Progress and Prospects," *Computers and the Humanities*, XI (1978), 265–278.

10 Silbey, *The Shrine of Party: Congressional Voting Behavior, 1841–1852* (Pittsburgh, 1967); Thomas B. Alexander, *Sectional Stress and Party Strength: A Study of Roll-Call Voting Patterns in the United States House of Representatives, 1836–1860* (Nashville, 1967); Bogue, Clubb, Carroll R. McKibbin, and Santa A. Traugott, "Members of the House of Representatives and the Processes of Modernization, 1789–1960," *Journal of American History*, LXIII (1976), 275–302; Clubb and Traugott, "Partisan Cleavage and Cohesion in the House of Representatives, 1861–1974," *Journal of Interdisciplinary History*, VII (1977), 375–401. Another approach to political development is found in: Van Beck Hall, *Politics Without Parties: Massachusetts, 1780–1791* (Pittsburgh, 1972). See also the summary articles cited in n. 9.

area than in American political and economic history. The work of Malin, Owsley, and Curti during the 1930s, 1940s, and 1950s demonstrated the utility of analysis of the nineteenth-century manuscript agricultural and population census rolls. But it was Thernstrom's study of the social mobility of Newburyport's residents in the nineteenth century that caught the imagination of numerous graduate students during the late 1960s and served as a precursor of an outpouring of research on social mobility in American urban settings.[11]

During the 1960s a number of talented young scholars examined broader community and family processes in various colonial towns in New England. Such efforts were soon duplicated in other regions and periods of our history. Numbers of historians became interested in ethnic history. Social historians joined economic historians in assessing inequality and demographic trends in American history. Not only were these historians applying quantitative analysis in social history to a greater degree than formerly, they were developing the basic substance of American social history from scratch in greater degree than was true of either the political or economic historians, whose predecessors had bequeathed a massive accretion of research to their successors, old fashioned or one sided though it may be. Many of the new social historians have studied social attitudes and values and aspects of social process in which quantification appears less easy to effect. One recent authority concluded that, "on the whole . . . the union of social history and quantification remains incomplete."[12]

11 Note Kenneth A. Lockridge's acknowledgment of the influence of French scholars on the research which resulted in his book, *A New England Town: The First Hundred Years, Dedham, Massachusetts, 1636–1736* (New York, 1970), viii, and in Lockridge, "Historical Demography," in Charles F. Delzell (ed.), *The Future of History: Essays in the Vanderbilt University Centennial Symposium* (Nashville, 1977), 53–55. Although Lockridge reported that he used "many techniques of social-science analysis," he presented his findings in narrative style. By contrast, Stephan Thernstrom found precedents for his influential study of social mobility in the published work of the American sociologist, W. Lloyd Warner, and that of Oscar Handlin, Merle Curti, and Frank L. Owsley. See Thernstrom, *Poverty and Progress: Social Mobility in a Nineteenth Century City* (Cambridge, Mass., 1964), 3; *idem*, "The New Urban History," in Delzell, *The Future of History*, 45–46.

12 Particularly noteworthy were Lockridge, *A New England Town*; John Demos, *A Little Commonwealth: Family Life in Plymouth Colony* (New York, 1970); Philip J. Greven, Jr., *Four Generations: Population, Land, and Family in Colonial Andover, Massachusetts* (Ithaca, 1970). Note, however, that modern town studies predated the work of this trio and Sumner C. Powell, *Puritan Village: The Formation of a New England Town* (Middletown,

Within the last fifteen years, American and Canadian scholars have published hundreds of articles and dozens of books that rested upon the use of quantitative data to some degree. During this same period, quantitative historians have won some of the major scholarly book prizes in the United States. The editors of established journals have increasingly opened their pages to quantitative scholars during the 1970s and the *Journal of Interdisciplinary History, Social Science History,* and *Historical Methods* developed particularly to serve this consistuency. At the same time other new, or relatively new, journals, such as the *Journal of Social History* and the *Journal of Family History* included a significant number of quantitative historians among their contributors.

How many quantitative historians are there in the United States? This we cannot say with certainty; some quantitative historians do not restrict themselves to numerical analysis. But during eighteen months of low-keyed solicitation in the mid 1970s, the organizers of the Social Science History Association obtained membership pledges or first-year dues from some 1,200 individuals, including a relatively small number of foreign scholars. The number of individual subscribers to the *Journal of Interdisciplinary History* at this time was about the same and no doubt the two groups overlapped to a considerable degree. But not all such subscribers are committed to the use of quantification in their own work. In 1979, Kousser estimated that some 750 junior faculty and graduate students had attended summer programs in quantitative historical methods since the late 1960s at the University of Michigan under the auspices of the Inter-University Consortium for Political and Social research, at the Center for the Study of the Family and Culture at the Newberry Library, and in the History Department of Johns Hopkins University. Nonrecurring summer programs have probably introduced another hundred or more young American historians to aspects of quantitative methodology. These numbers are at least equalled by

1963), included various quantitative exhibits and won a Pulitzer Prize. Peter N. Stearns, "Toward a Wider Vision: Trends in Social History," in Kammen, *The Past Before Us,* 226; other aspects of social history are discussed in the same volume by Carl N. Degler, "Women and the Family," 308–326." See also John B. Sharpless and Sam Bass Warner, Jr., "Urban History," in *American Behavioral Scientist,* XXI (1977), 221–244; Allan N. Sharlin, "Historical Demography as History and Demography," *ibid.,* 245–262; Maris A. Vinovskis, "From Household Size to the Life Course: Some Observations on Recent Trends in Family History," *ibid.,* 263–287.

those who have enrolled in the increasing numbers of quantitative methods courses introduced in the regular curricula of graduate history programs during the same period.[13]

Although most of the first generation of cliometric historians received their training in the established east coast bastions of historical scholarship, the heartland of the country was more influential in nurturing the quantification movement than the universities of the eastern seaboard. Faculty members at Purdue, Iowa, Wayne State, Chicago, Wisconsin, Michigan, and Pittsburgh universities played a more important role in popularizing the use of quantitative methods than those of the Ivy League Schools. But some graduate directors in the eastern schools encouraged or allowed graduate students to investigate quantitative methods or to take advantage of interdisciplinary opportunities available in social science departments. And, in a secondary phase of development, various of the eastern schools appointed quantifiers to their history departments.

During the late 1960s and early 1970s quantifiers seemed destined to establish themselves rapidly in university history departments; at that time a significant proportion of job descriptions listed quantitative skills among the desired credentials. Such promises were not completely realized. Recruitment committees of traditional historians sometimes appointed ingratiating youngsters who paraded a tolerable command of long division or a passing acquaintance with computer programing in lieu of genuine skills in formal analysis. But general developments in the academic market place were more frustrating. When the changing demography of the pre-college age population began to predict a decline in the need for public and secondary school teachers and the objectives of liberal education came increasingly under challenge, college and university history departments suffered substantial declines in enrollment. Job openings usually reflected efforts to replace teachers lost through death, retirement, or to other institutions, rather than representing new positions, and in such cases the needs of continuing programs or inertia favored recruitment in the vacated specialty. Despite such developments, most major history departments now include some historians

13   J. Morgan Kousser, "Quantitative Social-Scientific History," in Kammen, *Past Before Us,* 449–450.

who understand the problems of applying quantitative analysis in historical research in some degree. Of the approximately fifty faculty members in the history department of the University of Wisconsin, ten have, at one time or another, developed research projects which were sufficiently quantitative in nature to suggest computer analysis, and others, such as David Herlihy, Philip Curtin, and Maris Vinovskis developed important quantitative projects while members of the department. Such concentration is unusual but it may well be a forecast of the future.[14]

Kousser has prepared time series beginning with the year 1961 that show the number of tables presented per 100 pages of text in various historical journals. Five of these were long-established publications that together serve the interests of most professional historians in the United States: the *American Historical Review*, the *Journal of American History*, the *Journal of Modern History*, the *Journal of Southern History*, and the *William and Mary Quarterly*. The mean number of numerical tables in these journals per 100 pages of article text was one during the years 1961–1965. That figure rose to 3.3 during the years 1966–1972, and stood at 4.8 between 1973 and 1978. Although this statistic clearly shows an increase in the use of numerical data, the implications of the index become clearer if we understand that the six tables per 100 pages of article text in volume LXV (1978–79) of the *Journal of American History* actually meant that four of eighteen authors (22 percent), or author teams, used tables and that their contributions occupied 75 of the 414 pages of articles (18 percent) presented. Only one of the contributors of the four quantitative articles used numerical analysis that was more sophisticated than the presentation of numbers and percentages. The authors of this piece used rank order correlation.[15]

Quantification has been much more common in specialized journals such as the *Journal of Economic History*, the *Journal of*

---

14 Some of the early background is sketched by Jensen in "History and the Political Scientist," and "American Election Analysis: A Case History of Methodological Innovation and Diffusion," in Lipset (ed.), *Politics and the Social Sciences*, 1–28, 226–243; developments of the 1950s and 1960s by Bogue, "United States: The 'New' Political History," in Walter Laqueur and George L. Mosse (eds.), *The New History: Trends in Historical Research and Writing Since World War II* (New York, 1967), 185–207. Handlin, Paul W. Gates, Roy F. Nichols, Owsley, and others successfully encouraged students to chart new paths.

15 Kousser, "Quantitative History," 438–443.

Interdisciplinary History and *Social Science History* than in the general purpose quarterlies. Whereas the six tables per 100 pages in the *Journal of American History* was the mean found in the main line journals in 1978–79, the equivalent number in JEH and JIH was around twenty and the first volume of SSH (1976–77) presented tables at the rate of thirty per 100 pages of article text. A considerable majority of the authors publishing in these journals used tables and approximately a quarter to one half of such contributors used techniques that reflected some understanding of classical statistics. During the course of the three volume years of JIH summarized in Table 1, the latter proportion rose from 28 to 52 percent of the authors publishing research articles or notes. But if χ^2 had been considered an elementary statistic, the percentages would have been greatly reduced.

The journal literature gives the best general picture of the state of quantification in history at this time. The members of the History Advisory Committee of the Mathematical Social Science Board initially planned that the volumes in "The Quantitative Studies in History" series should illustrate particularly useful or promising techniques in mathematical historical analysis. The contributions have in many cases, therefore, been more advanced in method than was usual in the field at the time of publication. Nor have these volumes necessarily reflected the relative degree of interest among quantitative historians in the various research problems under study in the subareas of quantitative history. The planners of the MSSB volume, *The History of American Electoral Behavior,* did not include an essay dealing with the relation between ethnocultural factors and voting behavior because they believed that the methodological problems of such analysis were already fairly well understood.[16]

To date, the bulk of quantitative history has been based upon simple quantification, in which numerical data is presented in the

16 The MSSB volumes currently available are: McCloskey (ed.), *Essays on a Mature Economy: Britain after 1840* (Princeton, 1971); Aydelotte, Bogue, and Fogel (eds.), *The Dimensions of Quantitative Research in History* (Princeton, 1972); Stanley L. Engerman and Eugene D. Genovese, *Race and Slavery in the Western Hemisphere: Quantitative Studies* (Princeton, 1975); Leo F. Schnore (ed.), *The New Urban History: Quantitative Explorations by American Historians* (Princeton, 1975); Aydelotte (ed.), *The History of Parliamentary Behavior* (Princeton, 1977); Silbey et al., *American Electoral Behavior*; Charles Tilly, *Historical Studies of Changing Fertility* (Princeton, 1978); Tamara K. Hareven and Vinovskis, *Family and Population in Nineteenth-Century America* (Princeton, 1978).

Table 1 Quantification in Journals of the "New" Histories

	ARTICLES PRESENTING TABLES[a]		PAGES IN TABLED ARTICLES		ARTICLES PRESENTING ADVANCED STATISTICS		PAGES IN ARTICLES WITH ADVANCED STATISTICS	
	NUMBER	PERCENT	NUMBER	PERCENT	NUMBER	PERCENT	NUMBER	PERCENT
	Social Science History							
Vol. I (1976–77)	13	68	350	77	7	37	196	43
Vol. II (1977–78)	12	60	300	74	4	20	111	27
Vol. III (1978–79)	13	62	363	77	5	24	154	33
Total	38	63	1013	76	16	27	461	35
	Journal of Interdisciplinary History							
Vol. VI	15	83	391	88	5	28	147	33
Vol. VII	19	90	368	82	9	43	185	41
Vol. VIII	20	87	461	80	12	52	303	56
Total	54	87	1220	85	26	48	635	44

[a] Does not include review essays.

form of raw numbers, means, and percentages. And some of this work has been of great significance in the reinterpretation of historical development. In the various fields of history in which quantification has become popular, the sophistication of the statistical methods vary roughly in proportion to the time when quantification became popular and to some degree also reflect the quantitative sophistication of the social sciences that have most strongly influenced that particular area of history. The functions, equations, and elaborately derived models of the economic historians demonstrate considerably greater mathematical and statistical skill and command of theory than the scaling techniques and correlation and regression analysis used by the more advanced political historians, and the methods of this latter group often reflect more mathematical and statistical skills than do the procedures of social historians.

Advocates of quantification credit its practitioners with a number of important general contributions. Quantitative analysis, they say, has enabled historians to give new or better answers to long-standing questions of importance: Was slavery profitable in the United States? Were the class divisions in American society at the root of individual and party political activity? Did the radical Republicans provide the leadership and policies that brought Union victory during the Civil War and the reconstruction at its close? Was there a high degree of social mobility, even among immigrant groups in American society? Often quantitative analysis has not produced novel answers to such questions but rather has demonstrated that one of several long-standing hypotheses is more worthy of acceptance than others. But have the answers been truly definitive—to invoke the criterion that some historians view as the Holy Grail of their craft? Perhaps not in the larger sense, but the historian who contends in future that slavery was unprofitable, or that the quantifier's answer to our other illustrative questions is wrong, must discredit a body of evidence that appears much more convincing than that mustered thus far in the defense of alternative explanations. Indeed, some discern the possibility that historians may finally be building a body of cumulative rather than heterogeneous knowledge.

The somewhat naive hopes of some quantitative pioneers that definitive answers to old controversies would immediately close the book in particular areas of research has not been realized.

Rather, quantitative answers have usually raised additional questions. Such questions have frequently involved the validity of the quantitative evidence and the appropriateness of the analytical methods used in evaluating them. These dialogues have both deepened professional understanding of the issues and helped to educate historians in quantitative analysis.

More interesting, however, has been the impetus that quantitative analysis has given in a variety of ways to the redefinition of research agendas. If, for instance, we can assume that slavery was generally profitable, we are in a position to consider the implications of that fact on the social and political structures of the South. If we can show that radical Republicans did not dominate the policy processes of the Civil War era, we can then search for a more satisfactory model of policy formulation than one in which a relatively small core of radical leaders forced their prescriptions upon compliant colleagues and a reluctant president, or in which a farsighted, but apparently moderate, president used the radicals as the advance agents of the policies that he actually favored. If spatial mobility was common in the United States and social mobility significantly present (provided particular definitions are accepted), it becomes appropriate to explore the implications of these facts systematically and to investigate other questions about the social, economic, and political structure of America in the past that assume high rates of mobility.[17]

The use of quantitative data has changed the patterns of historical research in another respect. This form of evidence facilitates comparison which has predisposed some quantifiers to emphasize the analysis of collectivities or categories of historical phenomena rather than the isolated event or sequence of events. Now the focus of interest becomes the status of slaves in a whole

17 The first undeniably econometric answer to the question of profitability was the article by Alfred H. Conrad and John R. Meyer, "The Economics of Slavery in the Ante Bellum South," *Journal of Political Economy*, LXVI (1958), 95–130. It continued to be an issue until (and past) the publication of Fogel and Engerman, *Time on the Cross*. But it is important to note that much of the dialogue among econometric historians between 1958 and 1974 involved issues of technical elegance and that the controversy over *Time on the Cross* within the same fraternity has not focused in any appreciable degree upon profitability. T. Harry Williams, *Lincoln and the Radicals* (Madison, 1941); James G. Randall, completed by Richard N. Current, *Lincoln the President* (New York, 1945–1955), 4v.; Hans L. Trefousse, *The Radical Republicans: Lincoln's Vanguard for Racial Justice* (New York, 1969).

region rather than on one or several plantations, not just key legislative votes but all of those in major categories of legislation, or even all votes in a series of legislative sessions, and not just an isolated presidential election but series of elections at the various levels of political activity found in the United States. Rather than examining a few robber barons we can study the leadership of an industry, and instead of focusing upon the participants in a dramatic strike or the strike leaders we can consider all of the workers of an industry town or city. Where once the attributes of elites drew our attention, the birth, death, and mobility patterns in regional or national populations have become of much more interest to us. History in such terms can, say some zealots, be written from the bottom up.

But the examination of the unique individual or event and the study of collectivities are by no means mutually exclusive. Indeed the study of individuals or phenomena en masse will allow the researcher to explain better the unique event. And surely such an investigator will think twice before emphasizing a causal agent that was apparently of little importance in analogous situations. The comparative process reveals the necessity of explaining the unique features of any particular pattern.

The quantification and computer processing techniques of the last generation have made it feasible to use quantitative data bodies, hitherto believed to be too unwieldly for intensive use. Such research has advertised the existence of neglected sources. But the quantifiers have also produced a great stock pile of machine-readable quantitative data that may be used for new research as well as the replication of earlier studies. Governmental budget data, corporate and individual income and expenditure data, the personal and agricultural census returns of individuals, popular and legislative voting records at various levels of aggregation, elite biographical data, will and probate inventory files, federal land disposal records, and a variety of miscellaneous quantitative sources have been converted to machine readable form and are available to researchers generally, often through the agency of the Historical Data Archive of the Inter-University Consortium for Political and Social Research. As a result many historians may now start their research without having to transcribe their basic data from the sources, code, keypunch, or otherwise transform them into machine-readable form. Much research effort has been saved.[18]

The accumulation and management of the "intellectual capital" represented in machine-readable data is in some respects controversial, calling, some believe, for a more cooperative professional ethic than historians have displayed in the past. But conservatives refuse to abandon the old rule that research notes are forever the property of the investigator. The authors of a number of important studies in the new quantitative histories have refused to make their data available to other researchers. But the concentration of machine-readable data in a relatively limited number of depositories is the source of some concern as well, as has been the failure of research and university libraries to develop facilities for the storage and administration of such resources. The official archival agencies at all levels of government in the United States and abroad have been slow to meet the challenge of adapting to the widespread use of machine-readable data anlysis or to realize that machine-readable data may indeed allow economies of storage that will offset the costs of the new technology to some degree. But there are still very considerable technical problems involved in the storage of machine-readable data—depositories now face substantial costs in guarding against losses of research material due to tape deterioration and in upgrading data formats to keep pace with the changing practises of the data-processing industry. All of these problems demand the close attention of the research community.[19]

The influence of quantifiers has produced a broadening in the training of historians. Kousser's recent survey of the curricula of the 125 major graduate departments of history in the United States showed that at least fifty-three departments were offering one or more quantitative methods courses. But only five institutions required such a course and we suspect that quantitative methodology formed only a part of the curriculum in these cases.

18 Bogue, "The Historian and Social Science Data Archives in the United States," *American Behavioral Scientist*, XIX (1976), 419–442; other contributions to the March/April issue of this periodical. See also: Bogue, "Data Dilemmas: Quantitative Data and the Social Science History Association," *Social Science History*, III (1979), 204–226; Val R. Lorwin and Jacob M. Price, *The Dimensions of the Past: Materials, Problems, and Opportunities for Quantitative Work in History* (New Haven, 1972).

19 In addition to the items in 18n. see also, Kousser, "The Agenda for 'Social Science History,'" *Social Science History*, I (1977), 383–391; *idem*, "Quantitative History."

Such courses and the summer programs in quantitative methods have introduced hundreds of young historians to quantitative methods but the word "introduced" should be stressed. These offerings have not prepared individuals adequately to engage in quantitative research. Additional courses in statistics or social science departments have been essential but Kousser discovered that only two history departments had developed articulated sequences providing such training. In summary, Table 2 shows significant progress, but anything but complete acceptance of the necessity of including social science methods within the history curriculum. And these offerings, of course, were designed primarily for graduate students; the faculty of history departments have largely ignored undergraduates in such curriculum building.

This is perhaps to put too grim a face on the situation. History graduate students can currently acquire methodological skills in the course of completing minor requirements or in lieu of language training. A few of our most impressive young quantitative historians acquired their skills by putting themselves in the hands of sympathetic social scientists in related disciplines or used knowledge obtained in a "quickie" summer course to chart a substantial program of training in social science methods. But the quantitative training offered in departments of statistics or the social sciences does not usually demonstrate how the methods under discussion can be applied to historical data. Many history

Table 2 Quantitative Methods Offerings in U.S. Graduate History Programs[a]

PROGRAMS(125)	GRADUATE HISTORY DEPARTMENTS (NUMBER)	PERCENT OF RETURNED QUESTIONNAIRES (83)	PERCENT OF SAMPLE
Offer some course in methodology and statistics	53	64	42
Including bivariate regression	42	50	34
Including multiple regression	33	40	26
Offer some social theory course	8	10	6
Require methodology course	5	6	4
Require calculus	0	0	0

[a] Based on J. Morgan Kousser's data in "Quantitative Social Science History," in Michael Kammen, *The Past Before Us*, 448–449.

students require preliminary instruction of that sort before they encounter the offerings of professional statisticians or social scientists.

Adequate training in the methods of quantitative analysis is not necessarily a passport to success; that follows only if such skills are used appropriately in confronting important historical problems. Some believe that quantitative methods are most appropriate in historical analysis when used in research designs that address aspects of major social theories. Are history graduate students prepared for investigations of this kind? The formal history graduate curriculum revealed in the Kousser survey (Table 2) shows little evidence of such tendency. Only one history department reported a required course in social science theory and, in actuality, that course apparently does not touch upon aspects of theoretical model building or the mechanics of research design.[20]

The situation is unfortunate in another respect as well. During the last thirty years the social sciences in general have become much more quantitative in approach. Typically in the past, these disciplines have provided historians with their understanding of the determinants of human behavior. In that sense, all history students should have sufficient statistical training so that they can easily read the research journals of at least one or two social science disciplines. The lag in the history department curriculum has contributed to the production of a generation of history majors who are often ignorant of current research in the most important related discipline. And as social scientists now begin to recapture the interest in the historical dimension that was largely lost in their fields for a generation, there is a growing tendency for them to produce their own historians. This development threatens both the intellectual and political future of history, as we have known it, in the university community.

Although scholars applying quantitative methods to historical issues have indeed accomplished much during the last fifteen years, many have severely criticized their contributions and indeed, in some instances, have argued that their work is positively

---

20 Two useful introductions to statistics for historians have appeared: Dollar and Jensen, *Historian's Guide to Statistics*; Roderick Floud, *An Introduction to Quantitative Methods for Historians* (Princeton, 1973).

harmful. Barzun maintains, for example, that the new historians have not clearly demonstrated a new method, proven the superiority of their approach, nor moved convincingly from the individual to the collectivity; they have asked nonhistorical questions, used unfamiliar and grating language, substituted pompous abstractions for the concrete and simple, and restricted the mind of the historian from ranging free. Although Barzun may be largely dismissed as a Luddite and a curmudgeon, or his opinion disregarded as contrary to fact, some criticisms of the new histories are more worthy of serious consideration. I use the electoral historians as an illustration.[21]

Critics have charged that the new political historians have ignored conventional sources. They have shown relationships between party voting and ethno-religious reference groups, but they have not thoroughly canvassed the foreign language press and local records for additional evidence that would confirm quantitative relationships and explain the reasons underlying them. Would greater use of foreign language materials give specific or different explanations for the behavior of foreign language groups than that deduced from the quantitative voting patterns and English language documents? Perhaps so, but many literary historians who have written electoral history are guilty of the same sins. In general, they have used *neither* quantitative evidence *nor* the foreign language press in depth. Unquestionably it would be desirable for historians to use all the relevant evidence. But in practise this is often impossible. Certainly the traditional historian often lacks the skill to use quantitative evidence. Most desirable would be an atmosphere of mutual trust in which the traditional and quantitative historians depend upon each other's contributions.[22]

Some critics have suggested that the causal relationships posited by some of the "ethnocultural" historians are unconvincing. The latter have frequently demonstrated that there are strong correlations between the numbers in ethnocultural groups and

21 Barzun, *Clio and the Doctors*, 39–41.
22 Illustrative charges are found in: Robert W. Johannsen, Review of *The Kansas-Nebraska Bill: Party, Section, and the Coming of the Civil War* by Gerald W. Wolff, *Agricultural History*, LIII (1979), 540–542. Donald Pienkas, "Politics, Religion, and Change in Polish Milwaukee, 1900–1930," *Wisconsin Magazine of History*, LXI (1978), 179–209, esp. 188–191.

political party voting totals. Some of the new political historians have explained these relationships by arguing that religious doctrinal or world view positions are reflected in the programs and membership of American political parties. Although qualified by its proponents in various respects, this position can be stated in specific terms as follows: "the more pietistic (or evangelical) the faith of an American religious group during the nineteenth century, the greater the tendency for its members to be found in the ranks of the Whig or, subsequently, the Republican Party." Critics, including some of the new political historians, have suggested that the structure of inference and substantive evidence involved in this interpretation of voting relationships is less than fully convincing. This line of argument has some merit.

Critics also maintain that quantitative political historians have overemphasized the importance of the electoral process, although it is only one part of the political system. They have paid little attention to policy-making processes and to the impact of policy. This is the case, but quantitative historians are moving to remedy this deficiency. In addition the American political system is three tiered—local, state, and federal and, with a few significant exceptions, the first two categories have been relatively understudied. This remains true, but actually new political historians have taken the lead in emphasizing the local and state dimensions of American politics.[23]

There have been suggestions also that quantitative historians have used inadequate or inappropriate quantitative methods. In specific cases such allegations have been correct; it could hardly be otherwise when conventionally trained historians have tried to master the new techniques on their own initiative. And when literary historians have directed the quantitative research of grad-

---

23   For more extended discussion of these issues see James E. Wright, "The Ethnocultural Model of Voting: A Behavioral and Historical Critique," in Bogue, *Emerging Theoretical Models,* 35–56; McCormick, "Ethno-Cultural Interpretations of Nineteenth-Century American Voting Behavior," *Political Science Quarterly,* LXXXIX (1974), 351–377. Melvyn Hammarberg, *Indiana Voter: The Historical Dynamics of Party Allegiance During the 1870s* (Chicago, 1977), *passim.* Paul Kleppner responds to some of the criticisms of the "ethnocultural school" in *The Third Electoral System, 1853–1892: Parties, Voters and Political Cultures* (Chapel Hill, 1979), 357–382. Allan J. Lichtman, "Critical Election Theory and the Reality of American Presidential Politics, 1916–40," *American Historical Review,* LXXXI (1976), 317–348, develops various criticisms of the research dealing with electoral realignment.

uate students, who had picked up a smattering of quantitative methods in courses in related disciplines, the blind in effect have guided the one-eyed.[24]

Although we have used political history as the focus of these criticisms, they may be generalized and stated as problems relating to source use, specification, the appropriateness of methods used, and issues of inference. Similar criticisms have been made of the work of the new economic and social historians, sometimes with justice and sometimes quite unfairly.

Generalizing about the progress of quantification in history is difficult because its background and development in economic history, political history, and social history all have differed in essential respects. No one theoretical foundation, system of research design, or statistical technique has been applied universally in the three provinces of history. The historians who "revolutionized" American economic history were for the most part trained in economics, the social science discipline that has been most successful in developing a body of sophisticated theory and in operationalizing models derived from that theory in mathematical and statistical terms. The political or social historian has seldom thus far developed a true equivalent to the mathematical simulation or counterfactual modelling of the economic historian, although research of that sort is less dominant in economic history than is generally believed.

Modern political and social theory underlies much of the new political and social history but, despite major substantive contributions to that history by social scientists, scholars trained as historians have played the major role in developing the new political and social histories. Not only is the theory that illumines or shapes their work less elaborate, and its variables less well defined than is true of economics, the new social and political historians have been less alive to the nuances and complexities of that theory and much less well prepared to operationalize it than

---

24 Kousser, "The 'New Political History': A Methodological Critique," *Reviews in American History*, IV (1976), 1–14. For comparative purposes, Richard S. Alcorn and Peter R. Knights, "Most Uncommon Bostonians: A Critique of Stephan Thernstrom's *The Other Bostonians: Poverty and Progress in the American Metropolis, 1880–1970*," *Historical Methods Newsletter*, VIII (1975), 98–114; Thernstrom, "Rejoinder to Alcorn and Knights," *ibid.*, 115–120.

has been the case among economic historians. The latter frequently disagree with each other about the "specification" of their models, in other words, the degree to which they have built a model that effectively tests the propositions that they advance in explanation of economic events and that uses variables that do indeed measure the processes under study. The skills of the political and social historians in specification seem relatively less well developed than those of the economic historians.

The new historians have invested much effort in the quantitative description of phenomena—economic, political, and social. Such endeavor was part of the stock in trade of the old economic historians and not unknown among conventional political and social historians. But this component has been much more common in the new histories than in traditional history. Such additional emphasis on quantitative data has been rewarding. Historical analysis has become more rigorous as a result and, in addition, such evidence allows historians to study economic, political, and social processes more systematically. In particular, they are able to use methods that allow more precise estimation of the varying degrees of association between causal (independent) variables and affected (dependent) variables. This emphasis is the very essence of the new histories.

The political historian of the 1940s typically described a variety of factors that "explained" particular electoral results and either stopped at that point or identified the most important of these determinants by analyzing the opinions of contemporary observers or, perhaps, by using mere intuition. Electoral historians of the 1970s, however, are able to break down the electorates of the past into component social groups and measure the degree to which the various groups contributed to outcomes and to chart shifts in support over time. Although inference has not been banished from such research, quantitative analysis moves the new political historians beyond their predecessors by several analytical steps and broadens the perspective of their research.

In endeavoring to measure association between variables or suggest causal relationships, the new political and social historians have used a great variety of statistical measures during the last generation, ranging from simple tables of percentages, through controlled cross tabulation to multiple correlation and regression, analysis of variance and factor analysis (to note the most commonplace) and have often applied significance tests to the results. In adopting regression analysis the political and social historian began to use what economists have sometimes considered their most useful tool.

Although the effort to distinguish the relative importance of causal variables in a rigorous fashion is the distinguishing methodological characteristic of the new histories, a particular type of research design has also been characteristic of the new political and social historians. This has been the frequent use of the case study method; aspects of political or social behavior and structure are intensively studied in a community, township, county, or state during time periods of varying length, often, unfortunately, of relatively short duration. Again, such focus has not been unique to the era of the new histories, nor do cliometricians restrict themselves to this research design alone, but quantitative studies of state electoral activity and community social structure and mobility have been their most typical product.

In the development of quantitative methods in the various provinces of history, techniques have tended over time to become more sophisticated, but the process has often been slow. Electoral history, again, illustrates such evolution. In 1957, McWhiney was, perhaps, the first American political historian of the current era to use correlation coefficients when he endeavored to test the familiar generalizations that the Whig party was particularly strong in those southern regions where slavery was most common and that this relationship showed that large planters were particularly supportive of the Whig Party. Using county electoral returns and census data in Alabama, McWhiney calculated correlation coefficients between the proportion of slaves and the Whig vote across a number of elections, using the rank order coefficient, Spearman's rho. His quantitative data justified the use of the more precise and illuminating Pearson's r but the size of the coefficients was probably little affected by this research strategy. They ranged from .49 to .67 and McWhiney concluded that the relation was too weak to sustain the traditional interpretation.[25]

If McWhiney had used Pearson's r and obtained coefficients of comparable strength, the coefficient of determination (r^2)

25 Grady McWhiney, "Were the Whigs a Class Party in Alabama?" *Journal of Southern History*, XXIII (1957), 510–522.

would have shown that between 24 and 45 percent of the variation in Whig voting from county to county was associated with the number of slaves present. Those proportions are not trivial; the conventional wisdom was more correct than McWhiney admitted. But his results also revealed that the presence of slaves was not alone sufficient to predict the size of the Whig vote. Although McWhiney failed to use the most precise measure of association and he misinterpreted the results of his analysis somewhat, he made an important methodological breakthrough and demonstrated that quantification could sharpen and qualify long-standing historical generalizations. His results encouraged further investigation of party characteristics and objectives in Alabama. Such research documented that the number of slaves was indeed the most important single predictor of Whig voting in antebellum Alabama.[26]

Appearing in 1961, Benson's *The Concept of Jacksonian Democracy,* provided the conceptual apparatus and inspiration for dozens of younger scholars who have since ranged across the full sweep of American national history and proclaimed the importance of ethnocultural factors in American politics. Although considerable quantitative analysis underlay Benson's book and the Bureau of Applied Social Research at Columbia University placed its punch card sorters at his disposal, his quantitative methods were relatively simple. He presented no summative statistic more sophisticated than a percentage. But he did include one table showing the economic status and Democratic voting performance of various New York towns arranged in rank order so that the reader might judge the degree of relation between wealth and the Democratic vote—an "eyeball" correlation. Another table, showing the proportion of voters in various ethnocultural groups that voted Democratic or Whig, was apparently prepared by extrapolating the voting of relatively pure constituencies to the ethnocultural groups at large.

26 Alexander, Kit C. Carter, Jack R. Lister, Jerry C. Oldshue, and Winfred G. Sandlin, "Who Were the Alabama Whigs?" *Alabama Review,* XVI (1963), 5–19; Alexander, Peggy Duckworth Elmore, Frank M. Lowrey, and Mary Jane Pickens Skinner, "The Basis of Alabama's Ante-Bellum Two-Party System: A Case Study in Party Alignment and Voter Response in the Traditional Two-Party System of the United States by Quantitative Analysis Methods," *Alabama Review,* XIX (1966), 243–276. The Alexander group used Spearman's rho in the first article but employed multiple correlation and regression procedures in the second.

Benson was an early exponent of multivariate analysis but for him this essentially involved the control of one variable in the process of examining the relationship of two others in cross tabulation. He included no methodological gloss in the first edition of the *Concept of Jacksonian Democracy*; in retrospect his quantitative methods were rather blunt instruments. Although, Parsons brought multiple regression analysis to bear on the definition of Nebraska Populists in 1963 and the Alexander group at the University of Alabama published an illustration of such analysis in 1966, the general development of expertise in electoral analysis moved much more slowly.[27]

When the Inter-University Consortium for Political Research and the Historical Quantitative Data Commitee of the American Historical Association sponsored a summer institute on the quantitative analysis of electoral and legislative data at Ann Arbor during the summer of 1965, easy chairs were arranged around a large coffee table at the rear of the conference room on which various reprints were displayed. Among these was Robinson's article, "Ecological Correlations and the Behavior of Individuals." Participants, who had not read it previously, now learned of the "ecological fallacy"—that the correlation between characteristics of aggregates denoted by Pearson's r tended to rise with the level of aggregation and most particularly that such relationships could not be generalized to the individuals involved. Although Robinson's message undoubtedly discouraged some aspiring quantifiers, many pressed on. Some tried to circumvent the fallacy or to blunt its force by trying to discover pure or banner precincts in which individuals with particular ethnic, religious, or other characteristics were so widespread that numerical totals must be assumed to reflect individual voting behavior. Others wrote of constituencies instead of individual voters or regarded correlation merely as a means of discarding irrelevant variables. Others gladly accepted the message that Robinson's qualifications did not actually extend to the regression coefficient and advocated its use instead of Pearson's r. After some hesitation, still others followed the lead provided by Goodman, a statistician, and used regression analysis to

27 See particularly, Benson, *Concept of Jacksonian Democracy*, 149, 155, 185, 262. Stanley B. Parsons, "Who Were the Nebraska Populists?" *Nebraska History*, XLIV (1963), 83–99; Alexander et al., "Alabama's Ante-Bellum Two-Party System."

estimate the proportion within particular reference groups that voted for particular parties.[28]

Some of the solutions were more satisfactory than others. The use of banner precincts, for example, involved the dubious proposition that the members of particular reference groups behaved in the same way, whether concentrated in large numbers or widely disseminated within a larger population. And the use of selections of constituencies, such as "German counties" in which some lower bound (20 percent for example) of German-born residents differentiated them from counties at large, produced truncated regression lines in which the slopes were perhaps different than a more inclusive selection of constituencies would have provided.

Despite the occasional early use of advanced statistics by quantitative political historians, their electoral analysis passed through several stages. Benson's quantitative methods of 1961 were very simple but typical of those used at that time; data were presented in percentage form or in tabular rankings that suggested correlation. The wave of books and articles, that his book had in part stimulated by the end of the decade, displayed zero order correlation coefficients, standard deviations, and acquaintance with the concept of significance, but the use of multiple regression was rare. By the mid 1970s, a new level of sophistication was apparent. This was marked particularly by the appearance of Kousser's *The Shaping of Southern Politics,* in which the author used Goodman's method of regression estimation to test earlier generalizations about the southern system of voter exclusion, and Hammarberg's *Indiana Voter,* based upon the analysis of a skillfully-drawn sample of voters from compendia of biographical information about county residents.[29]

28 W. S. Robinson, "Ecological Correlations and the Behavior of Individuals," *American Sociological Review,* XV (1950), 351–357. L. A. Goodman, "Some Alternatives to Ecological Correlation," *American Journal of Sociology,* LXIV (1959), 610–624. There was some discussion of this technique at the Ann Arbor summer institute of 1965 but few electoral historians accepted it with enthusiasm, perhaps because of reservations expressed by some political scientists. Two research notes helped particularly to advertise it: E. Terrence Jones, "Ecological Inference and Electoral Analysis," *Journal of Interdisciplinary History,* II (1972), 249–262; Kousser, "Ecological Regression and the Analysis of Past Politics," *ibid.,* IV (1973), 237–262. These contributions cited earlier descriptions in social science publications.

29 Particularly noted in the wave of publications that drew heavily upon Benson's example were Kleppner, *The Cross of Culture: A Social Analysis of Midwestern Politics, 1850–*

Controversy over the appropriateness of particular statistical methods has not diminished. Many agree, for example, that regression analysis may in many cases be used to make useful estimates of the proportions and numbers of individuals possessing two attributes, although only the numbers of individuals possessing one of the two attributes is available. Thus Kousser estimated the number of black Republican voters in southern states during the late nineteenth century although only the number of adult male blacks and the number of Republican voters in the various reporting units were known. But some scholars have extended such analysis to develop estimates of the proportion or number of voters who changed partisan allegiance through time. When the elections examined were separated by a relatively short period of time the method is undoubtedly useful. But when the intervening time period was several years in duration, the mobility of nineteenth-century Americans guarantees that the two electoral universes were by no means identical; some therefore view estimates of this kind with considerable suspicion.[30]

The full implications of quantitative historical data and their analysis are not always apparent to the casual reader. Scholars have estimated the size of electorates and ethnocultural groups in some years by interpolating between census or other reporting years. The number of voters in religious groups have been estimated on occasion from reports of the seating capacity of houses of worship or from church records that perhaps reflect denominational chauvinism and differences in reporting practises from group to group. Extended series of correlation coefficients showing the election by election commitment of particular groups to a particular party are much rarer in the literature than one might anticipate.

1900 (New York, 1970); Jensen, *Winning of the Midwest: Social and Political Conflict, 1888–1896* (Chicago, 1971); Ronald P. Formisano, *The Birth of Mass Political Parties: Michigan, 1827–1861* (Chicago, 1971). Kousser, *The Shaping of Southern Politics: Suffrage Restriction and the Establishment of the One-Party South, 1880–1910* (New Haven, 1974).

30 Ray M. Shortridge, "The Voter Realignment in the Midwest during the 1850s," *American Politics Quarterly*, IV (1976), 193–222, both illustrates the technique and provides statistical justification for its use in election series. For other interesting substantive uses of the method see: Peyton McCrary, Clark Miller, and Dale Baum, "Class and Party in the Secession Crisis: Voting Behavior in the Deep South, 1856–1861," *Journal of Interdisciplinary History*, VIII (1978), 429–457; Baum, "Know-Nothingism and the Republican Majority in Massachusetts: The Political Realignment of the 1850s, *Journal of American History*, LXIV (1978), 959–986.

If we reflect upon the research of the electoral historians since 1961, there is good reason to believe that some of it will fail to stand the test of more rigorous scrutiny on methodological grounds. One young historian, exceptionally well-trained in statistics, mused without any effort to be sarcastic, "I wonder what Lee Benson's research would have shown had he used the proper statistical techniques?" Crude methods, however, often capture meaning in quantitative data that more sophisticated analysis only refines.

The convergence of the conclusions of many scholars in the new political history, using a variety of methods, suggests that there is a reliable core of fact in the findings of electoral research. The task of reevaluating and refinement will continue, however, and rightly so. In this respect, quantitative political history may duplicate experience in economic history. Typically one or more inventive studies have precipitated replicative or parallel research and controversy about the most appropriate methods of analysis. As in the debate over the profitability of slavery, critics have in turn suggested methodological solutions that more clearly illustrate elegance and perhaps refine or modify the original conclusions; usually the result has been a genuine advance in substantive knowledge.

The Agenda for the Future: What should be the agenda for advocates of quantification during the 1980s and 1990s? The experience of the last generation surely tells us that predictions based on past experience are less than dependable. Promising lines of research have failed to fulfill their promise in the recent past but intimidating obstacles were successfully surmounted in other research areas. We can suggest a number of developments that would be beneficial, if quantification is to be most useful in the historical enterprise during the years ahead. We may be sure that we shall fall short in some respects, exceed expectations in others, and find our energies diverted into unexpected channels.

But in whatever develops, it would be beneficial for both quantifiers and nonquantifiers to realize that there are many different kinds of histories that fulfill useful purposes if they are well done. Some of these genres require the skills of the quantifiers; others do not. We need a profession in which this fact is recognized and in which many members can also conscientiously say:

"we are literary historians and we are quantifiers, as the need of the moment dictates."

Substantive Thrust: The selection of research topics is influenced, both directly and indirectly, by very complex combinations of world and local events, political, economic, and social, by the pressures of public opinion, and by the training, objectives, values, and group origins and allegiances of researchers, as well as by the institutional setting in which they work and by the priorities established by funding agencies. Who, thirty years ago, could have forecast the lively interest in American colonial studies that was to develop among historians? We know that historians will continue to work in economic, political, and social history and that current research thrusts will be projected into the future to some degree. I have suggested elsewhere that the research networks of the Social Science History Association should develop research agenda in their areas of interest, stressing both the bodies of theory and the related quantitative indicators that can be most profitably developed in the future. If prepared, these may be valuable, but we can be sure that they will not be perfect blueprints of what actually occurs. Given this fact we should emphasize developments in the tools of research and in the setting of investigation that will prepare us for the unexpected, as well as for activity that we now believe desirable.[31]

Research Training: Our first priority should be to eliminate the persistent diletantism that we affect in trying to explain the human behavior of the past. A distinguished historian has cautioned against the development of programs that so emphasize "statistical methodology, model building, and knowledge of the social sciences" as to prevent the acquisition of the "broad historical knowledge and wisdom" and the command of sources essential to the historian. Another endorses the practices of "star gazing . . . vagrant earflapping . . . stackstalking . . . [and] crisscross shoptalking" as well as "suit-to-cloth cutting" as satisfactory avenues to interdisciplinary knowledge.

Neither counsel is adequate to our needs. We must eliminate quantitative illiteracy among history students, both undergraduate

---

31 Bogue, "Data Dilemmas," 210–211.

and graduate, and try to make that process as attractive as possible to them. We should provide history courses in which the usefulness of quantitative analysis is demonstrated and statistics presented within the context of historical research. We should also encourage history majors to take the courses in calculus, matrix algebra, and geometry which are essential to a full comprehension of statistical concepts and formulas. We should, at the minimum, require graduate students to meet a quantitative methods requirement sufficiently rigorous to insure that they can understand the literature of quantitative social science. We should also provide them with a range of more advanced optional offerings and workshops that provide a sound understanding of the statistical methods appropriate to historical research and the data-processing expertise necessary to apply them to machine-readable data.[32]

In a world of diminishing resources and shrinking distances the enhancement of cultural understanding appears increasingly vital; one, therefore, hesitates to reduce the language training component in doctoral studies by allowing students to substitute statistical methods for one of the foreign languages that has been traditionally required in the United States. Perhaps we should instead increase the "tool" component in history graduate training absolutely and compensate by reducing the substantive history requirements. Possibily an additional year of training should be required in the doctoral program.

No one can referee manuscripts for historical journals for any period of time without concluding that history graduate programs should place more emphasis upon training in social theory and the logic and methods of research. The manuscripts that cross the referee's desk are often more drastically flawed in these respects than in the marshalling and analysis of quantitative data. The emergence of the new histories and the traditional backlash that it has inspired has left many young historians confused about the proper design of a research article. Overt acceptance of hypothesis testing sometimes leads the traditional editor to complain, "this manuscript does not tell a story." Often the compromise is to pose a question—a device that still robs the result of dramatic

---

32 Lawrence Stone, "History and the Social Sciences in the Twentieth Century," in Delzell, *The Future of History*, 36–37. Hexter, *Doing History* (Bloomington, Ind., 1971), 113.

impact in the eyes of the traditionalist and yet foregoes the precision and rigor of the argument keyed to models and hypotheses.

All historians have preconceptions or theories about human behavior that shape their research in execution and presentation. But is such theory to lurk implicit in narrative description of events or to be stated explicitly? Is history to be dramatic story, legal brief, the step-by-step recital of the detective who advances clue by clue, some genuine, some false, to a solution of a mystery, or the multivariate analysis of quantitative variables in the search for relationships that may explain mass behavior, events, or processes? (And these alternatives do not exhaust the possibilities.) We should not try to rob literary historians of their stock in trade, but we should equip students to understand the various objectives and alternative explanatory forms and methods that are available to them. This involves introducing them to classical theories of social, political, and economic behavior and to modern variants as well. Since nothing is more ridiculous than the use of inappropriate theory, students should learn that, in many cases, they must build their own models. To do so requires training.[33]

Even the work of practicing historians of eminence sometimes displays confusion or carelessness in treating matters of causation and proof. What should be regarded as "root" determinant and what as intervening variable? How can ideological determinants and socioeconomic or ethnocultural variables be incorporated in the same causal explanation? This is perhaps the most important single methodological problem confronting political historians today. What constitutes conclusive evidence or proof? How can research be best designed so that it is not challenged on such grounds? Formal training in social science theory, model building, and in the logic and methods of research is as legitimate and necessary as in quantitative methodology. We should introduce courses, or establish requirements in appropriate departments, to provide such training on both the undergraduate and graduate levels.

33 There is a considerable body of literature that points the way: Hubert M. Blalock, *Theory Construction: From Verbal to Mathematical Formulations* (Englewood Cliffs, 1969); Jerald Hage, *Techniques and Problems of Theory Construction in Sociology* (New York, 1972); McClelland, *Causal Explanation and Model Building in History, Economics, and the New Economic History* (Ithaca, 1975).

Techniques of Quantification: Historians have changed their quantitative technique as they have become familiar with more appropriate measures or as the nature of the historical problems under study has changed. Certainly knowledge of the basic concepts and methods of classical statistics is essential for any quantitative historical researcher of the future, and some argue convincingly that even the political and social historian would do well to develop a full understanding of the econometric applications that have proven so useful across a wide range of problems in economic history. But on the basis of developments in political and social history since 1955, a sound working knowledge of the following areas of statistics seems essential: measures of central tendency and dispersion; probability basics and significance tests, confidence levels, and sampling methods; analysis of variance; regression analysis; the range and details of contingency coefficients; and factor analysis and scaling.

The ability to apply classical statistical techniques to historical data at the level of proficiency demonstrated in the most sophisticated political and social history studies is probably inadequate for the needs of the future. Regression analysis in historical research appears generally thus far in the linear model; curvilinear models should become standard tools. But the basic premises or procedures of classical regression analysis are in various respects constraining. Alternatives or variants are being developed, such as multiple classification, probit, and discriminant analysis. Logit analysis is bringing new power to the analysis of nominal data. We shall hear more of these and other techniques and should understand their uses.

As these latter developments suggest, there is a good deal of reconsideration under way among statisticians today, sparked in part by the inadequacies of the classical methods. Increasingly some statisticians have argued for methods that better fit the unique character of particular data bodies and some advances have been made in the development of "robust" methods of analysis. Stem and leaf and other display techniques, two way decomposition of tables, and other simple methods hold promise. And some of the basic foundations of classical statistics may be used to support quite different analytical procedures in the future.

The intent in improving the statistical abilities of historians should not be, however, to foster such knowledge for itself but rather to insure that they will use the most effective techniques available when they confront quantitative evidence. These methods will not necessarily be the most complex, but rather those guaranteed to extract the most meaning from the data. In the major recent contribution to the theory and philosophy of history that relates most specifically to the new histories, Murphey has emphasized that historical data frequently fail to meet the basic premises of the statistics that are currently available to us. Although unduly pessimistic, the message is an important one. We need a cadre of quantitative historical statisticians to pioneer in the development of statistical methods that are particularly appropriate for the analysis of historical data and in the problems of inference that they involve. (The historian, for instance, confronts missing data problems that his colleagues in related disciplines may currently regard as insuperable.) We should encourage development of methods that are particularly appropriate for historical data but, aside from an improbable crash program of foundation assistance, the route must lie in the dissemination of mathematical and statistical literacy generally among historians. And of great assistance in such developments should be a new text in quantitative methods for historians. Useful though they have been and still are, those now available fall far short of our needs.[34]

The Research Environment: Our general approach to quantitative research can be improved in various respects.

1) We should accept machine-readable data acquisition and maintenance as a routine and essential component of university and other research library budgeting. University librarians and administrators should stop regarding this type of research material as an unwanted and troublesome step-child.

2) The data processing industry at long last should achieve essential breakthroughs in data storage devices, perhaps in terms of the use of fiche, or permanent metallic tape, or some of the other devices currently under development, that will provide a safe, long term, storage medium for machine-readable data.

---

34 Murray G. Murphey, *Our Knowledge of the Historical Past* (Indianapolis, 1973), 134–206. Dollar and Jensen, *Historian's Guide to Statistics*; Floud, *Introduction to Quantitative Methods*.

3) The computer industry should perfect an optical reader scanner that will allow the conversion of book text to machine readable form without respect to type font, or at least with minimal restrictions of the latter kind. This will put the computer at the service of the intellectual historian who analyzes the themes and ideas of other writers. There is an unrecognized implicit quantitative bias in the work of such historians, and computerization of literary classics would enhance this tendency by allowing such quantification to be systematic, thereby greatly simplifying the task of literary analysis of texts. A simple computer command could bring all references to particular themes or ideas, or conjunctions of themes and ideas in an author's works, to hand immediately for study. Not only would this revolutionize intellectual history, it might also go far toward modernizing the attitudes of research librarians, since most would then understand the desirability of having machine-readable versions of standard literary texts freely available.

4) Researchers should have the foresight and organizing ability to prepare the research theory and resource agenda necessary to identify the most desirable types of quantitative data for conversion to machine readable form. Once that essential step has been taken, researchers should organize to ensure the conversion of essential data, building on the experience of the past in these matters.

5) The changing scholarly ethics of the profession should be confirmed to the point where it becomes a matter of course for researchers to place their machine readable data files in depositories at an early point in their research, where they will be easily available to other scholars for replicative and other research. Research funding agencies uniformly should make this an *enforced* requirement of grants in aid of research projects. Accompanying this change should come improvement in general knowledge about the construction of data files so that researchers can use files developed elsewhere with a minimum of difficulty and so that data depositories are not required to expend resources in "cleaning" data files before they can make them available for researchers.

6) All major funding agencies should adjust their support of research in such ways as best to facilitate the foregoing developments.

7) Hysteria over privacy and confidentiality should be muted to the point where public agencies cease efforts to destroy or

indefinitely close valuable sources of quantitative research data and begin constructively to develop policies that make such resources freely available to qualified researchers.

Most of the participants in a recent symposium on "the future of history" in the United States resolutely concentrated upon the past and present of American historiography; they were, their contributions suggest, unwilling to embark upon the treacherous waters of prophecy. Each of us inevitably reads the future differently and must accept the almost certain possibility that our successors will ignore or disagree with our assessment of opportunities. From this writer's perspective, however, various developments in quantitative history appear particularly attractive. The history of American agriculture and rural life before 1850 must be rewritten, utilizing quantifiable data derived from wills and probate inventories. Students of wealth and income have publicized the use of these sources and others have recognized their broader potential. Research of this kind will emphasize the need of sampling methods that are designed to maximize the opportunities of linkage with other data sources, and of providing systems of weighting for age and wealth strata, that are appropriate for the analysis of a society in which the use of the probate process was more common in some segments of the population than in others. The improvement of the analytical techniques of contingency table and regression analysis will be called for in this area of research.

Although extremely useful federal census information about individual farmers and rural residents is available for the years 1850–1880, the student of that era must link the use of probate data to the information derived from census samples. And, as yet, we have too few such samples. Because the Bureau of the Census has destroyed much of the farm-by-farm enumeration data collected since 1900, satisfactory substitutes must be developed for such sources in research on twentieth-century agriculture. These same sources—probate and manuscript census materials—hold great promise for the continuing development of family history.[35]

35 Delzell, *Future of History*. On probate research particularly see Alice Hanson Jones, "Wealth Estimates for the American Middle Colonies," *Economic Development and Cultural Change*, XVIII (1970), 4, pt. 2, 1–172; idem, "Wealth Estimates for the New England Colonies about 1770," *Journal of Economic History*, XXXII (972), 98–127; idem, *American*

In political history the poll-book data that are available in unanticipated richness for the years between 1790 and 1860 promise a veritable revolution in our understanding of antebellum political behavior. These records will not allow us to examine the political behavior of individuals in the detail permitted by modern panel survey analysis. But they will allow us to go part of the way to achieve a deeper understanding of the strengths and weaknesses of the aggregate analysis now in use, and to acquire greater comprehension of the degree to which we can safely apply in antebellum research the theories generated by modern survey analysis.[36]

Such suggestions involve micro-level analysis. Clearly similar opportunities await scholars interested in research at the macro level. Modernization theories have fallen into disrepute, but the individual processes and variables of some developmental analysis are of considerable interest in their own right and may in the future be fitted into more useful models of long-range historical development. We need to develop indices that reflect long-run trends in social, economic, and political processes at both the national level and at lower levels of social and political aggregation. Measures of extraction, distribution, differentiation, democratization, centralization, elite composition, and many others should be constructed, improved, or extended.

A generation of researchers has diligently multiplied case studies in many areas of history. Now scholars should try to fit the findings into broader patterns of historical development, a task that is more difficult than might appear at first glance because of the idiosyncracies of some case studies. In general, we should view the case-study method as permissible only in the initial probing of a research problem. Thereafter, thematic comparative

Colonial Wealth: Documents and Methods (New York, 1977), 3 v., esp. 1. Lawrence M. Friedman, A History of American Law (New York, 1973), 220–221, notes the differential incidence of probate activity.

36   Paul F. Bourke and Donald A. Debats, "Identifiable Voting in Nineteenth-Century America: Toward a Comparison of Britain and the United States before the Secret Ballot," Perspectives in American History, XI (1977–78), 259–288; idem, "Individuals and Aggregates: A Note on Historical Data and Assumptions," Social Science History (forthcoming); see particularly David A. Bohmer, "The Maryland Electorate and the Concept of a Party System in the Early National Period," in Silbey et al., American Electoral Behavior, 146–173.

analysis should be the rule. In this respect too, there will be rich rewards if we can break out of the excessive compartmentalization that has characterized much research. We must view the political system as a whole and avoid excessive concentration on one aspect only, particularly electoral behavior. Recent findings of research in social history or economic history have had more implications for political history than specialists in that field have acknowledged. And there is a particular need also for studies of social, economic, and political change that are developed within a comparative framework from the beginning. Improved understanding of the methods of comparative time series analysis is necessary if such work is to be fully useful.

Other scholars will see even more promising avenues of research in other areas of quantitative history. If these are as potentially fruitful as those touched upon here, the next twenty years of American historiography could be among the most exciting eras in the development of the American historical enterprise.

The New History
The 1980s and Beyond (II)

Economic History in the 1980s

Peter Temin

The Future of the New Economic History The "new" economic history is at a crossroads. Despite its impressive accomplishments during the past two decades, it is losing its ties to economics. Having turned its back on history, it is in danger of drifting aimlessly between two shores. But the new economic history can find its way back to terra firma by giving attention to a particular problem—the "second industrial revolution"—and a particular methodology—the explicit recognition of diverse modes of behavior. Paradoxically, it may be possible to land on both shores at once, to build a land bridge between the disciplines.

I begin by reviewing briefly the accomplishments of the new economic history and its current condition. I then describe the problem of the second industrial revolution and, finally, the method I propose to investigate it. The model of economic behavior lying at the core of this method can be applied generally; it is not restricted to the problem selected for analysis here. On the contrary, I suggest that the general application of a model like this one offers a key to understanding a wide range of economic and historical phenomena.

The new component of the new economic history was its tie to economics. Old economic history is a branch of history; new economic history, a branch of economics. Much was gained by this transfer of allegiance, but—inevitably—some was lost as well. Specifically, the methodological rigor of the new economic history needs to be allied with the willingness to contemplate diverse modes of behavior characteristic of the old economic history.

Phrased differently, the psychology of economics is excessively narrow. It has served the field of economics well, and it has served economic history as well in the investigation of certain

Peter Temin is Professor of Economics at The Massachusetts Institute of Technology. He is the author of *Taking Your Medicine: Drug Regulation in the United States* (Cambridge, Mass., 1980).

0022-1953/81/020179-19 $02.50/0

problems described below. But as our conception of interesting problems changes, so too must our theoretical framework. And for some of the most interesting problems facing us today, a broader strategy—one that admits of alternate modes of behavior—is needed.

The economist's model of a competitive economy provided the theoretical framework for the intellectual explorations of the new economic history. Individuals were seen in isolation, working to accomplish their unwavering goals by a series of discrete exchanges. Firms were conceptualized—in the manner of the United States Supreme Court's construction of the Fourteenth Amendment—as additional individuals, acting similarly to accomplish straightforward goals by means of fair exchanges.

The question for research also came from economics. Economic growth was the topic of the day in that discipline, and economic historians joined the attack on it. Abramovitz and Solow showed in the late 1950s that the economist's model of production explained only a tiny fraction of the United States' economic growth in the twentieth century. The challenge was taken up by Rostow—among others. His *Stages of Economic Growth* provided a vocabulary and a flash point for controversy in the historical approach of economic growth.[1]

North's survey of American economic growth before the Civil War set the stage for a detailed investigation of early industrialization in the United States. That country was, and is, the focus of the new economic history for a combination of reasons. As a result of the decennial census, more complete data for the nineteenth century exist in the United States than in any other country. In addition, since the academic support for the new economic history came from departments of economics at American universities, it was natural to work on the United States. And, finally, the new economic history is by and large an English-language activity.[2]

---

1 Moses Abramovitz, "Resources and Output in the U.S. since 1870," *American Economic Review, Papers and Proceedings,* XLIV (1956), 5–23; Robert M. Solow, "Technical Change and the Aggregate Production Function," *Review of Economics and Statistics,* XXXIX (1957), 312–320; Walt W. Rostow, *The Stages of Economic Growth: A Non-Communist Manifesto* (Cambridge, 1960).
2 Douglass C. North, *The Economic Growth of the United States: 1790 to 1860* (Englewood Cliffs, 1961).

North said that the United States, like Gaul, was divided into three parts, and he raised questions about the divergent patterns of growth in the three regions and about their interaction. Fogel and Fislow analyzed the role of railroads in effecting the unification of the country's economic regions, debunking some earlier extravagant claims for the iron horse that had been made in an excess of historical enthusiasm. They investigated the railroad as a construction activity and as a means of transport, but not as an organizational form. As with most economics, the internal workings of railroad organizations were ignored. This appears to be the result of an implicit assumption that the organizational form used to accomplish an objective does not matter. As economists often say in the classroom, it does not matter whether capital hires labor or labor hires capital.[3]

Zevin and David examined the cotton textile industry in America, attempting to measure and explain the pace of technological change in the premier industry of the industrial revolution. I examined technological progress in the iron and steel industry in a similar vein, providing a counterpart to the focus on cotton and iron in most accounts of the English industrial revolution. More generally, a variety of people fiercely debated Habakkuk's suggestion that the cause for all of this American inventiveness lay not in Yankee ingenuity, but rather in the high cost of American labor.[4]

These investigations, and numerous others that followed them, were directed at the question of technological change and through that question at the puzzle of economic growth. The new economic historians' interest, or even their obsession, with slavery—as shown in the myriad responses to the classic work of

3 Robert W. Fogel, *Railroads and American Economic Growth: Essays in Econometric History* (Baltimore, 1964); Albert Fishlow, *American Railroads and the Transformation of the Ante-Bellum Economy* (Cambridge, Mass., 1965).

4 Robert B. Zevin, "The Growth of Cotton Textile Production After 1815," in Fogel and Stanley L. Engerman (eds.), *The Reinterpretation of American Economic History* (New York, 1971); Paul A. David, *Technical Choice Innovation and Economic Growth: Essays on American and British Experience in the Nineteenth Century* (Cambridge, 1975), 95–191; Temin, *Iron and Steel in Nineteenth-Century America: An Economic Inquiry* (Cambridge, Mass., 1964); H. J. Habakkuk, *American and British Technology in the Nineteenth Century: The Search for Labour-Saving Inventions* (Cambridge, 1962); Temin, "Labor Scarcity in America," *Journal of Interdisciplinary History*, I (1971), 251–264; David, *Technical Choice*, ch. 1 and the references cited there.

Conrad and Meyer and the more recent, controversial, account by Fogel and Engerman—constitutes an exception to this rule. But, as we shall see, it is an exception that proves a rule.[5]

The accomplishments of the new economic history during the 1960s were summarized in a series of collective volumes. Davis, Easterlin, and Parker edited a volume consisting of invited essays by a dozen new economic historians and summarizing the findings of the subdiscipline to that date. Its subtitle, *An Economist's History of The United States,* clearly signalled the authors' renunciation of traditional history. A contemporaneous volume edited by Fogel and Engerman reproduced no less than three dozen articles of the new economic history. Its title, *The Reinterpretation of American Economic History,* similarly proclaimed the break with the traditional methods and results of economic history.[6]

What were the accomplishments of this research? They may be grouped under three headings. First, we now possess a much more complete description of the American economy before the Civil War than anyone believed possible a generation ago. Second, we have a collection of observations—one hesitates to call them conclusions—about the nature of technological change. And third, we have a test of the competitive model. In the words of Parker:

> This is in good part what the new economic history is about: it is a gigantic test of the hypothesis of economic rationality of a system and of the behavior of individuals within it. It turns out that after all the market has really worked very well. Should the southerners have invested in slaves? Yes, they were earning a normal rate of return. Should the railroads have been financed by generous land grants? Yes, the returns were just sufficient to cover the risks of such an investment. Should the Pennsylvania iron industry have clung to charcoal as long as it did? Yes, there was a good cost justification for its shifting to anthracite, then to coke just when it did. Should the reaper have been introduced in the 1850s? Yes, any earlier its introduction would not have been profitable.[7]

5 Alfred H. Conrad and John R. Meyer, "The Economics of Slavery in the Antebellum South," *Journal of Political Economy,* LXIV (1958), 95–130; Fogel and Engerman, *Time on the Cross* (Boston, 1974), 2 v.

6 Lance E. Davis, Richard A. Easterlin, and William N. Parker (eds.), *American Economic Growth: An Economist's History of the United States* (New York, 1972); Fogel and Engerman, *Reinterpretation.*

7 In addition to the sources already cited, see National Bureau of Economic Research,

The new economic history's contributions to the history of slavery can be seen in this context. First Conrad and Meyer and then Fogel and Engerman more strongly asserted that even an institution so far removed from the free market as slavery operated in America in ways predicted by the competitive model. Although not part of the general inquiry into economic growth, the study of slavery both contributed to our knowledge of the early nineteenth-century economy and "tested" the economists' model. It would not be a gross distortion to say that the storm that greeted Fogel and Engerman's study was induced by professional opposition to the extension of the economists' model of free choice to "the peculiar institution."[8]

It would be difficult to say that many strong conclusions about the nature of economic growth have emerged from this inquiry. Our knowledge has been summarized in a fragment from a larger, unpublished work characterizing nineteenth-century American economic growth. Abramovitz and David showed that the United States' economic growth in the nineteenth century came from the shift of workers out of agriculture into other occupations and the concomitant rise in the capital employed per worker. This shift started at the beginning of the century and was largely exhausted by its end; nineteenth-century American economic growth thus differed from the kind of economic change both preceding and following it.[9]

The new economic historians therefore followed the intellectual track of the economics profession. For economists had begun to realize as the 1970s began that economic growth was too complex to be understood easily and too slow for its consequences to be seen quickly. As the economic consequences of the Vietnam War and the OPEC price rise began to be felt, economists turned their attention toward macroeconomic questions.

Unfortunately, most macroeconomic questions are short run

Trends in the American Economy in the Nineteenth Century (Princeton, 1960); *idem, Output, Employment, and Productivity in the United States after 1800* (New York, 1966). On the nature of technological change see, for example, David, *Technical Choice*; Nathan Rosenberg, *Perspectives on Technology* (Cambridge, 1976). Parker, "From Old to New to Old in Economic History," *Journal of Economic History*, XXXI (1971), 6.

8 See David et al., *Reckoning with Slavery* (New York, 1976).

9 Abramovitz and David, "Towards Historically Relevant Parables of Growth," *American Economic Review, Papers and Proceedings*, LXIII (1973), 428–439.

in nature, and the investigation of them has been ahistorical. New economic historians consequently continued to work in their accustomed fields, while the discipline of economics moved away from them. Occasionally forays into macroeconomic history, like Friedman and Schwartz's *A Monetary History of the United States,* my much more modest analysis of the Great Depression, and accompanying studies, provided a bridge between the new economic history and economics proper, but one that was seldom crossed.[10]

Southern economic history provides another tenuous link between economics and the new economic history.[11] The attempt to chronicle the progress of the southern economy and of freedmen within this economy after the Civil War casts light on the current problems of integration in the United States. But although historical studies have begun to illuminate a relatively dark area, economists have preferred to analyze discrimination in a typically ahistorical way. As with macroeconomics, problems of integration have provided more of a potential than an actual bridge between the subdisciplines.[12]

The independence of economic history is in part an inevitable result of its growth. Any group of scholars acquires a separate identity as it grows larger. But there is reason to think that the new economic history is too small a field to "go it alone." There are no departments of economic history in the United States, and economic historians consequently need to be accepted as peers either by economists or historians to find employment. Having rejected links to historians in the 1960s, it is dangerous to have renounced the concerns of economists in the 1970s.

American economic historians can do well by repairing bridges both to traditional historians and to at least some economists. This is possible because there is a convergence of interest between some historians and economists that offers a fruitful field for research.

If the old questions can be seen as an inquiry into the nature

10 Milton Friedman and Anna J. Schwartz, *A Monetary History of the United States* (Princeton, 1963); Temin, *Did Monetary Forces Cause the Great Depression?* (New York, 1976).

11 For example, Roger L. Ransom and Richard Sutch, *One Kind of Freedom: The Economic Consequences of Emancipation* (Cambridge, 1977); Gavin Wright, *The Political Economy of the Cotton South* (New York, 1978).

12 See Gary S. Becker, *The Economics of Discrimination* (Chicago, 1957).

and causes of the industrial revolution, the new questions can be described similarly as an inquiry into the nature and causes of the "second industrial revolution" of the late nineteenth and early twentieth centuries. And if the results of the old inquiry described the nineteenth-century American economy as conforming to the economist's model of a competitive economy, the results of the new inquiry should be an analysis of the shift away from those conditions that began approximately a century ago.

The changes taking place in the Progressive period can be—and have been—described in many different ways. Abramovitz and David approached them abstractly. They first noted that the growth of real gross domestic product per capita was almost exactly the same in the latter half of the nineteenth century as in the first quarter of the twentieth. They then observed that although less than one third of the nineteenth-century growth could be attributed to the rise in conventional factor productivity, close to nine tenths of the twentieth-century growth could be attributed to this component. The latter result replicates Solow's classic finding. The former shows how great the contrast was between the period studied by Solow and the preceding epoch.[13]

Changes in conventional factor productivity are calculated as residuals, and they have been characterized as a measure of our ignorance. Nonetheless, most economists and economic historians regard them as evidence of changes in technology. Under this interpretation, the Progressive period witnessed a decisive change in the rate of technological change.

This change, in addition to increasing the output from given inputs, gave rise to a new form of business organization. Chandler characterized a modern business organization as a firm which has many different operating units and which is managed by a hierarchy of salaried executives. He then chronicled the way in which technological changes gave rise to modern business organizations, first separately in distribution and production and then in firms that combined both of these activities. These organizations had not arisen before the late nineteenth century because of the absence of a railroad-based distribution network. They used the railroads

13   The contrast is even sharper than the aggregate numbers show, since the shift of labor out of agriculture into more productive activities in the nineteenth century might have been expected to raise conventional factor productivity more rapidly than in the twentieth. Abramovitz and David, "Parables of Growth."

both as a means of transport and as an organizational model, and they appeared in different industries as new technologies were introduced in these industries. While it may be going too far to characterize Chandler as a technological determinist, changes in technology seem in his narrative to be the exogenous events that induce changes in businesss organization.[14]

Changes in the organization of product markets were mirrored in changes in the organization of labor markets. Before the late nineteenth century much of the work in factories was done by a subcontracting system. The manager of a factory contracted with a foreman to get a job done, and the foreman then allocated, augmented, or diminished his labor force to do the job. Although managers retained some control over the way work was done, this control was limited by the institutional framework within which it was done. As modern business organizations grew, they exerted more direct control over the work processes for which they paid. They circumvented and eliminated the traditional foremen and substituted a hierarchy internal to the firm for the previous hierarchies within occupational classes. With cavalier disregard for the meaning of words, the new hierarchy has been termed by economists "the internal labor market."[15]

The changes in product and labor markets were not lost on contemporaries. They felt themselves to be in the midst of a rapid and important transformation of their economic lives. And, according to most modern observers of the scene, they felt themselves dislocated by the change. This sense of frustration has been described similarly by different authors. Hofstadter noted that: "All groups with claims to learning and skill shared a common sense of humiliation and common grievance against the plutocracy." Wiebe concurred and extended the thought: "The incomprehensible ways of the corporation were also alienating a multitude of wage earners. Rapidly losing control over their working lives, they knew only that decisions made somewhere else pushed them about like so many cattle." And Haskell summarized the perception in a vivid metaphor: "Like a sheet of chain mail

14 Alfred D. Chandler, *The Visible Hand: The Managerial Revolution in American Business* (Cambridge, Mass., 1977).

15 Daniel Nelson, *Managers and Workers: Origins of the New Factory System in the United States, 1880–1920* (Madison, 1975). Peter Doeringer and Michael Piore, *Internal Labor Markets and Manpower Analysis* (Lexington, Mass, 1971).

stretched taut, the individual links of what had been a remarkably slack society lost a degree of freedom and found themselves constrained by forces transmitted through adjacent links." The similarity of these quotes is striking. If it represents the results of independent research, as opposed to the progressive development of a single idea, it shows the pervasiveness of the chronicled attitudes.[16]

Feelings of humiliation, alienation, and constraint generated a demand for government action. This action was directed at the perceived cause of the problem: the modern business organization. The Interstate Commerce Act of 1877 implemented one approach to the problem. By creating the Interstate Commerce Commission, the federal government accepted the existence of large business firms and attempted to regulate their actions for the public good. The Sherman Antitrust Act of 1890 articulated another approach: refusal to accept the existence of these firms. The debate over these positions, about whether to regulate or to outlaw monopoly firms, continued throughout the Progressive period. Congress' failure to resolve the issue is shown by the passage in 1914 of acts embodying both approaches. The Clayton Act expanded on the cryptic Sherman Act and made specific anticompetitive actions illegal. The Federal Trade Commission Act established another regulatory commission for the purpose of maintaining competition through regulation.[17]

The conventional narrative that ties these events together sees the growth of large business organizations as the result of profit opportunities opened up by new technologies. Government intervention was a response to the new firms, an attempt to destroy or control them. This story, attractive though it is, has problems. In particular, it fails to resolve two problems of increasing interest to scholars. First, the motives controlling the growth of large firms is not clear. Various people have suggested that large firms were created to increase capitalists' control over workers or to increase firms' control over markets, not to exploit new technol-

16   Richard Hofstadter, *The Age of Reform* (New York, 1955), 149; Robert H. Wiebe, *The Search for Order, 1877–1920* (New York, 1967), 36; Thomas L. Haskell, *The Emergence of Professional Social Science: The American Social Science Association and the Crisis of Authority* (Urbana, Ill., 1977), 36.
17   William Letwin, *Law and Economic Policy: The Evolution of the Sherman Antitrust Act* (New York, 1965).

ogies.[18] Second, people have noted that many of the government's actions missed their apparent mark and that many of these actions—those that were both on and off target—had curiously little effect on the problems that they were designed to cure.[19]

These problems with the conventional story can best be resolved by recasting the traditional story. This recasting will be accomplished by introducing a new vocabulary and then applying it to the second industrial revolution.

In the presence of uncertainty, people act differently, depending both on who they are and what situation they face. The different types of behavior can be grouped into three distinct "modes" of behavior without asserting that anyone follows any single mode all the time. On the contrary, most people switch from one mode to another as conditions vary or as they are called upon to play different roles in society.

The first mode may be characterized as *instrumental*. This is the type of behavior that economists assume prevails in market settings. It is represented most often by the abstraction of the *homo economicus* or the profit-maximizing firm, ceaselessly striving to attain a unitary goal against the constraints imposed by the actions of other, similarly-minded individuals or firms. Since a person or firm in the instrumental mode acts consistently, in the sense that no sequence of his actions leads to an outcome in conflict with an outcome reached by a different chain, instrumental behavior is often called rational.

Economists assume almost automatically that people engaged in market behavior act instrumentally or rationally. Other social scientists almost automatically assume that they do not. The necessity to choose between the polar alternatives has isolated economics within the social sciences, although there are isolated signs of rapprochement. Instead of choosing sides, however, I propose a middle ground which asserts that people act in this way part of

18 For a general statement of this position, extending beyond the United States in the late nineteenth century, see Stephen A. Marglin, "What Do Bosses Do? The Origins and Functions of Hierarchy in Capitalist Production," *Review of Radical Political Economics*, VI (1974), 13–54.

19 See, for example, W. A. Jordan, "Producer Protection, Prior Market Structure and the Effects of Government Regulation," *Journal of Law and Economics*, XV (1972), 151–176.

the time. The question is not whether people act this way, but when they act this way.[20]

The second ideal type of behavior is *customary* or traditional behavior. People acting in the customary mode do today more or less what they did yesterday. I say "more or less" because it often appears to them that they are repeating their previous pattern when they are in fact deviating from it. This can happen because of faulty memories, because the context in which the actions take place has changed, so that familiar actions no longer seem familiar, or because a variation introduced by someone else has become incorporated into the tradition. It can happen because the customs or habits are not hard and fast, not published in a code of regulations. They are implicit in people's actions, not explicit.

An example of customary behavior is provided by the organizational theory of the firm. Industrial firms are repositories of customary behavior in this theory. They operate by means of rules of thumb that are honored so long as they produce results that provide a minimum level of organizational well-being. When the rules of thumb fail to achieve this minimum level, they are replaced temporarily by a search for better rules—that is, by instrumental behavior.[21]

The third mode of behavior is *command* behavior. This mode is the product of a context in which one person can order another to perform or refrain from performing a specific action and can impose penalties for noncompliance. In some contexts these sanctions may be legal. In others they may consist of excluding the noncomplier from the context of the order, as in firing a recalcitrant employee. In still others the sanctions may be various forms of physical violence. Although firms as a whole may exhibit customary behavior, they rely on command behavior in most of their internal workings.[22]

There are two striking differences between customary and

20 See Richard R. Nelson and Sidney G. Winter, "Toward an Evolutionary Theory of Economic Capabilities," *American Economic Review, Papers and Proceedings,* LXIII (1973), 440–449; Oliver E. Williamson, *Markets and Hierarchies: Analysis and Antitrust Implications* (New York, 1975); Herbert A. Simon, "Rational Decision Making in Business Organizations," *American Economic Review,* LXIX (1979), 493–513.

21 R. M. Cyert and J. G. March, *A Behavioral Theory of the Firm* (Englewood Cliffs, 1963).

22 The terms customary and command are taken from John R. Hicks, *A Theory of Economic History* (London, 1969), 9–15.

command behavior. Change comes about in the former without the consciousness of the people involved; it appears in the latter as a result of the decisions of identifiable individuals. And while customary behavior constrains all actors more or less equally, command behavior recognizes a hierarchy in which only some people have the ability to direct behavior and make the changes in behavior to which I have just alluded.

The form of personal interaction differs between modes. The characteristic means of communication in instrumental behavior is explicit exchange. People barter or pay money for goods or services that they want; they can balance the benefit to themselves of having these goods or services against the cost. The characteristic means of interaction in command behavior, clearly, is a command or order. And in the customary mode, the typical means of personal interaction is reciprocity, with the affect that accompanies it. As befits the nature of this mode, reciprocity is informal and nonquantitative. Reciprocity cannot be added up like a price, nor can it be formally itemized like an order. Yet we all experience reciprocity in our daily lives, and only the most callous would deny its importance.[23]

This discussion of communication can be stood on its head to suggest a way of telling which mode of behavior is being observed. Since each mode has its characteristic form of communication, the mode of behavior in use can be inferred from the type of communication observed. But this test, although unobjectionable on logical grounds, often is difficult to apply. Reciprocity and affect can be implicit in a relationship and difficult to observe without a careful inquiry. Their qualitative nature eludes quantification, giving rise to possible conflicts of interpretation. And although they always are present in customary relationships, they may also appear in the context of other modes of behavior. This test needs to be supplemented with another.

Just such a second test emerges naturally from the description of the three modes of behavior. A person acting in the instrumental mode evaluates actions by their results. He compares the *output* of his activities against some explicit or implicit standard. A person acting in the customary mode ignores the results of his

23 George Homans, "Social Behavior as Exchange," *American Journal of Sociology*, LXIII (1958), 597–606; A. W. Gouldner, "The Norm of Reciprocity: A Preliminary Statement," *American Sociological Review*, XXV (1960), 161–178.

actions; he concentrates on the actions themselves, on the *inputs* to a set of activities. He compares the actions he performs with a set of loosely defined—if explicitly defined at all—norms.

Command behavior differs from both instrumental and customary behavior in these same dimensions. In contrast to the former, a person acting in the command mode evaluates actions by examining the actions themselves. And in contrast to the latter, he evaluates these actions by reference to an explicitly formulated set of directions emanating from an identifiable source.

Institutional arrangements or structures can be grouped into three types, parallel with the three modes of behavior. Customary behavior thrives in what we may call *community* settings, where informal interactions and continuing relationships are the norm. The existence of a community allows the informal reciprocity characteristic of customary behavior to take place, and the continuity of a community encourages the growth of affect that accompanies the reciprocal actions. Instrumental behavior can be used to its best advantage in *market* settings, where the explicit exchanges needed to pursue a unified set of goals are facilitated by the institutional surrounding. And command behavior needs *hierachical* institutions, whether formal or informal, for its operation.

This three-fold classification scheme of institutions follows from and parallels the division of behavior into three modes. As with the modes, this list of institutions consists of ideal types, and any particular institution may partake of qualities of more than one of the ideal types. For the purpose of this argument, all that is needed is that actual institutions may be grouped easily and consistently into these three categories and that transitions between institutional forms can be identified and distinguished from the ongoing operation of continuing institutions.

Transitions, of course, are critical. Each type of institution is linked to a mode of behavior, and each mode of behavior similarly is linked to a different class of institutions. There is, as a result, a tendency for behavior and institutions to come together according to the correspondence between them, although this tendency may be worked out over a long period of time—or not at all if conditions change in the interim. And, changes in behavior have stronger effects on the structure of institutions than changes in institutions have on the mode of behavior, so that a change in the mode of behavior is more likely to lead to an institutional change than an insitutional change is to produce a change in the mode of behavior.[24]

The late nineteenth century produced many changes in the daily lives of ordinary people. As already noted, these changes had many dimensions, among which was the weakening of local communities and the integration of individuals into national markets both as consumers and as workers. Even though local consumption and production had been responsive to national and even international market forces before this period, the last few stages of distribution and the unit of employment had been local. The local organizations performing these functions progressively were absorbed into national firms at the end of the nineteenth century.

This movement weakened the hold of local communities on behavior as well as altering the conditions of both consumption and employment. Most people acted customarily in their ordinary actions before this transformation, and these people—like business firms no longer earning satisfactory profits from their customary rules of thumb—found themselves forced into an instrumental mode of behavior as they adapted to the rapidly changing conditions. The "closing of the frontier" is better understood as the destruction of the local community structure than as the end of land settlement.

Some people responded to the change in their local environment by adopting instrumental behavior. Their role in the formation of large firms followed along the lines described by Chandler. But many more people, I suggest, responded to the new conditions by switching into command behavior and generating a demand for new hierarchies.

It is not possible after a century to reconstruct motives with great exactitude, but two kinds of evidence suggest the prevalence of command behavior. First, as Chandler noted, not all large firms were started in response to profit opportunities newly opened up by an emerging technology. Many new firms were formed, only to fail because they did not lead to any economies of production or distribution. Second, although some firms did exploit profit opportunities and flourish, it is difficult even now

24 Temin, "Modes of Economic Behavior," *Journal of Economic Behavior and Organization,* I (1980), 175–195.

to discover where in the production process those profit opportunities lay. Many of the entrepreneurs who were successful must have been similarly unable to comprehend the implications of the new technology. They were lucky rather than smart, and the proportion of entrepreneurs acting instrumentally was smaller than the proportion of new firms that succeeded. Third, people tried to create hierarchies outside the manufacturing sector where technological change was not apparent. Being unable to put together a national organization unaided, these other groups enlisted the government in a variety of regulatory and licensing arrangements. These arrangements differed from the large business firms, but they still imposed hierarchical structures on people's behavior.[25]

This approach resolves some of the problems with the conventional story. It recognizes a variety of motives, many unconnected with the exploitation of specific new production methods, for the formation of large firms. The conventional story is admitted as part, but only part, of the transformation of American industry. In addition, the "failure" of government action to suppress or control this activity is seen to be failure only in terms of the conventional story. Much of the government action represented attempts to parallel the hierarchical constructions of the private economy. Its aim was to add to the movement toward a new organization of the economy, not to oppose it.

This approach also clarifies another debate in the literature, one which focuses on the motives of entrepreneurs. One school, represented by Chandler, assumes that entrepreneurs responded to profit opportunities. A quite separate line of inquiry denies the importance of profits in favor of social control. In this view, the governing motive for organizational change was power, not profits. Changes in organizations were episodes in the class struggle, and technology was developed in response to the needs of owners to control their work force.[26]

The difficulties of investigating questions of causation are well known. To observe that events accompany each other is

25 Chandler, The Visible Hand, 315. Lawrence Friedman, "Freedom of Contract and Occupational Licensing, 1890–1910: A Legal and Social Study," California Law Review, LIII (1965), 487–534; Morton Keller, Affairs of State: Public Life in Late Nineteenth Century America (Cambridge, Mass., 1977).
26 Katherine Stone, "The Origins of Job Structure in the Steel Industry," Review of Radical Political Economics, VI (1974), 61–97.

only to suggest that there is some relationship between them. The observation itself seldom gives direct evidence on the nature of the relationship. A model with assumptions about behavior is necessary to specify the connection, and more than one model may fit the observed data. In the case in point, we observe neither the profits of the large firms at the point of creation nor the locus of power on the shop floor. We infer both of these from other events according to our view of the world. If we assume that businessmen were concerned only with profits, then it is natural to see the expansion of certain business forms as the response to profit opportunities. But if we think that businessmen were oriented toward questions of power, then it is equally easy to see the expansion of these forms as an attempt to seize power. Since most changes probably involved both profits and control, it will be difficult to find evidence to exclude one motive or another.

Toharia recently described one episode where the motives appear distinct. He analyzed the mechanization of the foundry in the McCormick reaper works in 1885–86. This department was the locus of intense union activity, and the new casting machines obviated the need for the unionized, skilled workers. Toharia argued that this change in the technology was an attempt by McCormick to seize control from the union of a critical part of the production process. Although Toharia could not observe the profits from using the new machines directly, he did note that they were abandoned shortly after the union was broken. Other explanations of this sequence are possible, but he interpreted this sequence of events as a deliberate attempt to shift the balance of power, in which new machines were used only to shift the power balance and not to increase production or lower costs. Whether this conclusion can be maintained and generalized is an open and intensely interesting question.[27]

The new approach acknowledges the debate between profits and control to be irreconcilable. It is not clear that the two motives are distinct, that it is not necessary often to exert control in order to make profits. More important, to the extent that the changes were an attempt to provide institutions conformable with command behavior, there was no need for the participants themselves

27 Luis Toharia, "The Division of Labor and the Historical Development of the Internal Labor Market: A Case Study of the McCormick Works of Chicago, 1848–1902," unpub. Ph.D. diss. (MIT, 1979).

to make discriminations between alternative objectives. In other words, the existing debate focuses on the goals of actions, whereas the revised story concentrates on the actions themselves. The conventional story inquires into goals; the new one, into processes.

It follows from the new approach that attempts to turn back the clock and regain the institutional structure of an earlier period are doomed to failure. Neither destroying the profit incentives nor the opportunities for social control—if that were possible— would change the mode of behavior and the consequent drive to create hierarchies. People have turned away from the market as an institution, and demonstrations that it can achieve a stated goal will only seldom overcome people's dislike for market institutions.

These conclusions have been stated baldly and without an overwhelming array of sources. But that is as it should be. The purpose of this article is to propose hypotheses and approaches to problems that can be confirmed, refuted, or modified by future work. The preceding statements therefore should be taken as tentative hypotheses which should become the subjects of more careful studies.

Future studies could follow several lines. The analysis of modes and institutions could be expanded and formalized.[28] Such an analysis could be applied to specific industries or changes in government actions. In each case, attention needs to be directed to the processes involved, not just to the results. This will be a big step for economists, since the normal procedure in that discipline is to ignore the processes internal to large organizations. There are exceptions to this tendency, as noted above, and I want to encourage students to concentrate on the exceptions rather than the norm.

The role of the railroad provides a case in point. New economic historians have looked at the financing, the construction, the profitability, and the cost-reducing effects of the railroads, but not at the internal operations of the railroad firms themselves. These historians have assumed implicitly that the organization and operation of railroad companies were not difficult or interesting tasks, that noting the existence of economies of scale was

---

28   I have begun such an analysis in Temin, "Modes of Economic Behavior."

a sufficient explanation for the emergence of large railroad companies. Business historians, by contrast, have looked on the railroads as a new kind of activity which developed techniques of operation later used throughout the economy. Scheduling, management of cash flows, security, internal communication, and cost accounting are the kinds of tasks noted by these historians. Their implicit assumption is that the discovery and implementation of techniques to deal with these problems was neither trivial nor costless.[29]

In the terms introduced here, the creation of large firms was the creation of new hierarchical institutions. In the economist's jargon, new economic historians have looked on the creation of these hierarchies as a movement along a known production function, whereas business historians have looked on it as a shift of production function—as technical change. The latter view seems to offer the larger possibility for study. The spread of the institutions could be studied in the way that other technical changes have been analyzed, and the relationship of the new institutions to individual behavior can be explored through the behavioral theory of the firm and the theory of internal labor markets.

Government regulation of medicinal drugs provides another example. The Food and Drug Administration has imposed a variety of institutional structures on the sale of drugs in the United States. Every drug has to be approved by the FDA before it can be marketed, and most drugs need in addition to be prescribed by a doctor to be sold. This hierarchy looks quite dissimilar from the hierarchy in a large firm, and it appears to have arisen from dissimilar causes. Yet the mixture of customary and command behavior seen in the large firm can be seen also in the selection of prescription drugs, and the creation of this hierarchy was the result of changes in the environment that induced people to abandon customary behavior, much as the changes in the economy in the Progressive period led to a similar and more general shift.[30]

The analysis of government policies raises policy questions that the study of private corporations does not. For we can—to some limited degree—choose the extent of governmental hierar-

29 Compare for example, the treatment of railroads in Fogel, *Railroads,* and Fishlow, *American Railroads,* with their treatment in Chandler, *The Visible Hand.*
30 Temin, *Taking Your Medicine: Drug Regulation in the United States* (Cambridge, Mass., 1980).

chies that we want. And although individuals have rejected customary behavior for choosing potent medicines, doctors rely on this mode far more than is generally acknowledged. The value of medical customs consequently is an important question for current policy. Understanding the evolution of regulatory structures will aid in the re-examination of these institutions as they operate today.

Economists are beginning to acknowledge that the world does not conform very well to their abstractions, and that the fit has diminished over the last century. Yet they have been unwilling to abandon their powerful tools of analysis in favor of the less formal ones of other social sciences. The approach outlined here does not reject the economic model of behavior. It sees it as one model among several, suitable for the analysis of some—but not all—problems. It suggests that economic historians are well situated to work at the edge of the economics discipline and document the limits of any particular construction of behavior.

Historians who have been ambivalent, at best, toward the new economic history can see this approach as an attempt to broaden the new economic history, to bring economic history and, perhaps, economics into greater touch with the diversity of human behavior that has been the mainstay of all history. The new economic history, like the Phoenix, could emerge with new strength from its current parlous condition.

Economic History in the 1980s

Barry Supple

Old Problems and New Directions   Practitioners
of what has been called "good, old-fashioned economic history"
will no doubt be alarmed at the prospect of even more rapid, if
not always radical, change in the 1980s—if only because many of
them are just becoming accustomed to the changes which have
washed over the discipline in the last twenty years or so. Now,
however, even devotees of the former mode argue that it must
give way to something different, perhaps broader and more "hu-
mane" in scope and orientation. Although many traditionalists
have firmly resisted the new methodology, others have tried to
accommodate themselves to it; and, having made an effort to find
their bearings aboard a relatively new ship, they will be chastened
to learn either that it is sailing in the wrong direction or that it is
probably going to sink anyway. Recent contributions to the field
reflect serious dissatisfaction with the core topics of—or the most
publicized trends in—economic history as it has recently evolved.
A common concern, therefore, is to find ways in which the
discipline might be revived and reincorporated into broader
streams of historical scholarship.

Two approaches to the methodological discussions are of
particular interest. The first envisages a shift in the focus of analytical attention. Peter Temin's article in this volume is a good
example, advocating a reform which concentrates on economic
structures and approaching an institutional understanding through
the use of conceptual tools fashioned around the *diversity* of human
behavior. The second approach is less concerned with spelling
out a new sub-field of research and argumentation than indicating
ways in which economic history has become isolated, and advocating a more positive recognition of its basic community of
interest with the newly fashionable—and rapidly proliferating—
fields of social and cultural history.

Barry Supple is Professor of Economic History at the University of Cambridge. His most
recent book is *Essay in Business History* (Oxford, 1977).

0022-1953/81/020199-7 $02.50/0

My own comments begin with questions which have been raised about developments in Britain. British economic history has been increasingly characterized by quantitative techniques and large-scale projects, but it has lost none of its notorious insularity. Its methodologies and research topics (although they reflect innovative tendencies over the last generation or so) are likely to be constrained by institutional rigidities and inertia; and, quite apart from the dangers of conceptual aridity, there is a sense in which British economic history is defining itself into a contraction. The principal evidence for this is not only the proliferation of regional and thematic specialisms within economic history, but also the rise to a new popularity (perhaps a new dominance) of social history in a variety of seductive forms.

Such trends as these do not all give grounds for comparable anxieties. We cannot even extrapolate them all and maintain consistency. For example, we may occasionally worry about stagnation or even contraction of an area of scholarship—but these are relative terms, and (as Stone argues at the end of his article) even family history cannot grow forever, just as growth in universities or in economies cannot continue smoothly, let alone indefinitely. More important, not only does the large-scale manipulation of data lend itself to a fruitful proliferation of the topics with which economic historians are concerned, but there has also been a striking development of sub-specialties as well as techniques—a growth which enriches the subject by diversification. From the outside, diversification may seem like splintering and the isolation of separate parts; from the inside it may be the inevitable accompaniment of intellectual evolution.[1]

The degree to which academic and intellectual trends are causes for anxiety or calls to action depends in large part on how we explain them. Although the intellectual costs and risks of separate institutionalization within economic history should not be forgotten, the spirit which lies behind specialization can also be warmly welcomed. For it can also reflect a new sense of the appropriate *regional* contexts within which to study economic as well as social and cultural processes; a healthy dissatisfaction with excessively *general* treatments of those processes; and a desire to

1 Lawrence Stone, "Family History in the 1980s: Past Achievements and Future Trends," *Journal of Interdisciplinary History*, XII (1981), 87.

define and thereby concentrate attention on, say, agricultural structure and techniques, the economic role of transportation, the dynamics of population change, or the evolution of cities.

In these respects economic history is no different from other types of historical scholarship or, indeed, from the social sciences in general: specialization can be the product of the worst sort of exclusive trade-union or introspective guild mentality; but it can also flow from a perfectly reasonable desire for sophistication and deeper understanding. This is not to say that the results of specialization are always healthy: they can be arid, antiquarian, and anecdotal. But the fact remains that (as in those other disciplines which exemplify the trend towards specialization) we are dealing not with a fashionable whim, but with the outcome of broad and powerful influences: the devising of more powerful techniques; the development of a much greater appetite for precision in generalization; the ability to locate and deploy—occasionally even to create—a much richer supply of data; and the reverberations of the sheer accumulation of knowledge. Specialization in this context is both inevitable and desirable.

Specialization has its costs—most notably in the avoiding of big and interesting questions—yet at the end of the day its best practitioners will have to come to terms with larger themes. Such a reintegration of knowledge and research is already evident in such specialist areas as demographic, urban, and agricultural history, the practitioners of which address themselves to all-embracing questions concerning social and economic evolution. The inner logic of the subject (as distinct from the managerial influences of research councils or even conference organizers) will contrive to press the boundaries outwards—as they are also manifestly being pressed outwards in the best examples of social history.

This last parallel is not fortuitous, for the most important issue relates not to the splintering of economic history but, rather, to the boom in social history—its transformation from what we may call its proto-Trevelyan stage to its apparent conquest of economic history in the battle for the hearts and minds of students and professional scholars.

The origins of this shift seem to lie less in any explicit dissatisfaction with the tools and topics of "classic" economic history in the 1960s and 1970s than in the mood and mode in which intellectuals (and especially Western intellectuals) came to perceive modern society in the 1950s and 1960s. That perception was in part a recognition of the subtle, complex, non-quantifiable aspects of the social condition—the inner relationships of things: of drains, environment, culture, and *mentalités,* rather than growth rates and real wages. But the new-found popularity of social history was only partly related to the intrinsic scholarship which generated it. That response also reflected the ever-present desire for easy generalization and intellectual short-cuts. The fact is that some social history, like some sociology, *does* appeal to the desire for *easy* knowledge, for the confirmation of social prejudice. And in that respect an understanding of the flowering of social history depends not only on a grasp of what, at its best, it is trying to do, but also of what, at its worst, it appeals to in the mythology of semi-popular cultural analysis.

There is, however, another level worth examining when we contemplate the respective popularities of social history and economic history. There is no doubt that radical approaches to the past, which used to find their professional home in economic history, have moved increasingly into the more accommodating mansions of social history. The implications of that transition are very important—and closely related to Temin's advocacy of a revitalized economic history which would take note of the social relations and hierarchies within the institutions of the second Industrial Revolution. One could even say that the *dominant mood* of the new social history—at least in its non-quantitative form— is critical, radical, and populist.

There are various possible explanations of this fact, not the least important of which involves an appreciation of the influence of environment and of historical lags. It could be argued that the economic experience of the West in the 1950s, 1960s, and early 1970s—and even more the implications of the study of economic history as it evolved over the twenty-five or thirty years after World War II—weakened the hold of a radical critique of society *on purely economic grounds.* And since neither the iniquity of the origins of industrialization nor the impending collapse of contemporary economies could then be easily demonstrated in terms of economic analysis alone, it was to quality not quantity, attitudes not achievement, and social class not economic performance, that the critics of industrial society turned.

This is the reverse side of the coin to the characterization of the new economic history as neo-classical in its implications and conservative in its conclusion. For economic history, too, was influenced by prosperity and by the presumption that it was, in some sense, assured.

If the adequacy and character of contemporary economic performance is an important determinant of intellectual perspectives, then there may (alas) still be scope for an energetic revival of *economic* history. Postwar prosperity has turned out to be transitory—or, at least, not continuous. And if, as seems to be the case, we have not "solved" basic economic problems, then questions—including historical questions—of economic growth, structure, and distribution are still very much on the academic agenda. In that respect alone, historians of lifestyle, culture, and social dynamics will again come to appreciate the primacy of economic performance and economic patterns.

Any such popular renaissance of economic history is bound to be more subtle than its original incarnation. Given our ignorance of economic growth, it is inevitable that, if and as they turn to it once more, economic historians will resort to more varied tools of analysis and more adventurous conceptual frameworks. In this respect it is interesting that Temin's offering to us should, precisely, be an argument in favor of studying modern economic growth in terms of a diversity of models of human behavior, rather than the model on which we (as economic historians) have been forcibly fed these last twenty years. (This argument is important even though the particular proposals embedded in Temin's article hardly seem very novel on close examination.)

There are two points worth making about the argument that it is premature to write off economic history, or to assume that it will not tackle, perhaps with renewed vigor, the fundamental economic questions in varied ways. First, it will probably happen more or less of its own accord as economic historians appreciate either the limits of the analytical techniques that they have inherited or the significance and interest of new topics of research and discourse. This already seems to be happening, for example with the recent interest in institutional analysis and property rights; or in the sort of problem raised by Temin; or in the case of demographic history where, as E. A. Wrigley points out elsewhere in this volume, the original concerns of historians have inevitably led to an indispensable interest in the social and cultural phenomena of the family. Problems breed answers. And answers breed problems.

Second, I do not think that economic historians should feel too burdened by the obligation to cross erstwhile frontiers. For they are needed every bit as much as they have needs. Even the best of the new social and cultural historians cannot operate in an economic vacuum. If the frontier between economic and social history is no longer a clear and linear one, the ambiguities of subject-matter and therefore of methodologies apply equally to citizens of each country. In that respect, the dependence is mutual.

Short as this contribution is, it does offer some explicit conclusions. First, the influences which shape academic research and the choice of subject matter are not really amenable to management or even to precise divination. There is a prior logic of scholarship, which it is best to acknowledge and respect. In this context it may be unwise to follow Temin too far in his view that the cutting edge of economic history is always honed on the frontiers of economic theory and preoccupation. In fact, the discipline has not been, nor ever was, cut adrift from the mainstreams of historical concern.

Second, the likely influences on economic history are sufficiently powerful and varied to ensure not one but a multiplicity of developments in substance and technique. It is still a mistake to think of economic history as a single subject involving a single methodology. Specialization will, quite properly, continue. But so—with lags and caution—will attempts at larger syntheses and generalizations. But those syntheses will have neither the sweep nor the confidence of their antecedents: in economic history, as in other academic fields, we live in a less ambitious (because more demanding and knowledgeable) age than earlier, heroic generations. It would be unrealistic to anticipate, in the 1980s, contributions to the subject with the sweep and certitude of a Richard H. Tawney or a Michael M. Postan, let alone a Karl Marx or Max Weber.

Third, there is still a good deal of life and scope for growth in the subject, and it will be neither dominated nor atrophied by the new economic history. Rather, the new approach will take its place alongside other techniques and presumptions. The use of statistical analyses and economic theory which we have seen over the last twenty-five years *has* been remarkable and, in spite of its frequently recondite character, it has also been important—and extremely fruitful. There seems to be no reason to regret its presence and influence any more than those of other preoccupations or methodologies. For many significant historical problems the new economic history—or something very like it—will therefore continue to lead the field. By the same token, however, for many problems (for example, our understanding of human motivation or the inner workings of economic and social institutions) it will be less relevant, and will be acknowledged so to be.

Finally, and much more generally, it is well to remind ourselves of the historical roots of economic history. The new techniques alone are not, in the last resort, satisfying because they do not address themselves to the foundations of historical concern— a narrative of the past as it unfolded, in its roundedness and interrelatedness. To write narrative history should not be a matter simply of telling the story of individual events, and certainly not of dispensing with systematic analyses and models. Yet, even in economic history, our best hope is to narrate and explain a *particular* past. Admittedly, that past is also created by us, and changes as historical conceptions change. But, whatever form it takes, it cannot be adequately approached without an understanding of the full and complex range of causal relationships in a real world. For that reason economic history—like other histories— will never be able to retain the purity of its newest technique or the holiness of its latest fashion.

Population History in the 1980s

E. A. Wrigley

The Prospects for Population History   If historical population study is to occupy a distinctive intellectual terrain within history, it is not enough to foster a rising tide of substantive studies of demographic behavior in the past. There must also be a complementary development of organizing concepts to link population characteristics to their socioeconomic context and to do justice to the mutual interaction between the two. The technical sophistication of some of the pioneering work in demographic history published in the 1950s and 1960s was not always matched by a willingness to balance the study of the interplay of strictly demographic variables by an investigation of other related features of the communities under examination. For example, some of the early reconstitution monographs, such as Henry's *Crulai,* were in a sense timeless, since they were focused on biological, demographic, or general behavioral questions. They did not attempt either to advance the understanding of birth, death, and marriage in a particular community at a particular period and place, or to clarify the general nature of such relationships. Or again, where the controlling influence upon population change has been seen as mortality fluctuation, controlled in turn by the arbitrary action of exterior events, notably the weather and the vagaries of infectious disease, it has seemed vain to hope to integrate population history with cognate branches of history. An event such as the irruption of pneumonic plague into fourteenth-century Europe may have momentous effects, but, like an earthquake, a typhoon, or a great flood, it is external to the normal functioning of society. Consequences flow from such events but the links all run in one

E. Anthony Wrigley is Professor of Population Studies at the London School of Economics and is the Co-Director of the Cambridge Group for the History of Population and Social Structure. He is the author, with Roger S. Schofield, of *The Population History of England, 1541–1871* (London, 1981).

0022-1953/81/020207-20 $02.50/0

direction. Societies may fall victim to them but they cannot influence them.[1]

Equally fatal to a serious interest in population history has been the long-standing tendency to view population trends in each community as determined by its economic structure and fortunes. If, for example, it is assumed that the supply of labor always responds to changes in the demand for labor in such a way as to keep the level of real wages close to some prevailing conventional standard as in David Ricardo's formulation of the "iron law of wages," then once again the attractions of studying population history may prove to be limited. Although there will be an interest in the relative importance of fertility and mortality changes in securing expansions or contractions in labor supply, many features of the resulting situation will be known in advance. Population stands downstream from the features of society and economy which will deserve first attention. The commanding heights lie elsewhere.

In short, if it is true that population is treated either as a dependent variable, or as a primarily biological or genetic phenomenon, its place in historical description and analysis is likely to be modest. Conversely, if the fertility, mortality, and nuptiality characteristics of a population appear to exercise an important influence on other aspects of social and economic behavior, population history is likely to attract more serious attention. In the course of the last quarter century there has been a substantial shift from the former toward the latter view of population in the history of European peoples.

It is in this context that the discovery of a distinctive pattern of marriage in early modern Western Europe has assumed such importance. In other traditional societies marriage, at least for women, was a biologically controlled event. Sexual maturity was soon followed for all except a negligible minority of women by marriage and reproduction. Fertility was not always high in these circumstances, even though there was seldom any conscious attempt to limit fertility within marriage. The spacing of births may vary substantially even where natural fertility prevails. But it was normally substantially higher than in societies where

---

1 Etienne Gautier and Louis Henry, *La population de Crulai, paroisse normande* (Paris, 1958).

women spent the first decade or so of their lives after menarche unmarried, where many women never married, and where illegitimate fertility was far lower than legitimate fertility. Where fertility was high, mortality was of necessity also high, since the ability to support population grew only slowly before the industrial revolution. Where it was lower, mortality too could stabilize at more modest levels. A low-pressure equilibrium between population and the resources available to sustain it was consonant with relatively high standards of living. A high-pressure equilibrium was inevitably one entailing for the bulk of the population a life lived close to the margin of existence, where incomes had to be devoted chiefly to food plus a minimum of expenditure on clothing, shelter, and fuel, constituting what Malthus termed a "Chinese" situation.[2]

It was Malthus indeed who first gave shape to the debate, the recent development of which partly accounts for the present status of population history. Although in the first edition of the *Essay* he sketched a rather rigid system, in which the positive check predominated in controlling population growth and economic expansion, or contraction entailed a virtually automatic sympathetic movement in population, in later editions he moved away from this simplistic scheme as he came to appreciate more fully the immense importance of the preventive check in much of Western Europe, and hence of the operation of customs influencing marriage behavior. If, as Malthus came to believe, the presence or absence of restraints upon marriage can make a major difference to the economic constitution and fortunes of a society, and if the influences which dispose some societies to marry late and others to marry early are not necessarily themselves chiefly economic, then the condition necessary to encourage the study of marriage and demographic behavior generally is met.

The seed planted by Malthus' work has taken a long time to reach a state of vigorous growth, and not only because of the influence of Ricardian or Marxist views of the functioning of society and economy. The range of issues which commanded the

---

2 "In some countries population appears to have been forced; that is, the people have been habituated by degrees to live almost upon the smallest possible quantity of food. . . . China appears to answer this description . . . the lower classes of the people . . . are glad to get any putrid offals that European labourers would rather starve than eat." Thomas Robert Malthus, *An Essay on the Principle of Population* (London, 1798), 130.

attention of historians rarely included matters to which Malthus' ideas were relevant until the last half century or so. Over this period however, the increasing attention given to economic and social history, with its concomitant interest in the behavior of the common people rather than the elite, has changed the scope of historical inquiry. At the same time historians have displayed an increased interest in the writing of sociologists and anthropologists for whom the study of the institution of marriage has long been a major element in the examination of social structure, action, and change. With a new consciousness of the potential importance of knowledge about population behavior in general and marriage in particular, there came a matching growth in the search for suitable source materials and in the effort devoted to devising new methods for the most effective use of the information which came to light.

The result has been a vast increase in empirical knowledge about population behavior in the past, and a substantial refinement of ideas concerning the interplay of economic, social, and demographic variables in European history from medieval times onwards. Moreover, the context in which population history is viewed has changed. If marriage is central to European population history, then questions such as the transmission of property between successive generations, authority structures within the family, patterns of co-residence and support, the institution of service, inheritance customs, and cognate matters, can scarcely fail to attract study. And if marriage were long delayed after sexual maturity for both men and women, the period of adult life spent single must hold a special fascination, since it is essential to the function of delayed marriage as a means of reducing fertility that its effect should not be frustrated by high levels of extramarital fertility. The institution of service is significant in this regard, no less than in relation to delayed marriage itself.

THE TECHNIQUES USED IN HISTORICAL DEMOGRAPHY   Historical demography was long faced with a teasing technical problem. Demographic measurement depends upon the ability to assemble information both about the number of events of a certain type occurring in a population (for example, deaths among men between the ages of twenty and twenty-four) and about the numbers at risk for the event to occur (in this instance, the size of the male population in that age group). This presents no difficulty in the era of the modern, bureaucratic state since both types of information are routinely collected. The census periodically reveals the numbers at risk, and the vital registration system records births, deaths, and marriages. Both stock and flow are measured.

Before the nineteenth century, however, there were very few instances of detailed and comprehensive censuses, although in many European countries ecclesiastical registers of baptisms, burials, and marriages afford a tolerably complete record of vital events from a much earlier date. There was therefore a pressing need for technical innovations which would enable a knowledge of the flow of events to be converted into measures of fertility, mortality, and nuptiality, even though the stock at risk was not separately recorded. In the course of the past quarter century two methods have been developed which offer a partial solution to the problem: family reconstitution and aggregative back projection. The nature of the two techniques has exercised a powerful influence upon the range of questions which have been tackled by those interested in population history, both in work on demographic matters and in studies with a broader scope.

The first of the two new methods to be developed was family reconstitution. Ironically it was perfected by a man whose interest lay almost solely in the purely demographic question of the nature and components of natural fertility. Henry turned to history out of frustration with the difficulty of finding accurate modern data for a population in which there was little or no deliberate control of conception. He needed very detailed and precise information, but this was available in the contemporary world only for populations in which birth control was widely practised. In those parts of the world where fertility was not controlled accurate data were not collected. Henry first made use of the genealogical work already carried out on the Genevan bourgeoisie, and later showed in his work on Crulai that the same information could also be abstracted from a suitable parish register, thus proving that the behavior of a substantial sample of an entire community could be studied, rather than that of an elite group only.[3]

Henry's essential innovation was not the articulation of scattered information about the lives of individuals into coherent

3 Henry, *Anciennes familles genevoises* (Paris, 1956).

family histories. Genealogists had done the same for centuries. It lay rather in his formulation of rules defining for each individual within a reconstituted family the period of time that he or she could properly be regarded as at risk to experience a particular class of event; how long, for example, a woman might be regarded as at risk to bear children taking into account the information available about other individuals in the same family. It is essential that observational rules be framed in such a way as to eliminate, or at least minimize, any source of bias. This Henry achieved.[4]

In 1958 when *Crulai* was published, Alfred Sauvy in his introductory observations pointed out that it conformed to the new trend in historical studies by covering a whole community and not just the powerful and prominent. He expressed the hope that it would be widely replicated.[5] He may well have been surprised, however, to see how amply his wish has been fulfilled. That so many reconstitution studies have been undertaken is due only in part to an interest in demography, whether historical or "pure." It is also and increasingly due to another feature of reconstitution—that it is based upon a logic of nominal record linkage which has proved applicable to a very wide range of historical source material. For it soon became apparent that the creation of structure out of a welter of initially unrelated snippets of information about individuals could be used to examine many other aspects of social behavior as well as nuptiality, fertility, and mortality.

Reconstitution provided an initial marshaling of information about individuals and families to which to attach other nominally ordered information drawn from wills and inventories; census lists; civil, ecclesiastical, and manorial court records; Poor Law records; and so on. Once articulated in this fashion, many features of local society could be examined—for example, the operation of social control, social and geographical mobility, or local land transfer and inheritance systems. It is often illuminating to study

---

4   The technique of family reconstitution was first set out in Michel Fleury and Henry, *Des registres paroissiaux à l'histoire de la population. Manuel de dépouillement et d'explitation de l'état civil ancien* (Paris, 1956). Later the same two authors published a revision and extension of their earlier work, *Nouveau manuel de dépouillement et d'exploitation de l'état civil ancien* (Paris, 1965). See also Henry, *Manuel de démographie historique* (Geneva, 1967).
5   Gautier and Henry, *Crulai,* 11–12.

the interplay of social, economic, and demographic factors in this way. The operation of the Poor Law is much easier to follow, for example, if the age and family circumstances of the recipients of relief are known. It is probable, indeed, that the long-term importance of family reconstitution to history will be far greater outside a strictly demographic framework than within it. Narrowly defined, it is a device for extracting demographic measures from unpromising material, but the idea of introducing structure into nominally ordered data to facilitate systematic analysis has a more general relevance.[6]

Family reconstitution, however, possesses singular disadvantages as well as great virtues. It involves a heavy expenditure of time in order to study even a small community, and will continue to do so in future even though there may be great advances in the computerization of record linkage, because the input of the original data requires many scores or even hundreds of hours of key punching. This inhibits work on large communities, or upon a substantial sample of parish populations drawn from an entire country. Further, because it is difficult to keep track of migrants, the results obtained by reconstitution studies are sometimes the subject of dispute as to their representativeness for the population as a whole.

There has therefore been need of other methods to overcome the problems posed by the absence of censuses during much of the period for which parish registers serve as a source for vital registration. Lee pioneered a new approach to this problem when he devised the technique which he termed inverse projection, and his initiative has been carried further by recent work at the Cambridge Group for the History of Population and Social Structure. Lee showed that a knowledge of totals of births and deaths over a period of time could be converted into estimates of fertility and mortality, expressed as gross reproduction rates and expectations of life at birth, given a starting population with a known size and age structure. His method suffers, however, from two significant limitations. It assumes population closure (that there was either

6 Some of these issues were discussed by the contributors to Wrigley (ed.), *Identifying People in the Past* (London, 1973). Subsequently nominal record linkage has figured prominently among the techniques which have been most discussed by demographic and social structural historians, notably in articles appearing in *Historical Methods* and the *Journal of Interdisciplinary History*.

no migration or that immigration and emigration were in balance in all age groups); and a system that moves forward in time, which makes it necessary to estimate population size and age structure at the earliest date covered by the exercise, when uncertainty is likely to be at its greatest.[7]

The Cambridge Group has developed a method which overcomes these two limitations. The technique involves moving backwards in time from a date at which the size and age structure of the population is known, and yields estimates of net migration as well as providing quinquennial "censuses." The conditions necessary for obtaining conventional measures of fertility and mortality are thus met, and, given certain assumptions about the age structure of fertility and mortality, it is a comparatively straightforward matter to produce estimates of the gross reproduction rate and expectation of life at birth.[8]

Back projection and family reconstitution complement one another. Although back projection can be used to trace the history of small populations down to the level of the individual parish, it is especially valuable for regional and national analyses which, because of the high cost of full reconstitutions on large populations, can only be tackled with family reconstitution methods if the data base is restricted to a small sample of parishes.

Back projection can provide a firm outline of the history of fertility and mortality, whereas reconstitution may serve to clarify the mechanisms which underlay the major changes in fertility and mortality levels, and therefore the reasons for fluctuating population growth rates. For example, back projection shows that the remarkable rise in population growth rates in eighteenth-century England (from a zero growth rate at the end of the seventeenth century to a peak rate of about 1.5 percent per annum early in the nineteenth) was due principally to a substantial rise in fertility which accounted for about three quarters of the acceleration which took place. But the technique cannot yield any information about

7 Ronald Lee, "Estimating Series of Vital Rates and Age Structures from Baptisms and Burials: a New Technique, with Applications to Pre-industrial England," *Population Studies,* XXVIII (1974), 495–512.

8 Back projection is described briefly in Wrigley and Roger S. Schofield, *The Population History of England, 1541–1871. A Reconstruction* (London, 1981), ch. 7. It is more fully described in appendix 15 of the same work.

marital fertility levels, nor about most aspects of nuptiality change. Reconstitution, however, is well able to do so. It provides evidence which suggests strongly that marital fertility scarcely altered but that age at marriage fell considerably. There is also evidence that proportions never marrying fell (culled indirectly from back projection).[9]

Reconstitution therefore, makes it clear that although the proximate cause of the rising rate of population growth was higher fertility, the underlying reason for the change was a marked increase in nuptiality. This in turn immediately suggests the importance of trying to identify the causes of the changes in marriage behavior which produced such momentous consequences. The explanation was not far to seek. Throughout early modern English history nuptiality was responsive to changes in real wages, though with a substantial time lag, and fertility was so strongly governed by nuptiality that it followed suit.

The work done in recent years on English population history provides more than an illustration of the capacities of new methods of demographic measurement. It serves both to alleviate doubt about the possibility of accurate knowledge in the pre-census era, and to exemplify the danger of assuming that population behavior can be relegated to the position of a dependent variable for most analytic purposes.

On the first score it is worth noting that one of the advantages of back projection is the ease with which it is possible to carry out sensitivity tests. If, for example, it is suspected that corrections to raw data which were intended to offset all causes of underregistration still leave births 10 percent below their true number and deaths 5 percent too few, it is a simple matter to make alternative runs using revised data sets and thus to see how far the initial results would be altered on different assumptions. The "stability" of the findings can thus be established. Again, if it is known, say, that net migration was relatively small and on balance outward, it will be obvious whether the main run results are plausible, and also which among the results produced by alternative assumptions can be entertained as possibilities. Moreover,

9 Wrigley and Schofield, *Population History of England,* Fig. 7.12, Tables 7.29, 7.25, 7.26, 7.28.

there are a number of ways in which the results produced by back projection are by implication mutually self-checking.[10]

THE LOGICAL STATUS OF POPULATION HISTORY   The central importance of marriage in English population history must be the starting point for any consideration of the second issue: the relationship between demographic change and the socioeconomic system. The changes in nuptiality in England in the early modern period were on a large enough scale in themselves to move population growth rates between the minimum and maximum to be found in pre-industrial societies (apart from the short periods when major epidemics were rampant). They were demonstrably the most important influence on secular changes in the growth rate, and there is clear evidence *both* that they were responsive to long-run economic trends via the real wage *and* that there were important causal links running in the opposite direction from demographic to economic change. There was for example, a remarkably close relation between changes in population growth rates and changes in secular price trends, and through the latter in turn with real wage trends. A coherent pattern linking price and real wage trends with changes in other elements of the socioeconomic system, for which Phelps Brown and Hopkins searched in vain in the course of their pioneering work a quarter of a century ago, is vividly clear with the new information now available about population growth rates, nuptiality, and fertility.[11]

10 For example, an approximate estimate of the proportion never marrying can be obtained by allocating first marriages occurring over a period of time to successive marriage cohorts according to a marriage age schedule. Each successive block of persons marrying for the first time allocated to a given cohort is then advanced to an age, say age fifty, above which very few first marriages took place, and reduced in number in accordance with the cohort life tables produced by back projection. The cumulative total of all those who had both married and survived to age fifty taken from the successive groups of entrants into marriage in the given cohort represents the proportion ever married in that cohort. The difference between this total and the total of *all* those surviving to age fifty in the cohort is the proportion never marrying. If either the marriage or death totals were significantly inaccurate, or the population totals, age structures, and mortality estimates produced by back projection were wide of the mark, it is highly improbable that the estimate of proportions never marrying would follow a coherent and plausible path. Only a general accuracy in the data and techniques employed, or a very remarkable set of offsetting errors could lead to acceptable results.

11 "For a century or more, it seems, prices will obey one all-powerful law; it changes and a new law prevails; a war that would have cast the trend up to new heights in one

If it is true that population trends and characteristics exercised a powerful influence over other aspects of economic and social life; that both gross trends and more detailed aspects of population change can be measured with fair accuracy; and that the inter-relationships among the demographic, economic, and social characteristics of a society were contingent and intricate, then the investigation of its population history is necessarily an important part of the history of any society, whether a local community or a national entity. Like any other branch of historical investigation, population history may lack appropriate source materials for the resolution of a particular problem, but this may be more of a stimulus than a deterrent, provided that another requirement is met. An example from a cognate branch of history may illustrate the point.

The economic history of eighteenth-century England is handicapped by the difficulty of obtaining data on certain key matters. For example, it would be helpful in deciding between alternative models of economic growth to have accurate knowledge of the output of agricultural products, of changes in yield per acre, of the changing balance of different crops and between crops and livestock, of farm size and the numbers employed in agriculture, of changing food consumption patterns, of male and female agricultural wage levels and work patterns, and so on. In some cases existing knowledge may be substantially improved with sufficient effort. In others it would be excessive optimism to expect great improvement. But the difficulty of obtaining all the empirical data which might prove illuminating is not perceived as a reason to abandon work on English agricultural history. On the contrary it is certain to continue to attract attention because the significance of agricultural change to the understanding of economic growth is unquestioned. The logical status of the exercise is clear, and it is this, far more than the abundance or

---

dispensation is powerless to deflect it in another. Do we yet know what are the factors that set this stamp on an age; and why, after they have held on so long through such shakings, at last they give way, quickly and completely to others?" E. H. Phelps Brown and Sheila V. Hopkins, "Seven Centuries of the Prices of Consumables, Compared with Builders' Wage Rates," in Eleanor M. Carus-Wilson, *Essays in Economic History* (London, 1962; orig. pub. 1955), II, 188. For evidence of the pattern linking demographic trends with secular economic change see Wrigley and Schofield, *Population History of England*, chs. 10, 11.

quality of the data, which determines the proportionate attention devoted to a particular topic.

The great change which has occurred in population history in recent years does not lie ultimately in its yield of empirical information or in the proliferation of developments in technique but rather in its logical status. In the course of the last half century it became impossible to imagine an adequate history of any society which did not encompass its economic history. The same is becoming increasingly true of population history. As long as population history was a catalog of fact, a history of cataclysms which could be viewed as acts of God, or a feature of the past the characteristics of which were believed to be readily determinable from a knowledge of some other aspect of the society in question, it was a matter of peripheral interest only. When it became demonstrable that the demographic constitution of a society had an important bearing on many of its other characteristics and it was impossible to regard its demographic constitution as secondary to some other aspect of its economic or social makeup, it also became essential to change its logical status.

It is arguable that the single most important publication tending to create a new logical status for population history was Hajnal's article on European marriage patterns. In it he returned to the question which had intrigued Malthus and treated it more rigorously and systematically. His essay belongs more closely to the statistical than the sociological strand in population study but its importance was manifold both in relation to purely demographic questions and to wider issues. He showed that both the timing and incidence of marriage for women (age at marriage and proportions never marrying) in Western Europe were radically different from those found anywhere else in the world and that this pattern is visible from the sixteenth century onwards. Other things being equal, this marriage pattern implies a lower level of fertility than elsewhere and makes possible a different balance of population and resources—a "low-pressure" rather than a "high-pressure" equilibrium. It suggests different relations between the generations, different patterns of coresidence within the household, and different life-time patterns of saving and expenditure. It is linked indirectly to a long-standing element in European historical writing present since Hegel's time—the attempt to explain the nature of the difference between Western civilization and other great civilizations, and to provide reasons for the greater dynamism of Western civilization in the recent past.[12]

The most significant feature of Hajnal's article, however, and one which places him in the tradition of the later Malthus, was simply that he placed marriage once again squarely in the center of the stage, thereby suggesting the most appropriate institutional vehicle for use in the study of population history. It has been the convergence of studies concerning the independent influence of the demographic characteristics of society with studies of social processes on the micro-scale in a common setting focused on the history of marriage, family, and the household which has produced a new breadth and richness in population history. The family was long a curiously neglected institutional form among historians. The happy coincidence of the appearance of new methods of marshaling evidence about the family in the past with a new acceptance of the strategic importance of achieving a fuller understanding of its structure and function has helped to give substance to the new logical status of population history by suggesting a wide range of cognate studies which have greatly enriched and diversified it.

The new appreciation of the place of population history in relation to other related branches of the subject has been marked by a parallel reappraisal of the source materials available for its study. At one time the fear was widely expressed that the paucity or incompleteness of the source materials would necessarily leave the subject impoverished and peripheral. But each step toward an enhanced awareness of the conceptual richness and complexity of the subject has been matched, as might be expected, by a new insight into the opportunities offered by source materials that were well known but previously regarded in a different light. In part this has been a matter of improved technique. A parish register can be made to yield far more, and far more accurate information about fertility and mortality now than was feasible thirty years ago. But in the main it is a question of seeing with new eyes. Manorial court rolls, for example, have been pored over by generations of medieval scholars, but their immense value for the study of familial forms, kinship ties, social mobility,

12 John Hajnal, "European Marriage Patterns in Perspective," in David V. Glass and David E. C. Eversley (eds.), *Population in History* (London, 1965), 101–143.

marriage decisions, the treatment of widows, inheritance and land transfer, illegitimacy, and the like was obscured or ignored until an acquaintance with the concepts which suggest the significance of these matters to the fuller understanding of medieval society had become more widely disseminated. Although conceptual richness cannot produce sources where none exist, it can radically transform the value and use of sources long familiar. It is now common to hear complaints about the burdensome volume of sources bearing upon the population history even of a single small community, a sure sign of the replacement of conceptual poverty by conceptual wealth.[13]

Once again, there are parallels between recent developments in population history and those occurring earlier in economic history. A history of prices, for example, can be no more than a simple listing of empirical material or, equally, if it is linked to an appropriate body of theory concerning the determination of relative price levels and movements, it can provide an insight into the functioning of an economy, the constraints under which it operates, the nature of the shocks to which it is subject, its degree of articulation into a single market system, and so on. And it will suggest a range of further investigations to be undertaken on other bodies of data. The value of the exercise will normally be determined more by the conceptual richness or otherwise of the study than by the quantity or precision of the data. The latter is always important but, if the relevance of a particular type of information can be established on theoretical grounds, it is frequently possible to find some data source which bears sufficiently closely on the question at issue to allow progress to be made, even though it may fall well short of the ideal.

MARRIAGE AND REPRODUCTION   As in economic, so in population history the crucial advances have not consisted of the discovery of new documentary evidence, nor even of the development of new techniques for squeezing information out of unpromising

13 For example, in the five-year period 1313–1317 the court rolls of the manor of Redgrave, Suffolk, contain references to almost 1,500 individuals. For each named individual there are on average about 2.7 entries, or more than 4,000 individual nominally ordered items of information. Redgrave was a manor of about 400 tenants (customary and freehold) at this period. I owe this information to Richard M. Smith of the Cambridge Group who has worked extensively on the manor of Redgrave and its neighbor Rickinghall in the later thirteenth and early fourteenth century.

sources, but chiefly of a new appreciation of the significance of the interplay of the forces which govern the population characteristics of a community. Just as the rise of economic history as a subject for investigation testifies to the recognition of the central importance of production to a society, so the parallel development of population history reflects a similar recognition of the significance of reproduction. And the two are linked by more than verbal similarity, for the nature of the balance between production and reproduction is necessarily a fundamental issue for the history of every society.

If access to the fruits of economic production may be envisaged as determined by the operation of the market, so, equally, access to reproduction is determined by marriage (often described as a market). Since this involves a transfer of resources, a change of status in the community for the individuals concerned, the creation of a new cell within the body social, and the granting of a licence to reproduce, it is always an institution of great consequence. The maturing of population history has occurred as the limitations of purely demographic investigation have grown evident and the existence of a natural focus of interest in marriage and the family has become clearer. The boundaries between the different branches of historical investigation are always indistinct and shifting, and there is no clearly etched boundary between population history and its neighbors, nor even any major increase in the visibility of imaginary lines of demarcation. It has not been changes at the periphery which have made the difference in recent years, but rather a greater coherence and richness at the center as studies of fertility, nuptiality, mortality, family and household structure, inheritance, kinship and neighborhood ties, social and geographical mobility, male and female roles, and local authority structures have increasingly found a common theoretical focus and have made use of cognate analytic techniques.

What then are likely to be the chief concerns of population history in the near future? If the foregoing is an accurate appreciation of the slow sea change in historical writing and research in the recent past, it is to be expected that the emergence of the distinctive West European marriage system will continue to attract attention. In the fifteen years since the publication of Hajnal's article it has come to seem more doubtful whether his view that it was of recent origin in the sixteenth century is correct. Fourteenth-century English poll taxes appear to show clearly that men at that time conformed to the West European marriage pattern. The evidence for women is more ambiguous, principally because the problem of assessing the scale of omissions from the returns is more acute, but there is probably better reason to suppose that the same was true of women than the reverse. Similarly, medieval English evidence suggests that household structure and patterns of co-residence were little different from those found in early modern times. Live-in servants were numerous but resident kin outside the conjugal family were rarely found. There is also evidence from Holland to suggest that among the ruling classes men and women married late and that many never married. The pattern was already firmly set by the beginning of the sixteenth century, when data are first available, and did not alter significantly thereafter until the recent past.[14]

The classic West European marriage pattern involved late marriage for both sexes, a small mean age gap between spouses (with many first marriages in which the wife was the older partner), and a relatively high proportion of persons of both sexes never marrying. At the other extreme in Eastern Europe marriage for both sexes was early and virtually universal. But there were also intermediate forms. In fourteenth-century Tuscany, male marriage characteristics were "Western" but women married young and there was in consequence a substantial mean age gap between spouses. This "Mediterranean" pattern was found in much of southern Europe and persisted until a very late date. To establish the boundaries between Western and Mediterranean marriage patterns, their persistence over time, and the social and economic concomitants of the two systems offers a fruitful field for work both of a monographic and comparative type.[15]

Malthus, incidentally, in the later editions of the *Essay on Population* exemplified the value of the comparative study of marriage systems. He set an example which might with profit be followed more frequently. When Kipling posed the rhetorical

---

14 R. M. Smith, "Some Reflections on the Evidence for the Origins of the 'European marriage pattern' in England," in Chris Harris (ed.), *The Sociology of the Family* (Keele, 1979), 74–112. Henk van Dijk and D. J. Roorda, *Het patriciaat in Zierikzee tijdens de Republick* (Rotterdam, 1980), ch. 2, esp. Tables 2.8, 2.11.
15 David Herlihy and Christiane Klapisch-Zuber, *Les toscanes et leurs familles* (Paris, 1978), 393–419.

question, "What should they know of England who only England know," he raised an issue which is relevant no less to population history than other contexts. A better understanding of each local or national situation will depend as much on knowledge of comparable situations elsewhere as upon further local work. Width is no less important than depth to population history.[16]

Moving closer to the present there is much to be done in the population history of the last two centuries. Far more is known now than ten years ago about the spread of fertility control within marriage in the West in the nineteenth and twentieth centuries in the sense that the timing of its onset and the subsequent pace of its fall has been measured on a uniform basis for several hundred regions of Europe as a result of the studies directed by Coale. But greater empirical knowledge has in some ways increased uncertainty about the causes of the change. The extraordinary near simultaneity of the onset of the fall throughout much of Europe poses a sharp challenge to interpretation which has not yet been successfully met. Equally, the striking contrast between France and the rest of Europe remains without a satisfactory explanation. In both cases the issue is complicated by the fact that national and regional units were not necessarily homogeneous. There were parts of Germany in which marital fertility declined early in the nineteenth century, and parts of France where it did not decline until toward the century's end.[17]

The move to small families was a momentous change, affecting sex roles, employment patterns, family composition, the relationship between successive generations, the upbringing of children, and much else. Furthermore, although the changes were not in all cases simultaneous, they effectively marked the end of the West European marriage system by cutting the previously

16   The phrase appears in Rudyard Kipling's poem, *The English Flag*.
17   Six volumes have appeared so far in the Princeton series initiated by Ansley Coale. They cover Portugal, Italy, Germany, Belgium, France, and Russia. Further volumes on the British Isles, Switzerland, and Scandinavia, with a second volume on France, are expected to be published. John Knodel, "From Natural Fertility to Family Limitation: the Onset of the Fertility Transition in a Sample of German Villages," *Demography*, XVI (1979), 493–521. There is evidence of a very late fall in marital fertility in some French departments. This was notably true of Brittany. In Côtes-du-Nord, Finisterre, and Morbihan, marital fertility was at a very high absolute level and showed no clear sign of dropping until about 1890. Etienne van de Walle, *The Female Population of France in the Nineteenth Century* (Princeton, 1974), 285, 306, 386.

close tie between the timing and incidence of marriage and the level of fertility. Marriage is now earlier and more nearly universal in England than at any other time in English history since the sixteenth century, and probably since a much earlier date.

The list of topics which promise well could be extended almost indefinitely. It might include the nature of the relation between short-term economic and climatic change and short-term changes in fertility, mortality, and nuptiality; the influences which determined the seasonal pattern of birth, death, and marriage; the circumstances in which remarriage occurred (comprising such questions as its declining incidence with age, intervals to remarriage, differences between patterns of widow and widower remarriage, its relation to the ownership of property, the number of children from previous marriages, the labor needs of the household, and the social norms of the community); the characteristic life-time patterns of earnings and expenditure in different groups within a population and their relation to family size, the dependency burden, marriage decisions, and so on; transfer payments between the generations within the same family; the relative importance of kin, neighbors, and community institutions in helping to meet the problems posed by illness, death, incapacity, old age, and widowhood; the circumstances in which young men and women left the parental household; the validity of concepts such as the "proto-industrial" family; attitudes toward childbirth, illness, and death, and how such attitudes may have affected or been affected by prevailing fertility and mortality patterns; the family as an agent of socialization; the connections between marriage, inheritance, and dowry arrangements; the nature of the link between fluctuations in legitimate and illegitimate fertility (and also what might be termed quasi-legitimate fertility—prenuptial pregnancy); and the institution of service in both its economic and demographic aspects.

In most such investigations occupational, class, and regional differences will attract much attention, as will their variation over time. And it is likely that there will be a rapid growth in the use of computers to simulate certain features of the functioning of the family in order to elucidate the relative importance of various influences upon its behavior. For example, it may prove convenient to examine in this way the possibility for transfer of resources from an older to a younger generation within a family on varying assumptions about marriage age, fertility and mortality, the characteristic pattern of life-time male earnings, dowry, opportunities for earning by the wife as a function of the number and age of her children, and so on.[18]

But attempts to produce comprehensive agenda for future research are foredoomed to failure. They are heavily influenced by the interests and prejudices of their authors. There is inevitably a sort of *hubris* attached to them.

Population history has been well launched by the developments of the last fifteen years or so. Its earlier history had comprised several disparate elements which for long appeared widely separated from each other. The recognition of statistical regularity in aspects of human experience which appear capricious and unpredictable in relation to individuals goes back to the work of Graunt and Halley in the case of demography, which was perhaps the first social science to perceive it. This has been a constant element in historical population studies ever since.[19]

The formulation of the key questions about the relationship between demographic and economic behavior and the identification of marriage patterns as of especial importance stands to Malthus' credit. In spite of his mathematical training, however, and his use of the distinction between arithmetical and geometrical progressions, Malthus approached the issue in a manner which was only quantitative by implication, preferring to conduct his argument in the main by general statements of underlying principles, liberally illustrated by particular examples.[20] And, as already noted, in his first *Essay* he treated population behavior as

18 There is a very telling example of the interplay between the long-term structural characteristics of a population and shorter-term variations in economic circumstances in Bernard Derouet, "Une démographie différentielle: clés pour un système auto-régulateur des populations rurales d'Ancien Régime," *Annales*, XXXV (1980), 3–41.

19 John Graunt, *Natural and Political Observations upon the Bills of Mortality* (London, 1676; 5th ed.), reprinted in Charles Henry Hull (ed.), *The Economic Writings of Sir William Petty* (New York, 1963), II, 314–435. Edmund Halley, "An Estimate of the Degrees of Mortality of Mankind, drawn from the Curious Tables of the Births and Funerals at the City of Breslaw . . ." *Philosophical Transactions of the Royal Society of London*, XVII (1693), 596–610.

20 Malthus was a sufficiently good mathematician to have been ninth wrangler of his year at Cambridge. His correspondence with his father reveals something of the range of topics studied and the nature of his interest in them. Patricia James, *Population Malthus* (London, 1979), 25–30.

a variable dependent upon the performance of the economy. The publication of the *Essay* did not therefore immediately afford a base for the development of population history. Only after the growth in interest in the family as an institutional form had taken place in the social sciences, and the independence of population behavior from economic trends had been vividly shown by the experience of the Third World after World War II, did the conditions exist to encourage an act of bisociation (to use Arthur Koestler's term), knitting together what had previously been separated. The recognition of the existence of a common nexus of interest centered on the family was facilitated by the development of techniques of description and analysis which have proved useful to all of the types of investigation now brought together.

The further development of population history will not depend solely upon intellectual considerations. It will also depend upon institutional developments in the structure of teaching and research in history, and upon the way in which its various components are disposed in relation to each other. Nomenclature may also play a part. Whether population history, named as such, will cover the range of topics discussed in this essay in, say, ten years time is a matter for conjecture. But it is reasonable to hope that the new conjunction of interests which has proved so invigorating in the past two decades will continue to develop in future and will further disseminate an understanding of the structural unity and wide-ranging significance of an aspect of the history of past societies which was once little appreciated.

Anthropology and History in the 1980s

Bernard S. Cohn

Toward a Rapprochement   History and anthropology are forms of knowledge, the creation, formalization, and practice of which are deeply embedded in the historical experience of Western Europe from the fifteenth century to the present. Until the eighteenth century anthropology was a part of history. Historians sought to understand otherness in time by postulating a relationship between the past and the present, the past being lineally and causally related to the present. The belief that the present was the result of the past, and the belief that the way men lived, their institutions of governance, and their social forms, as well as their ideas, had been shaped over time, was not merely part of the belief system of scholars, but become deeply embedded in European culture.

This past, which affected the present, could be studied and transmitted by identifying evidence of past action and thought in various collective representations embodied in texts, art forms, architecture, social practices, and customs. The European native theory of time itself was transformed into chronology, with the idea that time could be objectively measured and computed through the regular divisions of time into periods to which events could be assigned by dates.

Europeans believed that the world, animate and inanimate, had an absolute and datable origin. They had developed the idea of chronology in which time was conceived of in a linear fashion, which enabled them to order by date the reigns of kings, the lives of saints, and the events that affected polities. They also developed a distinction between what they thought of as true history and

Bernard S. Cohn is Professor of Anthropology and History at the University of Chicago. He is the author of *India: The Social Anthropology of a Civilization* (Englewood Cliffs, 1971).

Stephen Blum, Geoff Eley, Raymond Grew, Renato Resaldo, David Schneider, and Michael Silverstein read and gave me extensive comments on an earlier draft of this article. I do not think that I have met many of their criticisms nor answered most of their questions; I hope that I will next time.

0022-1953/81/020227-26 $02.50/0

fables, which were untrue or fictitious. Chronology, the capacity to sort events, ideas, persons, and lives into before and after statements, is the basic methodological assumption which underlies the practice of all historians. With the invention of chronology Europeans constructed a real world out of the past which they thought of in the eighteenth century—and we continue to think of—as natural and all-encompassing. Everything for Europeans has a history, and to discover the history of something, is to explain it.

Interlocked with the construction of a European past, a different kind of past was discovered by Europeans in what they thought of as the New World, Oceania, and the vaguely known worlds of Africa and Asia. The history which Europeans constructed for themselves was part of a growing process of control over space. In Europe, as Furet argues, the past as history was increasingly related to the definition of, and the marking of, the boundaries of states and nations. "From the sixteenth century to the Enlightenment, history . . . was above all the history of nations, i.e. of the peoples and states of Europe." Europeans saw themselves and their nations as the progressive elements in the world. The anthropologists' subject became primitive peoples associated with the natural or the fallen world, as distinguished from Europe, where the people were cultured, civilized, and progressive. In the nineteenth century, not only did Europeans dominate the land of the "primitives," but they also controlled directly or indirectly, the space of the once civilized Asia. The peoples of Asia were cast as backward, non-progressive, inert, once civilized and progressive, and Oriental. The history of these peoples might be reconstructed if they only produced the documents, chronicles, and annals of great political and military events.[1]

In the nineteenth century, Europeans tried to reconstruct the history of the Chinese, the Indians, and the Saracens in European terms as a reverse of the history that they constructed for themselves: as a history of peoples once powerful, creative, and progressive, who had lost direction and were now relegated to finding their history in a golden age of the once great. Their past or

---

1 François Furet, "History and Primitive Man," in Jerome Dymoulin and Dominique Moisi (eds.), *The Historian Between Ethnologist and the Futurologist* (Paris, 1973), 198.

their cleverness in inventing the concepts of zero, chess, and polo could be admired as one admires a piece of Greek statuary, but their civilizations were curiosities left to eccentrics and pedagogues to enjoy and ponder, and were relegated to the fossil bed of history.

By the end of the eighteenth century anthropologists were left to the study of the external others who were separated from the Europeans by space. Their field became a kind of non-history, since it dealt with societies which were unchanging, or at best slowly moving—societies which could not have history because they had no chronology. Even if they were literate, as were the ancient Indians, Mill argued that their texts were "destitute of historical records" and contain only "the miraculous transactions of former times."[2]

Anthropology in the first half of the nineteenth century concerned itself with "archaic" civilizations and the customs of "the primitives," the anthropologist's method being thought of as a form of history. Given the absence of datable documents and events out of which a chronology could be constructed, anthropologists reconstructed the laws of social development through the comparative method. This method was thought to be an extension of the methods of comparative philologists, who had demonstrated through comparison of grammatical features, phonologies, and lexical items that Sanskrit, Greek, and Latin had a common origin. Victorian anthropologists thought that this comparative form of reasoning could be applied to the history of religion, mythology, law, politics, marriage, and the family.

The classification system used by the comparativists was developed in the eighteenth century and was based on analytical units of customs, manners, morals, and institutions thought to be universal and rooted in the human condition. Society, as the concept was explored by the Scottish philosophers of the eighteenth century, was based on man's animal nature and his needs to acquire food, clothing, and shelter. These needs, combined with the long periods of dependency of the human child, lead, the Scottish philosophers thought, to the origin of the family. The dependency and interdependency within the family generated a principle of reciprocal services and cooperation which resulted

2 James Mill, *The History of British India* (London, 1820; 2nd ed.), 145.

in the creation of social institutions, the policy, the economy, law, religion, and education.[3]

For the eighteenth-century Scottish philosophers the idea of progress and the goal of happiness seemed to be self-evident. Everywhere the process of change was from simple to complex, from irrational to rational, and from superstition to enlightenment. Since society and culture were rooted in nature, the Enlightenment philosophers assumed that there would be commonalities of structure and function of institutions in all societies of particular types. Societies were scaled from simple to complex based on an index of techniques for subsistence: those peoples dependent on hunting historically preceded those dependent on pastoralism and agriculture. The scale could be used to translate space into history by the identification of subsistence systems of a group. Combined with the scale there was an inventory of domains or institutions, some of which were thought to be universal, such as the family, religion, and higher levels of organization, such as bands. The particular forms of these institutions could be associated with a stage or level of growth and compared to yield laws of growth or history.

By comparing such institutions as the family, the polity, and the law, anthropologists thought that they could write the history of these institutions. Maitland's frequently quoted and much misunderstood dictum that "by and by Anthropology will have the choice between being history and being nothing" was directed at "scientific sociologists" who claimed that there were general historical laws and not at those historians who tried to reconstruct the past of a particular people at a particular time. The comparativists' sources were accounts by travelers, missionaries, and colonial administrators, who reported on "Natives" and "native institutions"; classical texts; the writings of historians of the ancient world and Europe; and accounts of customs of the "archaic" folk within their own societies, recorded by antiquarians and folklorists.[4]

There have been sporadic efforts since the eighteenth century systematically to collect information about the customs and man-

3 John Sinclair, *Sketch of an Introduction to the Proposed Analysis of the Statistical Account of Scotland* (Edinburgh, 1802), 4–5.

4 Frederick W. Maitland, "The Body Politic," in *idem, Selected Essays* (Cambridge, 1936; orig. pub. 1899), 249.

ners of those primitive and archaic peoples who increasingly came under the control of European colonial powers. The attempt to construct these colonial sociologies was prompted by a combination of intellectual curiosity, scholarly interests, particularly relating to Asia, and pragmatic necessity in the colonies to control the colonized so that their labor and products could be made accessible to the metropolitan capitalist economies. Systems of colonial control rested on knowledge, whether it was the knowledge of both the language and the culture that a missionary needed in Fiji to translate the Bible; the insight that a British official had to have in India to define landed property so that taxes could be collected; the understanding of local politics that a slaver needed in West Africa; or the sensitivity that an Indian agent had to show in the Upper Peninsula of Michigan in order to "settle" Indians on their reservations.

While the sphere of interest of historians through the nineteenth century increasingly became nation states, anthropologists were relegated to the study of colonial peoples dominated by European nations. The history of European peoples could be found in archives; the customs of dominated peoples overseas were to be found in the "field." In the sixteenth century, missionaries, explorers, traders, soldiers, and administrators began writing accounts of the lives of the "exotics," which were studied by those constructing anthropological histories or accounts of primitive institutions. Governments and scholars sought more and more "facts" about those people who were to be civilized at home and overseas. In the metropolitan societies, censuses and surveys recorded facts about "dangerous classes" and the "unruly" to provide the basis for legislation and the development of institutions through which they could be controlled. Increasing efforts on the part of scholarly organizations and government bodies were made to draw up and circulate questionnaires to Europeans overseas so that they could collect systematic information about indigenous peoples.[5]

The data collected in this ad hoc fashion came to be seen increasingly as suspect and amateurish by a small but growing group of academically trained "scientists" in the United States,

---

5 James Urry, "Notes and Queries on Anthropology and the Development of Field Methods in British Anthropology, 1870–1920," *Proceedings of the Royal Anthropological Institute of Great Britain and Ireland for 1972*, 45–57.

Germany, and Great Britain. They viewed the practice of anthropology as a proto-laboratory science in which data had to be carefully collected before they could be used to test hypotheses about the nature of social laws. Expeditions were organized to collect data relevant for specific scientific and historical questions.[6]

By the 1920s, British and American anthropologists had turned radically away from the comparative studies of the nineteenth century. Two new anthropological projects now emerged. British scholars reasserted the Enlightenment project of a natural science of society, based on a description and analysis of the structure and functioning of social forms within bounded groups. For the Americans the object of anthropology became the construction or reconstruction of the uniqueness of individual cultures in relation to their histories, and the search for the mechanisms through which these cultures were transmitted. Although the projects of anthropologists began to proliferate and to vary as they have until the present, field work—the direct, first-hand observation of native peoples—continues to be the hallmark of anthropologists. Although Malinowski did not "invent" field work, his book, *The Argonauts of the Western Pacific,* published in 1922, was taken by most anthropologists as the *locus classicus* of the anthropological method. What a document is to historians, field work is to anthropologists.[7]

Malinowski stated that the ethnographer's "sources are in the behavior and in the memory of living men," which could only be obtained through direct observation. The goals of the ethnographer were to draw up, on the basis of these sources, "all the rules and regularities of tribal life; all that was permanent and fixed"; and to depict "an autonomy of their culture . . . and the constitution of their society." In addition, anthropologists recorded "the natives' views, opinions and utterances," and, by writing down texts in the natives' language, rendered "the verbal contour of native thought as precisely as possible." Through these texts, documents, or "native mentality," anthropologists had to

6 George W. Stocking, Jr., "From Physics to Ethnology: Franz Boas' Arctic Expedition as a Problem in the Historiography of the Behavioral Sciences," *Journal of the History of the Behavioral Sciences,* I (1965), 53–66; William H. R. Rivers, "A Genealogical Method of Collecting Social and Vital Statistics," *Journal of the Anthropological Institute,* XXX (1900), 74–82.

7 Bronislaw Malinowski, *The Argonauts of the Western Pacific* (London, 1922), 3.

"grasp the native's point of view, his relation to life, to realize *his* vision of *his* world."[8]

An indigenous language was not merely something which anthropologists had to learn, just as historians needed to know Latin or Greek to read texts, or German or Turkish to read documents, but it bound their objects of study to the assumption of one language, one culture. As nation states became historians' object of investigation in the nineteenth century, so the communities of language speakers became anthropologists' unit of study in the twentieth century.

Anthropological field work requires several significant epistemological entailments as it reduces the subject of enquiry to "my people"—those amongst whom anthropologists live and work and who appear in monographs. The object of field work becomes the establishment and reification of the "authenticity" of the peoples amongst whom the anthropologists work. This authenticity exists in the temporal frame, the "ethnographic present." The ethnographic present does not necessarily exist at the time and place in which anthropologists are working, but it is their reconstruction through long conversations with the natives of what the natives were like before the intrusion of European colonial domination. Anthropologists reconstruct the "ethnographic present" by "lopping off the more obvious results of colonial rule." If the study is one about law, then it is the chief's court in an African tribe or the memories of half-remembered conflicts, rather than the European judge's court or the contemporary squabbles on a modern reservation, that provide the data to be collected. When anthropologists study Hindu cosmologies, the account is drawn from shastric texts or discussions with pandits, and one never finds out how these concepts are reconciled with what is taught to many Indians in contemporary schools, where the students learn about a world which revolves on its axis every twenty-four hours.[9]

THE RETURN TO HISTORY   Ethnohistorians of native North America, Africa, Australia, and Oceania began a generation ago to try to write the history of their traditional subjects from the

8 *Ibid.*, 4, 21, 24.
9 Jack Goody, *The Social Organization of the LoWilli* (London, 1967; 2nd ed.), vi.

native's own standpoint. The sources used by ethnohistorians included documents written by European observers, the records of colonial governments, oral traditions, and the results of archaeological and historical linguistic research. They also drew on a variety of anthropological models and more recent ethnographic accounts to interpret older, and what had been thought to be less reliable or more biased accounts. Trigger, whose work on the Huron is among the most complete and sophisticated ethnohistorical accounts of a North American Indian people, locates the work of ethnohistorians between conventional historians and anthropologists, methodologically and chronologically between pre-history as reconstructed by archaeologists and the "ethnographic present" of field anthropologists.[10]

Traditional historians who have studied the history of the American Indians have been limited in their perspective because they used documents which were generated by white conquerors; hence, they accepted many of the assumptions of those who produced these sources. The Indian was seen either negatively or romantically as part of the environment, or as a problem to be overcome by the settlers. The basic analytical units which these historians used centered on the control and administration of the natives and on relations between whites and Indians in trade, warfare, and diplomacy.[11] Trigger points out that traditional anthropologists have difficulties locating and working with archival materials.

10 For a disucssion of the methods and problems of ethnohistorians see William Sturtevant, "Anthropology, History, and Ethnohistory," *Ethnohistory*, XIII (1966), 1–51; Cohn, "Ethnohistory," *International Encyclopedia of the Social Sciences* (New York, 1968), V, 440–448; Bruce G. Trigger, *The Children of Aataentsic: A History of the Huron People to 1660* (Montreal, 1976), I, 1–26; William Fenton, "Huronia: An Essay in Proper Ethnohistory," *American Anthropologist*, LXXX (1978), 923–934; James Axtell, "The Ethnohistory of Early America: A Review Essay," *William and Mary Quarterly*, XXV (1978), 110–144; Isabel McBryde, "Ethnohistory in an Australian Context: Independent Discipline or Convenient Data Quarry?" *Aboriginal History*, III (1979), 128–151; Urry, "Beyond the Frontiers: European Influences, Aborigines and the Concept of Traditional Culture," *Journal of Australian Studies*, V (1979), 2–16.

11 In the last decade scholarship on the history of American Indians has changed significantly from this traditional approach. See esp. Wilcomb Washburn, "The Writing of American Indian History: A Status Report," *Pacific Historical Review*, XL (1971), 26–281; Axtell, "Ethnohistory"; Robert Berkhofer, *White Man's Indian* (New York, 1978); Francis Jennings, *The Invasion of America* (Chapel Hill, 1975); Richard Drinnon, *Facing West* (Minneapolis, 1979).

When historical sources are used by anthropologists, it is usually to illustrate or support some particular point they wish to make. . . . Statements are considered without reference to their immediate context, and no effort is made to assess the biases or abilities of the recorder. The result is a mixture of arrogance and naiveté in the use of material which frequently repels the professional historian.[12]

Much of the more recent work of anthropologists on North American Indians deals with change; the assumption which is frequently made is that these changes can be measured from earlier ethnographic accounts which purport to be about the "untouched" natives. As Brasser and others have observed, however, "the Indian world had already been distorted before the first notes of ethnographic value had been jotted down." Hence, ethnohistorians must undertake a "detailed historical study of changes in Indian life." The chronological gap which ethnohistorians have to overcome is that of the time between the first direct or indirect white contact and the formalization of the ethnography of a particular Indian group.[13]

A major contribution of ethnohistorians has been to make historians and anthropologists increasingly aware that "authentic natives," the conventional objects of anthropological enquiry, had already gone through extensive changes before the first ethnographer appeared on the scene to record the texts and characteristics of their lives. In many parts of the world these changes preceded the establishment of direct European contact through the introduction of exotic microbes and viruses and the European demand for labor, resources, and objects, which often led to major ecological transformations.[14]

One of the many ironies which marks the history of European relations with the rest of the world is that many of what we

12 Trigger, *Aataentsic*, 12.

13 Ted J. C. Brasser, "Group Identification along a Moving Frontier," *Verhanlungen des XXXVIII Internationalen Americanistenkongresses* (Munich, 1968), II, 261; Trigger, *Aataentsic*, 4.

14 Alfred W. Crosby, Jr., *The Colonial Exchange: Biological and Cultural Consequences of 1492* (Westport, 1972); Urry, "Beyond the Frontiers," 2–16. Also see for example, Sherbourne F. Cook and Woodrow W. Borah, *Essays in Population History: Mexico and the Caribbean* (Berkeley, 1971–1979), 3 v.; *idem, The Indian Population of Central Mexico, 1531–1660* (Berkeley, 1960).

take to be authentic markers of the aboriginals of North America were created as result of European contact. The totem poles of the northwest coast, which adorn our parks and museums, could not have been constructed on the scale as we see them without the introduction of iron tools. The cultures and societies of the plains Indians were reconstituted after the advent of the horse. The crafts in Indian shops of the American Southwest and in most American airports, followed the arrival of the Spanish who brought sheep for the wool of Navajo blankets and tools to create the turquoise and silver jewelry adored by authenticity-seeking hippies.

CULTURE AS MEDIATED BY HISTORY   In the first half of the nineteenth century, Fiji, like most of the islands of the Pacific, was the scene of a complicated political, commercial, and theological war waged by European traders, labor recruiters, missionaries, sailors, planters, and administrators for the bodies, minds, souls, land, labor, and products of the indigenous peoples. For the Europeans, firearms, alcohol, trade goods, conversion to Christianity, and the occasional appearance of a European warship were the resources mustered to gain control over the peoples and their islands. The method primarily used was to enter into an alliance with local rulers in their battles with other Fijians by advancing them goods and services in return for the use of land and labor. Also involved were Tongans who themselves had come under European influence a generation before the Fijians, and sought to extend their hegemony over parts of the Fiji Islands. By 1860 the goal for most of the Europeans in Fiji was the permanent acquisition of land which could be exploited to grow sugar and cotton, this land being acquired from Fijian chiefs through grants, purchase, and fraud.[15]

Although Europeans had been active in Fiji since the beginning of the nineteenth century, no European power had annexed or claimed sovereignty over the Islands until 1874, when a "government" of Fijians and Europeans ceded the islands to the British Crown. Sir Arthur Gordon, the first permanent British Governor, arrived in 1875 to establish a government consonant "with the

15 J. D. Legge, *Britain in Fiji: 1858–1880* (London, 1958); Peter France, *The Charter of the Land: Custom and Colonization in Fiji* (London, 1969).

spirit in which native institutions have been framed, and endeavour so to work them as to develop to the utmost possible extent the latent capacities of the people for the management of their own affairs." One of Gordon's first tasks was to settle the question of the legal "ownership" of the land in Fiji through a commission established to investigate European and Fijian claims to the land. Gordon came to Fiji after being a colonial civil servant in New Brunswick, Trinidad, and Mauritius. He had a reputation for concern for the welfare of native peoples and believed that the Fijians should be ruled according to their own customs and institutions.[16]

In order to decide who owned the land, decisions had to be made about the nature of the indigenous political system and the position of chiefs or headmen in relation to the Fijian social groups of clans, lineages, and villages. Gordon believed that the Fijians should be ruled by their own chiefs, exercising their traditional rights; European officials were to be arbiters of conflicts among the Fijian rulers, and were to act as supervisors. Under the act of cession all land which had not been alienated previous to the act was to be declared Crown land. Europeans who claimed possession of Fijian acreage had to provide evidence of how their land was acquired and had to prove that its acquisition had not been by fraud. Gordon's policy was to maintain a substantial amount of land in local hands so that Fijians could develop "in accordance with their own traditional institutions."[17]

Before Gordon's arrival it had been assumed by Europeans that chiefs had a right to alienate land and this right was superior to any inferior's right to use the land; hence, land could be transferred outright to Europeans and the rights of users extinguished. Gordon was an enthusiastic follower of the anthropology of his time and believed in the theory of unilinear evolution propounded by Lewis Henry Morgan in *Ancient Society* (New York, 1877). Following Morgan's typology Gordon declared that the Fijians were just emerging from "barbarism" and were at a stage in

16 Arthur Gordon quoted in George K. Roth, *Native Administration in Fiji During the Past 75 Years* (London, 1951), 2; Peter France, "The Founding of an Orthodoxy: Sir Arthur Gordon and the Doctrine of the Fijian Way of Life," *Journal of the Polynesian Society*, LXXXVII (1968), 7.

17 *Ibid.,* 18.

which land was communally held and was therefore inalienable by any individual, be he chief or commoner.

Lorimer Fison, a Methodist missionary resident in Fiji for a number of years before Gordon arrived, who had collected information on kinship terminology in response to Morgan's questionnaire for his study, *Systems of Consanguinity and Affinity of the Human Family* (Washington, D.C., 1870), was also active in the debate about the nature of Fijian customs. Fison argued, on the basis of Morgan's evolutionary typology, that the Fijians were pre-feudal, a stage reached only after the production and use of iron, and were in the stage of middle barbarism because they were a stone-age people. In this stage the chief may be a commoner's lord, but could not be his landlord. Hence, the evidence that the Land Commission was collecting indicated that some Fijians indeed had what appeared to be private property rights in land but these rights were taken by Gordon and Fison to be evidence not of ancient Fijian customs and traditions, but of more recent practices due to European corruption.[18]

By the early twentieth century, a system of governance had been established in Fiji which consisted of a series of neatly graded social groupings at the base of which were villages, grouped into sections which had chiefs. These chiefs had superior chiefs who were grouped into territorially defined councils; the councils' chiefs were part of a Fijian-wide governing body. Land was declared to be communally held by kin groups who had chiefs to whom payments and services were owed by the communal groups. Except for those lands to which Europeans could establish title based on traditional custom, no foreigners—Europeans or the increasing number of East Indians who had been imported as indentured laborers on the European plantations—could acquire permanent rights over land not previously alienated. There was thought to be a uniformity of structure and custom throughout the 300 islands.[19]

18 *Ibid.*, 21–30.
19 Michael A. H. B. Walter, "The Conflict of the Tradition and the Traditionalized: An Analysis of Fijian Land Tenure," *Journal of the Polynesian Society,* LXXXVII (1978), 89–108; Tony Chapelle, "Customary Land Tenure in Fiji: Old Truths and the Middle Aged Myths," *ibid.*, 71–87; Marshall Sahlins, *Moala* (Ann Arbor, 1962); John Clammer, "Colonialism and the Perception of Tradition in Fiji," in Talal Asad (ed.), *Anthropology and the Colonial Encounter* (London, 1973), 199–222.

Fijians may not have been the originators of their reconstituted social order, but literate Fijians quickly learned about their "true and ancient traditions" from British officials, missionaries, and from British and Fijian publications. Following the anthropology of the late nineteenth century, Fijians "discovered" an origin myth which explained their history and their customs. Sahlins, who did field work in Moala, one of the Fijian Islands, in the 1950s, reported, "If you ask a Moalan today where his ancestors *originally* came from . . . you will probably receive the jarring reply, 'Tanganyika perhaps'." This interesting and erroneous piece of history, Sahlins continues, "is wholly of recent manufacture, perpetrated as much by speculative Europeans as by inventive natives." [20]

What the Moalans are referring to is the legend of the *Kaunitoni* migration: according to this tradition, a chief who had migrated from Thebes and had settled his people on the shores of Lake Tanganyika subsequently migrated in a great canoe, the *Kaunitoni,* eastward across the Indian Ocean and the Pacific until he landed on the rocky shore of Viti Levu, one of the larger Fijian Islands. From this landfall the people of the canoe and their descendants dispersed all over the Fiji Islands. This legendary origin of the peoples is now widely known; anthropologists have reported it since the early twentieth century, and archaeologists use it as the beginning point of their reconstruction of Fijian prehistory. [21]

The source of the *Kaunitoni* origin myth appears to have been compounded out of the speculations and "research" of three Europeans: Jesse Carey and Fison, missionaries who published a text book for Fijian schools on the "history" of Fiji, and the work of Basil Thompson, a British official and amateur anthropologist. Cary and Lorimer, on the basis of a study of place names, myths, and customs of ancient Thebes, and a study of tribes in Tanganyika and contemporary Fiji, tried to establish commonalities, which would "prove" an ultimate Thebean origin for the Fijians. In 1892 a Fijian language newspaper sponsored a contest "to select and preserve a definitive version of the legendary history of the

20 Clammer, *Literacy and Social Change: A Case Study of Fiji* (Leiden, 1970); Sahlins, *Moala,* 14 (italics in the original).
21 France, "The Kaunitoni Migration: Notes on the Gensis of a Fijian Tradition," *Journal of Pacific History,* I (1966), 107–108.

Fijian people." The winning account appeared to have been written for the paper by Illai Motonocoka, a Fijian employed as a clerk by Thompson.[22]

The process of the conversion of the European model of traditional Fijian social structure into a "native" model appeared to be so authentic that anthropologists in the 1950s took it as the base line from which social changes in the twentieth century could be assessed. In the 1960s and 1970s, as anthropologists, mainly through France's work, have become aware of how "traditional" Fijian customs were created and codified, they have sought once again, like the missionaries and administrators of the mid-nineteenth century, to seek "authentic" or original Fijian customs which lay behind the statements and practices of contemporary Fijians.

Why did Sahlins report that, when the Moalans told him that they had originally come from Tanganyika, it was "an erroneous piece of history" and the "product of recent manufacture"? He assumed that it was erroneous in terms of what he knew of "the history" of the peoples of the Pacific. Why can the *Kaunitoni* legend not pass the anthropologists' authenticity test? Anthropologists have no trouble reporting as authentic, i.e., very real to the people being studied, all sorts of "improbable and erroneous ideas" held by peoples everywhere. For the anthropologist authenticity, like chronology for the historian, is something natural—it has always been, therefore it has no history. Hence when the anthropologist is confronted, as was Sahlins, with something he knows was introduced from "outside," this is seen as an invention of particular persons whose intentions are knowable and can be dismissed as not being true or authentic in a particular native culture.[23]

The case of Fiji illustrates a process by which cultures have become constructed and reconstructed in much of the modern world, and have been accepted both by natives and others who study natives. Anthropologists cling to the idea that a people must have an "authentic" culture and their verification of this authenticity comes from studying the natives' point of view. This ver-

22 *Ibid.*, 103, 111–113.
23 Sahlins, *Moala*, 14.

ification is the counterpart of the positivist historians' conviction that the study of documents is the means by which a true or real account of what "actually happened" can be constructed.

What has been established in Fiji may be termed a colonial orthodoxy or a colonial sociology—a conscious model developed by the European rulers of what they took to be the traditional native social structure. This model was based on general theories of society and culture, which categorized the subjects in relation to their rulers as primitive, archaic, barbarian, savage, feudal, premodern, backward, or undeveloped. According to these categories and their implied theories the social groups were frequently assigned functional roles (such as warriors, rulers, peasants, intellectuals, artisans, and "traditional" elites) in a hierarchical order which was partially determined by a European construction of the history and culture of the ruled. Colonial sociology or orthodoxy defined temporal and spatial boundaries which marked off colonial territories one from the other, and institutions of the colonial control were established within them.

The native peoples who were the objects and subjects of these colonial control systems were caught up in a complex dialectic; they participated in the definition and compilation of the colonial sociology, not merely as informants, but frequently as the shapers and interpreters of the indigenous cultures. Everywhere the Europeans went they had guides to what was for them the "unknown," be it the indigenous trade routes of North America, the sources of gold and silver in Latin America, or the language and thought of the Vedas in India. To most of the places that the Europeans went, from the seventeenth century to the present, they carried sacred objects, which imparted to them magic and charisma—clothes, guns, books, clocks, cameras, printing presses, the telegraph, railroads, and ships—the ideas of heaven and hell, and orders, routines, and codes of conduct, all of which set them apart and made them powerful. In many places natives wanted the objects and the knowledge the Europeans had, and through force and attraction began to learn to understand and manipulate the ideas and objects the Europeans brought into their world.[24]

24 For examples of African, Melanesian, and American Indian representations of Europeans and their objects, see Julia Blackburn, *The White Men* (London, 1979).

ANTHROPOLOGICAL HISTORY   Since the early twentieth century, some historians have looked to anthropology, not just as one of the auxiliary sciences, but as a co-discipline. Thompson finds "the anthropological impulse chiefly felt, not in model building, but in locating new problems, in seeking old problems in new ways, in an emphasis upon norms or value systems and upon rituals, in attention to expressive functions of forms of riot and disturbance, upon symbolic expressions of authority, control and hegemony." Stone has commented that anthropologists are now taking more interest in the study of change, and in turn symbolic anthropologists, such as Mary Douglas, Victor Turner, and Clifford Geertz, are attracting the attention of some younger historians.[25]

The best French historians, writes Le Roy Ladurie, "from Marc Bloch to Pierre Goubert" have been "systematic systematizers" and have "practiced structuralism, deliberately or sometimes unconsciously." Braudel, not without some reservations, associates his work with that of Claude Levi-Strauss in the search for structural laws. The distinction made by the French historians between event-based history and history conceived of as "motionless" and of long duration, has led historians of this school, suggests Furet, to "rediscover the long economic states of permanence and the social and cultural inertias which have long characterized the societies of the ethnologist." LeGoff sees a "new" political history which "would be almost immobile if it was not linked, as political anthropology has shown it to be, to the essentially conflictual and therefore dynamic structures of societies." LeGoff, like Furet, expects that historians and ethnologists will be closer to each other after a divorce of 200 years.[26]

The ethnologists' concern with "repeated or expected events, feast days . . . events linked to biological and family history—birth, marriage and death . . . the liturgical element in a historical

25 Caroline F. Ware (ed.), *The Cultural Approach to History* (New York, 1940), 3–16; Edward P. Thompson, "Folklore, Anthropology, and Social History," *Indian Historical Review*, III (1977), 248; Lawrence Stone, "History and the Social Sciences in the Twentieth Century," in Charles F. Delzell (ed.), *The Future of History* (Nashville, 1977), 13–14.

26 Emmanuel Le Roy Ladurie, "Motionless History," *Social Science History*, I (1977), 118; Fernand Braudel, "History and the Social Sciences," in Peter Burke (ed.), *Economy and Society in Early Modern Europe: Essays from* Annales (London, 1972; orig. pub. 1958), 32; Furet, "History and Primitive Man," 203; Jacques LeGoff, "Is Politics Still the Backbone of History?" in Felix Gilbert and Stephen R. Graubard (eds.), *Historical Studies Today* (New York, 1972), 347.

society . . . the study of states of mind, mental outlooks . . . the role of magical elements, charisma" are now central concerns of historians. The anthropology projected by these historians is concerned with stability, structure, regularity, the local, the common, the small scale, and the expressive, symbolic, and magical. These features are typical of immobile or slow moving societies, which Levi-Strauss termed "cold" societies. In societies in which change seems cumulative, rapid, and transformative of the structures, then the anthropologically influenced historians look for those groups or categories within these "hot" societies who maintain aspects of this more immobile past—the engulfed and marginalized peasantry, the stubborn working classes, women who are mired in domesticity, and such semi-closed communities as academics, artists, and bandits.[27]

Doubts are raised by eminent historians about the fruitfulness of closer working relationships with anthropologists. Stone has seen social science's promise to revitalize the practice of history fade with the passing of decades. He seems worried that the marriage of one of Clio's daughters with anthropologists may go the way of the polyandrous union with economists, as entered into by Robert Fogel and Stanley Engerman. This union produced a child, Cliometrics, who was "intemperate and injudicious" and allowed "the tool to become an end in itself."[28]

Thompson, worried that the anthropological impulse could lead to barracking, cites the pointed exchange between Hildred Geertz and Thomas over his book, *Religion and the Decline of Magic* (New York, 1971). In commenting on this exchange, he suggests that research strategies are at issue and that historians can derive some stimulation from anthropologists but should not become ensnared in their debates and "ulterior assumptions."[29]

Le Roy Ladurie, even though he may be looking for "structural laws" and has admired "the efficacy of structuralist methods" as applied to New World kinship systems and mythologies, believes that these do not work as well on the European past. He

27 LeGoff, "The Historian and the Common Man," in Jerôme Dumoulin and Dominique Moisi (eds.), *The Historian Between the Ethnologist and the Futurologist* (Paris, 1973), 207.
28 Stone, "History and the Social Sciences," 28, 30.
29 Hildred Geertz, "An Anthropology of Religion and Magic, I," and Keith Thomas, "An Anthropology of Religion and Magic, II," *Journal of Interdisciplinary History,* VI (1975), 71–109; Thompson, "Folklore and Anthropology," 248.

also finds cultural anthropology "surer in its methods than in its achievements." Furet, who saw the divorce of anthropology and history as a result of European nationalism, predicts a new relationship between the two academic fields but cannot define what it will be. Higham, who suggests that anthropology, as practiced by Clifford Geertz, Turner and Douglas, is replacing literary criticism as a source of ideas for American intellectual historians, presumably is aware that their anthropology draws heavily on hermeneutics, analytical philosophy, and literary criticism.[30]

What has been questioned is the appropriateness for the study of the European past of the theories, models, and methods, which were developed by anthropologists in order to understand and interpret the non-European worlds. What is not clear analytically is whether this past is the same as, or analogous to, the non-European present. This is the same question which the nineteenth-century comparativists raised.

HISTORICAL ANTHROPOLOGY   Anthropology and history impart an understanding of the forms of knowledge which contributed to the construction of nation states in the European world, and to the creation of colonial control systems through which Europeans came to dominate other worlds. The capacity to control the past, by defining it as history, and to establish classifications which differentiate Europeans from others are central to the revolutions and transformations which are part of what we call the history of the modern world. In the last twenty years anthropologists and historians have become more conscious of the problematic nature of their definition of subject matter and their praxis, which has led, for anthropologists, to a deconstruction of their field, and, for historians, to a reformulation of their professional practices.

Historians have fared better professionally than anthropologists in this period of deconstruction and reformulation, as their academic departments, institutes, and professional organizations seem better able to accommodate new subject matter, methods, and theories without necessarily changing their basic orientations. Hence a history department can add fields, such as Middle Eastern

30 Le Roy Ladurie, "Motionless History," 118; Furet, "History and Primitive Man," 203; John Higham, "Introduction," in Higham and Paul Conkin (eds.), *New Directions in American Intellectual History* (Baltimore, 1979), xxvii.

History or Quantitative History, or split American History into sub-topics, such as Urban History, without unduly affecting the modes of thought and practice of their colleagues in more traditional fields.

The consequences of such deconstruction have had more radical effects on the practices of anthropologists and on their academic environments. The variety of projects which are now urged upon anthropologists is unmanageable. Some urge us to take an "interpretive turn"; others decry the "linguistic turn." There are polemics about "culture and practical reason" and "cultural materialism." Structuralism, old and new, phenomenology, Marxism, the study of world systems, political economy, sociobiology and symbolism all have their partisans and advocates. Anthropologists argue about whether culture is "on the ground," "in the heads of the natives," or made up of codes, metaphors, and texts. Discourse amongst anthropologists is filled with terms of abuse; one can be accused of being a utilitarian, a mentalist, an idealist, a materialist, a reductionist, a reflexionist, an extentionalist, and, worst of all, an eclectic. The challenge to "define one's terms" is the call to the field of battle. In anthropology, old debates never die; they just become enshrined in graduate curricula and text books. Thompson was right to warn historians not to buy used concepts from old anthropologists.[31]

Some anthropologists who are making these new turns invoke history to establish their intellectual legitimacy, when creating genealogies, and to resolve the inner contradiction between event and structure, and thought and action. In this revised interest in history on the part of anthropologists, and in the work of some historians, I see hope for establishing an agenda which would draw historians and anthropologists into a closer working relationship.

HISTORIES AS MEDIATED BY CULTURES   Anthropologists, in their study of others, encounter constructions by natives of pasts which do not fit the European idea of history as an objective, unmediated

31 Cohn, "History and Anthropology: The State of Play," *Comparative Studies in Society and History,* XXII (1980), 198–221; Paul Rabinow and William M. Sullivan (eds.), *Interpretive Social Science: A Reader* (Berkeley, 1979), Introduction, 1–21; Asad, "Anthropology and the Analysis of Ideology," *Man,* XIV (1979), 607–627; Sahlins, *Culture and Practical Reasoning* (Chicago, 1976); Marvin Harris, *Cultural Materialism* (New York, 1979).

account of what happened. The first reaction of anthropologists to the fact that natives had other kinds of pasts than they did was to apply their own conception of "real events" to statements that natives made about the past and to construct for them "objective" histories about what "really" happened. Much of the work of oral historians of Africa was based on the idea that by constructing "texts" out of oral traditions, comparing variants, collecting lists of kings' names and events, and by relating names, events, and place names in European documents to oral traditions, they could construct chronologies and histories in the Western mode. In doing so, African historians sought methods to circumvent the problem, raised by anthropologists working in Africa in the 1950s, of African histories as mythical charters, as statements about the present social structure, not as true reflections of an autonomous history leading to the present. As in sixteenth- and seventeenth-century Europe, so in late twentieth-century Africa, nineteenth-century India, and early twentieth-century Indonesia, history and the idea of the nation state came to be a political history of the pre-European past.[32]

In India, where there are texts which were the products and records of previous ages, European scholars quickly dismissed those accounts which were found in the Vedas, Brahamanas, the Puranas, and the Epics as "a maze of unnatural fictions, in which a series of real events can by no artifice be traced." The idea that India had no sense of history reached its apogee in MacDonell's statement: "Early India wrote no history because it never made any. The ancient Indians never went through the struggle for life, like the Greeks and Persians and the Romans in the Punic Wars, such as would have welded their tribes into a nation and developed political greatness."[33]

32 Jan Vansina, *The Children of Woot: A History of the Kuba Peoples* (Madison, 1978); David P. Henige, "Oral Tradition and Chronology," *Journal of African History,* XIII (1971), 371–389. For extension of this model of history for the Pacific, see P. M. Mercer, "Oral Tradition in the Pacific," *Journal of Pacific History,* XIV (1979), 130–153; Laura A. Bohannan, "Genealogical Charter," *Africa,* XXII (1952), 301–315; John Barnes, "The Perception of History in a Plural Society," in Simon and Phoebe Ottenberg (eds.), *Societies of Africa* (New York, 1960), 318–326. See the arguments between Donald Denoon and Adam Kuper, "Nationalist Historians: The 'New Historiography' in Dar es Salaam," *African Affairs,* LXIX (1970), 329–349; Terence O. Ranger, "The New Historiography in Dar es Salaam: An Answer," *ibid.,* LXXX (1971), 50–61.

33 Mill, *History of India,* 145; A. A. MacDonnell, *A History of Sanskrit Literature* (London, 1900), 11.

European and Indian historians of early India have struggled in the twentieth century with these assumptions and sought means to construct a chronological framework by demythologizing the Puranas and the Epics, by establishing genealogies of kings and other personages, and by collecting inscriptions for which rough dates could be established paleographically. The struggle for a chronology was part of a larger struggle for and by Indians to establish a political history, from which emerge Indian republics, empires, great rulers, great battles, rich and powerful merchants, declines and falls, bureaucracies, revolution, and even nascent capitalism.[34]

In the past few years an anthropological history has emerged which does not try to construct an African, Chinese, Indian, or Southeast Asian history as a reflection of European history. The texts and codified oral traditions are read not to establish chronologies nor to sift historical fact from mythical fancy, but to try to grasp the meanings of the forms and contents of these texts in their own cultural terms.

The method is carefully explicated by Errington in her discussion of a classical Malay *hikayat,* a genre of texts which relate stories of events and personages in the past. Her analysis proceeds by the examination of the form, and through this analysis captures the meaning of thought embodied in the *hikayat.* Malay verbs do not show tense and the events in the text are not temporally ordered; in this sense the *hikayat* is not a narrative, but a succession of images which convey the sense intended. To the Western reader, the "story" is filled with repetitions and the speeches of the characters are not personal but relate to their functions. There are no "individuated voices of characters" nor is there an "authorial voice." As is the case in other parts of South and Southeast Asia, the sound of words has a physical quality apart from what Westerners think of as the "meaning." "The imagery of sounds and silence in the text," Errington tells us, "is persuasive." She concludes by suggesting that in the Malay world the relation between event and form is thought about and is the reverse of

---

34 F. E. Pargiter, *Ancient Indian Historical Tradition* (London, 1922); Thomas R. Trautmann, "Length of Reign and Generation in Ancient India," *Journal of the American Oriental Society,* LXXXIX (1969), 564–577; Romila Thapar, "Genealogy as a Source of Social History," *Indian Historical Review,* II (1976), 259–281.

ours; it converts "the transitory events into something which endures."[35]

McKinley tells us how contemporary Malays conceptualize their relationship to history in what he terms "the epistemological ages in Malay culture." Malays have two concepts of history, one being *zaman*—era or age—which relates to what we would term a secular period, such as the Japanese occupation or the coming of white men to Malaya. The other term, *masa,* is used by Malays to relate periods or times in the "evolution of religious cosmologies in Southeast Asia." Siegel describes how the recitation and the nature of the *hikayat* of the Achenese of Sumatra are being transformed by the spread of literacy, other types of performances such as movies, and the recent political events in the region.[36]

The search for indigenous forms of knowledge in relation to the creation of national histories is not only an academic exercise but also lies at the center of the creation of nations out of multilingual and cultural entities which were given form during the colonial period. Moreover, the question of the past, the idea of history, the role which histories play in relation to social structure, the formation of hegemonic systems and polities, the internal forms which texts and narratives present in relation to wider forms of thought, and the creation of varied epistemologies have all been widely studied as part of Western thought and history. Europeans have fought since the sixteenth century over definitions of their past. The analyses of such topics as the "Norman yoke," the origin of the village community, the representation of French Revolutionary patriotism as a Roman virtue, the construction of German history and culture out of northern European mythology, and the symbolic significance of historical figures such as Napo-

35 Shelly Errington, "Some Comments on Style in the Meanings of the Past," *Journal of Asian Studies,* XXXVIII (1979), 231–244; see also James Siegel, *Shadow and Sound: The Historical Thought of a Sumatran People* (Chicago, 1979), 204–211, 244.

36 Robert McKinley, "Zaman Dan Masa, Eras and Periods: Religious Evolution and the Permanence of Epistemological Ages in Malay Culture," in Anton L. Becker and Aram Yengoyan (eds.), *The Imagination of Reality: Essays in Southeast Asian Coherence Systems* (Norwood, N. J., 1979), 300, 303–324. The essays in this work exemplify the conjunction of textual, linguistic, and anthropological study in the construction of culture. They provide an excellent introduction to contemporary anthropological method and thought. Siegel, "Shadow and Sound", 267–282.

leon, Cromwell, and Lenin have to be examined in anthropological as well as historical terms.[37]

REPRESENTATION OF ORDERS   Europeans not only write and read history; they represent it to themselves in a wide variety of ways. Our landscapes, towns, cities and capitals, public buildings, houses, streets, and public monuments individually and collectively convey a past and are central to the representation of order and authority in our society. Bourdieu and Tambiah have explained that the Thai and Berber houses are both statements about and are modeled on cosmographic ideas; they are expressions of the cultural construction of people and their lives, their relations to each other, their animals, and the supernatural. The ordering of space does not merely reflect social relations and social structure, but is the part of the actual constitution of the sociological order.[38]

Girouard's study of Victorian country houses demonstrates that the nineteenth-century English were no less enmeshed in webs of signification and representation than were the Berbers or the Thais. Architects in planning these houses had to separate the cooking of food from its consumption, as odors of all kinds were substantialized, much as the Malays substantialized sound. Passing of bodily wastes, care of the young, and household tasks of cleaning, storing, and washing were all sources of offensive odors. Victorian houses were also based on a series of separations of persons and activities, based on their status and functions in the household. English houses of the nineteenth century had names, emblems, genealogies, and histories in the form of documents which were attached to property, and were independent of fam-

---

37 Sue Nichterlein, "Historicism and Historiography in Indonesia," *History and Theory*, XIII (1974), 253–272.

38 Pierre Bourdieu, "The Berber House," and Stanley J. Tambiah, "Classification of Animals in Thailand," in Mary Douglas (ed.), *Rules and Meaning*, 98–110, 127–166. On the wider significance of spatial orders see Lucy J. Kamau, "Conceptual Patterns in Yoruba Culture," in Amos Rappaport (ed.), *The Mutual Interaction of People and their Built Environment* (The Hague, 1976), 333–363; Hilda Kuper, "The Language of Sites in the Politics of Space," *American Anthropologist*, LXXIV (1972), 411–415. The classic statement on the significance of spatial orders is Emile Durkheim and Marcel Mauss, *Primitive Classifications* (London, 1963).

ilies and lineages; persons were known by the names of their properties.[39] The polity, economic society, and domestic life in nineteenth-century England were all constituted and represented in relation to the Royal Family. Bagehot saw the attachment of the English to this family as the "dignified" part of the English constitution which brought to the government its "force" and "motive power." This allegiance excited "the reverence of the population" with "semi-filial feelings." The Crown was the "visible symbol of unity" which brought the "pride of sovereignty to the level of petty life" and was found in the "actions of retired widows and unemployed youth." The investitures, marriages, and funerals of the Royal Family and great public leaders are life cycle rites which provide occasions for lavish public rituals. The ancient universities and the Inns of Court are organized around the sharing of food. The offices of civil servants seem to be like sitting rooms, and banquets, lawn parties, teas, drawing rooms, and regimental mess halls all affirm the domestic nature of authority.[40]

Hocart maintained that lordship or kingship grew out of ritual and that kings were priests, charged with enhancing the well being and prosperity of their people as well as with maintaining social order. Hence their centers were modeled on or constructed to symbolize the cosmos.[41]

Cities were, and many still are, symbolic of the relationship of people to ruler and ruler to God. Washington, D.C. was planned to symbolize the constitution, with its separation of powers, and to represent the federative relationship of the constituent states in its layout of public buildings, streets, and circles. Paris was rebuilt in the second half of the nineteenth century to reflect the grandeur of a great world power. In the reconstruction of London in the nineteenth century, the Royal Palace was linked

39 Mark Girouard, *The Victorian Country House* (Oxford, 1971); Robert Kerr, *The Gentleman's House* (New York, 1972; orig. pub. London, 1871), 202. For a discussion of the cultural significance of houses, see Clifford E. Clark, Jr., "Domestic Architecture as an Index to Social History," *Journal of Interdisciplinary History,* VII (1976), 35–56; Robert Boyd, *The Australian Home* (Melbourne, 1952); Conrad Hamann, "Nationalism and Reform in Australian Architecture," *Historical Studies,* XVII (1979), 393–411; Anthony King, *Colonial Urban Development* (London, 1976); Rappaport, *House Form and Culture* (Englewood Cliffs, 1969).

40 Walter Bagehot, *The English Constitution* (London, 1963; orig. pub. 1867), 60–61, 82–86.

41 Arthur M. Hocart, *Kings and Councillors* (Chicago, 1970; orig. pub. 1936).

by a broad parade boulevard, which passed through a monumental square celebrating the great English naval victory over the French, to the newly built houses of Parliament, which were adjacent to the ancient religious center of the country. The British built New Delhi as an imperial capital with the form of a Mughal Durbar, in which the Viceroy's Palace overlooks the colonial bureaucracy and the princes of India, as well as the remnants of Hindu polities. The wilderness of the United States was marked off in mile squares and its cities locked into grid plans to symbolize the rationality of the Enlightenment.

The newly constructed capitals of the nineteenth century provided arenas in which the increasingly lavish political rituals of the nation-states were performed. As authority and its charisma moved from the semi-privacy of royal courts, and as politically influential circles were enlarged to encompass a national's public, the person of the rulers, elected or selected by inheritance, and their entourages had to be seen. Great state funerals, the openings of parliament, celebrations of national holidays, victories of the people, or defeats of kings and ruling classes were occasions for which new national and state ritual idioms had to be created. If colonial systems of control were based on colonial sociologies, then new public rituals were based on the new internal social orderings in which the internal others—the working class or the new middle class—had their place in the line of march or in the audience.[42]

It is relatively simple to suggest and explore subject matters which are of joint interest to historians and anthropologists. It is much more difficult to delineate a common epistemological space which

[42] On the rituals of the state and representations of authority and ideologies, see George Mosse, *The Nationalization of the Masses* (New York, 1975); Mona Ozouf, "Space and Time in the Festivals of the French Revolution," *Comparative Studies in Society and History*, XVII (1975), 372–384; Charles Rearick, "Festivals in Modern France: The Experience of the Third Republic," *Journal of Contemporary History*, XII (1977), 435–460; Henry Millon and Linda Nochlin (eds.), *Art and Architecture in the Service of Politics* (Cambridge, Mass., 1978); J. P. Cogherty, "Baroque and Picturesque Motifs in L'Enfant's Design for the Federal Capital," *American Quarterly*, XXVI (1976), 23–36; Roy Strong, *The Cult of Elizabeth* (London, 1977); Kenneth S. Inglis, "Australia Day," *Historical Studies*, XIII (1967), 20–41; Christopher A. P. Binns, "The Changing Face of Power: Revolution and Accommodation in the Development of The Society Ceremonial System," *Man*, XIV (1979), 585–606.

can be termed historical anthropology. Some of the historians who met to discuss "history in the 1980s" at the conference in Bellagio called for a reassertion of the historian's role as narrator, albeit a narrator whose story would be more complete, encompassing not only events but also structures which would yield a more complex and perhaps truer history of modern man. This history would include the findings of those historians whose social science interests have so broadened the subject matter of history. At the same time it would reject the more rigid methodologies used by these historians and the teleologies of most social scientific theories of change.

Many anthropologists who have turned to history have seen it as a means of escaping the assumptions of an unchanging, timeless native culture, and have thereby uncovered events which led to the reformulation of structures. Yet by situating their histories inside tribes and archaic kingdoms, anthropologists find that their narratives always end with the coming of the destructive others—the Europeans. Anthropological historians or historical anthropologists cannot deal with history only as the reconstruction of what has happened, and as the explication of the natives' own understanding of the encounter with Europeans. They must also deal with the fact that events have consequences for those people who are our "subjects" up to and including their total destruction. Historical anthropology then will be the delineation of cultures, the location of these in historical time through the study of events which affect and transform structures, and the explanation of the consequences of these transformations. This will not yield a "scientific" theory of social change such as nineteenth-century scholars sought, but rather a history of change.

Anthropology and History in the 1980s

John W. Adams

Consensus, Community, and Exoticism Anthropological concepts, which have been taken out of context and applied without full understanding, have been misused by historians of colonial North America. Part of the difficulty is due to the normal hazards of incorporating the work of another field in one's own; and part is due to the reluctance of historians to employ monothematic explanations. This latter difficulty has led historians to favor those concepts of anthropology which are not easily measured.

ANTHROPOLOGY, HISTORY, AND NATURAL HISTORY The interest of social historians in anthropology has been one-sided. Although historians are excited about the work of Clifford Geertz, Victor Turner, and Mary Douglas, they do not seem to feel the same enthusiasm for the work of such antropologists as John Whiting, Roy Rappaport, or Marvin Harris, or of Anthony Wallace, David Schneider, or Marshall Sahlins, who are of equal importance within the field. As a result historians have borrowed only what was most like history as currently practiced: studies concerned with ideas.

Anthropology has always been poised awkwardly between history and natural history, its practitioners usually preferring one of the two approaches, while granting that the other is also valid. A recent statement in the *Annual Reviews,* a convenient source for authoritative positions of this sort, sees the field divided into ideational and adaptational conceptions of culture, under the renewed influence of Marxist thinking.[1]

There is still no agreement as to whether anthropology is

John W. Adams is Associate Professor of Anthropology at the University of South Carolina.

0022-1953/81/020253-13 $02.50/0

1 Roger M. Keesing, "Theories of Culture," *Annual Review of Anthropology,* III (1974), 73–97. A recent addendum is Keesing's review of Marshall Sahlins, *Culture and Practical Reason* (Chicago, 1976), in *American Anthropologist,* LXXXII (1980), 130–131.

like a science which has laws. The statement by Geertz that we must be content with interpretations, not laws, may have been misinterpreted by many historians as a denial that there is much regularity in human affairs—and therefore as a license to search out what appears to be unique. Yet anthropologists of both persuasions stress that regularities and patterning underlie a diverse range of societies or their parts. Many seek broad trends in cultural evolution and explain them using a materialism which historians may find uncongenial. At the same time, most anthropologists deny that differences in cultures are attributable to the biological differences of their members or that history has any predetermined course. Thus the materialist position, best (and certainly most notoriously) represented by the work of Harris, declares that the factors of demography, ecology, and the economy are more fundamental than such superstructural ideas as the sacredness of cows to Hindus. This is an old controversy, but a real one to most anthropologists today. It raises problems for historians who might wish to borrow anthropological concepts, especially those which are ideational.[2]

UNITS OF ANALYSIS   A basic problem for any discipline lies in its choice of phenomena to study which are sufficiently well-defined that they can be located in actual data. Ideationalists focus on rules and symbols; materialists on subsistence strategies and population densities. Between these lie the great common-sense units of study such as marriage, family, and community, which have enabled anthropologists to uncover similarities within cultures around the world. It has been fairly easy to demonstrate that forms which Western Europeans accepted as perfectly natural were only one of several cultural variations on the same institution. But the range of examples discovered has been so great that some scholars doubt whether it is possible to construct a universal definition of these units. Are the most extreme examples really instances of the same thing. Is marriage universal? Do all kinship systems recognize both the father's and the mother's side of the family as kin? Are there families in all societies? Do all societies

2 Clifford Geertz, "Thick Description: Toward an Interpretive Theory of Culture," in *idem*, *The Interpretation of Cultures* (New York, 1973), 3–30; Marvin Harris, *Cultural Materialism* (New York, 1979).

have nuclear families? These and similar questions make it clear that anthropology is presently at the limits of its terminology.[3]

The choice of significant units entails various conclusions about human nature which become problematic for proponents of different theoretical approaches to the study of man. The task of choosing one for application in another discipline involves a definite choice of theoretical perspective. To choose symbolic dualisms or "role reversal" is to take a position in favor not only of doing a certain kind of history, but also of doing a certain kind of anthropology, and to risk some predictable criticisms. Ideational (or symbolic) anthropology is often seen as being too concerned with the strange, the wonderful, and the subjective at the expense of the ordinary.

A further, disconcerting problem for historians who wish to use the insights of anthropology is that anthropological concepts are not easily transferrable. Their particularity is not helped by the propensity of anthropologists over the years to study cultural processes which have often turned out to have existed only in the minds of the profession, for example the totemic complex, mother right, tribe, clan, and village. Even Turner, who first studied and named "communitas," reports that this concept is so evanescent that it is no sooner noticed than it disappears.[4]

CONSENSUS AND COMMUNITY   The most satisfactory, recent work on colonial America which uses anthropological insights is that by Boyer and Nissenbaum on the Salem witchcraft hysteria. By placing the dispute, and the parties to it, within the local network of kinship and marriage ties, they showed how such ties both united and separated the participants. This matter-of-fact account uses the well-replicated and thoroughly discussed findings of anthropology, particularly those of the British structuralist school. Such a study is, no doubt, exactly what Thomas hoped to encourage historians to undertake some twenty years ago when he reviewed the potential of anthropological findings for history.[5]

3 A useful discussion of these problems runs through Ira R. Buchler and Henry A. Selby, *Kinship and Social Organization* (New York, 1968).
4 Victor Turner, *The Ritual Process* (Chicago, 1968).
5 Paul Boyer and Stephen Nissenbaum, *Salem Possessed: The Social Origins of Witchcraft* (Cambridge, Mass., 1974); Keith Thomas, "History and Anthropology," *Past & Present*, 24 (1963), 3–24.

However, the early attempts to import the family reconstitution methods of the *Annales* and Cambridge schools and combine them with concepts from social anthropology have resulted in a misapplication of these concepts. For example, Lockridge, in his book on Dedham, Massachusetts, considers the village more or less in isolation from other villages in the Colony and treats it as a "closed corporate peasant community" which is "self-shaping." To anthropologists a basic attribute of peasant societies is that they are "part-societies with part-cultures" because they exist in relationship to a more urbanized elite. Thus there is a possible theoretical contradiction here between "peasant society" and "self-shaping" which should have been addressed. The basic documentation for the study was derived from town records which do not include the relevant materials from surrounding localities. With regard to marriage, for instance, New England villages during this period were only about 54 percent endogamous; some 46 percent of the young people found spouses in neighboring towns, which suggests that Dedham was not the isolated world of "relentless immobility" which Lockridge supposed.[6]

A different point of criticism would be to ask why a social history is so concerned with the Revolution at the expense of the theme of utopianism, which is stressed explicitly in the book but is never used as a controlling model. Lockridge might equally well have compared the town of Dedham with the many other utopian communities for which we have good records and have drawn some conclusion about the degree to which its fate was typical of the set. Such an examination, however, would have shifted the focus from history to social science. Moreover, we are asked to regard Dedham as a typical example of the transformation of "a world we have lost" into something prototypically American, though this generalization (also one of a social science) goes unsubstantiated. Only later did colonial historians begin to

6 Kenneth Lockridge, *A New England Town: The First Hundred Years* (New York, 1970), 18–19; George M. Foster, "Introduction: What Is a Peasant?" in Jack M. Potter et al. (eds.), *Peasant and Society: A Reader* (Boston, 1967), 2–14; Adams and Alice Bee Kasakoff, "Migration at Marriage in Colonial New England: A Comparison of Rates Derived from Genealogies with Rates from Vital Records," in Bennett Dyke and Warren Morrill (eds.), *Genealogical Demography* (New York, 1980); Lockridge, "The Population of Dedham, Massachusetts, 1636–1735," *Economic History Review*, XIX (1966), 318–344.

compare their findings about single villages in New England with each other, with other regions, and with Europe.[7]

Often in these studies the word "community" is used not only to denote a small-scale settlement, such as a village, but also to imply a warm and closely knit social group. This implied correlation should alert us to ideological preferences. In the experience of anthropologists small villages are by no means always warm and happy places; they typically have factions, feuds, and even witchcraft accusations as part of their regular functioning. Dissensus occurs with consensus, as happened in the case of Salem.

THE BALINESE COCKFIGHT   Recently, colonial historians have shifted from studying towns to trying to discover one social institution—a Court Day, horse racing, gambling, or duelling—which might be the equivalent of the Balinese cockfight which Geertz suggested was a focus of widely held values in Bali. However, the nature of the Balinese cockfight and its possible universality has never been discussed by historians. Is there any reason to believe that an equivalent might have existed in colonial America? To search one out is a task to which many anthropologists would assign a low-priority, for not every culture has a ritual which serves ethnologists as a unique focus for describing values.[8]

The Nuer, who otherwise have a culture of great paradigmatic value, have no institution which sums up their values, although cattle were said by Evans-Pritchard to be at the center of all Nuer interests. Someone searching for potential "Balinese cockfights" among the Nuer would be frustrated, or would have to redefine the concept substantially (making it more operational in the process) to uncover even a reasonable surrogate. Indeed, a more useful search might be for the reason why so few societies develop this kind of focal institution.[9]

Besides the Balinese, the two best known examples of societies which have focal institutions are the Trobriand Islanders,

7   For example, W. R. Prest, "Stability and Change in Old and New England: Clayworth and Dedham," *Journal of Interdisciplinary History*, VI (1976), 359–374.

8   Geertz, "Deep Play: Notes on the Balinese Cockfight," in *idem, The Interpretation of Cultures*, 412–453.

9   E. E. Evans-Pritchard, *The Nuer* (New York, 1940), 16–50.

who observe the Kula ring ritual, and the Kwakiutl, who have the potlatch. Both are original examples of what Mauss called "total social phenomena." But the Balinese, the Trobianders, and the Kwakiutl have all developed self-consciously stratified societies, and lack an ideology of upward social mobility. Both the Balinese and Kwakiutl conceptualize their societies as sets of permanent statuses which people occupy temporarily. Trobriand chiefs, however, look forward to the receipt, and temporary ownership, of legendary, named valuables which circulate in perpetuity, while their owners are quickly replaced. In all three cases the earthly order of things is permanent, and is suffused with a sense of the importance of etiquette for the proper management of status.[10]

The frontier of colonial America is an unlikely place to find the cultural equivalents of a Balinese cockfight, a Kula ring, or a potlatch, given that, for those settlers who were interested in the here and now, it was a new social beginning, and, for those to whom it was but a temporary way station, other considerations took precedence over earthly status. Yet there was a ritual in New England which summed up the values of the society which practiced it: Sunday church-going, with the whole community arranged in pews which reflected the relative social ranking of the parishioners, who came to hear a sermon embodying the dominant values. Although the medium for their expression may seem too prosaic to be a true equivalent of the exotic cockfight, the institution of church-going had the virtue, true as well of the cockfight, that the participants were undertaking a life-or-death wager, not on their social status, but on their chance for salvation.[11]

If we were to accept this as a reasonable surrogate for the cockfight, we would have to inquire as to whether other parts of the model applied as well. Was New England actually more stratified than is usually thought, or was it more worldly? Or were these attributes of our putative model of a focal ritual simply contingent? Perhaps other attributes were crucial. One possible line of inquiry might be to determine the degree to which such institutions bridge a disjunction between two audiences: the cock-

10 Marcel Mauss, *The Gift* (London, 1954).
11 Frederick Augustus Whitney, "A Church of the First Congregational Society in Quincy, Mass., Built in 1732," *New England Historical and Genealogical Register*, XVIII (1864), 117–131.

fight often pits members of one community against members of
another, as do the Kula ring and the potlatch. If we take this
condition as fundamental, then a Sunday church service in New
England would not be a viable example. Moreover, in all three
of the anthropological examples the rituals socially humiliate certain participants, without engendering any sense of religious hu-
mility in the process. They are the opposite of the ritual activity
which Turner has characterized as "communitas": an evanescent
historical moment in which a mood of human fellowship pervades
the social relations of people who are otherwise caught up in the
humanly divisive, hierarchical relations found in all societies. Potlatch, Kula, and cockfight, on the contrary, display social hierarchy.[12]

This is not the place to develop a model of such institutions,
but it is appropriate to consider them in order to suggest the kind
of comparative work that could be done by historians. No such
work was done by Beeman when he advised historians that an
unappreciated resource lay in Turner's concept of communitas.
In fact he proposed a misreading: Beeman mistakes it for something akin to Redfield's "community." Yet Turner's idea is precisely that communitas, being a transient mood, cannot be captured in any social institution, and that attempts to do so have
always failed. There is a certain nostalgia in Beeman's enthusiasm
for the concept (possibly true of Turner as well), which anthropology is being employed to erase. It is also symptomatic of the
preference for such ideological concepts that, although Beeman
should find Turner's work on communitas attractive, he has apparently overlooked the equally substantial contribution which
Turner made to the understanding of the politics of small villages
in which almost everyone was related and where witchcraft accusations were common. For that matter, which social historians
read *The Lele* or *Agricultural Involution*?[13]

Beeman seems to ask of Turner's work on communitas that

12   For a recent study which cites much of the relevant literature on stratification, see
William Pencak, "The Social Structure of Revolutionary Boston: Evidence from the Great
Fire of 1760," *Journal of Interdisciplinary History*, X (1979), 267–278.
13   Richard R. Beeman, "The New Social History and the Search for 'Community' in
Colonial America," *American Quarterly*, XXIX (1977), 422–443; Turner, *Ritual Process*;
Robert Redfield, *The Little Community* (Chicago, 1955); idem, *Peasant Society and Culture*
(Chicago, 1955); Turner, *Schism and Continuity in an African Society* (Manchester, 1957).
Mary Douglas, *The Lele* (London, 1954); Geertz, *Agricultural Involution* (Chicago, 1963).

it cure the theoretical disjunction which Beeman experiences between structure and psychology, that is, between a science of society which focuses impersonally on the structure of a group and a science which depicts lives of individuals in readily intuited psychological descriptions. Yet the dialectical oscillation between hierarchy and communitas is precisely Turner's way of dramatizing the ever-present gap between structure and psychology and his way of asserting that it can never be finally overcome.[14]

To investigate historical phenomena by means of concepts like communitas and the Balinese cockfight without examining them is to engage in *la pensée sauvage*. It is also utopian thinking in the case of communitas, and a complete misunderstanding of the nature of history and cross-cultural comparison in the case of the Balinese cockfight.

EXOTICISM   When a ritual event is alleged to be, in effect, the total activity of an entire town, as is the case in so many studies, it is essential to break through that sort of immaterial conception to place it in the more immediate context of ordinary daily life. Waters' characterization of Guilford, Connecticut, as made up of stem-family households is an example of deliberate exoticism used to suggest the rootedness of the settlers as contrasted with our own supposedly more rootless times. He ignores the fact that there must be sufficient people of the right sex and age in Guilford for stem-family households to be common, and that no such type, given the nature of the variables, can ever solely characterize a society. Indeed, if there is any law in anthropology, it is a law of exceptions: that variations will be found in every rule or pattern.[15]

The concept of the stem family household cannot be applied to New England, as computer simulation shows. Herein lies a potential trap for unwary historians who use ideas from anthropology: there is a widespread, persistent feeling that anthropologists study exotic customs, whereas it is truer to say that they study the mundane in exotic locales. As for the exotic itself, they seem always to reduce it to some (outlandishly) commonsense

---

14 Beeman, "New Social History," 431, n. 18.
15 John Waters, "Patrimony, Succession, and Social Stability: Guilford, Connecticut, in the Eighteenth Century," *Perspectives in American History*, X (1976), 131–160.

explanation, such as that ritual cannibalism is a response to protein deficiency.[16]

Far from examining only the curious ritual occasion, anthropologists begin by counting populations and mapping villages. They hope that, by spending a year in the field, they can shed light, not only on the natives' way of life, but on their unconscious expectations as well. Since the exotic is only so in relation to our own culture, anthropologists have a professional distrust of the exotic, and at times virtually refuse to recognize that it exists.

A major difficulty in the development of knowledge in both ethnography and history is precisely this culture of the investigator, which even now goes largely unexamined because it resists discovery. Outsiders see it readily enough, which makes fieldwork on an island in the Pacific both easy and intellectually satisfying in ways which elude students of their own backyards, including historians of colonial America. What we do need to find out is whether what we study is ordinary and mundane, or whether the ordinary and mundane is merely a more pernicious version of our culture's commonsense understanding of things. Similarly it is important for historians to continue asking why they study particular phenomena.

TOWARD THE 1980S   In the next decade both anthropology and history will themselves become topics for investigation, as natural history has become for historians. The emerging ethnology will be one which examines the ordinary and the folklife, not the unusual, the highbrow, or the exotic. As anthropologists we will undertake research which parallels that of history without people, and of processual history, while social historians will examine implicit assumptions of daily life, which are free of the officially declared, contemporary values, and have not been formally ritualized by the community. Demos' use of the implications for daily living of the sizes and locations of rooms in Plymouth houses and Boyer and Nissenbaum's uncovering of the network of kinship in Salem are examples of such research. The common sense of a culture dwells close to material constraints—and does not question them. It will be our job to discover the premises

16 Kenneth Wachter et al., *Statistical Studies of Historical Social Structure* (New York, 1978).

which underlie this common sense and justify behavior as perfectly natural.[17]

Anthropologists have had little feeling for how the daily activities of the peoples that they study could become historical. Theirs is a wholly different perspective on daily life from that of historians, who write with the advantage of hindsight. Which historians can look at people's lives and not think of those contemporaneous events which history has singled out as important? Historians implicitly scrutinize all behavior for its potential relationship to the eventful. Anthropologists have their comparable teleological flaw: that everything they see during their short stints of fieldwork must be integrated in some way. Foucault, a social historian, has presented a solution to this latter problem in his call for an archaeology of knowledge. He suggests that we regard the array of facts at a given moment as if it were one layer of an archaeological dig, in which some elements cluster in meaningful association, but where others simply happen to be there and elude connection with the clusters. Anthropologists might, in turn, remind historians of colonial America that not every action has a cumulative historical goal.[18]

Here are two very different conceptions of human activity: the anthropologist's, which seldom conceives of the possibility that the moments of daily life might lead to anything for the history books; and the historian's, which often must see in each and every moment a determinant of some significant future or an exemplification of some significant past. At best (or worst?) anthropologists think of mundane actions as representative of sociological principles—although these principles are *not* confused with the actor's motivations.

At first anthropologists considered human action as something of an end in itself, a timeless round of custom. But this false start gave way to the discovery of a repertory of goals which were commonsensical and maximizing: to obtain a good harvest, to outdo a neighbor in gift-giving, to marry well, to get better

17 On anthropology see Robert A. LeVine and Donald T. Campbell, *Ethnocentrism* (New York, 1972); on "history" see Ioan M. Lewis, "Introduction," in *idem* (ed.), *History and Social Anthropology* (London, 1968). Michel Foucault, *The Order of Things* (New York, 1970). John Demos, *A Little Commonwealth* (New York, 1970); Boyer and Nissenbaum, *Salem Possessed.*

18 Foucault, *The Archaeology of Knowledge* (New York, 1972).

land, or to maintain one's following. This discovery restored to the pages of ethnographic description a goal-oriented actor, but one who was concerned with everyday activities not epic deeds. To anthropologists who are not much concerned with action from its historical perspective, many historians of colonial America seem to have their ears always cocked to the distant rumblings of the Revolution. This teleology gives the work of historians an idealistic cast. Historians might try to forget the eventful in favor of a history of simpler, everyday life. There is after all a major difference between behavior which is self-consciously trying to be historical and behavior which turns out to be historical.

THE METAPHOR OF TEXT   Recently Geertz suggested the metaphor of social behavior as text as a supplement for, or replacement of, the current metaphors of role-playing and games. To anthropologists this would transfer the traditions of literary interpretation to the study of behavior and thereby reframe behavior in a less reductionistic manner by suggesting that it is at least as complex, meaningful, and ambiguous as a good novel or poem. If the metaphor of text were to be adopted generally as a perspective, social anthropology would be even less inclined to turn the salient institutions of one society into ideal types for use in examining the social life of neighboring societies.[19]

However, if text were to become fashionable as a way of bringing to anthropology the baggage of post-structuralist literary criticism, with its concern for conjunctures, the mirror phase, and intertextuality, the course of inquiry in social anthropology would probably shift to a rethinking of normative authority; to a deemphasis on the psychic unity of mankind in favor of uncovering the significant differences between ourselves and "The Others" whom we study; and to a concern with what is missing in a people's discourse and in our ethnographies.

What this refocusing would not emphasize is the sense of text as historians most frequently use it—as a vehicle for knowledge about the past. To be more relevant for historians the metaphor would have to be extended from the documents themselves

19   Geertz, "Blurred Genres: The Refiguration of Social Thought," *The American Scholar,* XLIX (1980), 165–179; see also Alton L. Becker, "Text-Building, Epistemology, and Aesthetics in Javanese Shadow Theater," in *idem* and Aram Yengoyan (eds.), *The Imagination of Reality* (Norwood, N.J., 1979), 211–243.

to the behavior described within them, behavior which is often ambivalent and polyvalent.

The sense of unity and decorum of a narrative, the sense of what is an integral part of any story is a basic part of the everyday culture in which it is told. When Greven tells us that the basic goal of the inhabitants of Andover was to remain in Andover, preferably on the family farm, but that demography and land shortage prevented them from doing so; that in the third generation the sons of Andover were obliged to migrate to new lands; and that this restlessness was a cause of the Revolution, we have not progressed very far from the old-fashioned history of events. Demography merely replaces Governor Thomas Dudley (or whomever) as the villain of the story. It behooves historians to learn about the general form of narrative. The metaphor of text should be useful in this discovery, especially since there has been a recent call to return to the narrative.[20]

Historians of colonial America, often portray their subjects as behaving with a view to their place in the history books. This is especially noticeable to anthropologists because we are so often unable to give any account of history in our descriptions. The subjects of ethnographies are usually constrained to behave only with regard to finite tasks in the realm of common sense. This perspective presents us with problems but, from the anthropologists' point of view, much of social history is misconceived because of the teleology of historians' hindsight.

My depiction of social history is obviously too dark and too much drawn with the parochial bias of an outsider. But it raises important issues for the writing of history and of anthropology. First, to what extent do our data really mesh? And second, to what extent does social life have a historical goal which transcends immediate situations? My answers are those of the skeptic.

Historians have worried about these same issues and anthropologists have not absorbed everything they might from the practice of history. The place of a historical consciousness in ethnog-

---

20 Philip J. Greven, Jr., *Four Generations: Population, Land, and Family in Colonial Andover, Massachusetts* (Ithaca, 1970). A useful introduction to narrative analysis is Claude Bremond, *Logique du recit* (Paris, 1973). Lawrence Stone, "The Revival of Narrative: Reflections on a New Old History," *Past & Present,* 85 (1979), 3–24.

raphy will have to be reassessed. First, historians who are interested in social or cultural history should try to eliminate exotica and fantasies of a Golden Age of community. Instead, they should turn more scrupulously to the mundane, with its pettiness and dissensions, as well as its cooperativeness. If historians borrow from anthropology, it should be with the intention of developing the concepts borrowed and of making, in return, a contribution to anthropology. Either social history is anthropology or it is nothing. Dabbling with it will do no good. Historians must reflect on what they borrow.

Second, as part of a general trend toward self-consciousness, both historians and anthropologists will study history and folk history in particular, and its uses in our own culture. What do ordinary people take to be history? Why do television writers see history as a series of lucky moments for the uniquely gifted protagonists of a true story? These are the kinds of questions which anthropologists ask of preliterate peoples. As they shift their attention to groups within our own culture, they will ask these questions of us.

Third, when anthropologists have identified the common sense of our culture, they will want to see how and when it was institutionalized. Research along these lines would be a useful extension of Foucault's attempts to uncover the archaeology of the more highbrow concepts in our society. An even more recent example of a historian's work along these lines is Ginzburg, "Morelli, Freud, and Sherlock Holmes."[21]

History must become more reflexive about its goals and about the means it uses to realize its ends. To anthropologists the lack of interest in theory among historians still seems great. But borrowing concepts from another discipline does not hold out much promise either if the concepts are simply misused in a thoughtless way.

21 For example, Foucault, *Madness and Civilization* (New York, 1965); *idem, Discipline and Punishment* (New York, 1979). Carlo Ginzburg, "Morelli, Freud, and Sherlock Holmes," *History Workshop,* IX (1980), 5–36.

Anthropology and History in the 1980s

Natalie Z. Davis

The Possibilities of the Past   The current interest of some historians in the work of anthropologists is not just a matter of *l'histoire immobile*. Nor is the connection between the two kinds of endeavor entirely new. Herodotus described the different customs of peoples even while he told the story of the Persian Wars. Hume wrote *The Natural History of Religion* at the same time as he recorded the histories of Scotland and England. Vico and Marx looked both for the systemic features of past societies and for the sources of historical change. It is in pursuit of these same objectives that historians are putting books on the Trobriand Islanders and the Azande next to their records of European and American witchcraft trials and Mauss next to their editions of Bloch.[1]

Anthropological writings have four features that make them useful for historians: close observation of living processes of social interaction; interesting ways of interpreting symbolic behavior; suggestions about how the parts of a social system fit together; and material from cultures very different from those which historians are used to studying. Historians may first turn to such texts because they are trying to make sense of an event known to fellow practitioners, but baffling in its meaning. Why did that holy man sit on his sixty-foot pillar for years and why did Syrian villagers flock to visit him in the fifth century? What did early medieval communities think they were doing when they punished one accused person with the ordeal by hot iron or immersion and allowed another to rally oath-swearers to his cause? How could there be such a thing as a greyhound who became a saint? Why

Natalie Z. Davis is Henry Charles Lea Professor of History at Princeton University. She is the author of *Society and Culture in Early Modern France* (Stanford, 1975).

0022-1953/81/020267-9 $02.50/0

1 Herodotus (trans. George Rawlinson), *The Persian Wars* (New York, 1942); David Hume, *The Natural History of Religion* (London, 1957); Giambattista Vico, *La Scienza Nuova* (Naples, 1744); Karl Marx, *Das Kapital* (New York, 1867); Marcel Mauss (trans. Ian Cunnison), *The Gift, Forms and Functions of Exchange in Archaic Societies* (London, 1969); Marc Bloch, *La société féodale* (Paris, 1939).

were processions bearing Our Lady of Impruneta still so important in Renaissance Florence? Why was there so much excitement
for several centuries about Christ's presence in the Eucharist? And
why was there such absorbtion in the nineteenth century in the
disordering of male sexuality? What do we make of popular
leaders who see visions or of popular religious movements where
converts give inspired sermons or speak in tongues? [2]

Events such as these have often been defined by historians as
irrational or superstitious, or as an arbitrary cover for real and
serious social and political conflicts. We, as historians, have explained situations in terms of rational interests, perceived or not
perceived by the historical actors. But anthropologists have such
events at the center of their observation: they have listened very
carefully (as did Métraux in Haiti) to the words uttered by persons
in a trance and discovered that there is a kind of truth-telling in
the process; and they have followed the intricate rhythms of
exorcism ceremonies in Sri Lanka to discover that the clowning
and the reaction of spectators establish a universe of belief and
cure the victims of their complaints. Such interpretations can be
useful to historians, offering them ways to look at analogous
material. [3]

2   Peter Brown, "The Rise and Function of the Holy Man in Late Antiquity," *Journal of
Roman Studies*, LXI (1972), 80–101; *idem, The Making of Late Antiquity* (Cambridge, Mass.,
1978), 54–101; Rebecca V. Colman, "Reason and Unreason in Early Medieval Law,"
Journal of Interdisciplinary History, IV (1974), 571–592. Colman's attempt to apply an
anthropological approach to early medieval law is more promising than that of Charles
Radding, who, using Jean Piaget's theories of development, sees medieval culture (and
primitive societies more generally) as expressing the cognitive egocentricity of children
aged five to eight ("Superstition to Science: Nature, Fortune and the Passing of the
Medieval Ordeal," *American Historical Review*, LXXXIV [1979], 945–969). Jean-Claude
Schmitt, *Le saint lévrier, Guinefort, guérisseur d'enfants depuis le XIIIe siècle* (Paris, 1979);
Richard Trexler, "Florentine Religious Experience: The Sacred Image," *Studies in the
Renaissance*, XIX (1972), 7–41; *idem, Public Life in Renaissance Florence* (New York, 1980);
Davis, *Society and Culture in Early Modern France* (Stanford, 1975), 152–187; Carroll Smith-
Rosenberg, "Sex as Symbol in Victorian Purity: An Ethnohistorical Analysis of Jacksonian
America," in John Demos and Sarane Spence Boocock (eds.), *Turning Points: Historical
and Sociological Essays on the Family* (Chicago, 1978), 212–247; B. Robert Kreiser, *Miracles,
Convulsions and Ecclesiastical Politics in Early Eighteenth-Century Paris* (Princeton, 1978);
Clarke Garrett, *Respectable Folly: Millenarians and the French Revolution in France and England*
(Baltimore, 1975).
3   Alfred Métraux, *Le Vaudou Haitien* (Paris, 1958), 106–127; Bruce Kapferer, "Ritual,
Audience and Reflexivity: Sri Lanka Exorcist Rites," in John MacAloon (ed.), *Rite, Drama,
Festival, Spectacle: Rehearsals toward a Theory of Cultural Performance*, forthcoming. Mary
Douglas' study on the meaning of taboos has been one of several anthropological works

Once into anthropological literature, historians are prompted to ask questions about familiar events which have been slighted, not so much because they are puzzling, but because they have been thought unimportant and better left to other fields. How many of us, for example, work on religious history and examine the social and ethical teachings of the churches, the motifs of sermons and polemical literature, the origins of the clergy and converts, the structure of ecclesiastical organization, and even the frequency of devotional practise, without ever considering what believers often thought of as most significant in their relation to the Lord: liturgy and prayer? And if we do consider these, do we know how to make them advance our understanding of a historical period? First we must study the texts themselves, the Missal, the *Forme des prières ecclésiastiques,* the Book of Common Prayer, and the like, and see what is said about them in the writings of literary and liturgical specialists. For suggestions about how the liturgical event can be an instrument for reproducing culture—for making statements about and establishing social relationships, for imposing forms of self-control, and for encouraging characteristic moods and sensibilities—we can turn to the work of Turner, Geertz, and other anthropologists.[4]

Ethnographic studies have also given historians a new awareness of informal or small-scale interactions which can express important linkages and conflicts. Historical work on the fear and prosecution of witches was among the first to benefit from ethnographic observation of sorcery and counter-sorcery. Earlier historical interpretation had relied on images of unenlighted persecutors projecting their fears of the unknown on to innocent

---

which has had much influence on historians (*Purity and Danger* [Harmondsworth, 1966]). Anthropologist William Christian, Jr., has himself turned to a historical study of the meaning of vows and relics in *Local Religion in Sixteenth-Century New Castile* (Princeton, 1981).

4 Gregory Dix, *The Shape of the Liturgy* (London, 1945; 2nd ed.); Helen C. White, *The Tudor Books of Private Devotion* (Madison, 1951); Margaret Doody, "'How shall we sing the Lord's song upon an alien soil?': The New Episcopalian Liturgy," in Christopher Ricks and Leonard Michaels (eds.), *The State of the Language* (Berkeley, 1979), 108–124; Evelyn Underhill, *Worship* (New York), 1936; Victor Turner, *The Forest of Symbols. Aspects of Ndembu Ritual* (Ithaca, 1967); *idem, The Ritual Process* (Chicago, 1969); Clifford Geertz, *The Religion of Java* (Glencoe, Ill., 1960); *idem, The Interpretation of Cultures* (New York, 1973), 142–169; Roy Rappaport, *Ecology, Meaning and Religion* (Richmond, Ca., 1978).

victims, or on images of terrorized or hallucinating women confessing to events that never happened. Now it is possible to envisage a range of political, social, psychological, and sexual issues being fought out in witchcraft accusations between central authorities and local people and among the villagers themselves. And it is possible to identify a number of activities, including medical and ritual ones, which neighbors might brand as sorcery.[5]

Similarly, our understanding of the mechanisms of exchange is being assisted by anthropological reflection on gifts and reciprocity, on varied entrepreneurial styles, and on different kinds of markets and bazaars. For those seeking new indicators for clientage systems and linkages beyond families, ethnographic work on godparentage and on naming practices is proving valuable.[6]

5 Among recent studies drawing upon anthropology to interpret historical witchcraft, see Keith Thomas, *Religion and the Decline of Magic* (London, 1971); Alan Macfarlane, *Witchcraft in Tudor and Stuart England* (London, 1970); Carlo Ginzburg, *I benendanti. Ricerche sulla stregoneria e sul culti agragri tra Cinquecento e Seicento* (Turin, 1966); Paul Boyer and Stephen Nissenbaum, *Salem Possessed: The Social Origins of Witchcraft* (Cambridge, Mass., 1974); Garrett, "Witches and Cunning Folk in the Old Régime," in Jacques Beauroy, Marc Bertrand, and Edward T. Gargan (eds.), *The Wolf and the Lamb. Popular Culture in France from the Old Regime to the Twentieth Century* (Stanford, 1976); Richard A. Horsley, "Who were the Witches? The Social Roles of the Accused in the European Witch Trials," *Journal of Interdisciplinary History*, IX (1979), 689–716. See also the annotated bibliography in Marie-Sylvie Dupont-Bouchat, Willem Frijhoff, and Robert Muchembled, *Prophètes et sorciers dans les Pays-Bas, XVIe-XVIIIe siècle* (Paris, 1978), 33–39.

6 Mauss, *The Gift*; Marshall Sahlins, *Stone Age Economics* (Chicago, 1972); Annette B. Weiner, *Women of Value, Men of Renown. New Perspectives in Trobriand Exchange* (Austin, Texas, 1976). Among historians using this approach are M. I. Finley, *The World of Odysseus* (New York, 1965); A. Y. Gurevich, "Wealth and Gift-Bestowal among the Ancient Scandinavians," *Scandinavica*, VII (1968), 126–138; Georges Duby, *Guerriers et paysans: VII-XIIe siècle; premier essor de l'économie européenne* (Paris, 1973); Lester Little, *Religious Poverty and the Profit Economy in Medieval Europe* (Ithaca, N.Y., 1978); Christiane Klapisch-Zuber, "The Medieval Italian Mattinata," *Journal of Family History*, V (1980), 2–27. Claude Meillassoux (ed.), *The Development of Indigenous Trade and Markets in West Africa* (London, 1971); C. Geertz, *Peddlers and Princes: Social Change and Economic Modernization in Two Indonesian Towns*; idem, "Suq: the bazaar economy in Sefrou," in C. Geertz, Hildred Geertz, and Lawrence Rosen, *Meaning and Order in Moroccan Society* (Cambridge, 1979), 123–313; A. L. Udovitch, "Formalism and Informalism in the Social and Economic Institutions of the Medieval Islamic World," in Speros Vryonis and Amin Banani (eds.), *Individualism and Conformity in Classical Islam* (Wiesbaden, 1977), 61–81. Sidney Mintz and Eric Wolf, "An Analysis of Ritual Coparenthood (Compadrazgo)," *Southwestern Journal of Anthropology*, VI (1950), 341–368; Julian Pitt-Rivers, *The Fate of Schechem, or the Politics of Sex* (Cambridge, 1977), 48–70; Françoise Zonabend, "La parenté baptismale á Minot [Cote-D'Or]," *Annales*, XXXIII (1978), 656–676.

How historians then connect such events and interactions to periods at large will depend in part on what theories of social systems they adopt. Both history and anthropology are heirs to similar traditions of thought about how the parts of a culture fit together: the *Zeitgeist* theory, where the spirit of an age leaves its single stamp on all the major institutions; the Marxist view and its variants, in which the material sector and the cultural sector are distinguished, the former ordinarily affecting the latter, the system itself marked by conflict; and the liberal theory and its variants, in which multiple institutions and forces interact, now one, now another playing a determining role. When anthropological theories of system are simply old *Zeitgeist* writ new, they may not be especially useful to the historian. Where they develop a finely drawn picture of balanced or changing ecosystems, as in Rappaport's *Pigs for the Ancestors* and Geertz' *Agricultural Involution,* they add much to the insights of French and American *géohistoire.* Similarly, where they argue for a carefully observed range of cultural meanings which make sense of practical activities like production and which mediate between the world of thinking and the world of doing (as in Sahlins' *Culture and Practical Reason*), then they can change our ideas about intellectual history and its stages.[7]

So too, notions of a gender system—of how men's and women's spheres of action and speech and male and female symbolism relate to each other—in a village in Amazonian Brazil, a forested region in northern Luzon, or the western highlands of New Guinea can give historians a set of new questions to put to known documents and can send them in search of sources that they never considered relevant before. Although ethnographers hardly see things the same way when they go into the field (Weiner's recent revisiting of Bronislaw Malinowski's Trobriand Islands is a case in point), nevertheless their daily encounters with their subjects can reveal the workings of a system relatively hidden

7 Rappaport, *Pigs for the Ancestors. Ritual in the Ecology of a New Guinea People* (New Haven, 1968); C. Geertz, *Agricultural Involution: The Processes of Ecological Change in Indonesia* (Berkeley, 1963); Ira Berlin, "Time, Space and the Evolution of Afro-American Society on British Mainland North America," *American Historical Review,* LXXXV (1980), 44–78; Mintz and Richard Price, *An Anthropological Approach to the Caribbean Past* (Philadelphia, 1976); Sahlins, *Culture and Practical Reason* (Chicago, 1976).

to the historian, who must slice into a culture through texts, pictures, and artifacts.[8]

Can a tribe in the upper Amazon really be of interest to a student of European history? If properly approached, it can. Historians have long made use of comparison, but have ordinarily confined themselves to western or "advanced" societies (English and French economic development; agricultural history in eastern and western Europe; feudalism in Europe, China, and Japan; slavery in the southern United States and in the Caribbean, etc.). With the opening toward anthropology, we have expanded our cross-cultural approach to include "primitive" or archaic societies or those quite different from our own. This may be done because the historian is investigating a topic like oral culture, which is viewed as "archaic": just as Lord found that the art of composition of the story-tellers of Yugoslavia could shed light on the art of composition of Homer, so historians may find that the memory devices and proverb usage of some African cultures could help them to visualize how things were said in sixteenth-century villages. Far-reaching comparison can also be fruitful when a subject has been studied so much with a familiar Western orientation that no new meanings are being discovered, or has been studied so little that few contours are discernible at all. Thus, the course of Jewish history in Europe might be better understood not merely by more research, but also by pondering the anthropological literature on caste and ethnicity; the history of sexual behavior in the West by reflection on sexual systems and sexual culture in other parts of the world.[9]

8 C. Geertz, *Interpretation of Cultures*. Emmanuel Le Roy Ladurie in his *Montaillou, village occitan de 1294 à 1324* (Paris, 1975) has done an admirable job in reconstructing the cultural system of his villagers. Yolanda Murphy and Robert F. Murphy, *Women of the Forest* (New York, 1974); Michelle Z. Rosaldo and Jane M. Atkinson, "Man the Hunter and Woman. Metaphors for the Sexes in Ilongot Magical Spells," in Roy Willis (ed.), *The Interpretation of Symbolism* (London, 1975), 43–75; Rosaldo, *Knowledge and Passion. Ilongot Notions of Self and Social Life* (Cambridge, 1980); Marilyn Strathern, *Women in Between. Female Roles in a Male World: Mount Hagen, New Guinea* (London, 1972); Weiner, *Women of Value*.

9 Albert B. Lord, *The Singer of Tales* (Cambridge, Mass., 1960). Students of the poetry of the troubadours have also been influenced by Lord's methods. John C. Messenger, Jr., "The Role of Proverbs in a Nigerian Judicial System," in Alan Dundes (ed.), *The Study of Folklore* (Englewood Cliffs, 1965), 299–307; Elinor Keenan, "Norm-Makers, Norm-Breakers: Uses of Speech by Men and Women in a Malagasy Community," in Richard Bauman and Joel Sherzer (eds.), *Explorations in the Ethnography of Speaking* (Cambridge,

There are, of course, hazards in the historian's drawing upon anthropology. One is sometimes raised by anthropologists themselves: historians are eclectic in their choice of mentors; they mix together indifferently ideas from professional opponents, from demographic and economic determinists and symbolic analysts, from those stressing meaning and language and those stressing function and power, from those who believe in evolutionary stages of culture and from those who do not. This does not seem to be a major problem. Historians will surely want to be aware of the different schools of anthropological interpretation (and of anthropological eclecticism) and integrate them effectively into their own vision of social organization. Surely we must read ethnographic material with enough care to understand the argument and the evidence for it. But need we import all the special reservations that anthropologists have about each other's work or all their infighting, any more than they need to import ours?

A more serious danger is the misapplication of anthropological interpretation and fieldwork to historical cases. We consult anthropological writings not for prescriptions, but for suggestions; not for universal rules of human behavior, but for relevant comparisons. There is no substitute for extensive work in the historical sources. There is no way that a ritual in New Guinea or Zambia can be used to establish the meaning and uses of a ritual, say, in sixteenth-century Europe; the evidence must come from the people and the institutions of the time. There is no way to relate the psychology of witchcraft accusations among the Azande to that of Europeans without considering how seventeenth-century notions of property, body, soul, health, social

---

1974), 125–143; Davis, *Society and Culture,* 227–267. George De Vos, *Japan's Invisible Race. Caste in Culture and Personality* (Berkeley, 1966); Fredrik Barth (ed.), *Ethnic Groups and Boundaries. The Social Organization of Culture Difference* (Bergen, 1969); Abner Cohen (ed.), *Urban Ethnicity* (London, 1974). For an effort to use caste theory to inform a historical study of the Jews, see Maurice Kriegel, *Les Juifs à la fin du Moyen Age dans l'Europe méditerranéenne* (Paris, 1979). Some of the ethnographic material on homosexuality is reported in Randolph Trumbach, "London's Sodomites: Homosexual Behavior and Western Culture in the Eighteenth Century," *Journal of Social History,* XI (1977), 1–33. For a remarkable view of a sexual system, see Raymond C. Kelly, "Witchcraft and Sexual Relations. An Exploration in the Social and Semantic Implications of the Structure of Belief," in Paula Brown and Georgeda Buchbinder (eds.), *Man and Woman in the New Guinea Highlands* (Washington, D.C., 1976), 36–53. For an example of a historical work effectively informed by a cross-cultural perspective, see Kenneth R. Dover, *Greek Homosexuality* (New York, 1980).

connectedness, and the like might have affected the fears that people had about each other.[10]

Anthropololgy is not, then, some kind of higher vision of social reality to which historians should convert, but a sister discipline with increasingly close ties to our own. For some forty years ethnographers have been studying urban and peasant cultures as well as tribal ones; as their interest has moved into "advanced" societies and contemporary Europe, they have become more and more concerned with the nature of historical change and with the study of the past. We should not only be borrowing from them with discernment, we should also be prepared to offer advice about their own work and about anthropological theory.[11].

When Mintz uses the spread of sugar production and consumption as an indicator of social change over many centuries, we can make suggestions about the contrasting production, sale, and consumption of honey. When we read anthropological texts that seem to overstress system and consensus at the expense of change and conflict, we can point out where the cracks, the sources of discord and resistance, and the mechanisms of transformation are likely to appear in a society. (Let us hope we will do better than turning to the "inevitable" forces of urbanization, commercialization, and industrialization to account for all

10 See the exchange between H. Geertz and Keith Thomas, "An Anthropology of Religion and Magic," *Journal of Interdisciplinary History*, VIII (1975), 71–109; the review article by Edward P. Thompson, "Anthropology and the Discipline of Historical Context," *Midland History*, I (1972), 41–55.

11 Robert Redfield, *The Folk Culture of Yucatan* (Chicago, 1941). Among many works one could cite: C. Geertz, *The Social History of an Indonesian Town* (Cambridge, Mass., 1963); Milton Singer, *When a Great Tradition Modernizes. An Anthropological Approach to Indian Civilization* (New York, 1972); Wolf, *Peasants* (Englewood Cliffs, 1966), with bibliography; William Mangin (ed.), *Peasants in Cities. Readings in the Anthropology of Urbanization* (Boston, 1970); Mintz, "Slavery and the Rise of Peasantries," *Historical Reflections*, VI (1979), 213–242; Sydel Silverman, *Three Bells of Civilization. The Life of an Italian Hill Town* (New York, 1975); Christian, *Person and God in a Spanish Valley* (New York, 1972); Susan Tax Freeman, *The Pasiegos. Spaniards in No Man's Land* (Chicago, 1979). For a remarkable study showing that allegedly static primitive peoples can have a sense of history, see Renato Rosaldo, *Ilongot Headhunting, 1883–1974* (Stanford, 1980). Historians and anthropologists have been working together in Paris, in the *laboratoire* of Claude Lévi-Strauss and in the seminars of the Ecole Pratique des Hautes Etudes en Sciences Sociales; and in England, Italy, and the United States. Collective volumes such as Jack Goody (ed.), *Literacy in Traditional Society* (Cambridge, 1968); Goody, Joan Thirsk, and Thompson (eds.), *Family and Inheritance. Rural Society in Western Europe, 1200–1800* (Cambridge, 1976); Barbara A. Babcock (ed.), *The Reversible World. Symbolic Inversion in Art and Society* (Ithaca, 1978) bear witness to this new collaboration.

change.) When we see a set of symbols or ritual acts explicated only within the context of a stable culture, let us speculate on what they might mean in a situation of change and controversy.[12]

Indeed, the impact of anthropology on my own historical reflection has been to reinforce my sense not of the changeless past, but of the varieties of human experience. There are sets of relationships that one is continually looking for, but evolutionary schemes do not necessarily hold. Markets do not always drive out gifts, centers do not always eliminate particular localities, and history does not always replace myth. Anthropology can widen the possibilities, can help us take off our blinders, and give us a new place from which to view the past and discover the strange and surprising in the familiar landscape of historical texts.

12 Mintz, "Time, Sugar, and Sweetness," *Marxist Perspectives*, II (1979/80), 56–72.

Anthropology and History in the 1980s

Carlo Ginzburg

A Comment The growing influence, in recent years, of history on anthropology, and vice-versa, is well known. The emergence of a common area of research at the border between the two disciplines has been triggered by two crises: the end of the structured, self-confident notion of history and the growing consciousness among anthropologists that the presumed native cultures were themselves a historical product. Both crises are connected to the end of the world colonial system, and to the collapse of the related unilinear notion of history.

Two features of anthropologists' work have had a powerful impact on a good number of historians: the emphasis on cultural distance, and the attempt to overcome it by emphasizing the inner coherence of every aspect of societies widely different from our own. Historians have tried to look at old topics (for instance, political power) or at old evidence (for instance, inquisitorial records) in a different way. Behaviors and beliefs traditionally seen as senseless, irrelevant, or at best marginal curiosities (for instance, magic and superstition) have been analyzed at last as valid human experiences.

The result of this intellectual effort has been a new way of presenting documentary evidence; the revival of narrative, as stressed by Stone in a recent article, has been deeply influenced by the practice of case studies among anthropologists. The emphasis on lived experience and the close reading of evidence are connected with the choice of specific literary devices. It is usual to insist on the rhetorical and emotional value of these literary devices; but it is necessary also to analyze their cognitive, as well as methodological and ideological implications. From a general point of view, it could be said that every history, even if it is filled with statistics and figures, is a story, a piece of narrative:

Carlo Ginzburg is Professor of Modern History at the University of Bologna. He is the author of *The Cheese and the Worms: The Cosmos of a Sixteenth-Century Miller* (Baltimore, 1977).

0022-1953/81/020277-2 $02.50/0

but different models of narrative have been selected by historians in different times. It would be naive to take for granted a model (borrowed by nineteenth-century novels) in which a God-historian knows everything, including the hidden motivations of his characters—individuals, groups, or social classes. An anthropological look at the ways in which anthropologists and historians communicate their findings would be useful to both disciplines.[1]

The growing number of detailed studies on circumscribed historical phenomena has often been lamented as a fragmentation of the historical discipline. It seems to me, however, that this is a price to be paid for elaborating more powerful analytical tools. Case studies obviously imply generalizations: but it is difficult to predict whether the general frame of reference for this kind of analysis will be provided by history, anthropology, or both.

1   Lawrence Stone, "The Revival of Narrative: Reflections on a New Old History," *Past & Present*, 85 (1979), 3–24.

Intellectual History in the 1980s

William J. Bouwsma

From History of Ideas to History of Meaning

Intellectual history, until recently, was regarded with particular respect. It was probably the most interdisciplinary area of historical study and therefore seemed both unusually demanding and unusually prestigious. It was considered important. But during the last two decades, the impression has grown among historians that the kinds of material likely to be studied by intellectual historians are not very useful for telling us what we most need to know about the past.[1]

As those of us who scrutinize the small number of job listings for our students have observed, intellectual history seems now to be considered less essential to the curriculum than other kinds of history. Fewer students care to be identified as intellectual historians, and the remaining practitioners of intellectual history are more and more uncertain about their methods and purposes. And it is increasingly difficult to say what, at least, in the abstract, intellectual history is about. For these reasons, as well as for others that will emerge later in this article, the question of the immediate future of intellectual history requires more radical treatment than may be appropriate for other dimensions of historiography.

The decline of intellectual history appears obvious, and probably irreversible. But despite a long identification with the problems and methods of intellectual history, I do not deplore this development. For although intellectual history has indeed declined as an isolated specialty, in another form it has never been more important. The resources of intellectual history, or of something related to and growing out of it, can be useful to historians

William J. Bouwsma is the Sather Professor of History at the University of California at Berkeley. He is the author of *Venice and the Defense of Republican Liberty* (Berkeley, 1968).

0022-1953/81/020279-13 $02.50/0

1 See, for example, the opening paragraphs of Robert Darnton, "Intellectual and Cultural History," in Michael Kammen (ed.), *The Past Before Us: Contemporary Historical Writing in the United States* (Ithaca, 1980), 327–354.

precisely in the degree to which intellectual history is not treated separately but is generally assimilated by other kinds of historians. This is what has recently been happening. That intellectual history is now disappearing as one of the conventional specialties into which historians segregate themselves is a sign of the growing maturity of intellectual history, and of historiography more generally. We no longer need intellectual history because we have all become intellectual historians: some of us, no doubt, unintentionally, reluctantly, and without fully realizing what has happened. Since the explanation for this situation will itself require some exploitation of the resources of conventional intellectual history, it will also provide an example of the tasks that even an old-fashioned and specialized intellectual historian can continue to perform in any decade, notably for other historians: in this case the liberation—not always welcome—that can result from identifying and laying bare for inspection our own deepest assumptions about ourselves and the world. This useful service may suggest that the specialized techniques of intellectual historians are worth keeping alive.

Conventional intellectual history itself has a history that is instructive about its present predicament. Since this history is still largely unwritten, my observations about the origins and lineage of intellectual history will necessarily be somewhat speculative; but the word "intellectual" here holds some promise as a point of entry. This word is an adjective, based on a noun that refers to a faculty alleged—in a certain venerable tradition of thought which historians have never found very congenial—to reside in the human personality. This tradition is that of philosophical idealism, which, since its beginnings in classical antiquity, has depended on—and constantly reinforced—a characteristic anthropology that has had a major influence on the understanding of the human animal in the West.

According to this view, the human personality consists of a hierarchy of discrete faculties, among which intellect—more or less closely identified with reason—is highest. In the earlier stages of this tradition, the intellect was believed to constitute the divine element in man and so to distinguish him from the other animals; and a sense of the peculiar virtue and importance of the intellect and its works, although variously expressed, has always been a major element in this tradition. The association of the intellect with the brain gave the head ethical significance and converted it into a potent metaphor; the highest became best. And for 2,000 years, in what was the main stream of Western thought, the erect stature of man was the visible sign of his distinction from and his superiority to nature. It raised him above the material earth and enabled him to contemplate the heavenly bodies, from which he first learned the eternal principles of order. As Plato himself had testified, this was the origin of philosophy, the noblest of human activities.[2]

This remote background helps to explain both the special prestige once attached to intellectual history and the reasons for its recent decline. Intellectual history was perceived as the study of the working and the works of the human intellect through the centuries; and, since the intellect was the highest faculty in man, it followed that intellectual history was the highest type of history. As Hegel believed, it also could be seen as the source of such clues as we could have to the direction and meaning of all history. These ideas are still very much alive in the notion, which pervades much contemporary social and political speculation, that man, by taking thought, can add cubits to his stature: that is, that "intellectuals" can shape the world for the better. Furthermore, since society, in this tradition, was also conceived—following the general principle underlying all order—as a hierarchy, this line of thought also directed historical investigation toward the intellectual activity of elites. And such notions exerted a power over us, even just half a century ago, that was all the greater because we were unaware of them. A generation of academically precocious youths, too myopic or too light to be good in sports, found compensation in turning from physical activity to the higher concerns of the intellect. In this context intellectual history had obvious attractions.

But the marriage between an intellectuality that was focused on the progressively clearer grasp of the eternal, and history, which tended increasingly to view all things as mutable and even its own presuppositions as historical artifacts, was uncomfortable from the outset; and even in its purer forms intellectual history, although it was often hardly very historical, did not succeed in being philosophical.

2   Plato, *Timaeus*, 47a.

Lovejoy's treatment of the history of ideas is an illuminating example. His detachment of his "unit ideas" from a larger context of changing human needs and conditions suggests the autonomy of intellect in the idealist tradition; but when he faced the question of the significance of such conceptions as the great chain of being, Lovejoy could only reduce them to mysterious psychological impulses, inexplicable cravings for simplicity or complexity which were themselves variations on what he called "metaphysical pathos."[3]

The satisfaction of dealing with the morphology of ideas at the highest level in courses entitled "intellectual history" was rarely sufficient for historians, and the teachers of such courses tended increasingly to analyze a conventional body of texts (the standard works of "great thinkers") with the tools of psychohistory or one or another approach to the sociology of knowledge. In the degree to which it was genuinely historical, intellectual history was thus undermining its own claims to special respect.

Meanwhile these developments internal to the profession were complemented by the more important changes taking place in the larger world that historians inhabited—changes that radically subverted the claims of intellect not only to receive privileged treatment but even to any discrete existence. It is hardly necessary to review the role of Charles Darwin, Karl Marx, and Sigmund Freud in disintegrating the intellectual conception of man, although of the three Freud may prove to have been the most radical in his impact on anthropology. For Freud associated man's upright posture explicitly with his fall from a condition of primordial bliss; he saw in the erect stature of the human animal the sign, perhaps even the prehistorical cause, of that schism in the personality which, perversely dividing *humanitas* into an honorable portion above the neck and a shameful region below the waist, produced not wisdom and order, but neurosis, conflict, and despair. At any rate we can hardly any longer define man as an intellectual animal. However we regard him, he is both less and more than this—and infinitely more interesting, which is the major explanation for the fact that an autonomous intellectual

3 Arthur O. Lovejoy, *The Great Chain of Being: A Study of the History of an Idea* (Cambridge, Mass., 1948), 10–14.

history is now likely to seem, like the discrete intellect of the old anthropology, at best an irrelevant abstraction from real life.

Nevertheless the materials with which intellectual historians have traditionally worked cannot be dismissed as without interest or value for students of the past. Rather they must now be understood in a new way, as expressive or adaptive behavior of a kind still identifiable as (probably) peculiar to the human animal, and also as a subset of a larger category of such human behavior, to which they now solicit our attention. This category consists of all efforts to discover or to impose meaning on our experience, although some sense of meaning is also both a condition and a product of experience. These efforts are not the work of the "intellect" or of any particular area of the personality. They are rather a function of the human organism as a whole; they are carried on both consciously and unconsciously; and they are presupposed by, and merge with, every more specific human activity, including the begetting of children and their upbringing within families. I cite these examples not in order to put such matters down, but to reinforce the general point that the concern with meaning, which I take to be the remnant chiefly worth saving from intellectual history, has been profitably appropriated for their own purposes even by historians of those dimensions of human experience farthest removed from the sublime concerns of intellectual history.

The amalgamation of concerns once primarily limited to so-called intellectual historians with other kinds of history by way of a (usually only implicit) concern with meaning is the most significant development of the recent past from the standpoint of my argument in this article. The works that have most interested those of us who have sometimes thought of ourselves as intellectual historians, and that also have made the greatest impact on historiography, are virtually impossible to classify in terms of our conventional categories, but they come into focus as studies in the construction of meaning. I would cite from my own field (not because it is unanimously admired or because all of its conclusions have been accepted, but because it stimulated a whole generation of Renaissance scholars in various directions and in this way transformed a major area of European historiography) Baron's *The Crisis of the Early Italian Renaissance*. The very title of this work lets us know that we cannot put it into one of our standard categories, and indeed that such classification would be useless for understanding it. It draws on the resources of both political and intellectual history, and it touches also on social and economic matters. But it is basically an extended account of a collective discovery of meaning in the destiny of the Florentine polis.[4]

A similar point could be made of May's *The Enlightenment in America*; although its title seems to classify it as intellectual history, it is also heavily concerned with political, social, and institutional analysis as it reveals how Americans, who must first be understood in their own complex setting, struggled to find meaning in a complex set of European ideas. Again we can only classify a work like Eisenstein's *The Printing Press as an Agent of Change* as an assessment of the impact of technology on the construction of meaning in various aspects of European experience. This work also provides us with an instance of the increasing tendency of historians to substitute the word "cultural" in places where they might earlier have employed the word "intellectual." No doubt this is partly because "cultural" seems less restrictive than "intellectual" but it also is an expression of an at least obscure association of "culture" with meaning in a larger sense.[5]

Thus, if I discern any trend in the work of historians who were once clearly (but have perhaps not recently been) identified with intellectual history, it is an increasing concern with the location, the description, and perhaps the explanation of what passes for meaning in a variety of historical situations. Once this is recognized, a good deal of what seems most vague (and perhaps therefore irritating) about intellectual history will come into focus.

It explains, for example, a tendency for intellectual historians to exploit artistic expression. From the standpoint of a strictly "intellectual" history, this presents a serious conceptual difficulty, for art and intellect are not obviously synonymous and, since Plato, have often been at odds. But the difficulty evaporates once we have recognized that the arts have always been a primary

4   Hans Baron, *The Crisis of the Early Italian Renaissance: Civic Humanism and Republican Liberty in an Age of Classicism and Tyranny* (Princeton, 1955). The works cited in this article were chosen for illustrative purposes. I have not surveyed recent literature, although I have tried to range widely enough with my examples to suggest that the tendencies described in my text are not confined to particular areas of study.

5   Henry May, *The Enlightenment in America* (New York, 1976); Elizabeth Eisenstein, *The Printing Press as an Agent of Change: Communications and Cultural Transformations in Early-Modern Europe* (Cambridge, 1979).

vehicle for the expression of meaning (or more recently, some-times, meaninglessness).

Intellectual historians have long sensed (without perhaps fully understanding) their affinities with art historians like Erwin Pan-ofsky. Baxandall's *Painting and Experience in Fifteenth-Century Italy* is an unusually valuable study of the artistic creation of funda-mental meanings by an art historian. The possibilities of collab-oration between art historians and a more general kind of cultural historian are suggested by *A Renaissance Likeness* by Partridge and Starn, which explores a whole milieu by the intensive study of a single painting. Schorske's *Fin-de-Siécle Vienna* combines an in-terest in artistic meaning with the use of psychoanalysis to pen-etrate to other levels of meaning, which again are hardly to be described as "intellectual."[6]

In reporting on the past and future of intellectual history, I am (somewhat to my own surprise) describing the metamorphosis of an old and familiar, although never very satisfactorily devel-oped, field of historical activity into something new and strange that is likely to be far more useful. In its new state, however, it can also be seen to assimilate various kinds of history, some of them clearly growing in interest, which are otherwise hard to classify. A distinguished example is Thomas's *Religion and the Decline of Magic*. How are we to classify this work in terms of our conventional categories? It is not exactly intellectual history, if only because intellectual activity as a high thing was almost by definition confined to the upper classes. That Thomas's book deals with structures of popular belief is hardly sufficient to call it social history, although the identity of social history sometimes raises difficulties for me almost as serious as those created by intellectual history. But if we recognize this work as an example of a new historical genre that might be called, for want of a more elegant term, the history of meanings, we have placed it within its own family of works, the members of which—once we recognize that they belong together—can illuminate each other.[7]

6 Michael Baxandall, *Painting and Experience in Fifteenth-Century Italy* (Oxford, 1972); Loren Partridge and Randolph Starn, *A Renaissance Likeness: Art and Culture in Raphael's 'Julius II'* (Berkeley, 1980); Carl E. Schorske, *Fin-de-Siécle Vienna: Politics and Culture* (New York, 1980).
7 Keith Thomas, *Religion and the Decline of Magic: Studies in Popular Beliefs in Sixteenth and Seventeenth Century England* (London, 1971).

Immediately one thinks of further candidates for membership in this group: some of the essays of Davis; Le Roy Ladurie's *Montaillou*; Levine's *Black Culture and Black Consciousness*, with its eloquent use of folklore; or Jordan's *White Over Black* which, whatever else it may be, is a report on the tragic results of one kind of assertion of meaning.[8]

In the same way other major kinds of recent work, too often ignored in historiographical discussions because they do not fit our conventional categories, can be seen as subsets of the history of meanings, and therefore well worth serious attention. One of the most important of these clearly is religious history, which is concerned in the most direct and ultimate way with the exploration of meaning, and in its institutional dimension with structures for the preservation, cultivation, and transmission of meaning. Thomas's work belongs partly in this category, and a substantial proportion of the activity of historians of every period and part of the world is now devoted to religious phenomena. Again this remarkable circumstance is easy to overlook because of an inherited system for the classification of historical scholarship in which it has no place.

The titles of a few major works concerned with the period with which I am most familiar convey some sense of the difficulty of classifying them according to our usual labels: among them are books by Reeves, Ozment, Tentler, O'Malley, and Rothkrug.[9]

Still other kinds of scholarship can be brought into focus in this way. One thinks immediately of the history of education, which has normally had as its primary purpose the transmission of meanings from one generation to the next; a recent example

---

8 For example, Natalie Davis, "The Reasons of Misrule" and "The Rites of Violence," in *idem, Society and Culture in Early Modern France* (Stanford, 1975), 97–123, 152–187. Emmanuel Le Roy Ladurie, *Montaillou, village occitan de 1294 à 1324* (Paris, 1975); Lawrence W. Levine, *Black Culture and Black Consciousness: Afro-American Folk Thought from Slavery to Freedom* (New York, 1977); Winthrop D. Jordan, *White Over Black: American Attitudes toward the Negro, 1550–1812* (Chapel Hill, 1968).

9 Marjorie Reeves, *The Influence of Prophecy in the Later Middle Ages: A Study in Joachimism* (Oxford, 1969); Steven Ozment, *The Reformation in the Cities: An Essay on the Appeal of Protestant Ideas to Sixteenth-Century Society* (New Haven, 1975); Thomas N. Tentler, *Sin and Confession on the Eve of the Reformation* (Princeton, 1977); John W. O'Malley, *Praise and Blame in Renaissance Rome: Rhetoric, Doctrine, and Reform in the Sacred Orators of the Papal Court, c. 1450–1521* (Durham, N.C. 1979); Lionel Rothkrug, "Religious Practice and Collective Perceptions: Hidden Homologies in the Renaissance and Reformation," *Historical Reflections/Réflexions Historiques*, VII (1980), published as a special issue.

is Straus's *Luther's House of Learning*. The history of historiography, and perhaps of other branches of learning, also assumes more general significance when it is understood to be centrally concerned with meaning; every work of historical composition is, after all, a bit of documentation of what passes for meaning in the community and period out of which it arises. Such studies as White's *Metahistory* may be highly "intellectual" (a term that now seems to mean something like "difficult to read"); but the awkward intrusion of the word "imagination" in the title suggests that it is not very usefully called "intellectual history." A similar point can be made about Pocock's *The Machiavellian Moment*. But meaning can also be expressed through institutions: constitutions, for example, judicial systems, or even bureaucracies. Thus Brentano's *Two Churches* is a distinguished investigation of the construction of meaning as well as utility out of materials not usually associated with such activity.[10]

The kind of history that I am describing is characterized not (like traditional intellectual history) by the sources that it utilizes but by the questions that it asks. By the same token, it does not exclude attention to the creation of meaning by elites; it leaves open the considerable possibility that this may be of the greatest interest. It may be objected, indeed, that this redefinition of intellectual history is far too broadly conceived: that, indeed, in an outburst of disciplinary imperialism from the most unexpected quarter, and by the most arbitrary redefinition of my assignment, I have claimed almost everything in historiography for my province. I hope that this is not the case; but I do see, in the conception of man as an animal who must create or discern meaning in everything that he does, the most promising resource that has yet presented itself for overcoming the consequences—so devastating for the historical understanding in the long run, no matter how convenient in the short—of our proliferating specialization. The only antidote for this tendency in historiography, now so widely deplored, is a shift in emphasis from raw historical experience

---

10 Gerald Straus, *Luther's House of Learning: Indoctrination of the Young in the German Reformation* (Baltimore, 1978). Hayden White, *Metahistory: The Historical Imagination in Nineteenth-Century Europe* (Baltimore, 1973); John G. A. Pocock, *The Machiavellian Moment: Florentine Political Thought and the Atlantic Republican Tradition* (Princeton, 1975); Robert Brentano, *Two Churches: England and Italy in the Thirteenth Century* (Princeton, 1968).

(i.e., what happens to people) to what human beings have made out of that experience. Such a shift should remind us, too, that the creative interpretation of experience also shapes experience, which is only in the abstract independent of the meaning imposed upon it.

As to the future, it is my hope that tendencies already discernible—the decline of traditional intellectual history as an area of specialization, the exploitation of its resources instead by historians who do not care to identify their work as intellectual history, and an expanded concern with the meanings expressed by every kind of human activity in the past—will grow stronger, be more explicitly embraced, and develop the more deliberate strategies that are likely to emerge when scholarship becomes conscious of what it is doing. I have one or two suggestions about what this might mean, but first it seems to me that a caveat against reductionism is in order.

I have referred to the role of Darwin, Marx, and Freud in the destruction of a traditional model of man; we owe them a great deal for this and will continue to benefit in various ways from the insights that they have released. But we should not, by following them, correct one kind of mistake only to make another. It is unlikely to help us much simply to reverse the hierarchy, and to put matter in the place of mind, or biological in the place of intellectual experience. This would still be too traditional; the structural principle—the principle that organizes phenomena as *sub* (or *infra*) and *super*—would remain the same. A more novel anthropology (which is at the same time very old, since it too has a history), an anthropology that is more wholesome (in the sense of integrated and therefore irreducible), is fundamental to the notion of man as a creator of meanings, a conception that can only engender a sense of the unpredictability of the human condition and therefore of mystery and awe, sensations as appropriate to the historical as to the poetic understanding.

History, as has often been observed, is parasitical; but as it changes, so does the host on which it feeds. Traditional intellectual history was chiefly nourished by traditional philosophy; but as intellectual history has been transformed, it has been turning to the arts. I expect this tendency to grow stronger and to expand from literary, and visual art into music and dance, and from elite to popular expression in all the arts.

But art as expressive and integrative behavior points finally to anthropology, now as an academic discipline, and especially to cultural anthropology, which is likely to be the fundamental external resource for the kind of study that is being born out of a dying intellectual history. This is so for several reasons. The anthropological model which generally (with some exceptions) informs anthropology as a discipline underlies the conception that I have outlined of man as a creator of meanings. This model largely rejects the conception of man as a hierarchy of discrete faculties. It accordingly rejects also the assignment of privileged status *a priori* to one or another area of human activity. Since it conceives of the human personality as a mysterious whole, it is opposed to all reductionism. And, of course, it is centrally concerned with the construction and symbolic expression of meaning in every dimension of human activity. In short it is useful to the historian precisely because it is the least specialized among the social sciences; this is why, increasingly, it insists on a kind of "thick description" that many historians are finding so congenial. Most anthropologists have been content so far with a kind of systematic and static description that is fundamentally ahistorical (although even this has been useful for the—almost equally static—study of *mentalités* by historians); and I have heard anthropologists confess that their discipline has not dealt very satisfactorily with problems of cultural change. But the recent work of some anthropologists, for example Sahlins, Bourdieu, and Bloch, has been increasingly historical. It may be that future work in anthropology will be even more useful for historians, and also that historians can be of some help to anthropologists.[11]

A second and closely related discipline that will probably be necessary for the development of intellectual history is linguistics. For if man (to quote once again a much-quoted remark) is "an animal suspended in webs of significance he himself has spun," he spins these webs primarily from—or with the help of—language. Through language man orders the chaos of data impinging on his sensorium from, in a singularly mysterious and problematic sense, "out there," organizing them into categories and so making

11 Marshall Sahlins, *Culture and Practical Reason* (Chicago, 1976); Pierre Bourdieu (trans. Richard Nice), *Outline of a Theory of Practice* (Cambridge, 1977); Maurice Bloch, "The Past and the Present in the Present," *Man,* XII (1977), 278–292.

them intelligible for himself, manageable, communicable, and therefore socially useful as well as essential to his private adaptation to the world. Indeed, as the humanists of the Renaissance maintained (the point was perhaps more profound than they could realize), language is the basis of society. The human and social world with which historians are all, in one way or another, concerned, might therefore be described as a vast rhetorical production; and rhetoric is also likely to become a major tool of the new intellectual history. For the operations that bring this human world into existence in consciousness and endow it with meaning are comparable to such basic rhetorical transactions as division and comparison, or metonymy and metaphor.[12]

A few historians have pointed in this direction; but the connections between a language and the perceptions of reality peculiar to those who speak it, as well as the significance of linguistic change, although often recognized in the abstract, have not yet seriously engaged historians.[13] Because of the basic role of language at once in perception, thought, and social existence, linguistics seems—in the most literal sense—of fundamental importance for historians, as indeed for other social scientists. Changes in language are likely to provide us with clues, of a kind previously lacking, to the human significance of various kinds of developments about which we have so far been able to form only the most unverifiable impressions. Here, indeed, might lie one of the possibilities, which may be rare in the kind of history with which I am concerned, for the application of quantitative methods.

I have noted that traditional intellectual history depended heavily on traditional philosophy, and, in conclusion, it is worth observing that traditional philosophy has been slowly dying, although with occasional remissions, during the same period, at about the same speed, and for probably the same reasons as traditional intellectual history. But it has gradually been replaced

12   The quoted remark is Clifford Geertz's paraphrase of Max Weber in *The Interpretation of Cultures* (New York, 1973), 5. Cf. Bouwsma, "The Renaissance and the Drama of Western History," *American Historical Review,* LXXXIV (1979), 10–11.

13   For example, Nancy S. Struever, *The Language of History in the Renaissance: Rhetoric and Historical Consciousness in Florentine Humanism* (Princeton, 1970); Pocock, *Politics, Language, and Time* (New York, 1971); Marjorie O'Rourke Boyle, *Erasmus on Language and Method in Theology* (Toronto, 1977).

by a quite different kind of wisdom than traditional philosophers were supposed to enunciate. It is thus possible that intellectual history, transformed in the manner that I have envisaged here, may also be able to renew its connections with philosophy, similarly transformed. Under new conditions, history and philosophy might once again have much to offer each other. Historians could help explain what has been happening to philosophy, and philosophers might help historians to scrutinize their own metahistorical assumptions. In this way one of the least historical among academic disciplines might at last join hands with one of the least philosophical. This is another possibility for the next decade.

Intellectual History in the 1980s

Joel Colton

The Case for the Defense   Any candid assessment would have to concede the ill fortune into which intellectual history has slipped. Indeed Ozymandias's epitaph might serve notice on those historians now enjoying more felicitous positions: "Look on my works, ye Mighty, and despair!"

In subtle and indirect ways it is, of course, possible to restore intellectual history to the position of esteem and prestige that it once occupied. One can assert that intellectual history has begun to suffuse all historical writing, enriching and reinforcing it—in the way the taking of vitamins invigorates the individual—and hence that intellectual history no longer has an independent *raison d'être*. But if intellectual history is everywhere, is it anywhere? If it is everybody's business, is it anybody's business? The issue needs to be joined: Does intellectual history have an autonomy of its own? [1]

To argue for intellectual history does not require either a mythology or a physiology that endows it with superiority over all other history because it deals with *homo sapiens* and not human animality. Nor is philosophical idealism required to justify its continued existence despite its possible origins in that realm. It is true that modern thought, and in particular the troublesome threesome, Charles Darwin, Karl Marx, and Sigmund Freud, helped

Joel Colton is Director for Humanities at the Rockefeller Foundation, on leave from Duke University where he is Professor of History. He is the author of *Léon Blum: Humanist in Politics* (New York, 1965) and, with R. R. Palmer, of *A History of the Modern World* (New York, 1978; 5th ed.)

0022-1953/81/020293-6 $02.50/0

1   For discussion and additional bibliographical suggestions, see Leonard Krieger, "The Autonomy of Intellectual History," in Georg G. Iggers and Harold T. Parker (eds.), *International Handbook of Historical Studies: Contemporary Research and Theory* (Westport, Conn., 1979), 109–125; Felix Gilbert, "Intellectual History: Its Aims and Methods," in Gilbert and Stephen R. Graubard (eds.), *Historical Studies Today* (New York, 1972), 141–158; Arthur Schlesinger, Jr., "Intellectual History: A Time for Despair?" a review of John Higham and Paul K. Conklin (eds.), *New Directions in American History* (Baltimore, 1979), *Journal of American History*, LXLI (1980), 888–893.

to dislodge an oversimplified rationalism, undermined the autonomy of mind and idea, and substituted biological, economic, or psychological determinism for self-standing ideas and ideologies. Yet even they taught us only that in the most rational of ideas there are elements that go beyond the merely intellectual. In their case the question remains: Who but the intellectual historian can explain the dethronement of reason and its consequences? The roots of Marx's dialectical materialism or of Freud's "irrationalism," in their own age and place, need to be explored—as some contemporary historians are successfully attempting to do.

Despite the evidence to the contrary, there are historians productively at work today whose writings demonstrate the vigorous contribution of the "older" intellectual history. Berlin is a leading example. Only his *Hedgehog and the Fox* and his recent *Against the Current* need be cited. No need to deny the importance of imagination, insight, and intuition as against cool and calculated reason—he assures us—but no reason to deny the independence of reasoned judgment as well. Schorske deserves mention because he shares a preoccupation with ideas and with their birthplace. Krieger can examine the idea of freedom in a given context, or Gay, the Enlightenment and other subjects, not on the basis of ideas divorced from their milieu but illuminated by an understanding of their environment. White, Hughes, Himmelfarb, and Manuel (author, with his wife, of an inquiry into the idea of utopianism in Western thought) are other examples.[2]

Three separate but at times overlapping entities are involved when we speak of intellectual history: the history of ideas or of idea-units, intellectual history proper, which links ideas to the society from which they spring; and cultural history, which con-

2 Isaiah Berlin, *Hedgehog and the Fox: An Essay on Tolstoy's View of History* (New York, 1953); idem, *Against the Current: Essays in the History of Ideas* (New York, 1980); Carl E. Schorske, *Fin-de-siècle Vienna: Politics and Culture* (New York, 1980); Krieger, *The German Idea of Freedom: History of a Political Tradition* (Boston, 1957); Peter Gay, *The Enlightenment: An Interpretation* (New York, 1966–1969), 2 v.; Hayden White, *Metahistory: The Historical Imagination in Nineteenth-Century Europe* (Baltimore, 1973); H. Stuart Hughes, *Consciousness and Society: The Reorientation of Social Thought, 1890–1930* (New York, 1958); idem, *The Obstructed Path: French Social Thought in the Years of Desperation, 1930–1960* (New York, 1968); idem, *The Sea Change: The Migration of Social Thought, 1930–1965* (New York, 1975); Gertrude Himmelfarb, *On Liberty and Liberalism: The Case of John Stuart Mill* (New York, 1974); Frank E. Manuel and Fritzie P. Manuel, *Utopian Thought in the Western World* (Cambridge, Mass., 1979).

veys something of the way society absorbs, adopts, and dissem-
inates these ideas. Lovejoy's discrete set of philosophical ideas or
idea-units, divorced from surrounding reality, has been discarded
as overly abstract and of marginal interest. So too have been the
ways in which philosophers, as at the University of Chicago,
have worried the ideas of liberty, equality, and progress—reconstructing discourse on these themes across the ages (Aristotle and
John Dewey, Thomas Aquinas and John Stuart Mill)—with no
relationship to the times involved.[3]

Philosophy itself has moved further and further away from
history in recent years. Linguistic analysis and logical positivism
have threatened to take over. But it is an exaggeration to say that
philosophy has abandoned its concern with the historical evolution of ideas. Philosophers still read Plato, Immanuel Kant, Jean-
Jacques Rousseau, and David Hume and there is even evidence of
a revived interest in political philosophy, as evidenced in the
writings of Skinner and Wolin. In any event, no matter what the
course of philosophy, history—especially intellectual history—
cannot abandon its concern with philosophers.[4]

Because cultural history seems to be holding its own, although taking new directions, what we see being abandoned is
the older challenge that intellectual history undertook—to grasp
and communicate the thought and the thinkers of the past and in
that way to convey as graphically as possible the *Zeitgeist,* or
intellectual spirit of an age. That holistic effort, once the noblest
challenge to intellectual historians, now lies in disrepute. John
Herman Randall, Jr., Preserved Smith, Paul Hasard, Perry Miller,
and Vernon Parrington are no longer in favor. Nothing comparable has appeared in our day to Randall's *Making of the Modern
Mind*, a synthesis of intellectual history on which many scholars
were nurtured. The book's mission was clear: "by entering sym-
pathetically into the spirit of the past, to make the thought of the
present more intelligible." It rested, Randall said, upon "a first-
hand acquaintance with the works of those who have expressed

3 Arthur O. Lovejoy, *The Great Chain of Being* (Cambridge, Mass., 1936); Charles Van
Doren, with foreword by Mortimer Adler, *The Idea of Progress* (New York, 1967).
4 Quentin Skinner, *The Foundations of Modern Political Thought* (New York, 1978), 2 v.;
Sheldon S. Wolin, *Politics and Vision: Continuity and Innovation in Western Political Thought*
(Boston, 1960).

the intellectual currents of their times." On the basis of those currents, he would search out the *Zeitgeist* of each age, from medieval Christendom to the then present. His synthesis, despite imperfections and weaknesses, especially in the treatment of more recent times, remains unmatched.[5]

We stumble here on a reason for the decline of intellectual history. Is it because we are now unclear about the *Zeitgeist* of the modern West? If there was one dominating Western theme, it was the idea of progress—the continuing advance of civilization in such areas as science, technology, rationalism, and tolerance. It was a thesis brilliantly but naively explored by Bury in 1920. But that belief in progress has been radically overhauled and transformed in the post-imperialist, post-Auschwitz, post-Hiroshima, post-Vietnam, post-Gulag-Archipelago era. If we can no longer believe in that *Zeitgeist* and are not sure of what has succeeded it—an age of anxiety? an age of disillusionment? an age of despair? — how can we explore the spirit of other ages? Yet the very undermining and transformation of the idea of progress demands the historian's effort to trace and reevaluate its career, as Nisbet (a sociologist and historian of social thought) has recently done, and as some other scholars are collaboratively attempting to do in other ways.[6]

No one should derogate the splendid contributions being made by some contemporary historians who are writing a newer kind of sociocultural history. Although they share some of the same concerns as intellectual historians, their emphasis lies elsewhere: on the percolation downward of seminal ideas; on the transformation of ideas into political programs; on the vehicles of transmission; on the economic and commercial transactions involved in intellectual enterprises; on the lesser rivulets rather than on the mainstream; or on the care and feeding of audiences.

It has been suggested that the decline of intellectual history can be explained in part by the post-1968 milieu in which contemporary historians are writing. Intellectual history deals perforce with elites and with ideas that emanate from elite minds;

5 John Herman Randall, Jr., *The Making of the Modern Mind* (Cambridge, Mass., 1926; rev. ed. 1940; reissued 1976), see foreword, 1940 ed., v.

6 J. B. Bury, *The Idea of Progress: An Inquiry into its Origin and Growth* (New York, 1955; orig. pub. London, 1920). Robert Nisbet, *History of the Idea of Progress* (New York, 1980); Gabriel A. Almond, Marvin Chodorow, and Roy Harvey Pearce (eds.), *Progress and Its Discontents,* forthcoming.

and elitism fell out of favor in 1968. To put it more sympatheti-
cally and constructively, historians are concerning themselves for
the first time in a systematic way with the history of ordinary
men and women, the 95 percent of past populations as against
the 5 percent—the inarticulate as against the literate and the vocal.
It may be understandable that the tide has been running toward
other kinds of history, which may also explain the current appeal
of anthropology. Historians in the contemporary world, moreover, must show that they are tough and do not deal with heady
fantasies, woolly notions, or romantic ideas.

If it is true that ideas grow out of one's time and place, there
need be no divorce between intellectual history, cultural history,
and social history, but rather an ongoing partnership. We should
be challenged to explore the relationships between minds, ideas,
individual human beings—and the societies which nurtured the
ideas and the individuals. We need not abandon the elite figures
or the elite ideas after all. We need not abandon the study of
individuals, nor yield to determinism, nor be party to skepticism
about the possibilities of human action and human freedom, past
and present. As Schlesinger has written in a challenging note:
". . . the unique subject matter for the intellectual historian is the
role thought plays in enabling men and women to accept and to
transform their environment. The unifying focus is the problem
how and why people change their minds." One can applaud his
conclusion that in that way one can thwart "the attempt to turn
intellectual history into a suburb of social history."[7]

Intellectual history may not provide the key to unlock the
mysteries of civilization, but neither can any of the other subdisciplines of history with which we are dealing. That must remain
a collective enterprise, and undoubtedly an unattainable one. But
intellectual history has its unique tasks, and an autonomous role
to play, custodial and critical. It remains the custodian of the great
thoughts and texts of the ages; and it must critically reexamine
and reevaluate those thoughts and texts for our own age. It must
explore the role, large or small, that thought itself plays in enabling men and women to understand—and to change—the world
in which they live. The task is a noble one, and essential to the
understanding of the human experience, for, as Randall reminded

7 Schlesinger, "Intellectual History," 893.

us, "ideas are much more lasting than anything else in man's civilization." If one may be permitted the phrase, intellectual history has a right to hold its head high. It may be suffering from malaise, but the report of its demise is exaggerated.[8]

8 Randall, *Making of the Modern Mind,* introduction, 1940 ed., 5.

History of Science in the 1980s

Arnold Thackray

Science, Technology, and Medicine   The history of science is Janus faced. It looks both to history and to science. It is subject not only to those constraints common to all forms of history, but also to those that derive from its special relationship to science. The tension inherent in this duality of roles goes far toward explaining the development and possible futures of the discipline. Here I approach the history of science through history, then through science.[1]

THE HISTORICAL CONTEXT   Over the past three decades the field of history has been profoundly affected by the shifting demography of the historical profession; by ramifying employment opportunities; and by the transformation of the scholars' tools. Each change will continue in the 1980s, in subtly altered ways.

First, the period since World War II has seen a great surge in the number of Ph.D. holding historians in the English-speaking world. The expansion has now slowed and the 1980s will see a rise in the number and also in the median age of historians; but age and experience offer many advantages. Second, the 1980s will see an acceleration of the movement away from history as mainly

Arnold Thackray is Professor of History and Sociology of Science at the University of Pennsylvania and is the editor of *Isis*. He is co-author of *Gentlemen of Science* (Oxford, 1981).

    This article owes much to Thomas P. Hughes, Nathan Sivin, Rosemary Stevens, and other colleagues in the Department of History and Sociology of Science at the University of Pennsylvania, who made many valuable suggestions.

0022-1953/81/020299-16 $02.50/0

1 Science here includes the physical, biological, and social sciences, technology, and medicine. The Janus metaphor comes from Henry Sigerist's early journal of medical history *Kyklos,* by way of Owsei Temkin's *The Double Face of Janus and Other Essays in the History of Medicine* (Baltimore, 1977). Recent historiographic guides include Thomas S. Kuhn, *The Essential Tension. Selected Studies in Scientific Tradition and Change* (Chicago, 1977), 105–164; I. Bernard Cohen, "The Many Faces of the History of Science," in Charles F. Delzell (ed.), *The Future of History* (Nashville, 1977), 65–110; Thackray, "The History of Science," Carroll S. Pursell, "The History of Technology," Gert S. Brieger, "The History of Medicine," all in Paul Durbin (ed.), *A Guide to the Culture of Science, Technology, and Medicine* (New York, 1980), 1–194.

an academic activity. We increasingly hear of public historians or of employment opportunities in business, in archives and museums, and in local, state and federal government. This shift may change the forms of discourse in the historical profession as much as did the earlier change from a norm of gentlemanly independence to one of academic employment. Third, the intellectual trend has been toward the pursuit of more complex goals using more elaborate tools. The multiplying patronage of philanthropic foundations and of government has broadened the scope of historical enquiry. Data banks of various kinds have been created, and their exploitation has encouraged the growth of team research. Computers have transformed both bibliographical and quantitative work. Archival research in its turn has depended increasingly on the information available in a growing array of printed guides, on microfilms, and on xerox copies. New tools mean that our histories are now routinely based on broader, more complex information. This is not to say that the histories in question are more subtle or more significant—but they are more fully documented. The financial constraints expected throughout the 1980s may slow but will not reverse this trend.[2]

In the case of the history of science, changes in demography, employment, and tools are present in sharply exaggerated form.

The demography of the history of science is remarkable. Only today are the first American-trained, professional historians of science reaching the age at which *Festschriften* are deemed suitable. Few "deaths" and many scholarly "births" mean a population that continues to grow rapidly. Over 25 percent of the subscribers to *Isis* are graduate students, and each annual crop of doctorates increases the pool of trained people by between 5 and 10 percent. Even so, the median age of scholars in the history of science is at last beginning to rise. If the last three decades have been characterized by the heroic labors of a small band of pioneer professionals, the next two belong to the many maturing craft practitioners of a routinized discipline. It is simple to recognize

2 Lindsey R. Harmon (ed.), *A Century of Doctorates. Data Analyses of Growth and Change* (Washington, D.C., 1978), 13. The "Philadelphia Social History Project" is an example of a project pursuing complex goals. Its funding sources include the National Institute for Child Health and Human Development, the sociology program of the National Science Foundation, and the Division of Research Grants of the National Endowment for the Humanities.

that this transition must alter the style of the subject, but difficult
to predict exactly how. One change may be away from bold,
imperial hypotheses (as in Kuhn's widely influential *Structure of
Scientific Revolutions,* conceived in the 1950s) to limited, empirical
studies (as in *Electricity in the Seventeenth and Eighteenth Centuries,*
written by Heilbron, Kuhn's first student).[3]

The employment situation is equally extraordinary. Thirty
years ago, North America could not boast more than two or three
dozen professionals in the field, all in academic employment. In
contrast, sixty-one *new* positions were advertized in 1980. Academic openings are still dominant, but archives and science museums are significant sources of employment. Industrial employers include organizations like General Electric, Bell Labs, and the
oil companies, and historians of science may be found in government agencies as varied as the Congressional Research Service,
NASA, the Department of Defense, the National Archives, the
National Science Foundation, and the Department of Energy. The
implications of growing non-academic employment have yet to
be felt fully in graduate programs, in research priorities, and in
publications.[4]

Finally, there has been the transformation of tools. Sarton,
the great pioneering crusader for the history of science, set up
Isis, his "Revue consacrée à l'histoire de la science" in 1912. One
of his overriding concerns was to establish and exemplify proper
professional standards. Despite the heroic labors of his lifetime,
the field enjoyed few reliable resources in 1950. The past three
decades have seen the situation altered not simply as regards those
elements common to all historical work, but also in the creation
of the special tools that define and mark off the territory of a
historical specialty. On the grand scale there are Charles Gillispie's
Dictionary of Scientific Biography (New York, 1970–1980) and Joseph Needham's *Science and Civilization in China* (Cambridge,
1954–). Together with the six volumes of the *Isis Cumulative*

---

3   Thomas S. Kuhn, *Structure of Scientific Revolutions* (Chicago, 1962) consisted of 171 text
pages and was delightfully free of scholarly impedimenta; John L. Heilbron, *Electricity in
the Seventeenth and Eighteenth Centuries* (Berkeley, 1979) required a 69 page bibliography.
Both books, it should be stressed, display great and ingenious learning. However that
learning is directed to far different ends.
4   Kathy Olesko, "Employment Trends in History of Science," *Isis,* LXXII (1981),
477–479.

Bibliography (London, 1971–1981), they give the historian of science extraordinary command of his field. (Matters are less satisfactory, but changing rapidly, in the subfields of the history of medicine and the history of technology.) Then there are the great editions of the correspondence of Marin Mersenne, Henry Oldenburg, and Charles Darwin, of the manuscripts of Galileo and (waiting offstage) of Albert Einstein and Thomas Edison. The point may be made most vividly by reference to the Newton industry—a voracious conglomerate which, since its modest beginnings in the late 1940s, has spawned seven volumes of *Correspondence,* and eight of *Mathematical Manuscripts,* together with two major biographies, a magisterial critical edition of the *Principia* (and one promised of the *Lectiones Opticae*), monographs on Newton's alchemy, theology, and history, literally hundreds of articles, and an erudite *Bibliography* of Newtoniana.[5]

The general constraints and opportunities controlled by demography, the market, and tools—in their magnified form—subtly condition the evolving discourse of historians of science. That discourse is also influenced by other factors which both emphasize the discipline's role in historical scholarship, and set it off from other varieties of history.

THE SCIENTIFIC COMMUNITY AND THE HISTORY OF SCIENCE   The history of science has always enjoyed a special relationship with the scientific community. Scientists, engineers, and physicians have served as patrons, practitioners, and audiences for the subject and have long been its only reliable constituency. The lofty sentiments of Leopold von Ranke, the curiosity of Henry Buckle, the crusades of James Harvey Robinson and his new historians, and the elegant apostrophes of Herbert Butterfield—these glorious exceptions cannot disguise the extent to which the history of science until recently has been met with studied indifference by the historical community. Sarton, himself a scientist turned philosopher, challenged this indifference by proposing to replace all previous history with a fresh synthesis built on science as the leading thread of civilization. The history department of Harvard

---

5 Full bibliographical details of these works, and further discussion, may be found in Thackray, "History of Science."

University responded to his lonely, imperialist vision with a polite, cold shoulder.[6]

The special relationship has given a particular flavor to the history of science. Recruits to the discipline have traditionally been long on scientific and short on historical training, although this is now changing. Kuhn may serve as a representative figure, with his doctorate in physics; or one might reach further back and point to Karl Sudhoff, with his medical degree; or, in technology, to Cyril Stanley Smith with his background in metallurgy. Patrons too came primarily from the sciences—as exemplified in the seminal roles of L. J. Henderson and James Bryant Conant at Harvard, William H. Welch at Johns Hopkins, and Sir Henry Wellcome in London. The teaching of the history of science has typically taken place under the auspices of science departments, or in engineering and medical schools. The agenda of questions to be answered has also been set by intellectual developments within the sciences as evidenced by historical research on the philosophical problems of modern physics, on evolution and genetics, and on the rise of physiology and scientific medicine. Patrons, practitioners, and audiences have been agreed that the history of science was a record of the success of science. It displayed the heroic achievements of great scientists and established an argument for science; it showed that science was not simply a momentarily useful set of devices, but was among the most impressive undertakings of the human race, with an illustrious past and limitless promise for the future.

What is new within the past decade or so—and likely to be of increasing importance in the days ahead—is the scientist's changing awareness of the nature and destiny of science. Stated simply, there is an end to triumphalism: the long march is over. Since the era of the Enlightenment, practitioners of the various sciences have most often seen themselves as standing on the side of a progress that was at once automatic and benign. Threats to that progress might lie in an imperfect grasp of scientific method or an insufficient appreciation and funding of scientific workers, but

---

6 Thackray, "The History of Science in North America, 1891–1941: the Pre-History of a Discipline," *Minerva*, forthcoming; *idem* and Robert K. Merton, "On Discipline Building: the Paradoxes of George Sarton," *Isis*, LXIII (1972), 473–495.

not in Western science itself. As C. P. Snow put it, scientists were confident that they had "the future in their bones." The heroes of science were those who precipitated that future by their brilliant discoveries, or by their invention of tools and techniques.

Today that confidence is waning. A suspicion of the professions has found clear expression in the public's uneasiness over nuclear power, genetic manipulation, and the role of "experts." The surface shift in consciousness reflects far deeper, slow-moving causes, such as the somber record of twentieth-century violence, and the great scale that science itself has assumed, with its consequent fragmentation, industrialization, and erosion of spirit.[7]

The shift in mood and perception is part of a redefinition of what constitutes science. There is less emphasis on great ideas, great doctors, and great inventions, and a new awareness that science is a profoundly social phenomenon, deeply imbedded in culture. The National Science Foundation now supports an Office of Science and Society; M.I.T. and Harvard jointly sponsor a journal entitled *Science, Technology and Human Values*; and courses proliferate in the field of medical ethics. Science is understood to contain within itself institutions and ideologies, while being inextricably linked to economics, politics, and philosophy; it is not the coherent, autnomous body of knowledge so familiar from elementary texts, but is a spectrum of activity with no sharp edges. In the medical field, there is a new awareness of the hospital, the medical center, and the team of health professionals. Methods of financing and delivering services, and deciding what services to deliver are inescapable parts of the subject matter of medicine. Technology in its turn is increasingly a matter of complex systems, such as the communication, energy, and transport systems with their political, economic, and organizational connotations. The development phase of innovation, and the diffusion of innovations across cultural barriers, are matters of growing concern. Science—in the inclusive sense of science, technology, and medicine—has become a vastly expanded enterprise, with

7 Philip Handler, "Public Doubts About Science," *Science,* CCVIII (1980), 1093. The scale of modern science is illustrated in the fact that *one* instrument, now under construction at Brookhaven, will cost over $500 million: *Science, CCX* (1980), 875–878. Jerome R. Ravetz, *Scientific Knowledge and its Social Problems* (Oxford, 1971).

quite different and less coherent boundaries than it was thought to possess in earlier times.[8]

The redefinition of science both mandates and carries with it a different style of historical awareness in the scientific community: one that is less certain of what answers it seeks, more eclectic, more willing both to embrace and to abandon historical discourse, and more dependent on the particular configuration of needs at stake. At the same time, the very size of the scientific community (some 50 to 100 times larger than the historical community), the great intellectual capital that continues to accrue within it, and the appeal of those subjects and problems on which scientists seek historical illumination—all combine to assure a continuance of the special relationship between scientists and historians of science.

THE CHANGING NATURE OF THE DISCIPLINE   Shifts in history and in science set the context for another and most important change: the emergence of a critical mass of historians of science trained within, rather than belatedly recruited to, the field of history. The change is at once intellectual, ideological, and generational, and it is no surprise that older voices have recently sung a chorus of lament about "history of science losing its science" or about "medical history without medicine." The change has gone farthest in the history of the physical and biological sciences, which today for the first time enjoys a cadre of practitioners no longer dependent on the patronage of those about whose fields they write. The new practitioners identify with one another and with the problems, techniques, and assumptions of "mere" historians. They study the scientific community, rather than belong to it. The change is also apparent in the history of medicine, because health and disease appear more accessible than science or technology to social historians without the specialists' expertise. Signs of a similar change are apparent in the fledgling field of history of technology, where the pioneer professionals are still producing the first generation of trained scholars. (The history of the social sciences is searching for its pioneer professionals.)

8   Mark B. Adams, "Sergei Chetverikov, the Kol'tsov Institute and the Evolutionary Synthesis," in Ernst Mayr (ed.), *The Evolutionary Synthesis* (Cambridge, Mass., 1981), 1–61; Thomas P. Hughes, "Emerging Themes in the History of Technology," *Technology and Culture*, XX (1979), 697–711; Rosemary Stevens, *American Medicine and the Public Interest* (New Haven, 1971).

Historians of science are increasingly historians, yet they also enjoy a special relationship to science. The duality hints at a further element which gives the field its special flavor—its interdisciplinary nature. Like other interdisciplinary fields of scholarship, history of science is perpetually in danger of losing its identity. Its subject matter spills over into, and may at any moment be subsumed by, other interests: American science disappears into studies of the professions, British technology into economic history, and French medicine into structuralist sociology. The danger is more apparent than real, for the history of science has always enjoyed and will continue to benefit from the attention of major figures in other disciplinary traditions: witness the work of Robert Merton, the sociologist; Alexandre Koyré, the idealist philosopher; or Michel Foucault.

The growing importance of historical concerns within the history of science, and the traditional openness of the field to other disciplines, together suggest that the subject will profit from the newer historical interest in sociological and anthropological methodology, and from what Geertz has called "the interpretive turn" in the social sciences. Indeed there are already whole genres of work available in the history of science that draw on, nourish, and modify these wider trends in historical enquiry.[9]

ACHIEVEMENTS AND OPPORTUNITIES   The achievements of the past three decades may be characterized in several ways. The field found its major patrons among natural scientists and profited from the exploits of its pioneer professionals. The sequence of events from Hiroshima to Sputnik spoke powerfully of the enhanced role of science in the affairs of nations, and scientists themselves sought new affirmations of the great and good heritage of an endeavor now armed with awesome powers. The trek to college of the baby boom generation created a context in which intellectual and social commitments to a particular vision of the scientific tradition could be translated into programs of graduate training and research. A nucleus of gifted men and women with extensive training (and, on occasion, wartime experience) in the physical sciences was drawn into teaching the history of science

9 Clifford Geertz, "Blurred Genres; The Refiguration of Social Thought," *American Scholar*, XLIX (1980), 165–179.

at the university level. The subtle, fine-grained philosophical analysis of past scientific texts practised by Koyré, captured the imagination of this group. The "Koyré paradigm" for the history of
science implied a program of work that was based on the practitioner's skills in at least one scientific discipline, that reinforced
the pattern of links with scientific and philosophical colleagues
which Sarton had imparted to the field, and that was congruent
with teaching aimed primarily at audiences of scientific, medical,
and engineering students.[10]

The achievements of this phase of the history of science were
concentrated on roots and origins—on rewriting the history of
medieval science and the "Scientific Revolution" to accommodate
the reality of that mixture of theology and philosophy, Herme-
ticism and neo-Platonism, and preconception and empirical enquiry, which nourished early modern science. Textual analysis
and the recourse to documents have shown how leading concepts
(e.g. inertia or momentum) were developed and refined. Scientific
knowledge was one key to this enterprise and will continue to
be essential, though less dominant, to it. The history of science
will not easily lose its science (if by that is meant the great ideas
of intellectual heroes), nor should we desire it to.[11]

A paradoxical achievement of this phase of research has been
that historians of science have triumphantly demonstrated how
little of the intellectual advance of science is given by nature or
by the immediate context, and how much depends upon the
subtle complexities of personality in key figures. Here again, the
case of Isaac Newton is instructive. In 1950 the main lines of
Brewster's century-old biography still stood intact: Newton—
with his prism and his silent face—was a solitary, rational man
uncovering physical facts and theories by the triumphant employment of scientific method. Today he stands as an enigmatic
figure, weaving a bizarre, speculative web in which theology,
alchemy, experimentation, history, and hypothesis are hopelessly

---

10 Alexandre Koyré, *Metaphysics and Measurement. Essays in Scientific Revolution* (London,
1968); Dorothy Stimson (ed.), *Sarton on the History of Science* (Cambridge, Mass., 1962).
11 Marshall Clagett, *Archimedes in the Middle Ages* (Madison, 1964–1978), 4 v.; Cohen,
Franklin and Newton: An Inquiry into Speculative Newtonian Experimental Science (Philadelphia, 1956); A. Rupert Hall, *The Scientific Revolution, 1500–1800* (London, 1964); Kuhn,
The Copernican Revolution (Cambridge, Mass., 1957); Walter Pagel, *Paracelsus: An Introduction to Philosophical Medicine in the Era of the Renaissance* (Basel, 1958).

entangled. More than that, he stands as a man of strange, compulsive psychological needs, and as a central figure in one social and political movement by which the Restoration settlement was given its ideological underpinnings. Newtonianism turns out to be a political statement, an ideology, and a way of life as well as scientific methodology.[12]

The Newton industry represents the most-developed but by no means the only example of the fascination exerted by a great man. Figures like Louis Pasteur, Joseph Henry, Thomas Edison, Sigmund Freud, and Albert Einstein are receiving increasing attention. "Great man" studies have fostered a keen attention to manuscript evidence, and a growing sophistication of analysis. The result has been a new realization of the elusive quality of their ideas and of the persistence and intricacy of their patterns of thought. That realization has done much to challenge stereotypes of science as an impersonal, value-free inquiry.

Adjusting to these new realities can be troubling both to students and to settled practitioners in the sciences. In a way again familiar for intellectual novelties, the challenge has not been appreciated fully by those who stand to gain most from it; as social scientists come to understand how little historical evidence there is for those mythologies of natural science on which they have depended for direction, we may expect fresh enthusiasm for "the interpretive turn" in the social sciences.[13]

The eclecticism that is now emerging in the history of science grows out of the earlier conceptualist enterprise, while radically transforming it by asking genuinely historical questions. The practitioners who will dominate the history of science in the years ahead are as interested in contextual and social history as any other group of young historians. At the same time, many of them are employed in situations where the demands of science are obvious and inescapable. Although certain inherited styles and common assumptions may continue to mark their work, that

12 David Brewster, *Memoirs of the Life, Writings, and Discoveries of Sir Isaac Newton* (London, 1855). Three convenient points of entry to the literature on Newton are Cohen, *Introduction to Newton's Principia* (Cambridge, Mass., 1971); Margaret Jacob, *The Newtonians and the English Revolution, 1689–1720* (Ithaca, 1976); Richard S. Westfall, *Never at Rest. A Biography of Isaac Newton* (New York, 1980).
13 Stephen G. Brush, "Should the History of Science be Rated X?" *Science, CLXXXIII* (1974), 1164–1172.

work will also be characterized by its considerable variety. One could consider the history of science as likely to contain within it variegated congeries of practitioners of more-or-less connected specialisms. There will be those who continue to visualize the subject as a series of enquiries, each closely linked with the concerns of its parent scientific subject: those who—following Sarton—will see the subject as a unitary and synthetic discipline, at least self-sufficient if not central to the progress of knowledge; those who will emphasize the social context of science and accordingly focus on particular periods (the ancient world or the twentieth century) or on national cultures (American science or Chinese science); those who may stress the links with cognate fields such as philosophy, sociology, or economic history, and define their problematics accordingly; and to conclude, though not to exhaust the possibilities, those who will be concerned with science policy and with the ethical implications of modern scientific knowledge.

No new consensus is about to dominate the field. At the same time, certain deeper concerns that characterize our present culture seem likely to have an enduring impact on the history of science. Public uncertainties about the value and virtue of science have helped to fuel both defensive and self-questioning moods in the scholarly community. A shift in the center of gravity of historical study from medieval and early modern to nineteenth- and twentieth-century science may be connected to this change of mood, and to changing employment opportunities. The by now unavoidable comparison of Western with Oriental and Third World cultures may also help to shape the agenda of the field.[14]

Can logical or historical distinctions between science and magic be sustained? Is science culture-free in anything other than a trivial sense? Are themes like "progress" or "truth" useful concepts around which to organize historical work? How are the patterns of growth and decay in scientific activity and scientific creativity to be conceptualized and measured? How are obvious differences in applied science (medical and technological systems, for example) in different regions to be most usefully explained? What is the proper relationship between scientific thought and

14 Special issue, "Science and Its Public: The Changing Relationship," *Daedalus, CIII* (1974), 1–207.

religious and ethical concerns? Is science essentially an ideology or form of oppression? There is currently no consensus on any of these questions.

Historians of science are skeptical as to whether nature itself can legitimately be understood as setting any definite, narrow limits to the ways in which scientific knowledge may develop. The hope for a true world science of which modern (Western) science is but the first foreshadowing appears only a little less delusive than the hope for world government based on a (Western) parliamentary model. Perhaps more realizable is the wish for a coherent understanding of how different scientific systems reflect the cultures which sustain them. Even such an anthropology of science remains far distant. For now, the ways in which the relations of man to nature are shaped by the moral and social realities of a given culture remain a matter for allusion, allegory, and speculative probing. More accessible and more concrete are the ways in which certain domains of enquiry seem likely to occupy center stage within the history of science, in response to the values and interests of the subject's audiences, patrons, and practitioners, and the tools, funding and traditions that those practitioners can command.[15]

One central task is to understand science as an aspect of culture.[16] If, as researchers within the Koyré paradigm have shown, scientific thought is under-determined by experimental factual knowledge, then the way is open to treat the whole past of science in a genuinely historical manner. This new, demanding program is now underway. The wider, historical concern to study movements and ideologies from the bottom up here coincides with the moods of public disenchantment over science, technology, and medicine. Undergraduate courses and public discussions on science and society have become popular (creating a demand for teachers, texts, and experts), and the problems and allure of a social explanation of scientific ideas are intellectually enticing. The shifting dialogue between Western nations and the Third World, and the difficulties encountered by missionary attempts to

---

15 Yehuda Elkana, "The Distinctiveness and Universality of Science: Reflections on the Work of Professor Robin Horton," *Minerva*, XV (1977), 155–173.
16 For some of the possibilities, see Susan F. Cannon's pioneering study, *Science in Culture: The Early Victorian Period* (New York, 1978).

implant modern scientific and technical systems in traditional cultures, reinforce the awareness that science is as much a social and cultural as an intellectual phenomenon. Historians now perceive the formal institutions of science—societies, laboratories, university departments, prizes, journals, and funding agencies—as strategic sites for research using both documentary and sociological techniques. For these among other reasons, the social history of science has developed rapidly and will continue to do so.

Much important work is already being published on scientific institutions: it includes a fresh examination of the Scientific Revolution and the origins of the Royal Society; studies of the work of the Royal Institution in London, the Academy of Sciences in Paris, and the Franklin Institute in Philadelphia; a re-interpretation of early Victorian science, and of the British Association; analyses of the Cambridge school of physiology, and of agricultural chemistry in America; histories of American, British, and French work on atomic energy and of physics in America. This last work offers one example of the way in which professionals are increasingly turning toward social histories of scientific disciplines within their various national and transnational contexts.[17]

In these histories, scientific ideas and research programs are being recognized not as something given by nature, but as evolving responses to intellectual, institutional, financial, political, and career pressures and opportunities. Early examples of this new genre include studies of chemistry, radio-astronomy, and geology

17 Charles Webster, *The Great Instauration: Science, Medicine, and Reform, 1616–1660* (London, 1975); Morris Berman, *Social Change and Scientific Organization: The Royal Institution, 1799–1844* (Ithaca, 1978); Robert Hahn, *The Anatomy of a Scientific Institution: The Paris Academy of Sciences, 1666–1803* (Berkeley, 1971); Bruce Sinclair, *Philadelphia's Philosopher Mechanics: A History of the Franklin Institute, 1824–1865* (Baltimore, 1974); Jack Morrell and Thackray, *Gentlemen of Science. Early Years of the British Association for the Advancement of Science* (Oxford, 1981); Gerald Geison, *Michael Foster and the Cambridge School of Physiology: The Scientific Enterprise in Late Victorian Society* (Princeton, 1978); Margaret Rossiter, *The Emergence of Agricultural Chemistry: Justus Liebig and the Americans, 1840–1880* (New Haven, 1975); Richard Hewlett and O. E. Anderson, *A History of the United States Atomic Energy Commission, I: The New World, 1939–1946* (University Park, Penn., 1962); Hewlett and Francis Duncan, *ibid.*, II: *Atomic Shield, 1947–1952* (University Park, Penn., 1969); Margaret Gowing, *Britain and Atomic Energy, 1939–1945* (London, 1964); idem, *Independence and Deterrence* (London, 1974); Spencer R. Weart, *Scientists in Power* (Cambridge, Mass., 1979); Daniel Kevles, *The Physicists: The History of a Scientific Community* (New York, 1978).

in Britain, biochemistry in America, and genetics in the Soviet Union.[18]

The historical study of scientific disciplines offers one important meeting ground for traditional concerns with scientific ideas, new interests in the politics of science, an awakening curiosity over scientists as social groups, the growing desire to treat modern periods and American problems, and the fresh awareness of contextual, cultural factors. Forman's widely-noticed study of quantum physics in Weimar Germany provides one especially rewarding example of the insights to be gained from sophisticated work in this area of social history. That study also indicates ways in which historians of science are turning toward questions in the sociology of knowledge, as their work reveals how little ground there is for treating science as a privileged form of communication. Theoretical treatments of the sociology of scientific knowledge are being rapidly joined by historical case studies; detailed treatments are already available of Newtonianism as an ideology, and of the uses of scientific ideas in various contexts including nineteenth-century America and England.[19]

With the new emphasis on science in its social and cultural setting goes a new set of methods. Epistemological questions about paradigms, research programs, and the truth content of science will continue to attract their followers, especially in the rich borderlands, where history of science dissolves into philosophy. However, the relativistic, agnostic mood that now characterizes Western society and Western history seems likely to nourish a different range of concerns. We should rather expect to see new emphases on the politics of knowledge, on ideas as tools,

18   Robert F. Bud, "The Discipline of Chemistry: The Origins and Early Years of the Chemical Society of London," unpub. Ph.D. diss. (University of Pennsylvania, 1980); David Edge and Michael Mulkay, *Astronomy Transformed: The Emergence of Radio Astronomy in Britain* (New York, 1976); Roy Porter, *The Making of Geology: Earth Science in Britain, 1660–1815* (Cambridge, 1977); Robert E. Kohler, *From Medical Chemistry to Biochemistry: The Making of a Biomedical Discipline*, forthcoming; Adams, *Science, Ideology, and Structure: Soviet Genetics 1948–1965* (Chicago, 1981).
19   Paul Forman, "Weimar Culture, Causality, and Quantum Theory," *Historical Studies in the Physical Sciences*, III (1971), 1–116; Barry Barnes, *Scientific Knowledge and Sociological Theory* (London, 1974); Jacob, *The Newtonians*; Everett Mendelsohn, Peter Weingart, and Richard Whitley (eds.), *The Social Production of Scientific Knowledge* (Boston, 1977); Charles Rosenberg, *No Other Gods: Science and American Social Thought* (Baltimore, 1976); Barnes and Steven Shapin (eds.), *Natural Order: Historical Studies of Culture* (London, 1979); Shapin, *The Social Use of Nature*, forthcoming.

and on the social dimensions of scientific thought. These emphases will require comparative analyses of institutions, societies, and civilizations: medicine in Brazil as well as in France; physics in Buenos Aires as well as in Copenhagen; and technology in China and Russia as well as in America. We should also expect work on teachers and students, on research schools, on lobbies and invisible colleges, and on the social bases of knowledge. The very scale of modern science also suggests an increased attention to quantitative methods, to prosopography, and to "histoire sèrielle." In these last areas, team research is already much in evidence.[20]

The history of technology and the history of medicine share to some extent in these changes. They also have their own agendas arising from the growing dominance of complex systems in electronic, aeronautical, and chemical engineering, and from the way that medicine assumes a rising portion of the gross national product in every developed country.

In the last several decades the histories of science, medicine, and technology have moved away from each other, as each subfield increased in size and professionalized in style. However, one of the most intriguing of all possibilities lies in the exploration of themes and methods that embrace all three areas. It may be that the days ahead will be characterized by the emergence of a new composite discipline embracing the separate histories of science, technology and medicine. Central to this discipline will be questions in the politics of knowledge, in the historical sociology of disciplines, institutions and systems, and in the role of entrepreneurs and key individuals.[21]

In all of this, the history of science will stand less apart from

20 Nancy Stepan, *Beginnings of Brazilian Science: Oswaldo Cruz, Medical Research, and Policy, 1890–1920* (New York, 1976); Lewis Pyenson, "The Incomplete Transmission of a European Image: Physics at Greater Buenos Aires and Montreal, 1890–1920," *Proceedings of the American Philosophical Society,* CXXII (1978), 92–114; Peter Buck, *American Science and Modern China, 1876–1936* (New York, 1980); Alexander Vucinich, *Science in Russian Culture, 1861–1917* (Stanford, 1970); Kendall Bailes, *Technology and Society Under Lenin and Stalin: Origins of the Soviet Technical Intelligentsia, 1917–1941* (Princeton, 1978); Forman, Heilbron, and Weart, "Physics *circa* 1900: Personnel, Funding, and Productivity of the Academic Establishments," *Historical Studies in the Physical Sciences,* V (1975), 1–185; Bud, P. Thomas Carroll, Jeffrey L. Sturchio, and Thackray, *Chemistry in America, 1876–1976: An Historical Application of Science Indicators,* forthcoming.

21 Certain academic departments and programs are now training practitioners with a competence in these themes. See Hughes, "Convergent Themes in the History of Science, Medicine and Technology," *Technology and Culture,* forthcoming.

other forms of history than it has in the past. At the same time, the history of science will remain a specialist endeavor, like other areas of historical enquiry. Just as French historians expect to visit Paris and to master French, so historians of science will "speak science"—that is, have not only as good instincts as historians but also a familiarity with the scientific culture that they study. That culture is just as complex as that of France and requires the full attention of its students. Historians of science appreciate the intellectual challenge of science, but their methods, their questions, and their goals are those of historians. Their work may thus erode the older sense of science as something fenced-off from the common concerns of mankind. The loss of this sense of separation should be welcomed. For with it comes the realization that science, as part of history, is neither more mysterious nor more uncontrollable than any other aspect of our heritage.

Toward the Future

Theodore K. Rabb

Coherence, Synthesis, and Quality in History

As the "new history" advances, there is a growing concern that our discipline's coherence is vanishing, and that works of synthesis are no longer possible. How seriously should such worries be taken? Is the prognosis true and, if so, should we be dismayed? Is there a continuing coherence beneath the surface disarray, transcending even the difficulty of synthesizing current research?

THE VARIETIES OF COHERENCE   The contrast between present and past coherences can easily be overdrawn. For in one crucial respect, the methods of its practitioners, historical research has never been a genuinely unified endeavor, as a comparison of Herodotus and Thucydides, born about thirty years apart, will quickly make apparent. What these two fathers of our discipline *did* agree upon was the kind of problem that they wanted to confront—for example, how and why do major military and political developments come about?

This divide between varied method and common subject matter has persisted ever since. Despite contrasts in approach, historians from Livy to Leopold von Ranke remained basically united in addressing a well-defined range of topics: the nature of politics and political change, the development of religious institutions and ideas, and the accomplishments of great writers and thinkers.[1]

That unity began to break down in the late nineteenth century as a result of a growing interest in economic history, various kinds of social history, and new forms of cultural history. Jacob

Theodore K. Rabb is Professor of History at Princeton University and is the co-editor of *The Journal of Interdisciplinary History*.

I would like to express my thanks to the participants at the Bellagio Conference and at a colloquium sponsored by the Department of History at Princeton University for their valuable criticisms of earlier drafts of this article.

0022-1953/81/020315-18 $02.50/0

1 None of the surveys of historical scholarship is satisfactory. One which provides at least some introduction to the works of historians from Livy onward is Harry Elmer Barnes, *A History of Historical Writing* (New York, 1962).

Burckhardt, Karl Lamprecht, Karl Marx, and Gustav Schmoller changed the subject matter as well as the method. Before World War I the dwindling of the old coherences was already visible: "history should not be regarded as a stationary subject which can only progress by refining its methods and accumulating, criticizing, and assimilating new material," wrote Robinson; "it is bound to alter its ideals and aims with the general progress of society and of the social sciences." He went on to criticize the use of terms like "decline" and "civilization," suggesting instead that "even a slight tincture of anthropology, reinforced by the elements of the newer allied branches of social and animal psychology, will do much to deepen and rectify the sense in which we use these terms."[2]

Despite these demands for reform, echoed by Marc Bloch and others, the community of historical endeavor did not disintegrate. Although new methods, like comparative studies, and new subjects, like the connections between religion and entrepreneurship, came to the fore, until World War II there was still confidence that all historians were pursuing related enterprises. The new questions and styles still fed into the great questions of the past. A widely read book by Hauser and Renaudet, first published in 1929, but still considered the standard account of the early sixteenth century long after World War II, could begin its 1946 revision by stating, with complete assurance, that "at the beginning of the sixteenth century, European history is above all the history of the Italian Wars."[3]

Starting in the decade after 1945, however, when an exponential increase in the number of new directions for historical research began to develop, confidence about subject matter became less and less attainable. The proliferation of innovations, supported by rapid growth in the volume of publications, the founding of journals, and the production of Ph.D.s, dwarfed the expansion of methods and topics that had taken place in the previous century. Assimilating all of this newness—whether it be the use of computers and psychoanalysis, the borrowing from demography and dendrochronology, or the study of hitherto non-

2 James Harvey Robinson, *The New History: Essays Illustrating the Modern Historical Outlook* (New York, 1912), 25, 92.
3 Henri Hauser and Augustin Renaudet, *Les Débuts de l'Age Moderne* (Paris, 1946; 3rd ed.), 5.

existent subjects, such as fertility and festivals, madness and magic—is the task facing historians today. It dazzles and dismays, because it appears to have ruptured the traditional bounds of the discipline beyond repair.

But has it been a change in degree, or in kind? Is it possible that, for all the differences in interest and approach among contemporary historians, the old coherence has remained essentially intact? Could it be that the number of individual parts has multiplied without drastically altering the whole? Although methods might be far more varied than they were in the days of Herodotus and Thucydides, a few central questions may still be recognizable across the discipline. If that is so, then, despite the absence of the kind of assurance that Hauser and Renaudet displayed, despite the bewildering plethora of modes and objects of historical inquiry, it may be possible to define a coherence for the field that is not altogether unlike its pre-twentieth-century antecedent.

The community and the synthetic capacity of late nineteenth-century scholarship have certainly disappeared. Yet in an age when art forms, once bound together by unified styles for years and decades, have dissolved into countless individual "voices" and preoccupations, why should history be any different from other modes of contemporary intellectual endeavor or creativity? Why should not historians go their own personal ways, accompanied at best by small schools? Is there an academic discipline that is more united?

One response, the notion that a powerful group could conquer the entire territory, is a chimera. Political and social historians do sometimes define their interests so broadly that they include almost every form of inquiry in the past. Similarly, intellectual history comes to cover perceptions, hence reality, and then the entire gamut of human experience. Depending on the polemicist's perspective, we are urged to learn our quantification, our psychology, our anthropology, and so on. At the other end of the scale, we are told that adequate explanations can be found only in a single psyche, or in the dynamics of a single village.

These programs cannot produce coherence. For all the individual schools which do connect groups of historians—for example, Warburgian scholars of high culture, or *annalistes* in France and elsewhere—it is inconceivable that one would give way before another, or that strong links could be forged among them. There is also a much more profound level at which historians are divided in their aims and their preoccupations. This division must be examined in some detail if we are to reach any conclusions about the possibility for coherence, especially the assumption that the current pluralism of historical research can be resolved by works of synthesis. The best way to take this closer look is to explore three particular concerns which exemplify the deeper divergences: the quest for meaning, the flight from materialism, and the epistemological implications of quantification.

THE QUEST FOR MEANING   This first concern appears in many guises. The interest in the emotional component of family life, the expansion of the traditional history of science, the search for the latent behind the manifest in social history, the acceptance of psychobiography, and the hope of differentiating profit from power in economic history all reflect the aim of uncovering purpose, meaning, or an underlying truth in the matter being studied. There is a pervasive anxiety that the individual is being left out of the latest historical endeavor, and that we must regain an appreciation for the way people felt as well as the way they behaved. The same need underlies the return to narrative that Stone has discerned in recent scholarly literature. We have to put human beings, and the small-scale, comprehensible societies in which they lived, back into the story, and it has to be a real *story*, not a dry and forbidding piece of analysis.[4]

The ambition is admirable, and it is likely to receive increased support in the 1980s, especially as anthropological viewpoints become more widespread. But its effects on the atomization of the discipline are not sufficiently appreciated. The recovery of meaning, whether through thick description, linguistic analysis, elucidation of symbols, or psychological insight is necessarily confined to small groups. Gone are the days when we can speak confidently of a "national spirit" or a "Baroque temperament." Feelings and assumptions are recoverable, if at all, only by painstaking and exhaustive anatomizing of a confined body of data— examinations of some of the inhabitants of a heretical village in France or an eccentric miller in Italy, the diary of a clergyman in

4 Lawrence Stone, "The Revival of Narrative: Reflections on a New Old History," *Past & Present*, 85 (1979), 3–24.

England, descriptions of a ritual in Bali or a New England town, or the works of a brilliant scientist or an Indian political leader. Ginzburg's prediction that historians are likely to pay more attention to works of art in coming years confirms that, as the types of data proliferate, their specificity remains unchanged. The quest for meaning only multiplies the pluralism of current research.[5]

The very process of recovering deeper motivations and attitudes, dragging the latent out of the manifest, requires such personal feats of imagination and rhetorical ability that questions about plausibility and proof are bound to arise. When two distinguished historians of the inner life of early modern Frenchmen can disagree so plainly about the implications of the same event, a carnival that led to violence in the town of Romans in 1580, the reader can be forgiven for growing more uncertain than ever.[6]

Another consequence of the desire to contextualize as thoroughly as possible is that it can cause larger patterns and questions to vanish. The wish to avoid the genetic fallacy—the assumption that significance is gained only by relating the past to the present—leads to a refusal to link the thoroughly explored phenomenon of one place or time to any other. Such has been the burden of recent interpretations of early Stuart politics, in which the civil war of the 1640s has become almost inexplicable. Even major achievements of the historical imagination, such as the reconstitution of the families of a single village, can produce such unique results that scholars are reluctant to generalize, or even to compare their findings with the situation in a village fifty miles away. Each book or article, like the events it describes, stands on its own, equal to any other in the sight of God. Because the meanings are so specific to period and location, it is exceedingly difficult to find links among them, except by analogy or inference. Yet without a larger vision, the details lose their significance.[7]

5 Examples of such work at its best are Emmanuel Le Roy Ladurie (trans. Barbara Bray), *Montaillou: The Promised Land of Error* (New York, 1978); Carlo Ginzburg (trans. John and Anne Tedeschi), *The Cheese and the Worms: The Cosmos of a Sixteenth-Century Miller* (Baltimore, 1980). Ginzburg's prediction was made at the Bellagio conference.

6 Compare Le Roy Ladurie (trans. John Day), *The Peasants of Languedoc* (Urbana, 1974), 192–197, with Natalie Z. Davis, "The Reasons of Misrule," in her *Society and Culture in Early Modern France* (Stanford, 1975), esp. 117–119. There is yet another interpretation: L. S. Van Doren, "Revolt and Reaction in the City of Romans, Dauphiné, 1579–1580," *The Sixteenth Century Journal*, V (1974), 71–100.

7 See Rabb, "Revisionism Revis'd: The Role of the Commons," *Past & Present*, forthcoming.

Even when the links are sought, problems become apparent. Are modern African tribes appropriate parallels for Thomas' Tudor villagers? Is demographic behavior in contemporary Bangladesh comparable to the experiences of the Amerindians in Spanish colonies? Or, to give the most recent example, can one draw generalizations about the place of violence in Western society from the tale of a small band of robbers in seventeenth-century northwest England, even if analogies are made to nineteenth-century Sicilians? The point is that the links are made within genres—a concept of imprisonment is compared with other such concepts, but not necessarily with other aspects of its own period. The links become generic rather than historic: what is being elucidated is the character of witchcraft, of processions, or of contraception rather than the qualities of a particular age. To the extent that the latter are muffled, one has to wonder whether the generalizations really advance historical, as opposed to theoretical, understandings.[8]

What is most noticeable in the search for meaning is its exclusivity. Alternative investigations, or findings from different fields, come to be regarded as inappropriate or irrelevant. Thus the English Revolution is explained by purely political and short-term conditions; the slower workings of social and economic history have no bearing on the subject. Similarly, an elite can lose all connection with its own society, and one senses what Bellow has called "the chastising of high culture by the masses." It is as if the diplomat cannot make contact with the innkeeper, the theologian with the parish priest. And each village, all on its own, is a world sufficient unto itself. Synthesis seems to recede further and further into the future.[9]

The quest for meaning, although undoubtedly an important and fruitful enterprise, hardly contributes to the restoration of coherence or pattern in history. On the contrary, it reduces the scope of monographic research and emphasizes the interpretations of a few brilliant but not easily replicable investigators. To the extent that the stories they tell are self-contained, they offer lim-

8 Examples of these attempts at cross-cultural and cross-temporal linkage are Keith Thomas, *Religion and the Decline of Magic* (New York, 1971); Alan Macfarlane, *The Justice and the Mare's Ale: Law and Disorder in Seventeenth-Century England* (New York, 1981).
9 Rabb, "Revisionism Revis'd"; Saul Bellow's comment is quoted in *The Times Literary Supplement* (Feb. 6, 1981), 132.

ited guidance and few lessons for the practitioners of other fields. We learn from them a great deal about individuals, about groups, about communities, and about vital features of certain societies; but they do not offer a confident and comprehensive vision that can inform the entire discipline.

THE FLIGHT FROM MATERIALISM   The obverse of the quest for meaning is an uneasiness with the material conditions of life that until recently seemed so compelling: the subjects of economic and demographic history, of the Annales school, and of the studies of geography, medicine, climate, and technology. A clear signal emerges from the doubts that have been expressed about the explanatory power of economic developments, and from the defensiveness of the economic historians themselves. As family history turns to emotional content, the demographers are treated as if they have performed a difficult mechanical task with enormous skill, but cannot now be expected to provide a real understanding of daily existence in the past. The demand is for a more elusive process of comprehension, to which such technical research can contribute, but only to a limited degree. Indeed, one is obliged to leave it behind, because it is such a blunt instrument; as mind sets, attitudes, and symbolic acts become more prominent, the material influences on human societies fade into the background.

It is almost as if there were a shrinking from the physical world. Yet it seems certain that concrete, physical topics like diet, illness, and weather will receive increasing attention from historians in coming years. For, despite the hesitations of previous investigators, especially their reluctance to generalize, the rewards seem promising and the attractions self-evident. These are, after all, virtually unknown subjects. In addition, they require interactions with scholars in esoteric and lively fields, such as isotope chemistry. Consequently, they are more likely to lead to new insights, to provide access to new forms of evidence and sources of support, and to bring us closer to problems that people worried about in their daily lives.

The effect of such investigations, however, can only be a further splintering of the discipline. One more divide will appear, this time separating the material from the meaningful. The connections will be as remote as they are between those who see unities in national history and those who do not, between those who seek and those who reject all-embracing syntheses, or between the advocates of history's impenetrable complexity and the believers in its essential lucidity. All that will be added will be another dimension to these dichotomies. Moreover, the instinct of economists or geographers is to stress durable and fundamental continuities. In this regard they may find common ground with the explorers of meaning, because both types of research lend credence to a view of the past as *histoire immobile*. Yet this construct has in turn created another divide, since many historians consider the heart of their subject to be the study and explanation of change. Behind all these divergences there lies an epistemological question that represents perhaps the most profound of current challenges to the unity of the discipline.

QUANTIFICATION AND EPISTEMOLOGY   For reasons related to the two topics that have just been discussed—the desire for meaning and the suspicion of materialism—quantification often becomes the touchstone of arguments among historians. As Fogel has recently pointed out, the profession seems to be partitioned into those who are comfortable with formal, numerical analyses, and those who are not. Nobody has gone so far as to excoriate any hint of measurement. But few seem likely to accept the quantifiers' recommendations for revamping graduate training so as to embrace advanced statistics. In general, the acceptance of quantification is grudging and limited, and its practitioners remain assured but isolated. The great hopes of the early days of the computer have apparently been disappointed; now there is a more limited role for those who wish to count.[10]

The sense of disillusion bears stressing, because it highlights an unavoidable aspect of the profession's recent creativity, namely faddishness. Some of the hostility toward the quantifiers (and the economic and demographic historians, too) appears motivated by resentment of their failure to provide the keys to world history that their more ambitious propagandists promised in the 1960s. As the work has multiplied, the methods have become familiar, and they have lost their initial revelatory power. Quantifiers cannot claim new excitement for themselves by redefining their pur-

10 Robert W. Fogel, "'Scientific' History and Traditional History," in L. J. Cohen, J. Kos, H. Pfeiffer, and K. P. Podewski (eds.), *Logic, Methodology, and Philosophy of Science*, VI, forthcoming.

poses, as have some economic or political historians. Yet their methods remain essential both to the definition of regularities in the past, and to the assessment of previously unmanageable evidence. A dismissal of their importance and relevance to current scholarship is akin to a dismissal of the value of archival research.

If the criticism of quantification is to be explained, even partly, by the constant quest for fresh specializations, then a similar fate doubtless awaits other approaches that now claim central significance. Nor can they expect to enjoy a long lifetime in the spotlight, because the term "traditional" nowadays encompasses far more than the subjects of nineteenth-century scholarship. By a nice twist, some of the latter appear non-traditional as they assume new guises—politics as the symbols of power, intellectual history as semiotics—whereas mid-twentieth century inventions like computer analysis soon take on the aura of the staid and true. Yet the reaction to quantification is especially revealing, because it adds wider implications to the meaning vs. materialism dichotomy in current scholarship.

What is at stake is a profound epistemological question, not just a disagreement over technique. Could it be that in the late twentieth-century scholars are becoming inherently dubious about claims for precision and rigor? One fascination of *mentalités* studies is that they are so very personal and intuitive. The insights are the products of Pascalian sensibilities, and they are justified by powerful rhetorical and imaginative methods. They appeal to an interest in behavior that is very different from our own, but they can never claim to be definitive. The materialists, however, and their relatives the quantifiers, offer their readers almost opposite virtues. Their findings may be hedged with limitations and qualifications by the dozen, but in the end they do provide a degree of replicable precision. It is the statistical, not the rhetorical, force that commands respect. A change of x percent explains y percent of the variation—not *all* of it, but that exact amount without a doubt.

The question that this distinction raises is whether the relativism and uncertainty of the twentieth century has caught up with us to such an extent that we consider even a small dose of unequivocal truth to be suspect or, more damning still, uninteresting. This may be one source of our rejection of the old coherences. For however pressing we find the need to revise the specific conclusions of our nineteenth- and early twentieth-century predecessors, the fact remains that the contours that they depicted in political, institutional, and intellectual history have survived remarkably intact. Their frameworks and organizing principles may not be adequate for all new forms of research, but the continuing validity of the chronologies and narratives that they established is unmistakable, notwithstanding occasional assertions to the contrary. We see much of Roman history through Mommsen's eyes, the Renaissance through Burckhardt's eyes, the politics of sixteenth- and seventeenth-century Europe through Ranke's, and the development of English law through Maitland's—a crucial characteristic of the discipline, as we will see.[11]

It may seem capricious to link disputes over quantification with arguments about the enduring relevance of nineteenth-century historians. But that is so only if we forget the epistemological basis of the pluralism of current scholarship—if we fail to realize that the issue is not just the opposition between meaning and materialism, or between coherence and fragmentation. Rather, the focus is on a more fundamental decision. Does one prefer the certainties, limited but generalizable, that can still be attained in various ways in historical research—through numbers, through clear-cut and replicable methodologies, or through the accepted verities of traditional forms of inquiry—or is one committed to an undifferentiated egalitarianism, free of discriminations, which regards a question like "is it true?" as either meaningless or irrelevant? To simplify the distinction, the first wants to prove, the second to persuade.

THE POSSIBILITIES OF SYNTHESIS   The issues outlined sometimes resolve into questions of whether works of synthesis are feasible and/or desirable as a means of establishing the coherence of historical research. The problem is that it has become so easy to argue that synthetic works are no longer possible. The *Journal of Interdisciplinary History* itself promotes a pluralism of approaches that renders synthesis ever more difficult. And quests for meaning, flights from materialism, and the substitution of the insights

11   Theodor Mommsen (trans. William P. Dickson), *The History of Rome* (London, 1862–1866), 4v.; Jacob Burckhardt (trans. S. G. C. Middlemore), *The Civilization of the Renaissance in Italy* (London, 1878); Leopold von Ranke (trans. Philip A. Ashworth), *The History of the Latin and Teutonic Nations from 1494 to 1514* (London, 1887); F. W. Maitland, *The Constitutional History of England* (Cambridge, 1908).

of sister disciplines for the concerns of traditional historical scholarship intensify the problem. One could well conclude that history
is too important to be left to the historians. So many neighbors
have come pouring over the borders that one can no longer
distinguish a definable group in command of the field.

Consequently, the establishment of an agenda for history, of
a set of methods or purposes indigenous to the discipline, or of
a special task for its practitioners, hardly seems plausible. Historians are united in their respect for the record, and in their observation of certain fundamental rules for using evidence that were
laid down between the Renaissance and the nineteenth century.
But neither of these skills is difficult to learn. Nor is the telling
of a sustained story a special mark of the historian these days.
Whether or not narrative is reviving, as Stone has argued, many
historians still prefer analytic investigations. At the same time, as
submissions to this *Journal* testify, there are many sociologists,
political scientists, and psychoanalysts who like to tell a good
story about times gone by.

If an interest in the past and a commitment to narrative are
no longer the defining qualities of a particular profession, and
thus a potential basis for historical synthesis, are we then moving
toward Becker's "every man his own historian"? Alternatively,
is material from the past proving to be but one among a variety
of instruments for a multi-faceted study of mankind? If either
proposition is true, can one imagine a coherence or a distinctiveness that could be ascribed to the discipline these days? Is there
a unity that could transcend the divisions that have already been
mentioned, let alone others? [12]

The one form of synthesis that has attracted considerable
recent attention, particularly from French scholars, is *histoire totale*,
which blends the disparate methods of current research in examinations of well-defined localities. Its import for larger entities,
however, is uncertain at best, and it has not yet established general
and convincing links among physical conditions, economic and
demographic developments, social arrangements, intellectual and
cultural assumptions, and political behavior. Braudel's master-
piece is breathtaking more for its sweep through all of these
subjects than for its ability to connect them. [13]

12   Carl L. Becker, *Every Man His Own Historian* (New York, 1935).
13   Fernand Braudel (trans. Siân Reynolds), *The Mediterranean and the Mediterranean World
in the Age of Philip II* (London, 1972–1973), 2v.

A rigorous exploration of such links might broaden the comprehensiveness of our efforts, especially if the scantily studied effects of physical conditions (such as diet or climate) turn out to be fruitful avenues of inquiry. But such findings would remain within the confines of the materialist approach; they would be severely quantified; and they would be of interest primarily to one segment of the profession, especially its economists and demographers. There would be little impact on what has here been called the quest for meaning, because the very definition of meaning would be so different. *Histoire totale* is unlikely to engender the synthetic vision that the profession now seems to lack.

In the absence of such a vision, the microscopic cannot relate to the macroscopic. What can the historian of large-scale, continent-wide structures have to say to the historian of the village, and vice versa, except to offer certain metaphors or information of general interest? Can the scholar who works on family reconstitution learn from the analyst of market mechanisms? Do they have significant interests in common? And what about the student of urban violence and the student of agricultural techniques? Or what about those who want to understand attitudes toward children, and their colleagues who hope to understand witchcraft? Or any other combinations of these specialists? In sensitive hands even a minuscule part of life, such as table manners, can illuminate an entire age; but are there always links between that set of insights and the generalizations that other scholars derive from funeral ceremonies or the organization of asylums? Where are the grand, overarching, unifying themes? It is not even necessary to cite the chasms between elites and masses, or among regions and nations. The problems of synthesis seem large enough already.

History could gradually break up into different fields, each attached to a particular aspect of the study of humanity, just as the sciences keep splitting off specific parts of the physical world. Influences will be felt across these new disciplines, and an occasional brilliant interpreter will find a larger unity in an age or a theme. Yet within these investigations there will continue to be room not only for those who wish to devote themselves to a period or a country but also for those who define themselves by method. As different forms of training—statistical, psychological, and so forth—grow more complex, it will become less easy to move from one field to another, or to make use of the discoveries in a distant area. Eventually, too, it will seem pointless to compare the new disciplines, or for one to criticize another by reference to some abstract conception of the nature of "history."

If this assessment of current tendencies carries any weight, then the conclusion is inescapable that synthesis has to be abandoned as a means of restoring coherence. Indeed, there is no reason to believe that the nineteenth-century view—that the cohesion of the discipline is exemplified by magisterial, comprehensive histories—must carry weight in other contexts and times. All-embracing works are useful benchmarks, especially for the teaching of the subject. But they are often partial or ideological; they cannot cover all fields any more; and they are outmoded so quickly by the torrent of contemporary research that there can no longer be a plausible expectation that an omnicompetent polymath or a paradigm setter will unite us all.

ENGAGEMENT AS A SOURCE OF COHERENCE   Yet the belief in an essential cohesiveness refuses to die. And it is more than a blind adherence to great traditions or academic labels. The feeling that a common purpose is still possible has deeper roots, and it is visible in the enthusiasm that has greeted the multiple forms of current research—especially the widespread determination to address and absorb the findings of all areas of inquiry. The sense of liveliness and excitement aroused by the work that has been done since World War II is unmistakable. That in itself, considering the heterogeneity of both research and researchers, is significant evidence that students of the past still share common interests and aims.

Enthusiasm and engagement are more important than a uniform agenda, particularly if they are inspired by the very diversity that impedes synthesis. Although differences in values may persist, a profession which thoroughly engages the passions of its members is no less of a unity than one which binds them together around a homogeneous set of goals. A discipline can continue to function effectively, even without the blessings of a polymath or a synthesizer, as long as it is capable of inspiring the loyalty, the commitment, and the dedication of its practitioners.

This may not seem sufficient to justify calling history a discipline. Yet it takes on that quality when historians not only acknowledge the successes of specialties distant from their own, but also find themselves able to assess the value of important findings, however esoteric, for the field as a whole. The ability to become engaged across the entire spectrum of subject matter—visible at Bellagio and at all such meetings—testifies to a fundamental unity of purpose. Anthropology may be forbidding to the demographer, and the history of science to the political historian, but a common ground of discourse always manages to emerge. The essence of this community is a set of assumptions about the kind of historical research that rises above special intentions or emphases in order to enhance our understanding of the past, and which therefore deserves the attention of all who are concerned with the discipline.

To the extent that we can define these common assumptions of the discipline, we can perceive the substantive criteria—beyond engagement alone—which still unite the profession. The heart of the matter is an agreement about the standards for judging quality, which is by no means a new way of establishing the coherence of the discipline. When the shared outlook of the late nineteenth century began to fragment as a result of the rise of new interests and subjects, the writer of the article on "History" in the great eleventh edition of the *Encyclopedia Britannica* was forced to conclude that a different kind of unity would have to emerge: "This expansion of interest has intensified specialization. Historians no longer attempt to write world histories. . . . Each historian chooses . . . his own subject, and spends his life mastering such traces of it as he can find. His work there enables him to judge of the method of his fellows." In the 1980s, too, it is that ability to judge one's fellows that is the core of the practice of history.[14]

QUALITY AS A SOURCE OF COHERENCE   Throughout the discourse of our profession, the one subject on which agreement can coalesce, despite endless diversity, is a concept of quality—that elusive standard which enables one to accept and appreciate excellent work, whether or not one fully understands its methods. This form of judgment is constantly at work, and the way it emerges is essential to a definition of the discipline. There is the objection that the argument for coherence reduces history to the status of a craft, which can judge workmanship, but little more. A profes-

14   J. T. Shotwell, "History," *Encyclopedia Britannica* (1910; 11th ed.), XIII, 532.

sion, by contrast, ought to be distinguished by its subject matter. That judgments of quality are related to subject matter we will see shortly, but the dichotomy is by no means as clear as it appears, and never has been, because one cannot evaluate excellence without considering content. The distinction is far too amorphous. To take the sting out of this objection, however, it might be best simply to acknowledge the value of the designation: to join with Bloch, and take pride in the fact that history *is* a craft. Even that degree of coherence has been questioned in recent years, as the methodologies and subject matters have multiplied. Nor should the term craft be thought of as a derogation, an implication that manual dexterity is required of the learned. Rather, it should stand for both cohesiveness and utility—an indication that the many-sided entity known as historical research is not just a pile of fragments, and that the absence of obvious unifying trends or directions has not weakened its capacity, as a special form of inquiry, to surprise, to excite, and to resonate in the late twentieth century.[15]

Yet we can do better than that. We can assert that the ability to reach agreement on quality is our central unifying trait, that it is a means of transcending craft standards, that it creates a sense of professional cohesion, and that we can define its characteristics as being vital and indigenous to the profession.

DEFINING QUALITY   The ability to illuminate a specific situation or process in the past, however it is achieved, is the main characteristic of historians. As long as all who share that objective can recognize the virtues of those who attain it, regardless of individual style or intent, history will remain a united endeavor, linking its acolytes in a broad partnership. It would be futile to try to devise completely objective *and* uniform means of judging why, in their own times and ours, such historians as Herodotus, Thucydides, Edward Gibbon, and Ranke have been regarded as masters of our craft. To say that they were all original is to tell us nothing about their merit as historians. But, if there are elusive but still discernible criteria for judging achievement and effectiveness which apply equally to Gibbon and to our kaleidoscopic contemporaries, and which draw scholars to study the past, then

15 Marc Bloch (trans. Peter Putnam), *The Historian's Craft* (Manchester, 1954).

the situation that the discipline faces today is by no means unusual or regrettable.

The elements that combine to establish, not only these standards of quality, but also the distinctiveness of history as a form of inquiry, are not altogether elusive. They would seem to include the following:

(a) *An indifference to method as long as the results are illuminating.* Discursive rhetoric is not necessarily more acceptable than a statistical table or an isotope chemical analysis. Yet there is one significant limitation. If the method requires a departure from the evidence, then the conclusions are suspect *as history,* though not as some other form of inquiry. Erikson may find Martin Luther's "fit in the choir" revealing, even though it probably never happened; and quantifiers may extrapolate tenuously so as to recreate missing data; but the outcome, while perhaps good psychoanalysis or statistics, will always be dubious history. Speculation has to remain within narrow confines to retain its disciplinary cogency.[16]

(b) *A focus on the understanding and explanation of situations, processes, or events, not on the theoretical means by which that understanding and explanation are reached.* To pose the difference at its simplest level: a goal for historians might be to explain how and why fertility changed, and what the effects were, in various times and places; the demographer's goal would be to know what general mechanisms caused fertility to change. One set of questions may be interesting to historians, another to social scientists. The edges are blurred, because there are many overlaps, both in interests and in academic structures, but the ultimate aims remain distinct. It is not impossible to perceive when Erikson is being a historian, and when a psychoanalyst.

(c) *A determination to enlarge and reinterpret the classical questions.* History is unique among the social sciences in its antiquity (and it is not outdistanced by any of the humanities either). Yet the continuity of its traditions is not mere window dressing; it is a powerful force, which shapes the profession's conception of quality. Although every form of learning has its cumulative aspects, history carries its past into all of its endeavors. Excellence derives

16 Erik H. Erikson, *Young Man Luther: A Study in Psychoanalysis and History* (New York, 1958), esp. ch. 2.

from the capacity to reformulate existing questions, to cast them in new light, or to add dimensions not previously seen. A study has to make us reconsider traditional issues, however unlikely its connection to them, if it is to carry weight and purpose. Although the degree of freshness is often the basis for assessing quality, it is the linkage to previous inquiry that establishes a work as history.[17]

(d) *An emphasis on temporal causation.* The way the historian establishes context, whether for change or stability, is by making connections with *antecedent* phenomena. The particular nature of the connection is less important that its plausibility, because the latter determines the quality of the argument that is made. This interest in causation sets the historian apart from the chronicler or antiquarian, and gives relevance to both microscopic and macroscopic studies. At the same time, it can be distinguished from the commitments of other social sciences in its insistence on empirical evidence from appropriate times and places. To some degree, therefore, a work is judged to be history, and its excellence is determined, by its success in joining separate pieces of information from the past in this special causal framework.[18]

(e) *A congeries of professional and traditional predilections.* This characteristic, although not as distinct or as weighty as the four criteria just outlined, allows for a number of inclinations which, if not essential to assessments of quality, do play some role in forming the self-image and attitudes of historians. Like any profession, we have our outward signs of grace. There are appointments, departmental boundaries, reviews, citations, and invitations to conferences. Although these means of proclaiming competence or quality are fundamentally flawed, because they can be affected by considerations that have little to do with the substance of research, they are not trivial in helping to define the practice of history and its most influential components. We accept these criteria because they are long-standing, and because, in line with our commitment to the classical questions, we take older

17 This criterion, like (b) and (d), sets history distinctly apart from the other social sciences.

18 The insistence on many-sided interpretations of historical events is by no means new: cf. Bloch's "History seeks for causal wave-trains and is not afraid, since life shows them to be so, to find them multiple," in his *Historian's Craft*, 194. What is crucial is that the evidence be empirical and from the right period, not theoretical or analogous.

standards seriously, even while applauding what is fresh and stimulating. A similar inclination, grounded in tradition, is the admiration for a well-told story. Since it can partake of the qualities of good fiction—although the drama has to rest on the historical record—it allows us to use art as well as science to understand the past. Tradition, too, helps ensure that the teaching of history, even today, revolves around the time-honored subjects: the stories of nations, periods, and major themes or changes, like the expansion of Europe or the Industrial Revolution. If our courses, like our approaches to a larger public, are not always shaped by the insights generated at the frontiers of research, that is not inconsistent with our belief that the new never fully supersedes the tried and true.

The extraordinary amalgam of conservatism and openness to change that characterizes these central elements of our definition of quality, and thus the discipline itself, makes history both an enduring and an easily revitalized form of inquiry. Consequently, the innovations that it has absorbed since World War II have not necessarily reduced its coherence, despite their multitude. Rather, they have added to its range and its excitement. As both the *Journal* and the present volume can testify, moreover, the shared purpose continues to survive amidst the diversity, nurtured by a sense of quality. Since the house has long had many mansions without ill effects, we can assert with Donne that history still "makes a little room an everywhere." [19]

19 John Donne, *The Good-Morrow*, line 11. It is appropriate that Donne himself offers this response to the gloom that he, like many historians, expresses on the subject of the "Atomies" into which knowledge has fragmented: *Anatomie: First Anniversary*, lines 114–115.

The Contributors

PETER H. SMITH is Head of the Department of Humanities and Professor of History and Political Science at M.I.T. His most recent book is *Labyrinths of Power: Political Recruitment in Twentieth-Century Mexico* (Princeton, 1979).

JACQUES JULLIARD is Director of Studies at l'Ecole des Hautes Etudes en Science Sociales in Paris. He is author of, among other books, *Contre la politique professionelle* (Paris, 1978).

PETER CLARKE is a Fellow of St. John's College, Cambridge. His most recent book is *Liberals and Social Democrats* (Cambridge, 1978).

JACQUES REVEL is co-editor of *Annales*. He has co-authored *La nouvelle histoire* (Paris, 1978).

LAWRENCE STONE is the Dodge Professor of History and the Director of the Shelby Cullom Davis Center for Historical Studies, Princeton University. Among his books is *The Family, Sex and Marriage in England 1500-1800* (London, 1977).

MILES F. SHORE is Bullard Professor of Psychiatry and Head of the Department of Psychiatry, Massachusetts Mental Health Center, Harvard Medical School. He is the author of "Cecil Rhodes and the Ego Ideal," *Journal of Interdisciplinary History*, X (1979), 249-265.

DAVID HERLIHY is the Henry Charles Lea Professor of History at Harvard University. Among other books he is the co-author of *Les Toscans et leur familles. Une étude du Catasto florentin de 1427* (Paris, 1978).

ALLAN G. BOGUE is the Frederick Jackson Turner Professor of History at the University of Wisconsin, Madison. He is the co-editor of *The History of American Electoral Behavior* (Princeton, 1978).

PETER TEMIN is Professor of Economics at The Massachusetts Institute of Technology. He is the author of *Taking Your Medicine: Drug Regulation in the United States* (Cambridge, Mass., 1980).

BARRY SUPPLE is Professor of Economic History at the University of Cambridge. His most recent book is *Essay in Business History* (Oxford, 1977).

E. ANTHONY WRIGLEY is Professor of Population Studies at the London School of Economics and is the Co-Director of the Cambridge Group for the History of Population and Social Structure. He is the author, with Roger S. Schofield, of *The Population History of England, 1541-1871* (London, 1981).

BERNARD S. COHN is Professor of Anthropology and History at the University of Chicago. He is the author of *India: The Social Anthropology of a Civilization* (Englewood Cliffs, 1971).

JOHN W. ADAMS is Associate Professor of Anthropology at the University of South Carolina.

NATALIE Z. DAVIS is Henry Charles Lea Professor of History at Princeton University. She is the author of *Society and Culture in Early Modern France* (Stanford, 1975).

CARLO GINZBURG is Professor of Modern History at the University of Bologna. He is the author of *The Cheese and the Worms: The Cosmos of a Sixteenth-Century Miller* (Baltimore, 1977).

WILLIAM J. BOUWSMA is the Sather Professor of History at the University of California at Berkeley. He is the author of *Venice and the Defense of Republican Liberty* (Berkeley, 1968).

JOEL COLTON is Director for Humanities at the Rockefeller Foundation, on leave from Duke University where he is Professor of History. He is the author of *Léon Blum: Humanist in Politics* (New York, 1965) and, with R. R. Palmer, of *A History of the Modern World* (New York, 1978; 5th ed.).

ARNOLD THACKRAY is Professor of History and Sociology of Science at the University of Pennsylvania and is the editor of *Isis*. He is co-author of *Gentlemen of Science* (Oxford, 1981).

THEODORE K. RABB is Professor of History at Princeton University and is the co-editor of *The Journal of Interdisciplinary History*.

ROBERT I. ROTBERG is Professor of Political Science and History at The Massachusetts Institute of Technology and is the author of *The Journal of Interdisciplinary History*.